To

Marion L. Burton

in profound admiration of his work and with deep sympathy for his ideals.

from

Benjamin Clark Cocker

Ann Arbor

January 1921.

THE THEISTIC CONCEPTION OF THE WORLD.

AN ESSAY

IN OPPOSITION TO CERTAIN TENDENCIES OF MODERN THOUGHT.

By B. F. COCKER, D.D., LL.D.,

PROFESSOR OF MENTAL AND MORAL PHILOSOPHY IN THE UNIVERSITY OF MICHIGAN;
AUTHOR OF "CHRISTIANITY AND GREEK PHILOSOPHY."

"Science discloses the method of the world, but not its cause; Religion, its cause, but not its method."—Martineau.

NEW YORK:
HARPER & BROTHERS, PUBLISHERS,
FRANKLIN SQUARE.

PREFACE.

THE present volume was announced in the preface to "Christianity and Greek Philosophy" as nearly ready for publication under the title of "Christianity and Modern Thought."

Several considerations have induced the author to delay its appearance, the most influential of which has been the desire to await the culmination among a class of self-styled "advanced thinkers" of what they have been pleased to call "the tendency of modern thought." No extraordinary sagacity was needed to foresee the issue, or to predict that it must soon be reached. The transition has been rapid from negative criticism of the Christian religion to direct assault upon the very foundation of all religion—the personality and providence of God. Distrust of a supernatural revelation, and denial of all authority to the teaching of the sacred Scriptures, has been succeeded by doubt of the existence of God in the proper import of that sacred name. The Theistic postulate is degraded to the rank of a mere hypothesis, which is pronounced inadequate to explain the universe. A "law-governed Cosmos, full of life and reason," eternal and infinite, must now take the place of a personal God, the Creator and Ruler of the universe. This is the "New Faith" which is to supersede the Old.

The question, "Are we still Christians?" has received a final answer in the words of Strauss: "If we would speak as honest, upright men, we must acknowledge we are no longer Christians."[1] And in giving this answer he is confident he speaks in the name of a large and rapidly increasing number of men who once believed in the truth of Christianity—"The We I mean no longer counts only by thousands."[2] The further question, "Have we still a Religion?" (understanding by religion "the recognition and veneration of God, and the belief in a future life") is also answered in the negative. Religion "is a delusion, to abolish which ought to be the endeavor of every man whose eyes are open to the truth."[3] The only question which now remains for the speculative intellect is, "What is our conception of the Universe?"—the conception which henceforth must take the place of a personal God. The answer of Strauss is explicit, and in his estimation final: "The conception of the Cosmos, instead of that of a personal God as the finality to which we are led by perception and thought, or as the ultimate fact beyond which we can not proceed, . . . assumes the more definite shape of matter infinitely agitated, which, by differentiation and integration, develops itself to ever higher forms

[1] "The Old Faith and the New," vol. i. p. 107. [2] Ibid. vol. i. p. 3.
[3] Ibid. vol. i. p. 158.

and functions, and describes an everlasting circle by evolution, dissolution, and then fresh evolution."[1]

This may be called pantheism or atheism, materialism or idealism, just as we please; Strauss has no solicitude about mere names. "If this be considered pure, unmitigated materialism, I will not dispute it. In fact, I have always tacitly regarded the contrast so loudly proclaimed between materialism and idealism (or by whatever term one may designate the view opposed to the former) as a mere quarrel about words. They have a common foe in the dualism which pervaded the conception of the world throughout the Christian era, dividing man into body and soul, his existence into time and eternity, and opposing an eternal Creator to a created and perishable universe."[2]

The end is reached at last—no soul, no God, no providence, no immortality! We have waited for a culmination, and now we are called upon to look, "not into the golden Orient, but vaguely all around into a dim, copper firmament pregnant with earthquake and tornado." Or, rather, we are called to look into an abyss, and, "shouting question after question into the Sibyl-cave of Destiny, receive no answer" save "the Everlasting No." It only remains for us to listen to Strauss's *De Profundis* and retire. "The loss of the belief in providence belongs, indeed, to the most sensible deprivations which are connected with a renunciation of Christianity. In the enor-

[1] "The Old Faith and the New," vol. ii. p. 35. [2] Ibid. vol. ii. p. 19.

mous machine of the universe, amid the incessant whirl and hiss of its jagged iron wheels, amid the deafening crash of its ponderous stamps and hammers, in the midst of this whole terrific commotion, man—a helpless and defenseless creature—finds himself placed, not secure for a moment that on some imprudent motion a wheel may not seize and rend him, or a hammer crush him to powder. This sense of abandonment is at first something awful. But, then, what avails it to have recourse to an illusion? Our wish is impotent to refashion the world; the understanding clearly shows that it indeed is such a machine. But it is not merely this. We do not only find the revolution of pitiless wheels in our world-machine, but also the shedding of soothing oil. Our God [the world-machine] does not, indeed, take us into his arms from the outside, but he unseals the well-spring of consolation within our own bosoms. . . . He who can not help himself in this matter is beyond help, is not yet ripe for our standpoint."[1]

There is a weighty and solemn lesson in this illustration of the "tendency of modern thought"—a lesson which even Strauss intended to teach the age, viz., that there is no discernible *via media* between "the Old Faith and the New"—between the belief in a personal God and the impersonal All. The "New Faith" must at last be the faith of all who reject *providence*, that providence which is pre-eminently revealed in history, instituting a king-

[1] "The Old Faith and the New," vol. ii. p. 213.

dom of God upon earth by a supernatural guidance and grace.

The issue, now so sharply and clearly defined, between *a God and no God*, has determined a change in the plan of our work, and justifies, we trust, the attempt we have made to restate and defend "The Theistic Conception of the World."

Those who have done me the honor to read "Christianity and Greek Philosophy" will detect in the present volume a radical change of views concerning the concepts Time and Space. This change of position is the result of patient reconsideration of this branch of the discussion, and we allude to it here simply to guard against the charge of unconscious inconsistency. The views presented in this volume must stand or fall on their own merits.

The author has to acknowledge many obligations to his friend, Dr. Bernard Moses, for material aid rendered in getting this work through the press.

UNIVERSITY OF MICHIGAN, *July*, 1875.

CONTENTS.

"To such readers as have reflected on man's life; who understand that for man's well-being Faith is properly the one thing needful; how with it martyrs, otherwise weak, can cheerfully endure the shame and the cross; and without it worldlings puke up their sick existence by suicide in the midst of luxury: to such it will be clear that for a pure moral nature, the loss of religious belief is the loss of every thing.

"All wounds, the crush of long-continued destitution, the stab of false friendship and of false love, all wounds in thy so genial heart, would have healed again had not its life-warmth been withdrawn.

"Well mayest thou exclaim, 'Is there no God, then; but at best an absentee God, sitting idle, ever since the first Sabbath, at the outside of his universe and *seeing* it go?' 'Has the word Duty no meaning; is what we call Duty no Divine messenger and guide, but a false earthly phantasm made up of desire and fear?' 'Is the heroic inspiration we name Virtue but some passion; some bubble of the blood, bubbling in the direction others *profit* by?' I know not; only this I know, If what thou namest Happiness be our true aim, then are we all astray. 'Behold, thou art fatherless, outcast, and the universe is—the Devil's.' "—Carlyle.

THE THEISTIC CONCEPTION OF THE WORLD.

CHAPTER I.

THE PROBLEM STATED.

As Archimedes demanded only one fixed point in order to move the world, so Descartes desired to find one certain and indubitable principle upon which he could plant his feet and lift himself out of the universal doubt which environed him. He found it in the proposition—I EXIST. This for me is the most direct, immediate, and certain of all intuitions. I can not doubt, I can not deny my own existence. Whatever else I doubt, I can not doubt that I, the doubter, exist. This I that thinks, that is conscious, is the fundamental *reality*.[1]

I see around me a plurality of personal existences who are self-conscious and self-manifesting beings—beings who think and feel, and display their activities in time and space, as I do; and I can no more doubt their existence than I can doubt my own. This combination of the content of external perception with that of internal perception gives the immediate consciousness of external *reality*.[2]

Besides these personal existences analogous to my own,

[1] Ueberweg's "History of Philosophy," vol. ii. p. 41.
[2] Ueberweg's "Logic," p. 91.

there are other objects which exist in relation to my corporeal organism—relations of position, distance, and direction, which are purely objective. These existences offer resistance to my muscular effort to displace them in space, and defy all my mental effort to reduce them to the category of subjective phenomena. These objects have specific properties or exist in certain conditions which, in their mutual relation with my sensitive organism, produce in me certain vital affections, as heat, light, color, and sound. These affections presuppose a force or energy outside of my consciousness, and distinct from myself. Thus I am constrained to believe that the earth on which I tread, the heavens that shine upon me, the forms and movements which surround me, are not vain shadows, unreal phantoms of my own creation, but real entities. The totality of existence called the universe is for me a *reality*.

The phenomena of the universe are in ceaseless flow and change. Bodies are aggregated and dissolved. Plants are evolved from germs, they live and grow, then decay and perish. Animals and men are born and developed to maturity, then they sicken and die. The earth itself is in constant change. The storms of heaven, the erosion of the atmosphere, the gnawing of the tidal wave, the mountain torrent, the flowing river, the earthquake and the volcano, are perpetually changing the aspect of the globe. There is perpetual *genesis*, ceaseless *becoming*, incessant *change*.

Beneath all these changes there is an enduring "something." There are abiding constants as well as fleeting changes; enduring realities as well as unstable phenomena. The same forms and relations, the same forces and laws, the same analogous functions, and the same archetypal ideas, remain amid all individual changes. There is an enduring *substance* which is the subject of all these changes. There is a permanent force, or *power*, which is the cause of all change. There are constant numerical proportions, determinate geometrical forms, specific ideal archetypes, and special ends, which give the law of all change. The universe is not a mere aggregation of phenomena, a mere concourse of things in time and space with accidental resemblances: it is a *unity*, a cosmos, a harmonious whole, both in its contemporaneous and successive history.

So much is and always has been known, with more or less clearness and distinctness by all men, and known by a spontaneous and immediate intuition. This intuition, like every intuition, even the commonest intuition of sense, has had a gradual development both in the consciousness of the individual, and in the consciousness of the race. It has always been immanent in human thought even when not articulately expressed in human language. To the native common-sense of our race, the world is a reality, not a dream; to the universal reason of mankind the universe is a harmony, not a chaos. Men have instinctively apprehended some ideal relations, some causal connection, some adaptation and purpose in nature, and they have always had some intuition, however dim and shadowy, of an *all-pervading unity*, and an *ultimate causative principle.*

But when the universe has become the object of *reflective* thought, when man has attempted a colligation of the individual facts, and an ideal construction and rational interpretation of the phenomena, when he has sought to grasp the manifoldness and diversity of nature in a higher unity of thought, and, above all, when he has attempted to pass beyond phenomena and their relations, and form a conception of *the absolute reality and ultimate cause*—then it is that difficulties have arisen and questions have presented themselves which have perplexed the discursive reason, and taxed the genius of the ablest thinkers of every age.

1. First of all, there have arisen the fundamental questions: Has the universe always existed, or had the Cosmos, with its changes and constants, its forces and laws, its forms and relations, a *Beginning?* Is its present condition but one link in an endless chain, one phasis in a series of changes, which had no beginning and shall have no end? Is the universe limited both in space and duration, or is it unlimited, unbeginning, and endless?

2. If the universe had a beginning, what is the ἀρχή—the originant, causative Principle in which or from which it had its beginning? How are we to conceive aright that First Principle of all existence and of all knowledge? is it material or spiritual, intelligent or unintelligent?

3. What conception are we to form of the nature and mode of that beginning? Was it a pure supernatural Origination — an absolute creation? or was it simply a Formation out of a first matter or first force—an artistic, architectonic, demiurgic creation? Was that beginning determined by necessity or by choice? Was it an unconscious emanation from, or a necessary development of, the First Principle; or was it a conscious forth-putting of power for the realization of a foreseen, premeditated, predetermined plan—a *mental* Order.

4. A supernatural Origination being assumed, then,

from that first initial act of absolute creation, has the process of formation been gradual, continuous, and uniform —a progressive *Evolution* from the homogeneous to the heterogeneous, from lower to higher forms, according to a changeless law of uniformity and continuity? or have there been marked, distinct, and successive stages of formation—creative epochs which may be called "new beginnings?" Is the historic unity of creation a unity of Thought, an ideal consecution? or is it simply a physical unity grounded in a material nexus—a genetic connection resulting from the necessary action of physical causes?

5. What is the relation of the Creator to the existing creation? Is the Deity, in any sense, immanent in, or does he dwell altogether apart from, and out of all connection with, the universe? Has any finite thing or being an independent existence? Have the forces of nature any reality apart from the Divine efficiency? Did the Creator, in the beginning, give self-being to the substance of the universe, and endow it with properties and forces, so that it can exist and act apart from, and independently of, the First Cause? or is God still in nature upholding all substance, the power of all force, the life of all life, shaping all forms, and organizing all systems? Is God not only the Creator but the *Conservator* of all things?

6. Is there any Ethical meaning, any moral significance in the universe? Is the physical order of the universe subordinated to a moral order in which freedom exists? Are there any indications that the existence of moral personality is the end toward which all the successive changes of nature have tended, and the progressive types of life have been a preparation and a prophecy? Was the earth

designed to be a theatre for the development of moral character, the education and discipline of moral beings? Does the course of history reveal "a power that works for righteousness," and aims at the highest perfection of rational and free beings? In a word, is there a *Providential* Government of the world?

7. Does man stand in a more immediate relation to God than the things of nature? Is each individual the charge of a providence, the subject of a moral government, and the heir to a future retribution? Has man a spiritual and immortal nature? Has he the power so to determine his own action and character that he can justly be held accountable, and treated as the proper subject of reward and punishment? In the final issue of things, will every human being meet his righteous deserts, and be rewarded or punished according to his works? In short, is man under *Moral Government?*

These are the great, the vital questions of to-day. In one form or another they have engaged the attention and stimulated the earnest thought of the ablest and best of minds in past ages; and, whether from the inherent demand of reason, or the promptings of instinctive curiosity, they have a deeper hold on the mind of this, than of any preceding age.

We approach the discussion of these questions with a profound conviction of their magnitude and difficulty, and an oppressive foreboding that our essay will be pronounced ambitious and vain. Their vastness seems to defy our admeasurement, and their complexity and difficulty may defeat our feeble efforts at solution. "The mer-de-glace of the Infinite is covered with myriads of philosophic insects which have been carried up there and lost." May we hope for any better fate? Do the problems permit any solution at all?

Of one thing, at any rate, we are sure: these questions are native to the human mind. They arise spontaneously in presence of the facts of the universe. However much of human effort to solve these problems has ended in failure and defeat, the human mind has never lost confidence in the possibility of their ultimate solution, and humanity has never abandoned them in despair.[1] A few impatient souls have plunged into Pyrrhonism and taken refuge in universal skepticism; while others have sought to organize nescience into a science. But patient, earnest souls have never cast away their faith in the integrity of universal reason, and have never ceased to believe that its ideas and laws are, in truth, the ideas and laws of the universe. These problems are the great problems of all philosophy, and all religion; and unless philosophy be a dream, and religion an illusion, they are capable of such a solution as shall satisfy the reason of man.[2] This con-

[1] This is mournfully conceded by Geo. Henry Lewes (an avowed Comtean): "No array of argument, no accumulation of contempt, no historical exhibition of the fruitlessness of its effort, has sufficed to extirpate the tendency toward metaphysical speculation. Although its doctrines have become a scoff (except among the valiant few), its method still survives, still prompts to renewed research, and still misleads some men of science. In vain History points to the failure of twenty centuries; the metaphysician admits the fact, but appeals to History in proof of the persistent passion which no failure can dismay; and hence draws confidence in ultimate success. A cause which is vigorous after centuries of defeat is a cause baffled but not hopeless, beaten but not subdued. The ranks of its army may be thinned, its banners torn and mud-stained; but the indomitable energy breaks out anew, and the fight is continued."—"Problems of Life and Mind," p. 7.

[2] "Every religion may be defined as an *à priori* theory of the universe. The surrounding facts being given, some form of agency is alleged which, in the opinion of those alleging it, accounts for these facts. . . . Nay, even that

viction, which is common to the mass of thoughtful men, will justify every attempt of philosophy to attain to an ultimate unity of thought. The ultimate harmony of physical, philosophical, and religious truth is the faith of all noble minds.

The signs of the times are propitious. To-day the conflict between reason and faith, science and religion, presents many hopeful indications of an approaching conciliation. Candid men in both fields are earnestly working, and patiently watching, and hourly catching clearer glimpses of the everlasting harmony which pervades the universe of being and of thought. Every, even the smallest, contribution made with an honest purpose to give confidence and collimation to this movement, will be welcome to all earnest minds. This may be our apology for attempting a task that belongs to stronger intellects than ours.

It is obvious, at first thought, that the questions before us admit of no loose and desultory treatment. Abysses are not to be concealed by laurel screens, or chasms bridged by flowers of rhetoric. If we are to reach any satisfactory conclusions, our procedure must be rigidly systematic and logically exact. We must have a fixed point of departure, and, if possible, a faultless method of advance. The fundamental question must be determined. The central problem must be ascertained, and we must deal with all correlative questions in their logical connection with the one fundamental inquiry.

First of all, then, can we place that central problem

which is commonly regarded as the negation of all religion—even positive Atheism, comes within the definition; for it, too, in asserting the self-existence of Space, Matter, and Motion, which it regards as adequate causes of every appearance, propounds an *à priori* theory from which it holds the facts to be deducible."—Spencer, "First Principles," p. 43.

clearly before our mental vision? Amid the diverse questions which spontaneously arise in presence of the diversified phenomena of nature, and the wonderful evolutions of humanity, can we fix upon the *one* question in which all others are involved—the grand underlying problem which comprehends them all?

A little reflection will make it apparent that the problem of all problems is this—

How shall we conceive aright the FIRST PRINCIPLE *and* ORIGIN *of all things, itself unoriginated and unbeginning, the source of all beginnings? Or again, what is that* FIRST PRINCIPLE *which, being assumed, shall be found a sufficient explanation of the motion and change, the order and adaptation, the life and feeling, the consciousness and reason, we call, collectively, the universe?*

This is clearly the fundamental question on which all the others are grounded, and in the solution of which they have their solution.

The universe presents itself to sense and sense-perception as a perpetual genesis, "a vast aggregation and history of phenomena conditioned in time and space which, by its diversity and mutability, is disqualified from being regarded as independent and self-existent." To our experiential knowledge, to our physical science in its highest generalizations, the universe is a product, an *effect.* And it is an effect for which the reason demands an explanation and a cause. It is a manifoldness and diversity which the logical understanding is ceaselessly endeavoring to reduce to a unity. Indeed, every movement of thought, from the first rude attempt at classification on the simple basis of resemblance, upward to the recognition of more profound ideal relations and uniform laws, until its culmination in the highest integration of reason, is but the effort of the mind to grasp the individual facts of nature in a unity of thought, and interpret the universe according to principles and ideas which the reason supplies.

The moment reflective thought is directed to the phenomenal world, the questions spontaneously arise—Out of what does the phenomenal come? By what agency or efficiency does it arise? Why does it present itself in this order rather than another? Or, more specifically—What is the abiding *reality* which sustains the array of phenomena? What is the invisible *power* which effects all the changes we see around us? What is that unseen *presence* which determines the forms, relations, and adaptations which every where present themselves to the reason of man? In a word, *What is that ultimate principle—the last or remotest in the order of analytic thought, the first in the order of being and of reason—which sustains and moves and organizes and governs all*—that fundamental, abiding PRIMUS which is everlastingly present behind the scenery and changes of the world—*that which always was, and now is, and ever shall be* FIRST? Or if we permit ourselves to regard the present order of things as a necessary out-birth from the past, still we are compelled by a laborious effort of regressive thought to climb upward through a series of changes to an absolutely FIRST of the series conditioning all the other members, but itself unconditioned. Few will now claim that this is the natural and adequate cosmical conception; but, even under this mode of conception, we can not but feel that a development without a beginning of the process, a series without a first term, is impossible. "The absolute infinity of a series is a contradiction *in adjecto.* As every number, although immeasurably and inconceivably great, is impossible unless unity is given as its basis, so every series, being itself a number, is impossible unless a first term is given as its commencement." Therefore the question still returns—What is that First Principle of all things?

In obedience to this demand of reason, or impelled by an innate "wonder"—"the feeling of the philosopher"—men have in all ages attempted an ideal construction and rational interpretation of the universe.[1] The Mythologies, Cosmogonies, Philosophies, Religions of the ancient world were the simple products of this innate tendency. Beyond the circle of thought illuminated by Divine revelation, the first movement of reflection was unmethodical and incomplete. Pursuing the inquiries objectively, that is, in the realm of outward nature, and not subjectively in the realm of reason, the human mind was perpetually entangled with dualistic conceptions. There were contrarieties, polarities, antagonisms, which the logical understanding could not cancel. Hence we have, as an early, perhaps the earliest, form of construction, an Oriental Dualism — as in the Adonis and Moloch of the Phœnicians, the Isis and Osiris of the Egyptians, the Ormuzd and Ahriman of the Persians, the Chaos and Love of Orpheus, the Plenum and Vacuum (Matter and Space) of Democritus, and even some lingering taint in the God and Necessity of Plato's "Timæus."

But all this was unsatisfactory to human reason, which is a *unity*, and which makes its imperious demand that *absolute unity* shall stand at the fountain-head of being. It has never been able to rest in an Ultimate which was not an Absolute—that is, a *unity* which by its very idea and conception is the negation of all plurality and mutability; a *unity* which is unconditioned, and yet which

[1] "Philosophy begins in wonder: he was not a bad genealogist who said that Isis, the messenger of Heaven, is the child of Thaumas (Wonder); for Wonder is the feeling of a philosopher."—Plato, "Theætetus," § 155.

conditions all; an "eternal constancy," the voluntary cause of all genesis and all change.[1] It is a law of reason, under which alone it can maintain its integrity, that the *First Cause must be* ONE, *and not many.* An absolute cause must be one in order to be absolute; two absolutes is a contradiction. With more or less clearness, men in all ages have apprehended that "the *First Principle must be one or nothing.*"

This is tacitly conceded in all modern systems of thought. Büchner, the materialist; Spencer, the dynamist; Hegel, the idealist; Cousin and Coleridge, the spiritualists, know no divergence here. Atheism, Pantheism, and Theism alike commence with unity at the fountain-head of being—a unity which is incomposite, absolutely continuous, every where present and eternal. Every system of philosophy is essentially an effort to show how the universe that now is has been originated by, or evolved out of, or has emanated from, a First Principle, an absolute Unity. To determine whether this absolute First Principle can be known, and, if known, how conceived and expressed aright, is the ultimate problem of all philosophy and all religion.

All the answers which have been given, and, indeed, all which can be conceived, are contained in the following four propositions:

1. *In the beginning was* MATTER—matter as the original substance or substratum, with its inherent, essential, and necessary attribute of force; this alone is eternal and infinite. "No force without matter—no matter without force." "Matter and its immanent force is immortal and indestructible." "The world is unlimited and infinite."[2] Matter, with its primary forces of attraction and

[1] Plato, "Timæus," § 9. [2] Büchner, "Matter and Force," pp. 1–27.

repulsion, cohesion and affinity, is fully adequate to the explanation of all the phenomena of the universe, physical, vital, and mental.

2. *In the beginning was* FORCE—force homogeneous but unstable, and necessarily tending to differentiation and heterogeneity; splitting into opposites, standing off into polarities, ramifying into attractions and repulsions, light, heat, magnetism, and electricity; and mounting up through the stages of physical, vital, and neural to the mental life itself, with all its varied and endless phenomena, as revealed in the languages, laws, institutions, arts, sciences, and religions of the world. Force is "the ultimate of all ultimates," the "Absolute Reality," the "Unconditioned Cause."[1]

3. *In the beginning was* THOUGHT—thought as an eternal process of self-manifestation and self-actualization, which in its necessary evolution reveals itself as force, and expresses itself in the varied types of existence and laws of phenomena, natural and spiritual. "*The Absolute Idea,*" as a perpetual process, an eternal thinking, is the supreme principle of all reality. "The idea of the Absolute Spirit comprehends the entire wealth of the natural and the spiritual world; it is the only substance and truth of this wealth, and nothing is true and real except so far as it forms an element of its being."[2]

4. *In the beginning was* WILL—an unconditioned Will as the indivisible unity and perpetual differentiation of *Reason* and *Power* and *Love.* This Unconditioned Will is the causative principle of all Reality, all Efficiency, and all Perfection—a causative principle containing, predetermining, and producing all the manifold forms and re-

[1] Spencer, "First Principles," pp. 235, 236.
[2] Hegel, "Philosophy of Religion," vol. i. p. 201.

lations, forces and laws of the universe in reference to a final purpose. This *Absolute First Cause* is a living personal Being, "from whom, in whom, and to whom are all things."[1]

The first and second of these propositions coalesce with the creed of *Atheism*, the third with the creed of *Pantheism*, the fourth is the creed of *Theism*, and, as we hope to prove in subsequent chapters, the only rational and adequate explanation of the facts of the universe.

[1] "Spiritual Philosophy of Coleridge," by Green, vol. i. pp. 1, 2.

CHAPTER II.

GOD THE CREATOR.

"In the beginning God created the heaven and the earth."—Gen. i. 1.

"God that made the world and all things therein. . . . He is Lord of heaven and earth."—Acts xvii. 24.

"The Eternal Will is the creator of the world as He is the creator of the finite reason."—Fichte.

God is the first principle, the unconditioned cause of all existence. This is the answer of Christian doctrine to the great problem presented for solution in the preceding chapter. Whether this fundamental presupposition shall be finally accepted as the only adequate solution of the problem of existence will depend in a large degree upon our apprehension of the Christian idea of God. We shall, therefore, open the discussion by asking the question—What is the content of our conception of God?

Dogmatic theology might rest satisfied with the simple affirmation, "*God is* God,"[1] as against all the captious demands of science, were it not necessary to render an account to itself of what, at first sight, might be pronounced a "sublime tautology." For, while it is hereby confessed that God in his essential being is incomprehensible and ineffable, so that to the Christian as well as to the philosopher He is "the great Unknown," still it is not hereby admitted that it is absolutely impossible to know God. To affirm that God is absolutely "the Unknowable" is simply to assert his unreality. Mr. Martineau has finely

[1] Isaiah xliii. 13; Exod. iii. 14: "I am that I am."

observed that this term is self-contradictory; for we affirm by the use of it that we know so much that He can not be known. Nay, it assumes the existence of God, and in the same breath separates us from Him forever. But if it be admitted that God *is*, it can not be absolutely impossible to know *what* He is. The knowledge of existence and the form of existence mutually condition each other. There must be something in the understanding answering to the term in the language of mankind, and there must be something in the realm of being which is the ground of the idea in the reason of Man. The heathen have a presentiment, a dim intuition of the "unknown God," and the inspired teacher may so "declare Him" in human language that his hearers may receive a definite notion, and attain to a practical knowledge of God.

The *idea* of God is a common phenomenon of the universal intelligence of our race, and must have been present to the thought of man even before he uttered the *name* of God.[1] The moment man becomes conscious of himself, and knows himself as distinct from the world, that same moment he becomes conscious of a *Higher Self*—a living Power upon which both himself and the world depend. For this Higher Self all nations have found a name. All languages have a term cognate with the Saxon "God," which expresses that spontaneous consciousness of a supernatural power which is common to all minds—that intuition of a supramundane existence

[1] "We can see the sun, we can greet it in the morning and mourn for it in the evening, without necessarily naming it, that is to say, comprehending it under some general notion. It is the same with the perception of the Divine. It may have been perceived, men may have welcomed it or yearned after it, long before they knew how to name it."—Max Müller, "Science of Language," 2d Series, p. 454.

which is the ground and reason of all other existence. Even Polytheism has a name for the abstract of all the gods, which sets forth the ideas of being, power, causality, and personality. And in Christian lands the term God, without any periphrasis, at once represents the idea of a Being distinct from self and the world, who is the Maker of the world and the Father of humanity. For all practical ends it is enough to say God is *God*. It is only when reflective thought seeks to express some more specific and determinate conception of the Supreme Being that we find ourselves under the necessity of adding other expletives to this term God.

It is therefore desirable that we should set down, in a provisional form, the general conception of God as it exists in the mind of the Theist and the Christian. I can not do this better than by selecting from the writings of three men of diverse schools of thought—one a Physicist, another a Metaphysician, the third a Theologian; and all in a greater or less degree influenced by the teaching of the Christian Scriptures.

My first selection will be from the "Meditations" of Descartes, who is regarded as "the father of modern philosophy." "By the name of God," says he, "I mean an infinite, eternal, immutable, independent, omniscient, omnipresent substance, by which I and all other things which are have been created and produced."[1]

My second selection is from the "Principia" of Sir Isaac Newton, a work which, by the general consent of the scientific world, is the greatest contribution ever made to science. Sir Isaac Newton was a Physicist rather than a Metaphysician; he will therefore represent to us the conception of God entertained by the scientific Theist. At

[1] "Meditations," vol. i. p. 313.

the close of this his great work he writes: "The true God is a living, intelligent, powerful Being, and, from His other perfections, it follows that He is Supreme, or most perfect. He is eternal and infinite, omnipotent and omniscient; that is, His duration reaches from eternity to eternity, His presence from infinity to infinity. He governs all things, and knows all things that are or can be done. He is not eternity and infinity, but eternal and infinite. He is not duration or space, but He endures and is present. He endures forever, and He is every where present; and by existing always and every where, He constitutes [or causes] duration and space. Since every particle of space is *always*, and every indivisible moment of duration is *every where*, certainly the Maker and Lord of all things can not be *never* and *nowhere*. . . . God is the same God, always and every where. He is omnipresent, not *virtually* [potentially] only, but also substantially; for virtue can not subsist without substance. In Him all things are contained and moved, yet neither affects the other. God suffers nothing from the motion of bodies; bodies find no resistance from the omnipresence of God. It is allowed by all that the Supreme God exists necessarily; and by the same necessity exists *always* and *every where*. . . . We know Him only by His most wise and excellent contrivances of things and final causes; we admire Him for His perfections; but we reverence and adore Him on account of His dominion. A God without dominion, providence, and final causes is nothing else but Fate and Nature. Blind mechanical necessity, which is certainly the same always and every where, could produce no variety of things. All that diversity of natural things which we find suited to different times and places could arise from nothing but the *ideas* and *will* of a Being necessarily existing."

My last selection is from the "Grammar of Assent," by John Henry Newman, formerly a Protestant, now a Catholic divine. Prior to his change of theological position he published a remarkable work "On the Development of Christian Doctrine in Aid of a Grammar of Assent," the design of which is to exhibit the influence of philosophic thought upon the evolution of Christian doctrine, and to bring it into harmony with the theories of Cosmical, Physiological, and Historical development, which seem for the present to be in the ascendant. For this reason I choose to employ his words, as setting forth the conception of God which is generally entertained by thoughtful men. At page ninety-seven of his last work, "The Grammar of Assent," I read:

"There is one God, such and such in Nature and Attributes. I say 'such and such,' for, unless I explain what I mean by *one God*, I use words which may mean any thing or nothing. I may mean a mere *anima mundi;* or an initial principle which once was in action and now is not; or collective humanity. I speak then of the one God of the Theist and of the Christian: a God who is numerically One, who is Personal; the Author, Sustainer, and Finisher of all things, the Life of Law and Order, the moral Governor. One who is Supreme and Sole; like Himself, unlike all things besides Himself, which all are but his creatures; distinct from, independent of, them all. One who is self-existing, absolutely infinite, who has ever been and ever will be, to whom nothing is past or future; who is all perfection, and the fullness and archetype of every possible excellence, the Truth itself, Wisdom, Love, Justice, Holiness; One who is All-powerful, All-knowing, Omnipresent, Incomprehensible. These are some of the distinctive prerogatives which I ascribe unconditionally and unreservedly to the great Being whom I call God."

These statements of the Theistic conception will be regarded by most men as adequate and satisfactory. They will be accepted by the scientific Theist and approved by the dogmatic Theologian. They present the idea of God within the sphere of Christian thought; that is, reflective thought informed and illuminated by the revelations of God which are given in the Christian Scriptures. At the same time it must be confessed that they are defective in scientific form, philosophical development, and logical articulation. They do not present the conception of God in harmony with any *principles of Rational Integration.* They show no attempt to combine the various elements of this conception in the unity of an *Absolute Principle*, an *Ultimate and Fundamental Idea.*

The aim of all true philosophy is to attain to the insight of First Principles, yea, to the insight of the Absolute First Principle from which whatever now *is* must be derived, and in which whatever *is* must have its intelligible ground and sufficient reason. There exists in man, as the essential characteristic of his humanity, a power or faculty of intelligence, best named the *Reason*, which awakens in him the desire and furnishes to him the law that enables him to fulfill the inherent desire of combining all his manifold knowledges in the unity of such *Absolute First Principle;* and the one fundamental law of this faculty is the *Law of Sufficient Reason*, which has been thus enounced by Leibnitz: "Whatever exists, or begins to be, must have a sufficient reason for its existence, and why it is as it is, and not otherwise;" or, to give the principle a fuller, and at the same time a legitimate expansion—For all genesis, or beginning, there must be an adequate *Cause;* beneath all appearance, all changeful and fleeting phenomena, there must be a permanent *Being* or *Reality;* beyond all the diverse and manifold, there must be an ultimate *Identity*, an incomposite indivisible *Unity;* and in all order and special adaptation, there must be a unifying *Thought*, a definite *Purpose* and *End.*

The Reason of man can find satisfaction and harmony only in the recognition of an Absolute First Principle which shall comprehend and unite all these universal and necessary ideas which are the correlates of the facts of experience; that is, an Absolute First Principle which shall be the Ultimate Reality, the Ultimate Cause, the Ultimate Unity, and the Ultimate Reason of all existence. In other words, the Reason is not and can not be satisfied without "the clear insight of a *Causative Principle* containing, predetermining, and producing all the actual results we see around us, with their orderly relations in reference to a final purpose, reason, or end; and which causative principle exists not only as the originative and constructive, but also as the conservative energy of all things;" a Being who "is before all things, and by whom all things consist," "from whom, in whom, and to whom are all things."

And now what is this Absolute First Principle, causative of all existence, which the spontaneous reason has always intuitively apprehended, and which the reflective reason has always found to be the adequate, and only adequate explanation of the universe? I answer in a word, it is AN UNCONDITIONED WILL OR SELF-DIRECTIVE POWER, SEEING ITS OWN WAY, AND HAVING THE REASON AND LAW OF ITS ACTION IN ITSELF ALONE. This always and every where has been intuitively apprehended, with more or less clearness, as standing at the fountain-head of all existence.

This, then, we shall postulate as the fundamental axiom of all rational integration, viz., AN UNCONDITIONED WILL, *the principle of all Reality, all Efficiency, and all Perfection.*

1. An unconditioned Will which realizes itself in IPSËITY—self-potency and self-affirmation; expresses itself in that august name of God "I AM;" and constitutes ABSOLUTE REALITY.

2. An unconditioned Will which manifests itself in ALTERITY—pluri-efficiency; utters itself in the "I WILL" of the creative fiat; and constitutes INFINITE EFFICIENCY.

3. An unconditioned Will which returns to itself in TOTALITY—a complete Ideal to be realized in Creation; which expresses its satisfaction in pronouncing all things "very good," and constitutes PERFECT PERSONALITY.

The changeless correlation and inherent harmony of these ideas of the reason (Reality, Efficiency, and Personality) may be rendered more obvious by the following formula, after the method of Coleridge's "polar logic."[1]

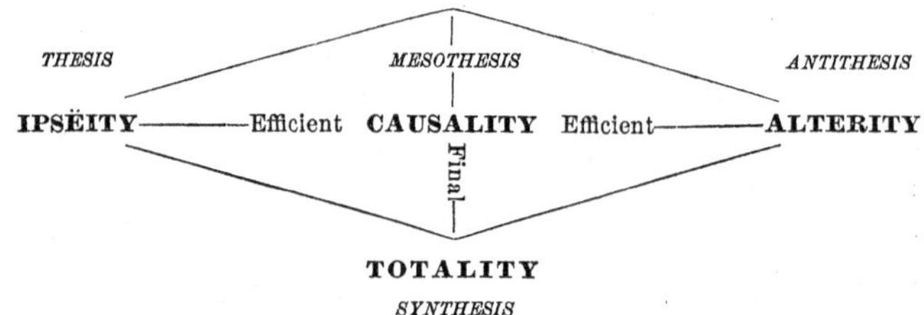

PROTHESIS expresses the absolute identity or eternal coinherence of Reason, Love, and Power (the Divine Es-

[1] "Works," vol. i. p. 218; vol. v. p. 18; Hamilton's "Philosophy," p. 176; Murphy's "Scientific Basis of Faith," p. 130.

sence). THESIS expresses Power in the form of Love (the Divine Self-sufficiency and Self-potency). ANTITHESIS expresses Reason in the form of Power (the Divine Efficiency). SYNTHESIS expresses the diversity in unity of Reason, Love, and Power (the Divine Perfection). And MESOTHESIS expresses the essential correlations which integrate the whole (the Triunity of the manifested God). Thus Absolute Reality, Infinite Efficiency, and Perfect Personality are all, as a triplicity, contained in the fundamental unity of an unconditioned Will, which has Love as its motive, Power as its agent, and Reason as its light and law.

And now let us retire within our own consciousness, and see if this fundamental axiom of rational integration—Will as the principle of all Reality, Efficiency, and Perfection—is not reflected in our reason, and evolved in our inner experience. Do we not find that the central point of our consciousness—that which makes each man what he is in contradistinction from every other man—that which expresses the *real essence of the soul* apart from its formal processes and regulative laws—is the WILL? Without Will man would fall back from the elevation which he now assumes to the level of impersonal nature: in a word, he would be a *thing*, and not a *power*. Power, spontaneity, causality, will—these, or similar forms, express, as nearly as can be, the essential nature or principle of the human soul.[1] Furthermore, it is obvious that mere Power or Energy does not suffice for the notion of Will—there must also be Reason and Affection.[2] Indeed, "Will is contemplated universally as the inseparable union and perpetual differentiation of Intelligence and originative

[1] Morell, "Philosophy of Religion," p. 3.

[2] Müller, "Christian Doctrine of Sin," vol. i. p. 28.

Power, and as such the sole ground of the intelligibility of all causation."[1]

A volitional act, a moral and responsible act, must be one which is performed under the influence of motives, and for which, when called to account, we can assign valid reasons. All true volition supposes a purpose or end to be realized, an inward appetency or motive which makes the end desirable, and the selection and adaptation of means to accomplish that end. Power divorced from reason is simply *blind force*, and can not be dignified with the name of Will. The mind of man is sometimes in a predominant state of *knowing*, sometimes in a predominant state of *feeling*, and sometimes in a predominant state of *determination*. To call these separate faculties, however, is altogether beside the mark. No act of intelligence can be performed without some determination of the Ego, no act of determination without some cognition, and no act of the one or the other without some amount of feeling being mingled in the process. Thus, while each mental state may have its distinctive characteristics, there is unity at the root—*the identical Ego, spirit,* WILL.[2]

Sensibility is the condition, Reason is the light, Will is the centre of human consciousness. Consciousness is a threefold phenomenon in which feeling, knowing, and self-determination are reciprocal elements, and in their connection and simultaneousness, and at the same time their differentiation, they compose the entire intellectual life.[3] The finite spirit or WILL unfolds itself, first, subjectively, in the spontaneous affirmation of self-being or self-potency (IPSËITY); secondly, objectively, in the exer-

[1] Green, "Spiritual Philosophy," vol. i. p. 2.
[2] Morell, "Psychology," p. 61.
[3] Cousin, "Elements of Psychology," p. 452.

tion of power to produce motion, change, phenomena (EFFICIENCY); thirdly, synthetically, in the unity of motive and intention, purpose and act, means and end (PERSONALITY).

Thus does "Will present the middle point, which embraces *thought* on the one hand and *force* on the other; and which yet, so far from appearing to us to be a *compound* arising out of them as an effect, is more easily conceived as the originative prefix (prothesis) of all mental phenomena. . . . It carries with it, in its very idea, the co-presence of thought as the necessary element within whose sphere it has to manifest itself; its phenomena can not exist alone; it acts on preconceptions, which stand related to it, not however as its source, but as its conditions, and are its co-ordinates in the effect, rather than its generating antecedents."[1]

Psychological analysis leads us inevitably to this conclusion, that all things are issued by Will, whether in the sphere of the finite or the infinite, and therefore we postulate an UNCONDITIONED WILL, A PERFECT MIND, at the source of all becoming. Thus, as Martineau truly remarks, *between the* FORCE *of the physical atheist and the* THOUGHT *of the metaphysical pantheist, we fix upon* WILL *as the true balancing-point of a moral theism.*

The intelligent reader scarce needs to be reminded that this is the conclusion reached by reflective thought in that best and fullest exhibition of it which is found in Greek philosophy. The great problem of Greek philosophy, as of all philosophy, was, "What is the αρχή, the First Principle—the ground and cause and reason of all existence?" The final answer of that age is found in Plato, for Platonism was the culmination, the ripened

[1] Martineau's "Essays," p. 188, 2d Series.

fruit of the ages of earnest thought which preceded Plato. He gathered up, co-ordinated, and grasped into unity the results bequeathed by the mental efforts of his predecessors. The Platonic answer to this great question of philosophy is clear and unequivocal. A perfect MIND is the primal source of all being — a Mind in which Intellect, Efficiency, and Goodness are one and identical. "Mind is the most worthy αρχή." "God is the most excellent of causes."[1] "Mind is king of heaven and earth."[2] "Motion and life and soul and mind are present with absolute being. We can not imagine being to be devoid of life and mind, remaining in awful unmeaningness and everlasting fixture."[3]

"Whatever begins to be, must necessarily be produced by some cause; for nothing can have its generation without a cause." "The Maker and Father of the universe . . . had no beginning of his being." He formed the universe according to the eternal model or archetype which his own reason supplied, and for motives which his own essential goodness proposed. "Let us now tell for what cause the Maker of this creation and this universe made it as it is. He was *good;* and he who is good grudges no advantage to any creature. Being thus free from envy, He willed that the universe should be good like Himself; and this, the special ground of the creation and the world, which we receive from the wisest philosophers, we must accept."[4]

It would be easy to show that the recognition of intelligent Will, as standing at the fountain-head of all the force which is manifested in the universe, is common to the first Physicists of this age.

[1] "Timæus," ch. ix.
[2] "Philebus," § 50.
[3] "Sophist," § 72.
[4] "Timæus," ch. ix. x.

Grove concludes his admirable essay on "The Correlation of the Physical Forces" with these words: "In all phenomena the more closely they are investigated the more are we convinced that, humanly speaking, neither matter nor force can be created or annihilated, and that an essential cause is unattainable [by science]—*Causation is the* WILL, *Creation is the act, of God.*"[1] Sir John Herschel has not hesitated to express his conviction that "it is but reasonable to regard the Force of Gravitation as the direct or indirect result of a consciousness or a WILL existing somewhere."[2] Dr. Carpenter, with his usual sagacity in penetrating to the essential point, remarks that the WILL "is that form of Force which must be taken as the type of all the rest;" "Force must be regarded as the direct expression of WILL."[3] "If," says Wallace, "we have traced one force, however minute, to an origin in our own WILL, while we have no knowledge of any other primary cause of force, it does not seem an improbable conclusion that *all force may be* WILL-FORCE, and thus the whole universe is not only dependent on, but actually is the will of higher intelligences or of one Supreme Intelligence."[4] In short, the present attitude of science in relation to this great problem is, I think, fairly represented by the Duke of Argyll: "Science, in the modern doctrine of the Conservation of Energy and the Convertibility of Forces, is already getting hold of the idea that all kinds of Force are but forms and manifestations of some

[1] "Correlation and Conservation of Forces," p. 199.

[2] "Outlines of Astronomy," pp. 233–4; also "Familiar Lectures on Scientific Subjects," pp. 462, 475.

[3] "Human Physiology," p. 542; also art. "On Mutual Relation of Vital and Physical Forces," *Philosophical Transactions*, p. 730.

[4] "Natural Selection," p. 368. See Mivart, "Genesis of Species," p. 298; Laycock, "Mind and Brain," vol. i. pp. 225, 304; Murphy, "Scientific Basis of Faith," p. 51.

one Central Force issuing from some one Fountain-head of Power." "This one Force, into which all others return again, is itself but a mode of action of the Divine WILL."[1] Even Spencer concedes that "the Force by which we ourselves produce changes, and which serves to symbolize the cause of changes in general, is the final disclosure of all analysis . . . all other modes of consciousness are derived from our consciousness of exerting Force."[2] "The order of nature is doubtless very imperfect, but its production is far more compatible with the hypothesis of an intelligent will than with that of blind mechanism."[3] Physical science is surely coming into harmony with metaphysical thought. It looks upon nature with the eye of reason as well as the eye of sense. And it reduces the phenomena to unity, not simply by comparative abstraction, which classifies under resemblance, co-existence, and succession, but by that rational integration which operates under the necessary laws of substance, causality, intentionality, and absolute unity. It regards the forces of nature as the product or manifestation of a higher force—a force which is not merely dynamical in its nature—a force which can compass not merely concurrent and antagonistic motions in space, but which is able so to adjust these concurrences and antagonisms as to construct agencies which shall realize designs—a force, therefore, which is thoughtful and percipient: in one word, intelligent—a force, in fine, which is not a mere mechanical dynamism in space and time, but a true Power existing in its type and fullness: in one word—God.[4]

[1] "Reign of Law," pp. 123, 129; Cooke, "Religion and Chemistry," p. 340.
[2] "First Principles," p. 235. See also Challis, "Principles of Mathematics and Physics," p. 681.
[3] Comte, "L'Ensemble du Positivisme," p. 46.
[4] M'Vicar, "Sketch of Philosophy," p. 8.

Thus does all reflective thought, whether directed to the phenomena of the human mind or the phenomena of nature, confirm the *à priori* intuition of an unconditioned Will unfolding itself in Thought and Power, and completing itself in a harmonious Totality, as the First Principle and Originative Cause of all existences and of all relations, of all individual beings, and of that harmonious whole men call the Cosmos.

And now we pass to the important question—How are we to bring all our acquired conceptions of God into harmony with this fundamental idea? Assuming that we have certain conceptions of God which are derived from verbal instruction, and ultimately from Divine revelation, can we bring these into unity under this First Principle? Or, in other words, can we logically evolve the attributes and perfections of God out of this fundamental Idea, and find the result in harmony with the Christian doctrine?

As the object of thought, even of Christian thought, God must necessarily be conceived by us under the fundamental categories of *Being*, *Attribute*, and *Relation.* All objects of thought must come under these categories, and out of or beyond these categories we can not think at all. Furthermore, we can not think of God as the unconditioned Being conditioning Himself, without conceiving Him as *Reality*, *Efficiency*, and *Personality.* These constitute the conception of the Divine essence whereby it is what it is. When we think of the Attributes of such a Being, we must necessarily conceive them as *Absolute*, *Infinite*, and *Perfect.*[1] And when we think of the Re-

[1] These terms are frequently and somewhat loosely employed as synonymous; but in reality each has its own peculiar shade of meaning. Here we employ the term *Absolute* to denote the underived, independent, incomposite,

lations of God to finite existences and finite consciousness, we are constrained to regard Him as the *Ground* and *Cause* and *Reason* of all dependent being.

In the unity and completeness of this categorical scheme of thought, we can not fail to recognize the following logical order:

BEING (Essentia)	REALITY }	EFFICIENCY }	PERSONALITY }
ATTRIBUTE (Related Essence)	ABSOLUTE }	INFINITE }	PERFECT }
RELATION (Free Determination)	GROUND	CAUSE	REASON OF END

In the Absolute Reality we have the ultimate ground; in the Infinite Efficiency we have the adequate cause; and in the Perfect Personality we have the sufficient reason or final cause of all existence.

1. BEING or ESSENCE, as *Reality*, *Efficiency*, and *Personality*. The intuition of Being is the most fundamental and the most abstract of all ideas. After every property and relation has been eliminated, there still remains the affirmation that something *is*. Non-existence, except as the negation of being, is inconceivable. But, at the same time, pure being is the most indeterminate of all ideas. Simple being, without attributes, and out of all relation to other ideas, is a notion without contents, and consequently indescribable and unknowable. For us, therefore, pure abstract being is equal to non-being, and the paradox of Hegel has some truth: Pure Being=Nothing. Distinction—differentiation, determination—is the

and immutable. *Infinite* is employed to denote the absence of all limitation—that which can not be bounded, measured, quantified. *Perfect* is employed to denote that which is complete, finished, self-sufficient—that which has no defect and no want. *The unconditioned* is a genus, of which the Infinite, Absolute, and Perfect are species—not conditioned by quantity, kind, or degree. For the Infinite there are no limits; for the Absolute no parts, no equals, and no change; for the Perfect no wants. See Calderwood, "Philosophy of the Infinite," p. 179; *North American Review*, Oct. 1864, pp. 407, 417.

condition of all reality. Real being must be determined, only pure nothing can be undetermined. The least *determined being* is the least real; the most determined is the most real, the most perfect being. Exactly in proportion as the nature of beings is differentiated and complicated do they rise in the scale of being. The vegetable has more determinations than inanimate matter; the percipient animal has more determinations than the vital plant; rational man has more determinations than the percipient animal, he is the most complicated, the most determined, and therefore the most perfect being in creation. An absolutely perfect being must be the most determined of all beings; he must contain within himself a fullness of determinations.

The pantheist Spinoza tells us that determination is negation—that is, limitation. "*Omnis determinatio negatio est.*" Nothing can be falser or more arbitrary than this principle. Its fallacy consists in the confusion of two things essentially different, namely, the *limits of a being*, and *its determinate characteristics*. A pure Ego, by determining itself to thought, affection, or action, is not thereby limited. The limitation or the illimitation depends simply upon the character of the thought, affection, or act as perfect or imperfect. "I am an intelligent being, and my intelligence is limited; these are two facts equally certain. The possession of intelligence is the constitutive characteristic of my being which distinguishes me from the brute. The limitation imposed upon my intellect, which can only see a small number of truths at a time, is my limit, and this is what distinguishes me from the Absolute Being, from Perfect Intelligence which sees all truths at a glance. That which constitutes my imperfection is not certainly my being intelligent; therein, on the contrary, lies the strength, the richness, and the dignity of my being. What constitutes my weakness and my nothingness is that this intelligence is inclosed in a narrow circle. Thus, inasmuch as I am intelligent, I participate in being and perfection; inasmuch as I am only intelligent within certain limits, I am imperfect."[1] Determination differs from limitation as much as being differs from nothing.

The Causative Principle of all reality must itself be *real*, that is, it must be a self-manifesting and self-conscious power, for there can be no reality without consciousness. Being which is not known to itself, and can not manifest itself, is as though it were not. Intuition, *sui conscia*, is the essence of reality. Here being and knowing are identical. It must also contain within itself a fullness of determinations, must be rich in ideas, must be the archetype of all possible existences. All forms and relations, all ideas and laws, all individual and special adaptations, all harmonious systems, must be present to the Absolute Reality. "Uncreated must be Mental Being. This seems an invincible necessity of all thought. Whatever else, or whatever more it is, it must be Mental Being"=REASON.

The Causative Principle of all efficiency must itself be *power*, pluri-efficiency, it must be self-determined and self-moved, and perfectly adequate to the production of being, motion, change, life, and intelligence objective to itself; in a word, it must be adequate to the realization of all the ideals which reason supplies; it must be unlimited Infinite Efficiency=SPIRIT.

The Causative Principle of all personality must itself be *personal*—that is, it must have a self-conceived, self-de-

[1] Saisset, "Modern Pantheism," vol. ii. p. 70.

termined purpose; must freely choose and wisely adapt the means to realize that purpose; above all, it must have a worthy motive, a best and highest reason for both purpose and act; and must make all conform to and result in a moral order in harmony with the blessedness and worthy the approbation of the All-perfect One. Intuition and choice, affection and conscience—these are the grand momenta of personality.

The necessary demand of reason is that the first and originative cause of all finite personality shall be Himself a person. Consciousness can not arise out of unconsciousness, reason can not be generated from unreason, personality can not have its birth from impersonality, no more than something can be born of nothing. There must be intelligence answering to our intelligence, freedom answering to our freedom, feeling responding to our feeling, and moral sentiment unisonant with our moral sentiment: in short, personality correlated with our personality, in the cause and author of finite responsible being. That perfection which is mirrored in our finite personality exists in all its fullness in the unconditionally perfect Being, the Perfect Personality whose name is LOVE.[1]

God, then, is the Absolute, Infinite, and Perfect Being in whom, by whom, and for whom the finite has existence and consciousness. He is *the unconditioned, conditionating Will.* The Divine Essence can not be apprehended or expressed in a higher universal. This is the first dim intuition of spontaneous reason, and the final goal of

[1] "The idea of God is the unity of three factors—the logical (intelligence), the ethical (love), and the physical (might)."—Dr. Martensen, "Die Christliche Ethik," § 19.

all reflective thought. The Divine Being is He who is before all, and who originates, destines, and conditions all. The Biblical idea of the unconditioned Being is in perfect harmony with the philosophical idea. In the language of Scripture, "the Will of God" stands for the remotest, inmost essence of the Godhead—a will which is the absolute identity, the eternal co-inherence of reason, power, and love. The Divine Will as efficient cause is never dissociated from the Divine Will as the formal cause and the final cause. That will is at once cause and law and reason of all things. God "effectuates all things according to the *counsel* (τὴν βουλὴν=deliberation, purpose, design) of his own Will" (Eph. i. 11). And not only according to the counsel, but "according to the *good pleasure* (τὴν εὐδοκίαν=the benevolent affection) of his own will" (ver. 5); a "good pleasure which He hath PURPOSED (προέθετο) in Himself (ver. 9). He "created all things, and for his own *pleasure* (θέλημα=will) they are and were created." Here "Will" is clearly more than power, more than efficiency: it is thought or purpose; it is reason or end; in a word, it is the identity and co-inherence of reason, power, and love. The unconditioned Will as revealed to us in Scripture is an *intelligent* Will —a will that thinks, deliberates, counsels, designs; and it is also a *benevolent* Will—a will that loves and delights in and desires the good of being. And in thinking and desiring it effectuates, for thinking and operating, desiring and doing, are one with God. "He speaks and it is done, He commands and it stands fast." Creation is a speech of God, a language in which He reveals his thoughts, his purposes, his benevolent designs, his will —that is, Himself. Every revelation of God is the development in us of the consciousness of the REAL BEING (τὸ ὄντως ὄν). All the proofs of the being of God—the etiological, the cosmological, the teleological, and the moral—are centred in the *ontological:* this is first and last. And just as our consciousness of the indivisible identical EGO as the unity and co-inherence of reason, feeling, and power is the exact arresting-point of psychological science, beyond which thought can not pass, so our intuition of the unconditioned BEING as the absolute identity of Reason, Power, and Love is the exact arresting point of Theological science, beyond which nothing can be known. Spirit, Light, Love—these designate essence or being. "GOD IS SPIRIT" (πνεῦμα=Spirit, not a Spirit—John iv. 24), the self-moving, efficient, animating principle, the unity and life-motion of the creative divine activity; *ἡ ζωὴ αἰώνιος*—vita absoluta—underived, eternal Life (John v. 26; xi. 25; 1 John v. 20). GOD IS LIGHT (1 John i. 5), the self-manifesting, intuitional, revealing principle=ὁ λόγος; the Eternal Reason, in which Spirit becomes objective to itself, and God is revealed to Himself (John i. 1; 1 Tim. vi. 16). GOD IS LOVE (1 John iv. 8, 16), the self-complete, self-sufficient, self-satisfying principle = τὸ τέλος, the Perfect One (Matth. v. 48). This Divine Love finds its fullest satisfaction in the κόσμος νοητός, the intelligible world as revealed and rendered objective to Himself in "the WORD." Reason, Spirit, Love are the simplest elements in the conception of the unconditioned Being: Reason as Reality, Spirit as Efficiency, and Love as Perfection.

The unconditioned Being is revealed, may we not say "incarnated,"[1] in the κόσμος αἴσθησις—the sensible world: 1, by the incarnation of the Spirit in the moving and animating forces of nature; 2, by the incarnation of

[1] Dr. Whedon, *Meth. Qu. Review*, Jan. 9, 1871, p. 164.

the Reason in the typical forms and permanent laws or relations of the universe, by which reality becomes known to finite minds; 3, by the incarnation of Love in the final causes, the benevolent purposes, which are realized in the completed Cosmos and the life of Humanity.[1]

2. Attribute or Related Essence. The knowledge of the Divine Essence is the root of the knowledge of the Divine Attributes, for in every conception of an attribute the Divine Essence is, in some mode or other, supposed. We may therefore define an attribute as a conception of the unconditioned Being under some relation to our consciousness. That conception may be either positive or negative, and the relation may consequently be one of causation or abstraction.

When we conceive of the Divine Essence as *reality*, our conception is in some measure determined by our consciousness of reality. The intuition of reality is immanent to our own consciousness. We know self as a reality, an indivisible, identical Ego—a unity, but yet a conditioned and dependent reality, which must have its ground and cause in an independent and unconditioned reality. Thus the pure intuition of reality is a preluding for the affirmation of absolute reality. We can not, however, affirm such reality on purely subjective grounds. To the eye of reason, which is the organ of necessary and absolute truth, the Divine Essence abstracts itself from the limits of space and time, and absolves itself from all the determinations of objective being. It is a reality which is not conditioned by *kind*, a reality which is independent

[1] As related to the purpose of Redemption. God the Father is the moving or actuating cause of Redemption, God the Son is the revealing and actualizing cause, and God the Spirit is the active and efficient cause. Father =Love; Logos=Revealer; Spirit=Life.

of, absolved from, undetermined by any other antecedent or contemporaneous being—absolute reality.

Furthermore, when we conceive the Divine Essence as *power* or efficiency, our conception is in some measure determined by our consciousness of power. We know ourselves as a power, a cause of our own volitions, and a power which can control and modify external nature, but yet a limited and finite cause. To the eye of reason the Divine efficiency transcends all limitation and mensuration. It is a power which is not conditioned by *quantity*. It is limitless power, spaceless, all-mighty presence, self-directive power, carrying its own light and seeing its own way—infinite efficiency.

And, finally, when we conceive of the Divine Essence as *personality*, again our conception is in some measure determined by our consciousness of personality. We are conscious of desiring and purposing, of determining and doing, of approving and delighting in our artistic and ethical creations, and in these we stand out from the plane of nature as persons and not things. But we are also conscious of limitation and imperfection. We fall short even of our own ideals; we feel we have unsatisfied longings and daily wants. The Divine Essence reveals itself to reason as exempt from all limitation by *degree*. "Pure personality is no more limited than absolute being, but it is deeper by all the contents of perfect consciousness." It is a personality which has no defect and no want: unconditioned, unlimited perfection—perfect personality.

Our conception of the Attributes of God may thus be formed through some relation to our consciousness, but by a process of immediate abstraction—the negation of all limitation by kind, by quantity, or by degree.

1. As related to our intuition of real being; by abstraction from all other being and personality—the *Immanent* attributes of God.

2. As causally related to finite, dependent existence; by elimination of all necessary limitation—the *Relative or Transitive* attributes of God.

3. As ethically related to finite personality; by elimination of all imperfection — the *Moral* attributes of God.

1. *The* IMMANENT *attributes.* The absolute reality (REASON) must necessarily be conceived as First, Supreme, and Sole; must be underived, and therefore eternal; must be absolved from all necessary relation to other being, and therefore independent; must be above all law of change, and therefore immutable; must have incomposite unity, and therefore indivisible; and must be the only one, for two absolutes would limit each other, and are thus inconceivable. Finally, absolute reality must be the fullness and archetype of all being in which every form and every relation, every totality and every harmony, conceivable or possible, must be ideally and eternally present.

ETERNITY (1 Tim. i. 17; vi. 15, 16; Rev. i. 4, 8; Heb. i. 8).

IMMUTABILITY (James i. 17; Psalm cii. 26, 27; Heb. i. 12).

UNITY (Isaiah xliv. 6; Eph. iv. 6; 1 Tim. ii. 5; John xvii. 3).

IDEALITY (Psalm cxxxix. 16; Rom. xi. 36; Acts xv. 18).

These are the immanent attributes of God.

2. *The* TRANSITIVE OR RELATIVE *attributes.* The In-

finite Efficiency (SPIRIT) must necessarily be conceived as all-mighty, all-present, and all-knowing. The Infinite Spirit fills, penetrates, moves, and vitalizes the universe. He is in all, and through all, and transcends all. He can not be bounded in space or limited in power, therefore He is spaceless and infinite. "He is every where present, not virtually but substantially, for virtue can not subsist without substance." And as the All-mighty is present every where, present to all things, so all things exist "in Him," and are present to Him in an immediate and intuitive vision—He knows all things.

OMNIPOTENCE (Psalm cxv. 3; Jer. xxxii. 27; Rom. xi. 36; 1 Cor. viii. 6).

UBIQUITY (Psalm cxxxix. 7–13; Jer. xxiii. 23, 24; 1 Cor. xv. 28; Matth. x. 29).

OMNISCIENCE (Psalm cxxxix. 1–6; Acts i. 24; Heb. iv. 13; Matth. vi. 8).

These are the relative or transitive attributes of God.

3. *The* MORAL *attributes.* Perfect Personality (LOVE) must by the very conception be wise and holy, righteous and blessed, for these are the attributes of personality, and may all be ultimately grounded in love. The reason of all existence and all personality is found, not in infinite causality, but in the free love of the perfect personality. This is the final cause of all existence. And if perfect Love be the final cause of all existence, it must know the end, and ordain the law and means. The highest end of the world is the perfect fellowship of man with God; the physical must therefore be subordinated to the moral order of the universe. The Perfect Personality must freely will to impart his fellowship to those who are obedient to his moral law; and it must be removed from fellowship

with and deny itself to evil, which is antagonistic to the ends of Love. Or, in other words, it must establish a fixed and changeless relation between righteousness and blessedness in the creature. It must approve the good and condemn the evil. And in making the righteous "partakers of his joy," He must be "well pleased." The absolute blessedness of God is found in the fullness and harmony of the Divine life. He has in Himself the eternal and absolutely worthy object of his love. But there is a Divine satisfaction, "a good pleasure of God," which is found in the communication of Himself to the creature. "He rejoiceth in the habitable parts of the earth, and his delights are with the sons of men." "He taketh pleasure in them that fear Him, in those that hope in his mercy."

WISDOM (Job xii. 13; Rom. xi. 33, 34; Eph. iii. 9, 10).

GOODNESS (Psalm xxxiii. 5; xxxiv. 8; cvii. 1, 8).

HOLINESS (Deut. xxxii. 4; Psalm v. 5; James i. 13, 17).

BLESSEDNESS (1 Tim. i. 11; vi. 15).

These are the moral attributes of God.[1] They are also called by pre-eminence the Perfections of God, because they are free determinations of the Divine nature, an everlasting "BECOMING," rather than an eternal "BEING." The immanent attributes of God are a necessary inbeing; the moral attributes of God are a voluntary outgoing, an eternally free, alternative forth-putting of choice for the right and the good.[2]

The doctrine concerning God above presented, in which

[1] The Justice, Truth, and Faithfulness of God are not properly regarded as attributes of the Divine nature, but as modes of Divine conduct or action, determined by the Holiness and Goodness of God. So Grace, Mercy, Compassion are but modifications of Divine Love viewed in relation to sinful, guilty, and suffering creatures, and their consideration belongs not to the doctrine of Creation, but of Redemption.

[2] Whedon, "On the Freedom of the Will," p. 316.

we fain would hope that philosophy and Christian thought are brought into harmony, may now be summarily presented in the following schema:

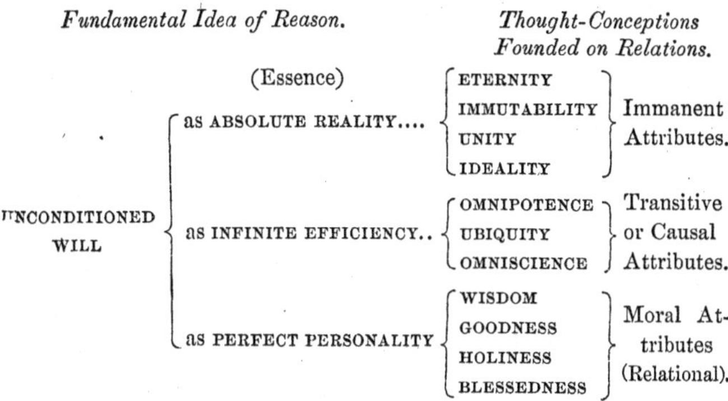

The references to the Sacred Scriptures already given will show the harmony between the conceptions of reason and the verbal revelations of God. Reason and Scripture unite in proclaiming that God is "the great and holy *One* that inhabiteth eternity," who "only hath immortality," "with whom is no variableness," and who "filleth all in all;" to whom "all his works are known from eternity," in whose book "all our members were written when as yet there was none of them," and whose "purposes," ideas, and plans are "eternal." These are mainly the immanent attributes of God, conceptions which flow from the very idea of the Absolute and Infinite Being. They are evolved from Real Being by the negation of all limit, all parts, all change; the canceling of time and space and matter, the recognition of God as pure Reason, pure Spirit, pure Love.

The Scriptures, however, deal more immediately with the causal, transitive, and relational aspects of the Divine attributes—that is, with the conception of God in his voluntary relations to finite being and finite personality. They speak of God in his historically known existence, as a Being who *voluntarily* conditions his Omnipotence and Sovereignty under concessions of self-reality, self-life, and freedom to finite beings, without Himself being conditioned by any thing—a *self-limitation* which in nowise detracts from the absoluteness and infinity of God—an *unconditioned conditioning Will.*[1]

The relation which God sustains to his works is not a *necessary* relation—it is a *voluntary* and self-imposed relation. Free Love is the highest determining principle for the efficiency of Divine Omnipotence. Power thus directed and conditioned by wisdom and love does not, can not detract from the perfection of God. The substitution of *choice* for necessity is, in fact, no real limitation; on the contrary, it ascribes to God the most *absolute perfection.*

The causal attributes of God, or those conceptions of God which are especially grounded upon his relation to the world and humanity, are properly divided into those which are Cosmical and those which are Ethical. The first, of course, embrace his relation to the world, the second his relation to personal, responsible beings. The content of the cosmological conception is Omnipotence, Ubiquity, Omniscience. The content of the ethical conception is Wisdom, Goodness, Holiness, and Blessedness. God as the Creator and Sustainer of the world, God as the Father, Teacher, and Ruler of humanity, are the two grand manifestations of the one infinite and perfect Being, and "*Elohim*" and "*Jehovah*" are his expressive and distinctive names, the first denoting the cosmical activity

[1] For an exhaustive discussion of this subject, see Müller, "Christian Doctrine of Sin," vol. ii. pp. 199–215.

of God, the latter his government and kingdom among men.

These two grand aspects of the Divine manifestation are marked in the Elohistic and Jehovistic portions of the first revelation given to the Semitic race. They are still more distinctly recognized in Paul's discourse before the assembled Athenian philosophers, where Christian theology was for the first time presented to the Greek mind—God the Creator and Conservator of the world (Acts xvii. 24, 25); God the Father, Teacher, Ruler, and Judge of humanity (Acts xvii. 26–31).

CHAPTER III.

THE CREATION.

God is the Absolute, Infinite, and Perfect Being, in whom, through whom, and for whom are all things. This is the Christian conception of God; and it is the only conception which furnishes an adequate and satisfactory explanation of all the facts of the universe. Here we have a First Principle, an Originative Cause which is sufficient to account for all existence.

But what conception are we to form of the nature and mode of this Origination? Was it a pure, supernatural Origination, an absolute Creation? or was it simply a formation out of a first substance existing coeval with and independent of God? Was that act of creation determined by necessity? was it an unconscious emanation from, or a necessary development of that First Principle? Or was it a conscious, free exertion of power for the realization of a foreseen and predetermined plan—a mental Order? What is the Biblical conception of Creation? This is the question we must now endeavor to answer.

Until very recently it has been the practice of theologians to attempt the determination of the Biblical notion of Creation on purely philological grounds. It is now generally conceded that this method is inadequate and inconclusive. The Greeks probably never conceived the idea of an absolute creation (commonly, though we judge incorrectly, styled creation *ex nihilo*), and consequently the Greek language has no terms expressive of a primal origination, an absolute beginning of the world. Ποιεῖν, the term employed in the LXX. (Gen. i. 1), and also by St. Paul (Acts xvii. 24), means to endow with a certain quality (ποῖος=*qualis*)—to construct, make, form, build, and evidently conveys the notion of *formation* rather than *origination*, the production of qualitative phenomena rather than real entity; κτίζειν is also ordinarily used in the sense of forming, fashioning, building, and seems to imply pre-existing materials.

There is also a wide difference of opinion among Oriental scholars with respect to the precise import of the verbs בָּרָא (bara), עָשָׂה (aysah), and יָצַר (yetsar), as employed in the Hebrew Scriptures. Some distinguished critics, as Parkhurst, Clarke, Lange, and Delitzsch, assert that בָּרָא means to originate *de novo*, to create in an absolute sense; and that עָשָׂה and יָצַר strictly mean to fashion out of pre-existent materials.[1] But Pusey, Kitto, Tayler Lewis, and some of the Rabbinical commentators (Aben Ezra especially), affirm that בָּרָא (bara), both

[1] We make no pretensions to critical acquaintance with the Hebrew, but will hazard this suggestion. עָשָׂה (aysah) is the most general term; its fundamental meaning is *to do, to perform, to work*, and may embrace both origination and formation. בָּרָא (bara) and יָצַר (yetsar) are more specific, the former denoting the origination of a new essence or substance, the latter formation or fashioning out of pre-existing materials. Thus we read in Gen. ii. 7: "And the Lord God formed [יָצַר] man [*i. e.*, the body of man] out of the dust of the earth." Here we have pre-existing matter. But in Gen. i. 27 we read, "And God created [בָּרָא] man [*i. e.*, the soul of man] in his own image." Here we have no pre-existing material, for matter can not bear the image of God. (See Acts xvii. 29.) *Bara* must therefore here mean origination. Even in Gen. i. 21, where *bara* is employed in regard to the production of *living creatures*, we have the origination of something new: for *vitality, sensitivity, perception* are not properties of matter, neither can they be educed from any organization of matter.

by its etymology and its connections, indicates *formation* as much as origination, and is, in fact, indifferent and neutral either as to a supposed creation *ex nihilo*, or a creation, that is, a formation from pre-existing materials. Furthermore, it is affirmed that the three Hebrew verbs are used indiscriminately in the Mosaic record. It is said in Gen. i. 27 that God created (בָּרָא) man, and that statement is amplified and explained at ch. ii. 7: "And the Lord God formed [עָשָׂה] man *out of the dust of the earth*."[1] An appeal to the merely verbal expressions of Scripture does not, therefore, promise any satisfactory and conclusive results.

By what method, then, are we to determine the Biblical notion of Creation? Clearly, not by a critical study of the several words which are employed to express the creative act—not by confining our attention to the visible embodiment of the Divine word, and neglecting the informing thought. We must ground our conception of creation upon the fundamental ideas and principles of Divine revelation, and determine it in harmony with the Christian idea of God, and the Christian doctrine of the relation of the world to God.

These fundamental principles we have already presented. They may be succinctly restated in the following propositions:

(1.) God is the one only self-existent, independent, unconditioned Being, "who alone hath immortality," "the incorruptible or immutable God" (ἀφθάρτος Θεός), "with

[1] We can not help regarding this mode of reasoning as superficial and misleading. Gen. i. 27, "So God created [בָּרָא] man in *his own image*," refers to the spiritual nature of man which alone can bear the "image of God," and must mean *origination*. Gen. ii. 7, "And the Lord God formed [עָשָׂה] man out of the dust of the earth," refers solely to the body of man. This distinction can scarcely be accidental.

whom is no variableness or shadow of change."[1] (2.) God is the sole causality of the heavens and the earth, in the most absolute sense. Whatever is, and is not God, is the creature of God. "By Him were all things created which are in heaven and which are upon earth, things visible and things invisible"—the objects of sense-perception and of rational intuition. The origin, development, and end, the principle, law, and reason of all existence, are in God and from God—πάντα ἐκ τοῦ Θεοῦ, ἐν τῷ Θεῷ, εἰς τὸν Θεόν.[2] (3.) The all of the finite is in ceaseless and complete dependence on the Divine causality—"He upholdeth all things," and "by Him all things consist."

Our interpretation of the formal language of Scripture, especially of the verbs which are employed to denote the act of creation, must therefore be informed and determined by these fundamental principles. If God is the unconditioned Cause of all existence, then the Creation must be the absolutely *free* and self-determined act of God. As such, it can not have been conditioned by any immanent necessity in the Divine nature itself, nor by any necessary existence out of and extraneous to the Divine nature. By this conception of God, and of his relation to the world, we are debarred from supposing the coeval existence of any thing besides God (*e. g.*, ἄπειρον, τὸ μὴ ὄν of Plato, the ὕλη of Aristotle, the "matter" of the modern Physicist) as the condition and medium of the Divine agency and manifestation. While, therefore, it is acknowledged that in Gen. i. 21, 27, בָּרָא (bara) denotes the *formation* of organic bodies out of pre-existent materials, we can not be restricted to this meaning of the term when dealing with verse 1, "In the beginning God created the heaven and the earth." We are compelled

[1] James i. 17. [2] Rom. xi. 36.

to believe that "bara" here means *origination*—origination *de novo;* first, because the primal act of creation must have been a supernatural, miraculous production of something which had not previously existed under any form—an unconditioned creation antecedent to nature; and, secondly, because we are informed that after this primal act of creation, "the earth was still *without form* and void." No possible ingenuity of criticism can construe that opening sentence of revelation to mean, "In the beginning God gave *form* to pre-existing matter." That first beginning is the *principium principiorum*, the beginning of all beginnings, and must be distinguished from the six new beginnings of the six days' work.[1] We must regard this sublime utterance, standing at the head of all God's communications, as affirming this foundation-idea of revelation—that God is the sole causality of the heavens and the earth in an absolute sense, the efficient cause of time, and all temporal relations; the all-mighty cause of space, and all spatial relations; the originator of the primordial substance, and all its qualities—in a word, the unconditioned Creator of all finite being, quality, and relation—"בְּרֵאשִׁית—ἐν ἀρχῇ—*in principio*—first of all (in the order of conception rather than the order of time) God originated, laid the foundations of, the heavens and the earth."[2]

And now that the Creation here affirmed was an absolute origination, a bringing into being of the primordial

[1] Lange's "Commentary," Introduction.

[2] We can not overlook the connection between Gen. i. 1 and John i. 1, and close our eyes to the light which the later announcement throws upon the former. It is most probable that by ἐν ἀρχῇ John means ἐν αἰῶνι, in eternity—that is, before all time-succession began. Ἀρχή here can have no relation to time. And why may we not accept the Platonic notion of "a creation in eternity," which itself constituted a beginning of time? Prior to finite succession and change, there can be *no time.*

elements out of which the heavens and the earth were subsequently "formed," is the doctrine of the best Hebrew lexicographers. It is held by many of the best authorities that the particle אֵת (ayth) means "the very substance of," "the very or real essence." Fürst, in his recently *published* Hebrew and Chaldee Lexicon, gives "being, essence, substance," as the meaning of "ayth." Gesenius, in his Hebrew Grammar, says "'ayth' means being, substance" (p. 216). And furthermore, he says "'*ayth*' is a substantive derived from a pronominal stem, and signifies essence, substance, being." "The particle '*ayth*,'" says Aben Ezra, "signifies the substance of a thing." Kimchi, in his famous "Book of Hebrew Roots," gives a similar definition. In the Syriac version, "*yoth*" takes the place of "*ayth*," and is very appropriately rendered in Walton's Polyglot, "*esse cœli et esse terræ*"—the being or substance of the heavens and the earth. It is not, therefore, a fanciful and altogether unauthorized reading of this opening sentence of Divine revelation which the Christian idea of God, and of his relation to the world, seems to demand—"*In the beginning God originated, brought into being, the primordial elements of the heavens and the earth.*"

For manageable clearness, in dealing with the Mosaic primeval history, we shall find ourselves under the necessity of accepting the distinction made by theologians between *creatio prima, immediata*, and *creatio mediata, formativa.*

1. *An absolute Creation*, a pure supernatural origination—the Beginning of all beginnings.

2. *An artistic, architectonic Creation*, a supernatural formation out of a first substance—the production of new

things or beings by aggregation, organization, and development according to pre-established laws and archetypal ideas.

The first notion of Creation is grounded on the Omnipotence of God, the second on the Infinite Wisdom of God, and both are united in and ultimately grounded on the unconditioned Will.

And now let us confine our attention to the first conception of Creation—*creatio prima, immediata, or* ABSOLUTE CREATION.

The fundamental Theistic conception which lies at the very root of the Biblical doctrine of Creation, and clearly distinguishes it from all Materialistic, Pantheistic, and Dualistic notions of the origin of the world, is that God is the *Absolute Personality*—the eternally self-conscious, self-complete, self-sufficient Being, all the determinations of whose *nature* and *action* are grounded in his absolute Will. The Divine essence, in its inmost, deepest ground, is not determined being, but *unlimited power of self-determination.* The primitive, root idea of the Godhead is an *ever-living, unconditioned Will* — an unconditioned Will as the indivisible unity and perpetual differentiation of *reason* and *power*, a will which realizes itself in self-affirmation (IPSËITY); manifests itself in self-determination and choice (ALTERITY); and completes itself in the actualization of a final purpose (PERFECTION).[1] The *nature* of God, as distinct from his *essence*, is absolutely his own act.[2] God, as the manifested God, is what He is by his

[1] "God being limited neither *in* nor *by* any other existence, is infinite in a positive sense, inasmuch as *his will alone* imposes all limitation."—Ulrici, "Gott und die Natur," 1862, p. 535.

[2] *Natura*—that which is produced or born, that which is always *becoming*. *Essentia*—the fundamental, permanent *being*. See note 1, following page.

own determination and choice. God is just, because He wills to be just; God is holy, because He wills to be holy; God is good, because He wills to be good, and not from any constraining, immanent necessity, otherwise He could not be the object of praise, adoration, and love. If God is not good by virtue of his own determination and choice, then there is nothing praiseworthy and adorable in his nature, and all the thanksgiving of sacred psalmody is meaningless; worship is groundless, religion has no significance, and love to God is impossible. A necessitated goodness can no more command our moral esteem than the uniform revolution of the planetary orbs, and where there is no moral esteem, there can be no love, no worship, and no praise.[1]

If, then, God is a personal Being, the Absolute Personality, another being can not proceed from Him except in virtue of his own free determination. *Creation must therefore be a* VOLUNTARY *act.*

And for the full comprehension of this fundamental principle, we must remember that volition is something more than a simple efflux of power, something more than

[1] "We Arminians hold that God is freely good from eternity to eternity, just as man is good freely and alternatively for one hour. Infinite knowledge does not insure infinite goodness. Infinite knowledge (which is a very different thing from infinite *wisdom*) is not an anterior cause of infinite goodness; but both Infinite Wisdom and Infinite Holiness *consist in* and result from God's volitions eternally, and absolutely, perfectly coinciding with, not the Wrong, but the Right. God's infinite knowledge=omniscience, is an eternal, fixed, necessary *be*-ing; God's wisdom and holiness are an eternal volitional BECOMING; an eternally free, alternative *putting forth* of choices for the Right. God's omniscience is self-existent; God's wisdom and holiness are self-made, or eternally and continuously *being made.* God is necessarily omnipotent and all-knowing through eternity, but God is *truly* wise and holy through all eternity, but no more *necessarily* than a man through a single hour. God is holy therefore, not automatically, but freely; not merely with infinite excellence, but with infinite meritoriousness."—Whedon, "Freedom of the Will," p. 316.

a mere developing tendency—an evolution or process without motive and without design. A voluntary act is a designed, an *intentional* act, the act of a being who can previously contemplate the act in thought, who can have a reason or motive for the doing of the act, and who can determine and condition the deed. This conception of creation as a voluntary act is unmistakably presented in the oft-repeated language of the Mosaic record, "God said, *Let there be—and there was!*" "The speaking of God most certainly indicates the thinking of God, and it thence follows that all the works of creation are *thoughts* of God (idealism). But it indicates also a will making itself externally known, an active operation of God; and thence it follows that all the works of creation are *deeds* of God (realism). Thinking and operating, however, are one in the Divine speaking, the primal source of language—his personality making Himself known (personalism). . . . Through creating, speaking, making, forming, the world is ever and again denoted as the *free deed* of God."[1] Furthermore, creation is a voluntary act in the most absolute sense—that is, it is an act of God to which He was not determined by any *inherent* necessity or want of his own nature, and an act which was not conditioned, in a necessary manner, by any thing out of, distinct from, and extraneous to the Divine nature.

1. *Creation was an act of God to which He was not determined by any inherent necessity or want of his own nature.*

If God is the eternally self-conscious, self-complete, and self-sufficient Being, He is under no necessity to create other beings in order to realize perfect self-consciousness, or to secure his own perfect blessedness. He does not

[1] Lange, "Commentary" on Gen. i., p. 180.

need "otherness"—that which is not Himself—in order to become manifest to Himself; neither does He "crave beings not Himself"[1] in order to his complete felicity. The antithesis of self and non-self—the *ego* and the *non-ego*—may be a necessary condition of finite personality, but it can not be a necessary condition of Absolute Personality. God is eternally revealed to Himself in an unconditioned manner as self-conscious Love, self-conscious Reason, self-conscious Energy—the Father, the Word, the Spirit; and He is from all eternity "the ever-blessed God," who has in the Divine Triunity the eternal and absolutely worthy object of his Love, independent of every relation to the world and humanity—"Thou lovedst Me *before* the foundation of the world" (John xvii. 24), "before the world was" (ver. 5).[2]

If, then, creation be the act of an Absolute Personality, the act of a Being who freely and unconditionally determines his own nature and conditionates all existence, then *the Will of God is the sole causality of the world*, and in his Will alone we have the unlimited, infinite ground-principle of all reality. Absolute Personality tolerates no other transition from the idea of God to the idea of the world than that of a Will which freely conditions itself by Love. This Free Love is the highest determining principle for the Divine efficiency. Therefore, in order to derive the essential existence of the world from God, the Scriptures postulate nothing beside or beyond an ever-living, intelligent Will which has its reason or motive, but not its necessitating cause, in Love—"*the benevolence* (εὐδοκία) *of his Will*" (Eph. i. 5). The Creation is nothing else than the free self-communication of God, who is Him-

[1] Poynting, quoted by Martineau in "Nature and God," p. 153.
[2] See also Heb. i.

self eternally self-complete and self-sufficient, but who from love alone wills that other beings shall have existence and, in fellowship with Him, eternal life.[1]

It is only by holding fast to these principles in all their integrity that we can escape the seductions of Pantheism, that perpetual temptation of metaphysical minds. The fundamental idea of Pantheism is "an indeterminate principle which is *necessarily* determined to become successively every thing. Absolute necessity is the beginning, middle, and end."[2] We can escape its iron grasp only by distinctly recognizing and firmly holding the Absolute Personality of God—that is, by affirming a perfect self-consciousness which is not conditioned by an antithetical not-self; a perfect self-determination which is not conditioned by an antecedent *natura naturans;* and a perfect self-sufficiency which knows no want. The first affirmation rejects the dialectical necessity of Hegel, the second excludes the mathematical necessity of Spinoza, the third cancels the metaphysical necessity of Cousin.[3]

2. *Creation as the free act of God was not conditioned by any thing out of and foreign to the Divine nature.*

A moment's reflection will suffice to convince us that a *limitation posited from without* would be as fatal to the idea of God as a supposed inherent necessity determining the Divine causality from within. The idea of God as the Being who is absolutely self-grounded, self-sufficient, and self-determined, equally excludes both. If God is the sole causality of the heavens and the earth in an absolute sense—the efficient cause of time and all temporal succession—the all-mighty cause of space, and of all spatial

[1] See Müller's "Christian Doctrine of Sin," vol. ii. p. 146.
[2] Saisset, "Modern Pantheism," vol. ii. p. 119.
[3] "History of Modern Philosophy," vol. i. p. 94.

relations—the sole originator of the primordial substance, and of all its qualities, then the creative act can not have been conditioned by *Time* or *Space* or *Matter*.

In his otherwise admirable essay on "Nature and God," Mr. Martineau asserts that we can have no conception of even the possibility of a creation except on the assumption of the coeval existence of something objective to God as the condition and medium of the Divine agency and manifestation. He therefore affirms the coeval and co-eternal existence of *Space* and *Matter*, *Time* and *Number*, "with Him, and yet independent of Him."[1] The idea of God's "*supplying Himself* with objectivity" is, in his judgment, "discredited by modern science." The creative act must therefore have been conditioned by something other than God, and independent of God.

Now it must be obvious to every thoughtful mind that this assumption tends to the invalidation of every proof of the existence of God. If it can be shown that any one thing exists aside from and independent of God—that any thing exists which was not created by God—then may we claim equal independence for every other thing, and He who claims to be the Creator of *all* things is discredited. As Herbert Spencer urges, with great force, "If we admit that there can be something uncaused, there is no reason to assume a cause for any thing."[2] With what reason can we say that some things do exist that never were created, but others can not so exist? If substances are eternal, why not attributes? If matter is self-existent, why not force? If space is independent, why not form? And if we concede the eternity of matter and force, why not admit the eternity of law—that is, uniformity of relations? And if so much is granted, why not also grant that a con-

[1] "Essays," 1st Series, pp. 158, 161. [2] "First Principles," p. 37.

sequent order of the universe is also eternal? If we admit that any thing besides God is self-existent, that any thing exists independent of God as "the *condition* of the Divine agency and manifestation," then God is not the unconditioned Absolute Being. "A limitation posited from without directly destroys the idea of God, for it contradicts the idea of the Absolute."[1]

Mr. Martineau admits that the assumption of "the coeval existence of matter as the condition and medium of the Divine agency" "rests on quite other grounds than those which support our belief respecting space."[2] We can conceive the non-existence of matter, but we can not conceive the non-existence of space. The idea of space is absolutely necessary, therefore "no one asks a cause for the space of the universe."[3] In making this assertion, however, Mr. Martineau betrays some want of acquaintance with the history of the philosophy of space and time. Many able and thoroughly philosophic minds have "asked a cause," and have assigned a cause for "the space of the universe." Sir Isaac Newton held that "God endures always and is present every where, and by existing always and every where *constitutes* duration and space."[4] This doctrine, thus generally stated, is held by Saisset to be incontestible.[5] McCosh also believes that time and space are not independent of God: "I am not necessarily obliged to believe that the infinity of space and time is independent of the infinity of God. . . . Who will venture to affirm that space and time, being dependent on God,

[1] Müller, "Christian Doctrine of Sin," vol. ii. p. 215.

[2] "Essays," 1st Series, p. 161. [3] "Essays," 1st Series, p. 203.

[4] "Deus durat semper et adest ubique, et existendo semper et ubique durationem et spatium, æternitatem et infinitatem *constituit.*"—*Principia, Schol. Gen.*

[5] "Modern Pantheism," vol. i. p. 180.

may not stand in some relation to God which is altogether indefinable and utterly incomprehensible by us."[1] Finally, Schleiermacher and Nitzsch do not hesitate to teach that "God is the all-mighty cause of space" and "the efficient cause of time."[2]

The question whether the idea of space is conditionally or unconditionally necessary can only be determined by the solution of the deeper question whether space is a real entity or a relation. If space is a real entity, it must have properties or attributes, but what philosopher of any reputation has ever attempted to set down the properties or attributes of space? They who assert that space is an uncreated, independent, and indestructible entity, ought to be able to define it and tell *what* it is. Dr. Porter tells us that space can not be defined, "We can not form a concept of this *entity* by means of generalized attributes or relations."[3] Can that be for us an entity of which we can form no concept, and which we can not determine in thought by any attribute or relation? The writer of the article on "The Philosophy of Time and Space," in the *North American Review*,[4] is an earnest defender of the objective reality of space as an independent and indestructible entity, and he has defined and analyzed the concept. "Space is *absolute vacuity*" (p. 91). "The idea of space is a triple synthesis . . . of three *negative* notions—receptivity, unity, and infinity; the first is the negation of matter, the second is the negation of divisibility, the third is the negation of limitation" (p. 95). Do these words convey any knowledge? Absolute vacuity is void, empty, inane. Absolute vacuity is pure nothing, and of course

[1] "Intuitions," p. 213.
[2] "System of Christian Doctrine," by Nitzsch, pp. 156–7.
[3] "The Human Intellect," p. 565.
[4] July, 1864.

there is nothing to be divided and nothing to be limited. Absolute vacuity is a negation, and unity and infinity are negations of a negation—that is, they are predicates of nothing. "Negative notions" must be predicates of *something*, otherwise they are a mere negation or absence of thought, and convey absolutely no knowledge. We may, if we please, assert with Hegel, that "Nothing is the same as Being," and then amuse ourselves with making affirmations concerning vacuity, nihility, and unreality to the disgrace of philosophy; but the common-sense of mankind will repudiate our absurdities. We can not think about nothing; all thought must be positive. Thought must have an object, and that object must be either an entity, or the attribute of an entity, or a relation between entities.

If pure space is regarded as "*absolute vacuity*"—pure nothing—then we may readily dispose of the argument on which Prof. Stewart relies with so much confidence. "Divine omnipotence can not annihilate space,"[1] therefore it must be an independent reality. We have simply to answer—the notion of annihilating nihility is an absurdity and a contradiction. There is nothing to be annihilated, and Omnipotence even must be inadequate to the annihilation of nothing.

If, with Leibnitz, Lord Monboddo, Calderwood, and many modern physicists,[2] we reject the notion of "abso-

[1] Stewart's Dissertation in "Encyclopædia Britannica," vol. i. p. 142.

[2] Even physical science rejects the notion of "pure space," and it may be reasonably doubted whether "absolute vacuity" has any place in the universe of God. As a question of science, the existence of the "vacuum" is doubtful. "It may be safely asserted that hitherto all attempts at producing a perfect vacuum have failed."—Grove, "Correlation of Physical Forces," p. 134. The general tendency of science is toward a denial of its existence (p. 137). As a question of metaphysics, the human reason can only find satisfaction in believing in a spiritual Being, a living Will which "inhabiteth eternity and immensity," and "filleth all in all" with living and

lute vacuity"—infinite space—and regard space as a *relation*—the relation of position, distance, direction—then, like all the quantitive relations of mathematics, it may be regarded as conditionally necessary—that is, bodies being given, they must necessarily have place, distance, and direction.[1] Space as a necessary relation is a reality, but a reality which is conditioned and conditional, and "God is the all-mighty cause of space." If all bodies were annihilated, there would be no position, no distance, no direction, and consequently space would be annihilated. There would remain nothing but the timeless, spaceless, Infinite One, who is the efficient cause of all existence, all qualities, and all relations. This, again, would be a sufficient answer to the sophism of Dr. Clark, quoted and indorsed by Stewart—"God can not annihilate the space in this room!" Annihilate the room, and the relative space in the room is no more—that is, the distance between the inclosing walls. Of "pure space" apart from the relations of bodies we have no conception, can have no conception; for to annihilate all bodies, in thought, we must annihilate our own body, and to a disembodied spirit there can be no *here* and no *there*. Place is a relation belonging to extension, and extension is a property of matter only.[2]

There has been so much confusion of thought generated by the mere word-jugglery of philosophers in the use of the terms *time* and *space*, *duration* and *extension*, *eternity* and *immensity*, that a revision of the whole terminology in the interest of true science is demanded. It is

life-giving fullness, so that "in Him we live and move and have being." —McCosh, "Intuitions of the Mind," p. 225.

[1] "By empty space I mean *distance*, I mean *direction*: that steeple is a mile off, and not *here* where I sit, and it lies southeast and not north." —Herschel, "Familiar Lectures on Scientific Subjects," p. 455.

[2] Taylor, "Physical Theory of Another Life," p. 26.

perilous to launch out upon this ocean of equivocal phraseology, called the philosophy of time and space, before taking our bearings, amid notions so closely related, yet so dissimilar, and endeavoring to fix some definite meaning to these terms, which, like points of the compass, shall enable us to find our position.

1. *Let us commence our effort with* SPACE, EXTENSION, *and* IMMENSITY. Some philosophers—Cousin,[1] Hamilton,[2] Spencer,[3] McCosh,[4] for example—confound *space* and *extension*, and all of them confound both with absolute *immensity*.[5]

Now if space is identical with extension, it must be cognized by the senses and the sensuous imagination. This is unhesitatingly affirmed by Hamilton: "We *see* extension," and "by the name extension we designate our empirical knowledge of space."[6] So also McCosh: "Of space in the concrete we have an immediate knowledge by the senses, certainly by some of them, such as the touch and sight."[7] Space in this connection can not therefore be regarded as an *à priori* cognition. It is equally obvious that if space is identical with extension, it must have color and form. This also is admitted by Hamilton: "I can easily annihilate all corporeal existence [in imagination]. I can im-

[1] "The idea of space—the idea of extension—is the logical condition of the admission of the idea of the body."—"History of Philosophy," vol. ii. p. 217.

[2] "Extension is only another name for space."—"Lectures on Metaphysics," vol. ii. p. 113.

[3] "Space and extension are convertible terms."—"First Principles," p. 48.

[4] See "Intuitions," p. 223, where the terms are employed as synonymous.

[5] L'immensité ou l'unité de l'espace."—Cousin, "Histoire de la Philosophie du xviiime Siècle," p. 121. "Infinity of extension."—McCosh, "Intuitions," p. 223. "Infinite immensity of space."—Hamilton, "Discussions," p. 36.

[6] "Lectures," vol. ii. pp. 114, 167.

[7] "Intuitions," p. 202.

agine *empty* space. But there are two attributes of which I can not divest it—that is, shape and color."[1] Now if space has "shape," that is, figure, it must have dimensions, and accordingly we find almost all philosophers speaking of the three dimensions of space—length, breadth, and depth. That which has length, breadth, and depth must be divisible, must have parts and proportions, must have susceptibilities of exact measurement, and therefore must be *finite.* This again is the doctrine of Hamilton: "Space is finite, and a finite, that is, a bounded space constitutes a figure"—a sphere.[2] The fundamental doctrine of Hamilton is that "space, like time, is only the intuition or the concept of a certain correlation of existence—of existence, therefore, *pro tanto, as conditioned. It is thus itself only a form of the conditioned.*"[3] But if space be only a correlation of conditioned, and therefore finite existence, how can he speak of it "being conceived as infinite,"[4] and, above all, how can he speak of "the absolute totality" and "the infinite immensity of space."

McCosh, also, though evidently with some hesitation, teaches that "we can conceive *proportion* in space, and if we take any of these proportional sections, and divide it into two, thought will compel us to say that the two make up the whole. In this sense the *parts* make up the whole—that is, the subsections make up the section. If the question be extended beyond this, and it be asked, Is infinite space made up of parts? I answer, that as we can have no adequate notion of infinite space, so we can not be expected to answer all the questions which may be put regarding it. *It is certain that neither infinite space nor finite space is made up of separate parts.* We can

[1] "Lectures," vol. ii. p. 169.

[2] "Lectures," vol. ii. p. 170.

[3] "Discussions," etc., p. 36.

[4] "Philosophy," p. 357.

speak intelligibly of *proportions* in finite space, and determine their relations to each other and the whole. I tremble to speak of the proportions of infinite space, lest I be using language which has or can have no proper meaning, and the signification attached to which by me or others might be altogether inapplicable to such a subject. Still there are propositions which we might intelligibly use. It is self-evident that *any proportion of space must be less than infinite space.* And if infinite space can be conceived as having *proportions,* and we could conceive all these proportions, then these proportions would be equal to the *whole!*"[1] Well may the author say that he is "in a region dark and pathless;" for the language here employed "can have no proper meaning" in regard to infinite space. Well may he "tremble to speak of *the proportions of infinite space,*" for what can proportion (*pro,* for *portio,* a part) mean except a numerical relation of parts? Proportions—numerical relations—are measurable quantities, therefore finite quantities, and no addition of finite quantities, can make the infinite. What confusion and contradiction is here wrought by this word-jugglery with "the whole and parts" of space!

Cousin, also, falls into the same inaccuracy and confusion. He tells us that "human reason can conceive of a space determined and limited,"[2] therefore divisible, measurable, and *finite;* and yet at the same time he teaches that "space is illimitable, absolutely continuous, an indivisible unity."[3]

And now let us note the contradictions which flow from this confounding of space with extension, and both

[1] "Intuitions," p. 208. [2] "History of Philosophy," vol. i. p. 77.
[3] "History of Philosophy," vol. ii. p. 224.

with immensity. Space is cognized *à posteriori*, space is cognized *à priori*. Space has parts and proportions, space has no parts or proportions. Space is divisible, space is indivisible—an absolute unity. Space is finite, space is infinite. Space is susceptible of exact measurement, space is immeasurable—that is, absolute immensity.

Space and extension are not identical. Extension is simply an attribute of body—the continuity of matter. Space is place, distance, direction, relations of bodies. *Space is a certain correlation of finite existences.* Immensity is the attribute of the unconditioned Being, the absolute Spirit—that is, God. He is incorporeal, boundless, spaceless, infinite.

2. The same confusion pervades the writings of philosophers in regard to TIME, DURATION, *and* ETERNITY.

Succession is confounded with duration,[1] duration with time,[2] and time with eternity.[3]

If succession and duration are identical, then, there is no permanent substance underlying the fugitive phenomena of the outer world, and no personal existence which remains the same through all the changes of our mental states. The human mind is simply "a series of feelings," a succession of mental states without any enduring ground principle constituting our personal identity, and we are thus landed in the constructive Idealism of John Stuart

[1] "When the succession of ideas ceases, our perception of duration ceases with it."—Locke, "Essays" (bk. ii. ch. xiv. § 4).

[2] Time and duration are confounded by McCosh ("Intuitions," p. 223), by Mahan ("Intellectual Philosophy," p. 22), and by Cousin ("History of Philosophy," vol. ii. p. 229).

[3] "Absolute time is eternity" (Cousin, "History of Philosophy," vol. i. p. 77). "L'éternité ou l'unité de temps" ("Histoire de la Philosophie du xviiime Siècle," p. 121). "Eternity is the synonym of pure time" (*North American Review*, April, 1864, p. 115).

Mill.[1] On the other hand, if there be a permanent substance or essence underlying all mental phenomena, whose continuance in existence is measured by phenomenal change, time succession, then duration can not be identical with time, any more than permanence can be the same as change. With finite duration there is necessarily given change; the past is like the future—always a minus in relation to the present.

Furthermore, if time is synonymous with eternity, then eternity is divisible, measurable, it has limits and parts. Time, say the philosophers, has one dimension, while space has three. "We," says McCosh, "represent time as a line,"[2] it must therefore be divisible, and, if divisible, it is legitimate to speak, with Hamilton, of "time and its parts." "Time has succession, or priority and posteriority."[3] And yet this same writer in the same work tells us, "Time has no limits," and "Time can not be divided into separable parts."[4] If time and eternity are identical, eternity has a past, a present, and a future—"eternity *ab ante* and eternity *a post*."[5] The eternity past is bounded by the present, it *ends* now; the eternity to come *begins* now. We may with propriety ask, How can that which has succession, which is capable of exact measurement, which has a beginning and an end, be infinite? That which had a beginning can not be unbeginning, that which will come to an end can not be endless. Is not the "eternity of *time*" a contradiction in terms? Is not "absolute time" an absurdity?

Mark, then, the contradictions which flow from the con-

[1] "Mind is nothing but the series of our feelings as they actually occur, with the addition of infinite possibilities of feeling" ("Examination of Hamilton's Philosophy," vol. i. p. 253).

[2] "Intuitions," p. 206.

[3] "Intuitions," p. 206.

[4] "Intuitions," p. 252.

[5] Hamilton's "Lectures," vol. ii. p. 527.

founding of succession and duration, time and eternity. Time has limits, time has no limits. Time is divisible, time is indivisible. Time is finite, time is infinite. Time is relative, time is absolute. Time is moving, "it flows;" time is immovable, "it does not flow."[1]

Duration and succession, eternity and time, are not identical. Duration is the continuance in existence of finite creatures, a continuance which is measured by the equable motion of planetary orbs, and imperfectly by phenomenal changes in our mental states. Succession is simply an order of phenomena, the recurrence, at regular or irregular intervals, of like changes, or the series of different states in the same existence. *Time is a certain correlation of successive existences.* Eternity is an attribute of the absolute Being—the *timelessness* of God. He is not subject to the law of change, and therefore not to the law of time, therefore his absolute being can not be measured by successive epochs.

Let us now endeavor to dismiss from our thought all this perplexing necromancy of words, and humbly pray, with Themistocles, for "some sweet voluptuous art of forgetting." Let us fix our mental gaze upon the *objects* of thought which are denoted by the terms *time* and *space*, and ask what are they? Are they existences or attributes, are they ideal or real, are they entities or relations? Have we any clear and definite notions of which these are the unequivocal signs? The solution of these questions is the essential condition of a true philosophy of time and space.

First of all, is it not self-evident that, if time and space are for us the objects of thought, they must be conceived under the categories of *Being* or *Quality* or *Relation?* If they can not be thought as real existences, or as attri-

[1] McCosh, "Intuitions," p. 205; Saisset, "Mod. Pantheism," vol. i. p. 193.

butes of existing things, or as relations among existing things, they can not be thought at all—they are non-entities, and we can not think about nothing. "Thought can only be realized by thinking *something* . . . this something must be thought as existing . . . and we can only think a thing as existing, by thinking it as existing in this or that determinate manner of existence; and whenever we cease to think of something as existing—something existing in a determinate manner of existence—we cease to think at all."[1]

McCosh asserts that time and space are "neither substances, modes, nor relations."[2] What, then, are they? He answers, "They seem to be entitled to be put in a class by themselves, and resemble substances, modes, relations only in that they are *existences, entities, realities*."[3] But if they are entitled to be put in a class by themselves, what is the name of that class, and by what characteristic marks shall we distinguish it? If they are realities, they must have being, or inhere in something that has being, or be relations of something in being. If they are existences, they must be the objects of *sense perception*, or *rational intuition*, or *immediate judgment*, otherwise they can not be cognized at all, for "the mind can not create objects of its own cognition."

We ask again, What *are* space and time? McCosh and Dr. Porter both answer: 1. They are not substances. This no one will dispute. They are not material substances having sensible qualities which can be the objects of sense perception. Space and time are not perceived by the senses.[4] Neither are they spiritual sub-

[1] Hamilton's "Logic," p. 55.
[2] "Intuitions," p. 211. See also Porter's "Human Intellect," p. 567.
[3] "Intuitions," p. 211.
[4] Strange as it may sound, Dr. McCosh says, at p. 202, that "we have an

stances. We do not know them as having power and performing acts. 2. They both reply, They are not attributes or qualities of matter or spirit. This, also, no one will dispute, if the word "time" is not used as a synonym for "eternity," and the word "space" is not used as a synonym for "immensity," because "eternity" and "immensity" are attributes of the absolute Spirit. 3. They both assert, They are not relations. This is disputed by many: by Leibnitz, by Hamilton, by Saisset, by Calderwood, and by others. Leibnitz says, "Space is the order of things co-existing. Time is the order of things successive."[1] Hamilton says, "Space, like time, is only the intuition or the conception of a certain correlation of existence."[2] Calderwood defines time "as a certain correlation of existence," and "space as the recognized relation of extended objects."[3] And Saisset regards time and space as standing in the same category with mathematical relations.[4] These are, to say the least, distinguished names in philosophy. The opinions of men who have for years pondered these profound problems are at any rate entitled to proper consideration, and if in opposition to their views it is affirmed that time and space as understanding-concepts are *not* relations, some reasons should be assigned. All the proof offered by Dr. McCosh is that "we know no two or more things which by their relation could yield space and time" (p. 211). We answer, promptly, *duration* and *change* do yield the relation of time. "The consciousness of succession in our mental states is in reality our consciousness of time."[5] The co-

immediate knowledge of space in the concrete by the senses," and here he asserts that "space is not a substance," and therefore can not be perceived.

[1] "Opusculа," p. 752.

[2] "Discussions," p. 36.

[3] "Philosophy of the Infinite," pp. 319, 331.

[4] "Modern Pantheism," vol. i. p. 192.

[5] "Philosophy of the Infinite," p. 300.

existence of two or more extended objects must yield the relation of space, for "empty space is nothing more than the relative distance of extended objects from each other, measured on a standard similar to that which applies to the bodies themselves. In this way it is equally accurate to say that there is a certain specified *distance* between the bodies, and that there is *nothing* between them, because space is nothing but their relation to each other."[1] Annihilate all finite existences, and what remains? Nothing but the immensity of God. Let one atom of matter be created, and we have extension. Let a second atom be created, and there is now a relation of distance, position, direction—that is, there is *space*.

The only remark made by Dr. Porter which has a direct bearing on this important discussion is that "Space and time are neither relations nor correlations, but *correlates* to beings and events" ("The Human Intellect," p. 568). It may seem an act of presumption in one who has spent much less time on these studies than Dr. Porter to offer a criticism on this final deliverance. But when he tells us that space and time are neither relations nor correlations, after having through four pages "On the relations of space and time concepts to motion" labored to sustain the doctrine of Trendelenberg that "the categories of space and time are derived from the universal and all-pervading motion which is common to both" (p. 526), we confess we are amazed. Let it be granted that the spatial and temporal relations can be, in their last analysis, resolved into motion, still the question remains, How can we conceive of motion except as the result of force?—that is, of power actually exerted somewhere. In the last analysis, therefore, the relations of space, time,

[1] "Philosophy of the Infinite," p. 331.

and motion are resolved into "*the relation of causality.*" The conclusion seems inevitable that time and space are *correlations of finite existences.* Annihilate all finite existences and finite duration, and there is neither space nor time—that is, there is "pure nothing." Or, more properly, there is the Omnipotence, the Immensity, the Eternity of God, whose causation may give existence to finite beings with all their necessary as well as contingent relations. "Whoever maintains a beginning of the world must also adopt *a beginning of time,* for only worldly being, which according to its notion has not its ground in itself, but is an originated being, can at all have time for the form of its existence."[1]

And now, in summing up, let us see if we can clearly disengage three classes of distinct notions:

1. The notion of concrete and finite EXTENSION as the essential quality of matter; and the notion of finite DURATION as a quality of changeful dependent existence.

2. The notion of SPACE as the relation of co-existing material things—that is, the relation of position, distance, direction, hereness, thereness; and the notion of TIME as the relation of successive existence—that is, the relation of priority and posteriority, of past, present, and future.

3. The notion of IMMENSITY and ETERNITY—that is, an absolute continuity and illimitability of being, the absence of all limit, all quantity, all beginning and end, the attributes of the unconditioned Being. Let us endeavor sharply to define these notions, which unhappily are too often confounded.

1. The external senses in their different degrees, especially sight and touch, give us the knowledge of objects that are *extended* and figured. The body I grasp with

[1] Müller, "Christian Doctrine of Sin," vol. i. p. 243.

the hand or survey with the eye has limits, outlines, angles, surfaces — that is, it has more or less EXTENSION. The inner sense gives us the knowledge of the changes and successions of our mental life. But, amid all these changes, I am conscious there is a something which *endures*. What is that permanent something which I apprehend under all the varying mental states? It is that principle of personal identity which I call *I—myself.* To feel and know that I am the same person under all modifications of my mental activity is to *endure*. Through the aid of memory, which enables me to recall past mental states, and the immediate consciousness of personal existence, through all these changes I obtain the notion of DURATION. The notions of Extension and Duration are clear to my mind.

2. Besides the notion of extended bodies, I have also the notion of position, distance, direction among extended bodies. They exist in various relations to each other; they are here or there, above or below, near at hand or indefinitely remote. It may be the distance between two particles of dust in the sunbeam, or the walls of the room, or between the earth and the sun, or between the sun and the outermost planet of our system, or between the earth and the remotest star which twinkles at the outposts of the universe. Position, distance, direction are all *relations*. And to all these relations I prefer, with Sir John Herschel, to give the generic name SPACE.[1] Then I have no confusion of thought, and no difficulty or contradiction in using the language of Cousin, Hamilton, and McCosh, when they speak of "determinate and limited space," "particular spaces," "parts of space," and "proportions of space."

[1] "Familiar Lectures," p. 455.

Along with the notion of duration (and succession of different states in the same existence), I am conscious that this duration is capable of admeasurement by common standards, and ideally divided into periods of longer or shorter duration. This duration may be measured by successive states of consciousness, or facts of domestic history, or, better still, by the succession of day and night, or the relative position of the sun in the heavens, the revolutions of the moon around the earth, or of the earth around the sun. These are really world-measurements of duration. Since, then, duration can be measured from any point and in any proportions, it is clear that measurement is a purely relative thing—a relation. Of any such thing as "pure time" or "absolute time" we have no knowledge. TIME *is the measure of finite duration*—the correlation of things successive. And if I confine myself to this usage, I am under no necessity of using the paradoxical language of many philosophers, "time is eternity!"

3. We come, lastly, to the notions or ideas of IMMENSITY and ETERNITY, and we ask, Are these necessary ideas of the reason, or can they be confounded with the relations of co-existence and succession on the one hand, or with the attributes of finite extension and duration on the other?

This is not a mere question of systems of philosophy or theology—it is a question of facts. Are the ideas of Absolute Infinity and Eternity necessary intuitions of the reason? The world of sense-perception, the world of science, is phenomenal and contingent. All that is offered to our observation is *limited* and *temporal.* The universe surrendered to our science is one of quantities and quantitative relations. It is conditioned by number and form. Its extensions, spaces, and motions are capable of admeasurement. Its worlds and systems are subject to numeration. The phenomena of the universe are all subject to change, they have beginning, succession, and end. But beyond the notions of the limited and the temporal, we find in consciousness the ideas of the *illimitable* and the *eternal;* the latter always appearing to reason as the necessary correlates of the former. The finite necessarily supposes the infinite; the temporal necessarily supposes the eternal. The two classes of notions are essentially different, and defy all attempts to generalize them under higher concepts. The infinite is not the totality of finite existences; eternity is not the prolongation of finite durations. Immensity and eternity are absolutely and unconditionally necessary ideas. I can easily conceive the non-existence of any finite thing. I can, without any contradiction, suppose the whole world to be destroyed. All which has a derived and a dependent existence may cease to be. But we can not conceive the source of all existence annihilated. There is one notion which it is impossible for me to annihilate in thought, and that is the notion of absolute being — underived, unconditioned, changeless, eternal being. Despite the destruction of all determinate extension and all finite duration, there remains a Supreme Reality, unlimited, unbeginning, and endless, as an absolute necessity of thought.

Here, then, are two absolute ideas found in the depths of consciousness—the ideas of IMMENSITY and ETERNITY; ideas as real, as natural, and as necessary as the notions of extension and duration. Immensity and Eternity are attributes of God. Extension and Duration are attributes of finite, dependent existence. Space and time are relations between co-existing things and successive events.

If by this somewhat abstruse and, perhaps, too lengthy discussion we have succeeded in proving that Time and Space are simply relations between co-existent things and successive events, which, apart from things and events, have no reality, and are "nothing but the bare possibility of body and change," then we have disentangled the Christian doctrine of absolute creation from the embarrassment occasioned by supposing "the coeval and co-eternal existence of Time and Space as the *necessary* conditions of the Divine activity." If Time and Space are relations between things and events, then God, as the almighty cause of things and relations, is the efficient cause of space and time, and the creative act was not conditioned by them.

The affirmation of the necessary existence of Space, Time, and Number as co-eternal with and independent of God,[1] prepared the way for and rendered plausible the further affirmation of "the coeval existence of matter as the condition and medium of the Divine agency and manifestation."[2] For if Space, Time, and Number are eternal, *why may not Matter be eternal?* But why stop with the assertion of the eternity of Space, Time, Number, and Matter? "If we admit that there may be something uncaused, there is no reason to assume a cause of any thing." If we admit the eternity of Matter, how can we deny the eternity of Force? We can not conceive of the existence of substance without some properties or qualities, and of all the properties of matter, gravitation or weight seems to approach nearest to an essential, necessary quality. And if we concede the eternity of matter and gravitating force, why not admit the eternity of law—that is, "uni-

[1] Martineau's "Essays," 1st Series, p. 158.
[2] Martineau's "Essays," 1st Series, p. 161.

formity of properties and relations;" uniformity in the results arising from the motions and changes of matter? And when so much is granted, why not grant that a consequent *Order* of the universe must also be eternal? why not grant that the universe is an infinite succession of orderly phenomena without a beginning and end? After the first concession that matter is uncreated and eternal, how can any one refute the doctrine of Hume that the universe never had a beginning, and that under some one or another possible phase—amid the infinite possibility of phases—it is both eternal and infinite? How, after this admission, can we deny that the universe is "a series of events existing eternally in a state of order without a cause other than the eternally inherent laws of matter?"

It would be easy to show that all those writers on "Natural Theology" who have made the least concession in regard to this fundamental question have involved themselves in entanglements and difficulties from which they could not logically extricate themselves.

Dr. Chalmers contends that the mere existence of matter with its properties and laws would not involve the affirmation of an Absolute First Cause. The proof, he says, lies solely in the disposition, collocation, and arrangement of these properties and laws in their relation to each other, so as to secure harmonious and beneficial results. So far as the argument for the existence of God is concerned, he provisionally concedes that *matter, with all its laws, may be eternal.*[1] True, he says that he grants the eternity of matter simply for the purposes of his argument. But what right has he to grant it for the purposes of his argument, and then to deny it in obedience to the decisive affirmation of a "well-accredited revelation?" If Divine

[1] "Institutes of Theology," vol. i. pp. 76, 79.

revelation teaches the non-eternity of matter, this is for the Christian a truth—a fundamental truth; and whoever surrenders or compromises a fundamental position must finally fail in his management of the Theistic argument. The intuitions of reason and the doctrines of revelation are but separate rays from the one eternal fountain of light; and if we ignore or compromise the fundamental truths of revelation, reason will refuse to place her *imprimatur* upon and give her indorsement to our lame and halting proofs. This is strikingly illustrated by Chalmers's failure to "construct an argument for a God" that satisfies the reason, after he has affirmed "the eternity of matter for the purpose of bringing out his conclusion" (p. 79). But Dr. Chalmers can not stop with the simple concession that matter is eternal. Only grant its necessary existence, and "it is impossible to imagine that along with existence it should not have *properties* . . . and *laws*" (p. 75). Now, if the admission that a finite, composite, divisible substance may be self-existent, and have eternal properties and laws, is not logically inconsistent, how can he show that these properties and laws in their eternal action and reaction are not adequate to the production of a series of phenomena which to our understanding may appear harmonious? Can eternal laws produce any thing but order? The existing order of things is the only possible order that could arise from the *necessary* operation of eternal laws, and there can be no choice, design, or purpose in the universe. Collocation, arrangement, adaptation, are only subjective anthropomorphic conceptions we impose upon nature. If matter and its laws are eternal, how will Chalmers extricate himself from this dilemma? By this admission he places a weapon in the hands of the anti-Theist, by which the latter may cut the teleological argument to pieces.

My esteemed friend, Dr. Mahan, in his zeal to overthrow the ontological proof of the being of God, and to vindicate for the etiological proof the sole claim to validity, has been betrayed into a similar inconsistency. That there is any *à priori* proof of the being of God is in his estimation a "wild chimera." "*Formation* from pre-existing materials" constitutes "the exclusive basis" of Natural Theology.[1] Matter, then, *may* be eternal, and an infinite series of events existing in a state of order is conceivable and possible. At page 85 of his "Natural Theology" he writes: "Mr. Hume has undeniably announced the truth *as it is* upon this subject, to wit, that the idea of a nature eternally existing in a state of order without a cause other than the eternally inhering laws of nature, is no more self-contradictory than the idea of an eternally existing and infinite mind who originated this order—a

[1] "Natural Theology," p. 23.

The practice so common among writers of Natural Theology of fixing upon one line of proof of the being of God as the only valid method, and then disparaging and endeavoring to show the invalidity of all others, is highly reprehensible. The strongest arguments employed by the Atheists have been culled from the writings of these eccentric theologians. In the celebrated public discussion between Mr. Holyoake, the leader of the Secularists in England, and Mr. Brindley, "On the existence of God," the most telling arguments of Mr. Holyoake were drawn from the standard works on Natural Theology. How much more rational and commendable is the course of the philosopher: "There are different proofs of the existence of God. The consoling result of my studies is that these different proofs are more or less strict in form, but they have all a depth of truth which needs only to be disengaged and put in a clear light in order to give incontestible authority. Every thing leads to God. There is no bad way of arriving at Him, but we go to Him by different paths."—Cousin, "History of Philosophy," vol. ii. p. 418.

The argument for the being of a God in its completeness is at once Ontological and Cosmological, Etiological and Teleological. It is in the concurrence and synthesis of these separate but harmonious lines of proof that we have an unanswerable demonstration. For ourselves, we are convinced, with Neitzsch, that the Ontological proof is first and last; they who seek to invalidate this cut the ground from under all the rest.

mind existing without a cause." After several pages disfigured by a labored effort to prove the possibility and logical consistency of an "infinite series of events existing in an orderly succession," he sums up with the imperious assertion that "the argument against the possibility of an infinite series of events stands revealed as a *logical absurdity*" (p. 88).

It is our deliberate conclusion, however, that the "logical absurdity" lies in the position of Dr. Mahan. "The idea of order in the Finite without a cause is no more self-contradictory than the idea of order in the Infinite without a cause." Mark the two points which stand out clearly in this strange assertion. First, the Finite here is nature—that is, matter and its laws. Secondly, the Infinite is the Supreme Mind. Dr. Mahan asserts that this *finite* may be conceived as *eternally* existing—that is, as existing through *infinite* time; in other words, *the finite may be infinite.* For a thing or being, or for a series of things or beings, to be at once "finite" and "infinite" Dr. Mahan says "is not self-contradictory." This is on a par with the logic of Hegel—"Contradictory opposites are identical." Again, we ask, Is there no difference between "finite matter" and "Infinite Mind?" Is not matter composite, extended, divisible, and limited? Is not Infinite Mind unextended, incomposite, indivisible, and illimitable? The mere existence of matter does not necessarily involve the idea of *Order.* There are nebulæ existing in the universe "utterly devoid of all symmetry of form, . . . irregular and capricious in their shapes and convolutions to a most extraordinary degree."[1] Wherever order is presented, we instinctively and infallibly ascribe it to mind. Mind for all of us, and forever, is the anal-

[1] Herschel's "Outlines of Astronomy," p. 511.

ogon and exponent of Order in every sphere, irrespective of all knowledge on our part as to when or how it had a beginning.

Furthermore, on the main issue we affirm briefly—if matter is extended, it is measurable; if it is measurable, it must have definite limits; if it has definite limits, it can not be infinite. Now that which is finite, limited, quantitive, conditioned, can not be self-existent, can not be infinite. Infinitude is illimitation by kind, quantity, or degree—illimitation by temporal, spatial, or numerical relations. An "infinite series" is therefore a contradiction *in adjecto*. "As every number, although immeasurably and inconceivably great, is impossible without *unity* as its basis, so every series, being itself a number, is impossible unless a *first term* is given as its commencement.... Even if it should be allowed that the series has no *first term*, but has originated *ab æterno*, it must always at each instant have a *last term*; the series as a whole can not be infinite."[1] If one thing more can be added to the number of existing things in the universe, then it is not infinite in number or in extent. In short, a series implies a succession of terms, or members, or links; if there is a last term, there must be a first term; if there is a last link, there must be a first. Through an Unconditioned First Cause, originating and conditioning all the members thereof, is a series conceivable or possible. To apply to number or quantity the designation of infinitude is surely *the* "absurdity" in presence of which all others pale. We grant that the term "infinite series" is employed by mathematicians in a loose manner, to denote that which exceeds our powers of mensuration or conception, but which nevertheless has bounds or limits—the *in-*

[1] *North American Review*, October, 1864, p. 428.

definite, but not the infinite;[1] such loose use of terms in philosophy, however, is inadmissible. The final reply of Dr. Mahan, "that the series under consideration is one which by hypothesis has no first," is the extreme of absurdity. It is as though a man should talk of a "round square" or a "bilinear figure," and when remonstrated with as to the contradictory character of these phrases, should reply, "Yes, but the 'square' under consideration is one which by hypothesis is 'round,' and the 'figure' is one which by hypothesis is formed by 'two lines!'" Men may make all kinds of strange hypotheses, but the strangest of all is that of an infinite-finite.

These incautious writers of "Natural Theology" all assert, as a fundamental doctrine, that God is the Absolute and Unconditioned Cause. We might ask, Whence do they derive this fundamental truth that God is "absolute and unconditioned," if not by an *à priori* rational intuition? We let that pass, however, to press the more pertinent question—How can God be "the absolute cause," if matter is coeval with and independent of Him? And how can He be the "unconditioned cause," if space, time, number, and matter necessarily exist as the *conditions* of the Divine agency and manifestation? If matter, with its essential properties and laws, exist independent of the Deity, do not these impose conditions upon the action of the Deity, and determine it to certain necessary modes? If so, God can not be the unconditioned Cause. Instead of one supreme, sole First Principle, there are at least two

[1] "By finite we generally mean that which is within reach, or may be brought within reach of our senses. . . . The powers, therefore, of our senses and mind place the limit to the finite, but those magnitudes which severally transcend these limits, by reason of their being too great or too small, we call *infinite* and *infinitesimal*."—Price, "Infinitesimal Calculus," vol. i. pp. 12, 13.

principles, God and Necessity, and may be more. No system of Natural Theology can maintain its integrity and consistency except by holding fast to the fundamental postulate—God is the Absolute and Unconditioned Cause of all things, of matter and form, quality and relation, purpose and law.

And now, in conclusion, we may properly ask, Whence arises the necessity for assuming the coeval and co-eternal existence of matter besides and independent of God? Why should the theologian feel himself under the necessity of prejudicing the Biblical conception of Creation by any such concession? The only reasons we have seen assigned are, first, that "creation out of nothing is discredited by the discoveries of modern science;"[1] secondly, that "an absolute origination is inconceivable and self-destructive."[2] In attempting an estimate of the weight of these reasons, we would first suggest that the question of *absolute* creation has been prejudiced by the persistent employment of the old formula of "creation out of nothing," as though "nothing" contained the cause of existence, and the universe was developed out of nothing. The Christian Fathers, who first employed the phrase κτίσις ἐκ τοῦ μὴ ὄντος, never indulged in such representations. The idea they sought to express was that the production of "*otherness*," the awarding of existence to something besides Himself, was an absolutely free act of God which was not conditioned by any thing external to Himself—in a word, that God is the positive original ground of all existence.

But who shall decide that this doctrine has been discredited by the progress of science? What special discovery of modern science has so revealed to us the ul-

[1] Martineau, "Essays, 1st Series, p. 161.
[2] Hamilton, "Metaphysics," vol. ii. p. 539.

timate constitution of matter, that we can affirm its absolute reality and its eternal existence? Nay, are the most advanced physicists and physiologists agreed as to whether, apart from our subjective, ideal conceptions, matter has any reality? If we are not utterly mistaken, the entire tendency of science is to reduce matter from the rank of entities to the rank of phenomena. "The old speculations of Philosophy, which cut the ground from Materialism by showing how little we know of matter, are now being daily reinforced by the subtle analysis of the physiologist, the chemist, and the electrician. Under that analysis matter dissolves and disappears, *surviving only as the phenomena of Force*."[1] We offer no opinion as to the validity of this new doctrine, but are sure it is the doctrine of modern science as represented by Faraday, Owen, McVicar, Bayma, Exley, Wallace, Poisson, Poyntong, Laycock, and, we think, Huxley. If modern science has resolved all our external sensations, even the feeling of resistance, into "phenomena of Force," then, according to the doctrine of Mr. Martineau, it had a beginning—"*phenomena demand causation*. . . . Supreme Entity needs no cause." "The universe resolves itself into a perpetual genesis," and "the Theist is perfectly justified in treating it as disqualified for self-existence."[2]

Sir William Hamilton contends that "an absolute commencement" is inconceivable. All the conception we can possibly form of Creation is "merely as the evolution of new forms of existence by the fiat of the Deity." "Let us suppose the very crisis of creation. Can we realize it to ourselves in thought, that the moment after the universe came into manifested being there was a larger complement of existence in the universe and its Author to-

[1] Argyll, "Reign of Law," p. 117. [2] "Essays," 1st Series, p. 206.

gether than there was the moment before in the Deity himself alone? This we can not imagine."[1]

There are, we presume, very few Hamiltonians who are prepared to indorse this bold statement of their master. Mansel, the editor and annotator of his "Lectures," has very distinctly and emphatically expressed his dissent. "Whether it be true or not that we can not conceive the quantity of existence to be increased or diminished, there is at any rate no such inability as regards the *quantity of matter*. It may be true as a fact that no material atom has been added to the world since the Creation; but the assertion, however true, is certainly not necessary. The power which created once must be conceived as able to create again, whether that ability is actually exercised or not. The same conclusion is still more evident when we proceed from the consideration of matter to that of mind. Of matter, we maintain that the creation of new portions is *perfectly conceivable*—as a result, at least, if not as a process; of mind, we believe that such creation actually takes place. Every man who comes into the world comes into it as a distinct individual, having a personality and consciousness of his own, and that personality is a distinct accession to the number of persons previously existing. . . . Every new person that comes into the world is a *new existence*."[2] Hence we are not justified in asserting that all actual existences are only different modes of one identical reality. We can not merely conceive, but we *know*, as a primary fact of consciousness, that the *sum* of existence, of personal conscious being, which is the most fundamental reality, may be increased in the universe.[3]

[1] "Lectures," vol. ii. p. 406. [2] "Prolegomena," p. 267–269.

[3] See Locke's "Human Understanding," bk. iv. ch. x., where a similar line of argument is pursued.

We readily confess that the act of creation—that is, *causing wholly new existence*—is utterly incomprehensible to us; so are thousands of other things. I am told by the physicist that eight hundred billions of ether-impulses impinge on the retina of the eye in a second of time to produce the sensation of deep violet;[1] and I believe it, but at the same time it is to me incomprehensible. My reason affirms that the First Cause must be infinite; and I believe it, but I can not comprehend Infinity. No logician of the present day teaches that comprehensibility is a test of truth. Is our finite capacity of conceiving or of doing a standard for Omnipotence? The only question here involved is, Can Infinite Power produce that mode of being we call matter? Does such an exercise of Infinite Power involve a contradiction? I conscientiously submit this question to my own reason, and I confess I am unable to see any contradiction. To my experiential knowledge matter presents "the essential characteristics at once of a *manufactured article* and a *subordinate agent*."[2] "This," says the distinguished Prof. Maxwell, "precludes the idea of its being eternal and self-existent. . . . It must have been *created*."[3] The notion of its origination by a Power which is unconditioned and every way unlimited, satisfies my reason, and affords the best solution of the problem of its existence. That it is self-existent, independent, eternal—"a second other God"—is directly contradictory. The original, primitive fountain of existence is *Mind*. This must stand at the fountain-head. God is the sole and absolute Cause of all things—of time,

[1] Schellen, "Spectrum Analysis," p. 45.

[2] Sir John Herschel, "Natural Philosophy," § 28.

[3] "On Molecules," Lecture at the British Association at Bradford, in *Nature*, vol. viii. p. 441.

and all temporal relations; of space, and all spatial relations; of the primordial element, and all its properties. *The creative act was not conditioned by Time or Space or Matter.*[1]

[1] "God is not merely spirit, but He has upon Himself a realistic *nature.* God did not create the world out of an absolute nothing. The something out of which God created it are his eternal *potentialities*—not merely logical (merely conceived by God), but at the same time also *physical* (essentially in God existing) potentialities. In these δυνάμεις God possesses both the something out of which He makes the world, and also the forces, instruments, and means by which He produces it. In this sense it is literally true: *All things are of God* (Rom. xi. 33). This admission of a supramaterial physis in God—this spiritual realism—furnishes not only an escape from the errors of a lifeless materialism and of an abstract spiritualism, but is the synthesis of the partial truth that is in both."—*Bibliotheca Sacra*, January, 1873, p. 191.

CHAPTER IV.

CREATION.—THE GENESIS OR BEGINNING.

"The laws of nature can not account for their own origin."—J. S. Mill.

Creation was the absolutely free act of God, unconditioned by any pre-existing thing. Matter with its properties and forms, its temporal, spatial, and numerical relations; Spirit with its life and feeling, its ideas and laws—these had all their origin in the creative Word of God. Whatever is, and is not God, is the creature of God. This is the Biblical conception of Creation.

Origination and formation are so immediately and inseparably united in the Biblical notion of Creation that the revelation of the one is the revelation of the other, and we can not deny the former without logically involving ourselves in the denial of the latter. He who gave to matter its forms must have given it its essential properties, upon which many of its forms depend; and He who gave to matter its essential properties must have given it *origination*, for how can we conceive of substance devoid of all attributes? Whether, therefore, the account in Genesis "be found to have in view, mainly or solely, a universal or a partial creation; whether the *principium* there mentioned be the particular beginning of the special work there described, or the *principium principiorum* — the beginning of all beginnings—the Bible is in either case a protest against the dogma of the eternity of the world, or of the eternity of matter."[1]

[1] Lange's Commentary, "Preliminary Essay," p. 126.

This notion of Creation as a pure supernatural origination is the only one which reason can accept as adequate, satisfactory, and complete. Formation without origination is a conception of creation which is logically incomplete. It fails to meet the demand of reason for an Absolute First Principle adequate to the production and explanation of all existence. There are outlying elements of the problem which it can not grasp in the unity of a Fundamental Idea. Matter with its properties, Number, Time, and Space, with their relations, are still lying outside of its field, and setting themselves up as self-existent and independent realities, which by their apparent or conceded independence must necessarily impose *conditions* upon the Divine activity, and perpetually embarrass the human mind in its effort to think of God as the free and unconditioned Cause. Reason demands that absolute unity shall stand at the fountain-head of being, and every system of philosophy which allows of more than one self-existent and independent and underived reality bewilders and staggers the understanding, and vitiates all its processes of thought. After this concession every argument for the being of God seems to us a *petitio principii.*

Reason and Revelation, then, are agreed in the affirmation that the Universe, both as to its matter and form, had its origin in the creative Word and Will of God. How far this affirmation is sustained by the *à posteriori* inductions of physical science is a question of the deepest interest, and to this we now invite attention.

This question naturally divides itself into two subordinate inquiries, one relating to the *form*, the other to the *matter* of the universe, which may be thus presented:

1. Had the existing *Order* of the universe a beginning? Had the forms, relations, laws, and harmonies of the universe a beginning?

2. Had that which is the ground of all forms, the subject of all changes and relations, a beginning? Had the *Matter* of the universe a beginning?

In regard to the first question, we remark in general: *The common conviction of our race in all ages has been that the existing order of the universe had a beginning, and will have an end.*

It has been affirmed by some mental philosophers that mankind has an intuitive and natural belief in the uniformity of nature, and the consequent stability and permanence of the universe. Reid, the father of the Scottish school of philosophy, says, "God has implanted in the human mind an original principle by which he believes in and expects the continuance of the course of nature." It is a matter of surprise that so acute a thinker should have fallen into so flagrant an error. He has evidently confounded our natural belief in causation with our acquired experiences of uniformity. That "like causes will always produce like effects" is a native intuition; but that "the same causes will always continue in operation, and always operate with the same intensity," is a mere presumption. Our faith in the uniformity and permanent stability of nature is an induction from experience, and not a natural and necessary intuition of the mind.[1]

Far from entertaining a belief in the permanence and stability of the present order of nature, the great mass of mankind in earlier times regarded the system of things as liable to constant interference on the part of supernatural powers. In all ages of the world the existing order of nature has been regarded as temporal, and the flow of terrestrial and even of cosmical events has been conceived as liable to be broken up by universal revolutions. The his-

[1] See Whewell's "History of Scientific Ideas," vol. ii. p. 287.

torical evidence of this universal belief in "geological catastrophes" has been fully brought forward by Dr. Winchell in his "Sketches of Creation."[1] Traditions of a primal chaos and of periodic cataclysms are found among the Greeks, Egyptians, Phœnicians, Chaldæans, Hebrews, Persians, Arabians, Hindoos, South Sea Islanders, and the Aztecs. And among those nations in which the physical sciences have been cultivated the same conceptions are still entertained. As science has extended our acquaintance with natural phenomena in all parts of the earth, and beyond the earth into the celestial spaces, men have gradually attained a belief in the uniformity of nature. But the doctrine of periodical catastrophes has not been abandoned by scientific men. When men now speak of the uniformity of nature, they use that term in a very large sense, and even loose sense, as including catastrophes and convulsions of an intense and extensive kind;[2] and, as we shall presently see, the most advanced and exact modern science teaches us to contemplate a grand final catastrophe in which all life will be extinguished on the earth, and the globe itself shall be "ensepulchred in an extinguished sun." The attempt, therefore, to represent the belief in the uniformity of nature as a universal and necessary truth is vain. We have no *à priori* ground for believing in the permanence of the universe.

The common conviction of our race that the universe had a beginning, that it has been the subject of great catastrophal changes, and that it will finally come to an end, is not to be regarded as an insignificant fact. As Herbert Spencer justly remarks, "We must presume that beliefs that have long existed and have been widely diffused . . . be-

[1] Ch. xxxiv.
[2] Whewell's "History of Inductive Sciences," vol. ii. p. 593.

liefs that are perennial and universal . . . have some foundation, and some amount of verity."[1] Universal beliefs must rest on some common ground. That common ground can not be experience. A belief which was as clearly and confidently held four thousand years ago as it is held to-day can not have been gradually attained by successive generalizations. It is grounded on the fundamental antithesis between Becoming and Being, phenomena and reality, the changeful and the permanent, the finite and the infinite, the temporal and the eternal, which has been a necessary form of thought to all minds in all ages. The human mind has never been able to conceive these contradictory opposites as predicable of the same subject. The universe as presented to sense is a perpetual genesis, a ceaseless change; therefore it can not be permanent. It is a time-march of phenomena; therefore it can not be eternal. It is limited by quantity and quantitative relations; therefore it can not be infinite. Thus reason has always conceived the universe as having a *beginning*, and has confidently predicted that it will come to an *end.* All systems of philosophy, and, indeed, many systems of religion, have been attempts to explain "the beginning or origin of things"—that is, they have been "*à priori* theories of the universe."[2] Even Atheism itself comes under this definition: it is an attempt to explain the origin of the universe and of man on the *à priori* assumption of the self-existence of Matter, Space, and Motion. Thus all systems of thought, ancient and modern, have had their birth in the innate conviction that there is something to be explained, and that human reason is adequate to the task of furnishing an explanation. They all assume that the universe had a be-

[1] Spencer, "First Principles," p. 4.
[2] Spencer, "First Principles," p. 43.

ginning, and their one, central problem is, "How are we to conceive aright the origin of things?"

In what does this differ from the problem of modern science? It is true that Comte would limit positive science to "the study of phenomena in their orders of co-existence, resemblance, and succession," an idea which the word "positive" by no means conveys. And Tyndall asserts that "the man of science, if he confine himself within his own limits, will give no answer to the question" as to the origin of things. At the same time he admits that "he can clearly show that the present state of things *may* be derivative."[1] The great masters of science, however, refuse to acknowledge any such arbitrary limitations. "The essence of science," says Sir William Thomson, "consists in inferring antecedent conditions, and anticipating future evolutions from phenomena which have actually come under observation."[2] If this be the *essence* of science, then we presume that it is competent to throw some light on the primitive condition of the universe, and give some prevision of its future destiny. Did not Comte himself teach that the solar system was once all nebula, and that it will yet collapse into an exhausted and extinguished sun?[3] Is it true, then, that physical science by its inductive inference of "antecedent conditions," does really furnish a solid confirmation of the *à priori* and native conviction of our race that the universe had a beginning? Then most assuredly even physical science is carrying us forward toward the ultimate unity of all truth—a unity which can be realized perfectly only by the constant mut-

[1] "Fragments of Science," p. 12.
[2] Inaugural Address before the British Association of Science, in *Nature*, vol. iv. p. 269.
[3] "Positive Philosophy," vol. i. p. 206.

ual determination of *à priori* and empirical knowledge, a synthesis and equipoise of physical and metaphysical truths.

This is the most obvious tendency of modern science in its relation to the question under consideration. Nothing is more remarkable in the present aspect of physical research than what has been aptly called "the transcendental character of its results." As George Henry Lewes observes, "the fundamental ideas of modern science are as transcendental as any of the axioms of ancient philosophy."[1] Palætiological science in general has advanced by sure and steady steps, through careful observation and experiment, inductive inference, and the application of exact mathematical calculus to the recognition of the truth long ago announced by Paul: "The things which are seen are *temporal*, the things which are not seen are *eternal*." Dynamical Geology, Astronomical Palætiology, Cosmogony, Molecular Physics, Abstract Dynamics, have all landed in the same inevitable conclusion that "the existing order of things had a beginning." Sir William Thomson's doctrine of the "Dissipation of Energy" leads us, by sure steps of deductive reasoning, to the necessary future of the universe—necessary, that is, if physical laws remain unchanged—"so it enables us distinctly to say that the present order of things has not been evolved through infinite past time by the agency of laws now at work, but must have had a *distinctive beginning*, a state beyond which we are totally unable to penetrate—a state which must have been produced by *other than the now acting causes*."[2]

[1] "Philosophy of Aristotle," p. 66.

[2] Prof. P. G. Tait, M.A., opening Address at the Edinburgh Meeting of the British Association of Science, in *Nature*, vol. iv. p. 271. See also Prof. Maxwell's Address at the Liverpool Meeting, in *Nature*, vol. ii. p. 422.

The science of Geology reduces all terrestrial phenomena to the great law of finite duration. If there be one scientific induction which may be fairly pronounced legitimate and irrefragable, it is this one—that the existing terrestrial economy had a beginning. "All organic existence, recent or extinct, vegetable or animal, had a beginning; there was a time when they were not. The geologist can indicate that time, if not by years, at least by periods, and show what were its relations to the periods that went before and that came after." He can carry us back to the time when man did not exist upon the earth, when no mammals existed; to the time when no birds, no reptiles, no fishes existed — when even Huxley's protoplasm had no being; "when all creation, from its centre to its circumference, was a creation of dead inorganic matter,"[1] and when there was not one spore or monad or atom of life throughout its dark domain. The form of the earth itself clearly reveals its history, and points us to that beginning. Its bulging equator and flattened poles, its pavement of congealed lava, which in some cases we name granite; nay, the oldest water-worn pavement composed of the detritus of the igneous rocks—all attest the emergence of our planet from a molten condition, and a temperature[2] in which no life could exist; so that even Tyndall admits "there are the strongest grounds for believing that during a certain period of its history the earth was not, nor was it fit to be, the theatre of life."[3]

The earth was once a molten mass heated to incandescence — a self-luminous globe. On this point there is

[1] Miller's "Testimony of the Rocks," p. 221.

[2] Sir William Thomson supposes that temperature to have been at least 7000° Fahr. See Thomson and Tait's "Natural Philosophy," vol. i. p. 716.

[3] "Fragments of Science," p. 158.

scarcely any difference of opinion among scientific men. Furthermore, a large majority of modern scientists regard themselves as justified in the affirmation of a still anterior nebulous condition. If the nebular hypothesis is accepted, then we are required to contemplate a period when the earth did not exist, and when even the matter which now enters into its constitution was an undistinguished part of the nebula from which the whole solar system was evolved.

Many exact observations and mathematical computations as to the secular cooling of the earth give results which are in strict accordance with this theory of its primitive igneous condition. The observed facts clearly indicate that the earth is becoming, on the whole, cooler from age to age, and that the natural current of events is carrying it inevitably to a state of total refrigeration.[1] The fossil remains now found within the arctic circle indicate that at a period, not extremely remote, tropical vegetation flourished, and forms of animal life subsisted there which are now confined to the torrid zone. Mammoths lived in the now uninhabited polar regions, and tree-ferns and the tropical shell-fish found there a home.[2] The surface of the earth was then warmed by internal heat which since that period has waned; that heat has been gradually dissipated in the surrounding space, as a red-hot ball suspended even in the warm air of a room must, according to the well-known laws of radiation and absorption, necessarily part with its heat.

Many experiments carefully conducted in our time show that the temperature of the earth increases with the depth

[1] Thomson and Tait, "Natural Philosophy," vol. i. p. 714. Winchell, "Sketches of Creation," p. 407.

[2] Mayer, "Celestial Dynamics: Correlation and Conservation of Forces," p. 315. The palæobotanist Heer has described many species of tropical plants from Greenland, Alaska, and Spitzbergen.

to which we penetrate: "In boring for the artesian well at Grenelle, which is 546 metres deep, it was observed that the temperature augmented at the rate of 1° Centigrade for every 30 metres. The same result was obtained by observations in the artesian well at Mondorf, in Luxemburg; this well is 671 metres in depth, and its waters 34° warm." As the result of many investigations in mines and borings, Sir William Thomson concludes that the average inference may be thus stated—there is on the whole about 1° Fahr. of elevation of temperature per 50 British feet of descent.[1] If this increase is uniform—and we have no reason to suppose the contrary—then at the depth of 50 miles there exists, says Helmholtz, a heat sufficient to fuse all our minerals.

The fact that the temperature of the earth increases with the depth necessarily involves a continual loss of heat from its interior by conduction outward into and through the upper crust, according to a well-known law of equilibrium of temperatures. "Hence, since the upper crust does not become hotter from year to year, there must be a secular loss of heat from the earth."[2] Thus it appears that from the surface of the earth and the ocean, from thermal springs, and from three hundred active volcanoes, the internal heat of the globe is incessantly radiated into space and is practically lost.

Now this average loss of heat may be at least approximately measured, and data are thereby furnished for determining the probable *age* of the earth, or, perhaps more correctly, its phase of life. If a man were to find a hot

[1] Thomson and Tait, "Natural Philosophy," vol. i. p. 714. Observations on over forty artesian wells in Central Alabama show an average increase of temperature of 1° for every 47 feet of descent.—Dr. Winchell, in "Proceedings of American Association," part ii. p. 102.

[2] Thomson and Tait, "Natural Philosophy," vol. i. p. 714.

ball of iron suspended in a room, and if he were carefully to observe the distribution of heat in the ball, he would be able easily to determine whether the ball were becoming hotter or cooler. If he found that the inside were hotter than the outside, he would conclude that the ball was cooling, and had therefore been hotter than when he found it. So far common-sense would be his guide; but with the aid of mathematics, and some knowledge of the physical properties of iron and air, he could go much further, and be able to calculate how hot the ball must have been at any given moment, if it had not been interfered with. Thus he would be able to say, The ball must have been hung up less than, say, five hours ago, for at that time the heat of the metal would have been such that it would have been in a state of fusion, and hence not capable of hanging as a solid mass. Precisely analogous reasoning holds with regard to the earth: it is such a ball; it is hotter inside than outside. The distribution of the heat near its surface is approximately known—1° Fahr. of elevation in temperature for 50 British feet of descent.[1] The properties of the matter of which it is composed are approximately known. The temperature at which granite rocks are fusible has been found to be about 7000° Fahr. This must therefore have been the temperature of the earth in its primitive igneous condition. From these data, Sir William Thomson has, by rigid mathematical calculations, reached the conclusion that the consolidation of the earth's crust commenced 98,000,000 years ago.[2] The rates of increase of temperature *inward* in a great amount of

[1] Pouillet estimates that the heat which reaches the surface of the earth from its interior at 200 cubic miles per diem. A cubic mile is the quantity of heat nécessary to raise a cubic mile of water 1° Centigrade in temperature.

[2] Thomson and Tait, "Natural Philosophy," vol. i. p. 716.

average rock at various periods after the commencement of cooling, from the primitive heat of 7000° Fahr., are estimated by Sir William Thomson as follows:

"At	10,000	y'rs after	commencement	of cooling	we should have	2°	per ft.
At	40,000	"	"	"	"	1°	"
At	160,000	"	"	"	"	$\frac{1}{2}$°	"
At	4,000,000	"	"	"	"	$\frac{1}{10}$°	"
At	100,000,000	"	"	"	"	$\frac{1}{50}$°	"

It is therefore probable that for the last 96,000,000 years the rate of increase of temperature under ground has gradually diminished from $\frac{1}{10}$ to about $\frac{1}{50}$ of a degree Fahrenheit per foot, and that the thickness of the crust through which any stated degree of cooling has been experienced has gradually increased during that period from $\frac{1}{5}$ of its present thickness to what it now really is."[1]

We freely admit our inability to sit in judgment on the validity of Sir William Thomson's conclusions. There are eminent geologists who entertain the opinion that the secular cooling of the earth has proceeded with much greater rapidity. It is, however, sufficient for our purpose that the most distinguished physicists of the day are agreed in teaching that *the existing terrestrial economy had a beginning.*

There are other terrestrial changes which engage the attention of the geologist, and which force upon him the conclusion that the existing terrestrial order had a beginning and must have an end. The surface of the earth has at intervals undergone great changes in the disposition of its land and water. That which is now dry land was once the ocean-bed, and the ocean waves now roll and murmur over what was once dry land. Sudden, or comparatively sudden,

[1] Thomson and Tait, "Natural Philosophy," vol. i. p. 721.

catastrophes have extinguished the then existing creations, and the earth has been repeopled by new orders of life. Changes are now in progress which are gradually reducing the populous regions of the earth to the condition of the Sahara of Africa and the Desert of Arabia. Upper and Lower Mesopotamia, the seat of the ancient monarchies of Chaldæa, Assyria, and Babylonia, now present "vast tracts of arid plain—yellow, parched, and sapless—which have now become a bare and uninhabited desert." That ancient continent drained by the Colorado, once as fertile as the Valley of the Mississippi, is now the Great American Desert. "Every freshet burdens the streams with a load of sediment; and the Mississippi bears daily to the Gulf material sufficient for a cotton plantation. From the slopes of the Alleghanies and the Rocky Mountains, from the broad acres over which the Mississippi and the Ohio reach their silver fingers to filch from the land, the sediments are stolen and carried away to the sea. The Western States are slowly traveling toward the Gulf. The hills are melting, and even the mountain cliffs are lowering under the ceaseless conflict with storm and frost. The summits of the Alleghanies have come down 3000 feet from their original altitudes. Give time enough, and the inequalities of the land will disappear. The ocean will be filled, and again assert a triumph over the continents which in the beginning were wrested from his dominion." Thus by the storms of heaven, the erosion of the atmosphere, the blasting power of frost, the gnawing of the tidal wave, the mountains are being leveled, and the rocks and soils carried onward by the rivers to fill up the basin of the sea. The headlong rush of the avalanche, the murmuring of the brook, the roaring of the sea, the voice of the storm—all proclaim, "The things which are seen are temporal!"—"The existing order of things had a beginning and must come to an end!"[1]

Astronomical Palætiology reduces all celestial phenomena to the same great law of finite duration. It teaches that planets, stars, systems, have their birth, their process of formation, their maturity, and their slow, protracted decay. The ephemeron perishes in an hour, man endures his threescore years and ten; continents and islands have their ages and æons; the stars of heaven are not exempt from this universal law of change and decay. According to the Nebular Hypothesis, the formation of this our system of sun, planets, and satellites was a process of the same kind as that which is still going forward in the heavens. One after another, nebulæ condense into separate masses, which begin to revolve about each other in obedience to dynamical laws, and form systems of which our system is a matured example. The present aspect of this planetary system is, however, but a passing phase in the history of its fleeting life. Our planet was once a self-luminous orb; it has now become opaque, and shines only with a borrowed light. The moon is probably in a state of total refrigeration; its lunar air and lunar seas have been changed by intensity of cold into the solid form.[2] The sun itself is radiating heat into space in quantities incomparably greater than it receives, and, as Helmholtz affirms, "the inexorable laws of mechanics show that its store of heat must be finally exhausted."[3] The planets in their motions encounter resistance from the interstellar ether; they must, therefore, necessarily move in shorter and short-

[1] See Winchell's "Sketches of Creation," chap. xxxvi.

[2] Proctor, "Other Worlds than Ours," p. 193. "More likely these have been totally absorbed by the lunar rocks."—Dr. Winchell.

[3] "Correlation and Conservation of Forces," p. 245.

er orbits, and at last fall into the sun. Thus the Nebular Hypothesis, combined with the doctrine of a resisting medium, teaches us that the solar system is wending its way, through successive changes, from a past of vaporous unity to a future of consolidated reunion. "It was once all nebula; it will, if left to physical agencies alone, collapse into an extinguished and exhausted sun."

The astronomer who has been accustomed to regard every question relating to his favorite science as almost exclusively a problem in mathematics, will pronounce the above "a crude and adventurous" attempt on the part of the physicist to solve a problem which belongs to "the calculus of variations." Is the universe a Conservative or a Dissipative system? Under its present laws will it run on forever, or will these very laws in the end lead to its subversion? Will the mechanism of the heavens finally run down as surely as the weights of a clock run down to their lowest position, or are we authorized on scientific grounds to assert the permanent stability of the solar system? This question has been earnestly discussed by the most distinguished astronomers since the days of Newton. Until recently, the general conclusion—reached mainly on mathematical grounds—seems to have been that the universe is a thoroughly conservative system, and that the celestial machinery by a species of perpetual motion will run on forever. But must not all applied mathematical reasoning obtain its data from the exact observation of material facts? The mathematician must also be a good natural philosopher; he must lay his account with all the facts of the universe, otherwise his symbols have no contents, and his reasoning, however faultless in its processes, will be fallacious in its results. The discoveries of the present century respecting the correlation of the various forms of energy, the nature of the solar light and heat, the motions of comets, and especially the new doctrine of the "Dissipation of Energy," have introduced new elements into the great problem, which seem to indicate that gravitation is by no means the only force by which the motions of the heavenly bodies are influenced, and that causes are now in operation which are slowly but surely undermining the system. We now find, therefore, such high authorities as Whewell, Sir John Herschel, Sir William Thomson, Balfour Stewart, Prof. Maxwell, Dr. J. R. Mayer, Helmholtz, Tyndall, Littrow, Comte, Adolph Fick, asserting that the solar system is not a self-winding clock which may run forever, but that it is a dissipative system which must ultimately lose all motion, unless some power capable of controlling the laws of material nature interfere to preserve it. We have no more valid reason for concluding that the Deity intended the system should be eternal than that He intended the earthly life of man should be eternal.[1] A few general statements may assist the reader in appreciating the merits of the discussion.

It has been observed since the dawn of science that changes are taking place in the motions of the heavenly bodies. The eccentricity of the earth's orbit has been gradually diminishing from the earliest observations to the present time. The moon, also, has been moving faster and faster from the time of the first recorded eclipses, and is now in advance by about four times her own breadth of what her place would have been had she not been affected by these accelerations.[2] In a few thousand years she will be half a month ahead of the place she would be in if her month were to remain constant. The moon is, therefore,

[1] *North American Review*, Oct., 1861, pp. 372–3.
[2] Mitchell's "Planetary and Stellar Worlds," p. 143.

approaching closer and closer to the earth; and if these changes go on uninterruptedly, without any reaction or adjustment, sooner or later the final catastrophe must come, and the moon be precipitated on the body of the earth.

Toward the close of the last century, Laplace, in his great work, the "Méchanique Céleste," attempted by certain mathematical computations to show that, nevertheless, the solar system is stable and permanent. The planets, by their mutual attractions, produce perpetual perturbations in one another's movements. Laplace believed he could prove that these were periodic; they reach a maximum value and then diminish, oscillating between very narrow extremes. He therefore taught that the machine would go on by a kind of perpetual motion, without any winding up or adjustment from without; and, consequently, the eternal continuance of the solar system is insured.

All the investigations of Laplace, and the computations of Lagrange, proceeded on two assumptions: first, that the planets are moving *in vacuo;* and, secondly, that they are solid throughout their entire mass. The latter assumption is certainly in conflict with well-determined geological facts; and there is no *à priori* ground for assuming that the planetary spaces are void and empty. On the contrary, the general analogies of nature would lead us to the very opposite conclusion, and all attempts at producing a perfect vacuum have hitherto failed. Furthermore, the great body of modern physicists, and nearly all modern astronomers, hold that the celestial spaces are filled with a "material ether," which must by its very nature offer some resistance to planetary motion.

"Scientific men," says Mayer, "do not doubt the existence of such an ether." The presence of such "material ether—dense, elastic, and capable of motion—subject to and determined by mechanical laws,"[1] is demanded for the explanation of radiant heat, light, and actinism. No other theory ever proposed has so beautifully and completely accounted for all the facts. Its reality must be admitted, until the positions established by Huyghens, Young, Fresnel, Foucault, and Fiziau are shown to be untenable. All the prominent experimental physicists of the present day agree in teaching that light and heat are transmitted by vibrations or wave-like motions in a material medium universally diffused through space, and permeating all material bodies. Light and heat are the ceaseless thrill which the distant orbs collectively create in the ether, and which constitute what has been called the *temperature of space.* If the existence of such material medium as the assumed ether be denied, we can not account in any conceivable or rational manner for the transmission of light and heat from the sun. And now, if the space between the celestial bodies contain no other matter than that necessary for the transmission of light, "that alone," says Littrow, "is sufficient, in the course of time, to alter the motion of the planets, and the arrangements of the solar system itself; the fall of all the planets and comets into the sun, and the destruction of the present state of the solar system, must be the final result of this action."[2]

But it is further claimed by Helmholtz, Mayer, and Sir William Thomson that the phenomena presented by Encke's comet furnish "direct proof" of the existence of such resisting medium. The observations on this comet made during the past thirty or forty years show that the

[1] Tyndall, "Fragments of Science," p. 135.
[2] Quoted by Mayer, "Celestial Dynamics: Correlation and Conservation of Forces," p. 271.

periods of its revolution are continually diminishing at the rate of 0.11° per revolution of nearly $3\frac{1}{3}$ years. In other words, the comet's mean distance from the sun is diminishing by slow and regular degrees. The solution which Encke himself proposed, and which Herschel informs us "is generally received,"[1] is that resistance is experienced from the medium in which the comet moves; such resistance diminishing its actual velocity and also its centrifugal force, thus giving the sun greater power to draw it nearer. It will, therefore, fall into the sun. A similar fate, says Helmholtz, threatens all the planets. "The analogies of nature, and the ascertained facts of physical science, forbid us to doubt that *every star*, and, indeed, *every body of every kind* moving in any part of space, has its relative motion impeded by the air, gas, vapor, medium, or whatever we call the substance occupying space immediately around them, just as the motion of a rifle-bullet is impeded by the resistance of the air."[2]

There are also indirect resistances, the effects of tidal friction, on all bodies which, like the earth, have portions of their free surfaces covered by liquids, which, so long as these bodies move relatively to neighboring bodies, must keep drawing off energy from their relative motions. "Thus, if we consider the action of the moon on the earth, with its oceans, lakes, and rivers, we perceive that it must tend to equalize the period of the earth's rotation on its axis, and of the revolution of the two bodies about their centre of inertia; because, so long as these periods differ, the tidal action of the earth's surface must keep subtracting energy from their motions."[3] As the tidal wave sweeps

[1] "Outlines of Astronomy," p. 308.

[2] Thomson and Tait, "Natural Philosophy," vol. i. p. 191.

[3] Thomson and Tait, "Natural Philosophy," vol. i. p. 191. Balfour Stewart, "Treatise on Heat," p. 372.

over the oceans and rushes into the numerous bays and estuaries, the motions which it produces in the waters necessarily involve an expenditure of power or *vis viva* in overcoming the resistance from friction. The energy of motion thus expended must be drawn from the set of machinery which produces the motions—that is, from the motion of revolution of the moon, and the motion of rotation of the earth. It can not be returned to the machinery, because all that is not spent in triturating the sand and other materials composing the ocean-bed, is transformed into heat and radiated into space.

It is true that in the present state of science we have not exact data for estimating the relative importance of tidal friction, and of the resistance of the interstellar medium; but, whatever it may be, there can be, says Thomson, "but one ultimate result for such a system as that of sun and planets if continuing long enough under existing laws. . . . That result is *the falling together into one mass, which, although rotating for a time, must in the end come to rest relatively to the surrounding medium.*"[1]

Another evidence that the solar system is temporal, and that the present cosmical order must come to an end, is found in the fact that the sun is radiating heat into space in quantities incomparably greater than it receives. If it were not so, we should receive, on the average, as much heat from every other quarter of the heavens as from the sun, and no vicissitudes of temperature would ever occur on the earth. Now, from what we know of the nature of heat, it is impossible that the supply contained in the sun should be inexhaustible. There is no apparent reason why the sun should form an exception to the fate of all fires, its

[1] Thomson and Tait, "Natural Philosophy," vol. i. p. 194; also Helmholtz, in "Correlation and Conservation of Forces," p. 242.

only difference being one of size and time. It is larger and hotter than ordinary lamps, but is nevertheless a lamp in which invisible molecular energy is consumed, and consumed, too, at a rate which baffles all conception. From every square foot of its surface the sun gives out energy equal in amount to seven thousand horse-power. The total amount of heat sent off from the sun in *one minute* is "five thousand millions of millions of units:" a unit of heat being the quantity of heat required to raise one kilogramme—or about one quart—of water one Centigrade degree.[1] This enormous consumption of energy must finally exhaust the original stock. Were the sun a solid block of coal, and were it allowed a sufficient quantity of oxygen to enable it to burn at the rate necessary to produce the observed emission of heat, it would be utterly consumed in five thousand years. Or if we suppose, with Thomson, that the initial form of the energy of the universe is the potential energy of gravitation in matter diffused through space, and if this potential energy (energy of position) is transformed into heat (molecular kinetic energy) by condensation or contraction of the sun, and this energy of molecular motion (heat) is again transformed into radiant energy and diffused through infinite space, it is obvious that this condensation can not be continued forever, and Thomson has shown in his article on the "Age of the Sun's Heat" that its power of radiation must come to an end. Various theories have been suggested for replenishing the solar heat, one of the most plausible of which is the falling of meteoric and cometary bodies into the sun. Prof. Thomson, who was one of the first to

[1] Winchell, "Sketches of Creation," p. 422. If the whole solar radiation were employed in dissolving a layer of ice inclosing the sun, it would dissolve a stratum ten miles and a half thick in one day.

adopt this view, has now abandoned it, or at least has denied its adequacy to account for the maintenance of solar heat. Even were the hypothesis accepted as valid, the supply of fuel is still finite. Time will drain the entire space inclosed by the orbit of the planet Neptune of all the meteors and comets. Even the planets must at length be ensepulchred in the sun. "As surely," writes Sir William Thomson, "as the weights of the clock run down to the lowest position, from which they can never rise again unless fresh energy is communicated to them from some source not yet exhausted, so surely must every planet creep in, age after age, toward the sun." Not one can escape its fiery end. And, finally, the heat of the sun itself—that is, its molecular energy—must be transformed into radiant energy, and diffused and lost as a working force in infinite space. "Thus do the inexorable laws of mechanics indicate that the sun's store of heat, which can only suffer loss and not gain, must *be finally exhausted*."[1]

There are thus special geological and astronomical facts which have long been regarded as indicative of the principle that the existing order of the material universe is *temporal*—it had a beginning, and must have an end. But the modern Theory of Energy,[2] with its three great

[1] Helmholtz, "Correlation and Conservation of Forces," p. 245.

[2] *Energy* is now defined as "*the power of doing work*," that is, the power, in *virtue of its position* (as a head of water, a raised mass, a coiled spring) or in *virtue of its motion* (as a falling mass, a current of wind, a projectile), to do work. The first is called *Potential*, the second *Kinetic* Energy. Besides these instances of *Visible* Energy, there is also *Invisible* Molecular Energy, divided into, (*a*) the Energy of electricity in motion; (*b*) the Energy of radiant heat and light; (*c*) the kinetic Energy of absorbed heat; (*d*) molecular potential Energy; (*e*) potential Energy caused by electrical separation; (*f*) potential Energy caused by chemical separation. Of these different *kinds* of Energy, the most available for work is Mechanical Energy, or Energy of visible motions and positions; the least available is universal heat, or radiant Energy.

laws of Conservation, Transformation, and Dissipation, must be regarded as a comprehensive, complete, and final settlement of the question. It has been shown, first, that no system of machinery can *create* force any more than it can create matter; and that the amount of energy in the universe, or in any limited system which does not receive energy from without, or part with it to external matter, is a constant or invariable quantity. This is the *Law of the Conservation of Energy*. It has been proved, secondly, as an experimental fact that, in general, one form of energy may, by suitable processes, be transformed wholly or in part to an equivalent amount of another form; and the sole and only function of all possible machines is the conversion or *transformation* of energy. This is the *Law of the Transformation of Energy*. This law of Transformation is, however, subject to the limitations which are imposed by the *Law of the Dissipation of Energy*, the discovery of which is mainly due to Sir William Thomson. He has shown that every machine does its work against friction. "A material system can never be brought through any returning cycle of motions without spending more work against the mutual forces of its parts than it gained from these parts, because no relative motions can take place without meeting with frictional or other forms of resistance." No known process of transformation is exactly reversible. Whenever an attempt is made to transform and retransform energy by an imperfect process, part of the energy is converted into heat, and the heat is *dissipated*, so as to become useless because incapable of further transformation. It therefore follows that, as energy is constantly in a state of transformation, there is a constant degradation of energy to that final unavailable form of uniformly diffused heat; and this will go on as long as transformations occur, until the whole energy of the universe has taken this form.[1] The reader will find an extended discussion of this great question in Thomson and Tait's "Natural Philosophy," vol. i. pp. 188–304, in which it is shown that the present material system is not a *dynamically conservative* but a *dissipative* system, and therefore that in such a system "perpetual motion" is an impossibility.

Indeed, the Law of the Dissipation of Energy is an intelligent and well-supported denial of the chimera of perpetual motion. There is a loose idea that perpetual motion is impossible to us, because we can not avoid friction with its consequent loss of energy, but that nature works without friction, or that, in general, friction entails no loss, and so here perpetual motion is possible; but nature no more works without friction than we do, and friction entails a loss of available power. The supply of invisible molecular energy in the sun is no more infinite than the quantity of matter in the sun is infinite. The sun is daily lifting huge masses of water from the sea to the skies, yearly lifting endless vegetation from the earth, setting breezes and hurricanes in motion, dragging the huge tidal wave round and round the earth; performing, in short, the great bulk of the endless labor of this world and other worlds, so that the energy of the sun is continually being given away without any corresponding restoration. The loss of force in the shape of radiant light and heat can never be weaned back to any other mode of available energy. Carnot, Clausius, Thomson, and Rankine have all from different points of view been led to the same conclusion. We can make no use whatever of the energy repre-

[1] See article "Energy," in *North British Review*, May, 1864, and Balfour Stewart's "Treatise on Heat," p. 370.

sented by equally diffused heat. If one body is hotter than another, as the boiler of a steam-engine is hotter than the condenser, then we can make use of the difference of temperature to convert some of the heat into work; but if two substances are equally hot, even though their particles contain an enormous amount of molecular energy, they will not yield us a single unit of work. Energy is thus of different qualities, mechanical energy being the *best*, and universal heat the *worst;* in fact, this latter description of energy may be compared to the waste heap of the universe, in which the *effete* forms of energy are suffered to accumulate without any further conversion.[1] If, then, when mechanical force passes into heat, *some* of the heat can never be brought back to be mechanical force, and if the change from mechanical force to heat be ever going on, all the force in the universe must at last take the form of radiant heat. But if that be so, then at last all differences of temperature must disappear, and every thing end in a universal death.

"We are come," says Adolph Fick, "to this alternative: either in our highest, most general, most fundamental abstractions, some great point has been overlooked, or the universe will have an END, and must have had a BEGINNING; it could not have existed from Eternity, but must at some date, not infinitely distant, have arisen from something not forming a part of the natural chain of causes—that is, IT MUST HAVE BEEN CREATED."[2]

So far, then, the deductions of science are found to be in striking harmony with the teaching of revelation—the existing order of the universe had a beginning; the forms,

[1] Stewart's "Elements of Physics," p. 357.

[2] "Die Naturkräfte in ihrer Wechselbeziehung," p. 89.

relations, laws, harmonies of the Cosmos had a commencement in time. We may now proceed to the consideration of the second question: Had that which is the *ground* of all form, the *subject* of all changes and relations, a beginning? Had the *matter* of the universe a beginning?

That we may fairly present the answer which modern science offers to this question, we must premise, in general, that it confesses its inability, in the present stage of physical knowledge, to determine what is the ultimate or internal constitution of matter. Many scientists of to-day are of the opinion expressed by Grove[1] that "probably man will never know the ultimate structure of matter." Others, as, for example, Thomson, Bayma, McVicar, and Challis, entertain the opinion that physical science is competent to discover all the minutiæ of molecular actions, and when this has been achieved, the question as to the ultimate constitution of matter can be finally determined. There is one guiding principle, recognized alike by the physicist and the metaphysician, namely, that substances, ultimate entities, are known, and can only be known in and through their respective phenomena. An exact enumeration and careful colligation of all the phenomena are therefore indispensable prerequisites to the solution of the problem.

Meantime nothing is more remarkable, even in the present state of physical science, than the fact that, under the subtile analysis of modern physics, much that we have been accustomed to regard as phenomena of matter dissolves and disappears, surviving only as phenomena of *Force*. The phenomena of heat, light, color, sound, electricity, and magnetism are now "modes of motion"—

[1] "Correlation of Physical Forces," p. 187.

manifestations of one and the same omnipresent energy, which is transferred from one portion of matter to another, and modified or transformed simply by the mechanical arrangements and collocations of matter. The opinion is rapidly gaining ground that even chemical action is a mode of motion, and Professor Norton does not hesitate in affirming that "*all the phenomena of material nature result from the action of force upon matter.*"[1] All that we mean by a Material Force "is a force which acts *upon* matter, and produces in matter its own appropriate effects."[2] It is not an attribute of matter, not a quality inherent in matter, but a mode or state superimposed upon matter.

There is a large, influential, and daily increasing class of scientists, among whom may be named Faraday, Prof. Owen, Dr. Laycock, Wallace, Dr. Winslow, Prof. Huxley, who do not regard matter as an ultimate entity, and who believe that all the phenomena of matter (so called), even extension, resistance, and ultimate incompressibility, may be resolved into phenomena of force. In other words, matter is only *phenomenal*, and, like all phenomena, demands a *cause.*[3] These men are perplexed with no difficulties as to the *origin* of matter. As a phenomenon it

[1] *American Journal of Science*, July, 1864.

[2] Argyll, "Reign of Law," p. 121.

[3] Sir Isaac Newton entertained a similar opinion. "We may be able," he said, "to form some rude conception of the *creation of matter*, if we suppose that God by his power had prevented the entrance of any thing into a certain portion of pure space which is of its nature penetrable, . . . from henceforward this portion of space will be endowed with *impenetrability*, one of the essential qualities of matter; and as pure space is absolutely uniform, we have only to suppose that God communicated the same impenetrability to another portion of space, and we should obtain in a certain sort the notion of *mobility*, another quality which is essential to matter."—M. Coste, Note in the 4th Edition of his "French Translation of Locke's Essay." (M. Coste reports the above from Newton's lips.)

must be a product of Creative Efficiency, and therefore had a beginning.

It is obviously unnecessary that we should here discuss the merits of this hypothesis which resolves matter into force. We shall encounter it at a subsequent stage of our inquiry, and may then attempt to gauge its merits. It is enough for our present purpose that Heat, Light, Color, Sound, Electricity, Magnetism, are recognized as forms of molecular Energy — phenomena of Force; that these forms of invisible molecular energy, together with all the energy of visible motions and positions, are regarded as flowing from one great central force, or fountain-head of power; and that there is a remarkable unanimity among the first scientific men of our age in acknowledging this power as the Creative Efficiency of God. These forces uniformly work in obedience to Law; and Law, whether viewed in the orderly movement of a planet or an atom, in the symmetrical arrangement of a crystal of the definite proportions of chemical combination, in the organization of a worm or of an elephant, is intellect, is *reason*. This is the ultimate principle upon which every condition of matter and form depends.

This conception of force will materially aid us in the conception of matter. It is simply "the recipient of impulses or energy"[1]—the mere passive condition for the exercise of power. "It does not generate the phenomena which it manifests. It is only the substratum—it does absolutely nothing but give to the phenomena their conditions of manifestation."[2] Every molecule of matter, every aggregation of molecules, every organism must be regarded as a machine upon which the forces of nature

[1] Prof. Maxwell, in *Nature*, vol. ii. p. 219.

[2] M. Claude Bernard, *Revue des Deux Mondes*, 1867.

play, and by which they are transformed and rendered available for the performance of work. Thus matter, by its very conception, must have been *created*, and fitted for the fulfillment of a predetermined function. Before the mechanism of the universe was set in motion, there was a preparation and collocation of its materials, and an adjustment of its minutest parts. As Sir John Herschel justly remarks, "Chemical analysis most certainly points to an origin, and effectually destroys the idea of an external self-existent matter, by giving to each of its atoms the essential character, at once, of a *manufactured article* and a *subordinate agent*."[1] The numerical relations between chemical elements are the expression of creative ideas. The maxim of the Pythagorean philosophers is daily receiving new illustration from science, "The world is a living arithmetic in its development, a realized geometry in its repose." There can be no arithmetic without an Arithmetician, no geometry without a Geometrician. Thus in the very elements out of which the universe is built, the blocks of nature's temple, we see the indications not only of a fashioning but of an *originating* intelligence—a Creating God. Design as truly appears in the primitive nature of matter as in its secondary formations. The primitive purpose is stamped on the primitive article.

"Every molecule throughout the universe bears impressed on it the stamp of a metric system as distinctly as does the metre of the Archives at Paris, or the double royal cubit of the Temple of Karnac.

"No theory of evolution can be formed to account for the similarity of molecules, for evolution necessarily implies continuous change, and the molecule is incapable of growth or decay, of generation or destruction.

[1] "Dissertation on the Study of Natural Philosophy," § 28.

"None of the processes of Nature, since the time when Nature began, have produced the slightest difference in the properties of any molecule. We are therefore unable to ascribe either the existence of the molecules or the identity of their properties to the operation of any of the causes which we call *natural.*

"On the other hand, the exact quality of each molecule to all others of the same kind gives it the essential character of a manufactured article, and *precludes the idea of its being eternal and self-existent.*"[1]

[1] Prof. Clerk Maxwell, F.R.S., "Lecture delivered before the British Association at Bradford," in *Nature*, vol. viii. p. 441.

CHAPTER V.

CREATION: ITS HISTORY.

THE universe had a beginning. It is not eternal either in its matter or form; it is neither self-originated nor self-sustained. The all of the finite, with its relations and laws, its adaptations and harmonies, had its origin solely and absolutely in the unconditioned will of God. This is the Christian doctrine concerning the world.

In the preceding chapters we have endeavored to show that this doctrine is in perfect agreement with the teachings of sound philosophy, and we have found that it is daily receiving fresh confirmation from the discoveries of modern science.

If the universe originated solely in the free determination of God, then we are assured there must be a sufficient and ultimate reason for its existence. This logically follows from the true conception of *Will*, for will is not unconscious force, neither is it groundless arbitrariness, but conscious, rational choice.

In the merely formal and indifferent sense of the word, an arbitrary action is one in which the agent yields to the blind impulse of caprice, and can assign no reason for his doing. An action is truly free only when the agent knows *what* he wills, and *why* he wills it. The self-conscious will is the only real will. Will is intrinsically something more than power, something more, even, than the power of spontaneous self-determination. Will involves precognition, deliberation, and alternative choice: it is the living synthesis of reason and power. "The mere moment of self-determination does not suffice for the notion of will, for this, in a certain sense, we must ascribe to unintelligent creatures, to the organic life of nature by virtue of its development from its own principle. Self-determination only thereby becomes will by its being a *conscious* determination—that is, the conscious subject is able to present to its own mind that which it brings to reality by its self-determination."[1] All real volition supposes a purpose or end to be realized, an inward motive or reason which renders the end desirable, and the choice and adaptation of means to accomplish that end. Consequently, if the universe is the product of the Divine Will, it must, both in its origination and its history, be the realization of an ultimate or final purpose, must have a perfect unity of plan; and the highest law of the universe must be a *teleological* idea to which all nature-forces and all causal connections are subordinated. This ultimate purpose forms, as it were, a complete network of higher teleological connections above the web of mere aiteological connections which pervades the universe.

This great principle that a teleological idea is the highest law of the universe has been recognized by all philosophers of the spiritualistic school from the time of Plato to the present day. Even Mr. Mill admits that "Teleology, or the Doctrine of Ends, may be termed, not improperly, a principle of the practical reason;"[2] and he advises those who would prove the existence of God "to stick to the argument from *design*." No saying of Bacon has been more often quoted or more grossly misunderstood and misapplied than his remark on final causes: "The search after

[1] Müller, "Christian Doctrine of Sin," vol. i. p. 28.
[2] "Logic," vol. ii. p. 527, 4th edition.

final causes is barren, for like virgins consecrated to God they produce nothing." If, however, we refer to his writings ("Advancement of Learning," bk. ii. p. 142), we find him adding, "*not because these final causes are not true and worthy to be inquired, being kept within their own province.*" A fair consideration of the context clearly shows that the remark was intended to apply to Physics, and not at all to Metaphysics. All that he intends to say is that in purely physical inquiries the search after final causes can have no practical application; and the error he would guard against is the assumption that what appears to man a final cause must be the ultimate final cause to the Infinite One.

The belief that a principle of adaptation to special ends pervades all existence, and that it must be assumed as the ground of the scientific explanation of the facts and phenomena of the universe, is avowed by the first scientists of the age. "We can not be content," says Dr. Laycock, "with simply determining the mere relations of things or events—an existence, a co-existence, a succession, or a resemblance—and not inquire into the *ends* thereof. Such a doctrine applied to physiology would, in fact, arrest all scientific research into the phenomena of life; for the investigation of the so-called functions of organs is nothing more than a *teleological* investigation."[1] "*A law of design is the higher generalization of the great uniformities of nature.*"[2] In his inaugural address at the meeting of the British Association of Science at Edinburgh, Sir William Thomson said: "I feel profoundly convinced that the argument from design has been greatly lost sight of in recent speculations. . . . Overwhelmingly strong proofs of Intelligence and Benevolent Design lie all around us; and if ever

[1] "Mind and Brain," vol. i. pp. 107–8.
[2] "Mind and Brain," vol. i. p. 261.

perplexities, whether of a metaphysical or scientific character, turn us away for a time, they will come back upon us with irresistible force, showing us through nature the influence of a *Free Will*, and teaching us that all living beings depend upon one ever-acting *Creator* and *Ruler*."[1]

Every enlargement of our knowledge of organic nature is an addition to the already numberless instances of recognized special adaptation which crowd us on every hand; and all scientific discovery is but an illustration and a verification of the *à priori* intuition of the reason that a principle of design is co-extensive with and the highest law of the universe. Not merely of each individual existence, but of the grand totality of existence, are we constrained to believe that it exists for a purpose. Above all special ends there is a great ultimate design of creation—a last or final end to which all intermediate ends are means; and though physical science can not fully compass that final purpose, yet in the light of its present knowledge of special ends it has abundant reason for assuming that there *must* be a final purpose, and that that final purpose is at once beneficent and wise.[2]

But while the final purpose of creation may not be discoverable by human science, we know that it has been revealed in the Christian Scriptures.

The most fundamental doctrine of Christianity is that *God is Love* (1 John iv. 8, 16), and that Love is the highest determining principle of the Divine efficiency. Creation, Providence, and Redemption are grounded in Love as the final cause (Gen. i. 31; Isa. lxiii. 9; John iii. 16).

The gravitating point of the Christian doctrine of "God the Creator" is not Omnipotence, nor yet Wisdom, but al-

[1] *Nature*, vol. iv. p. 270.
[2] See Murphy, "Habit and Intelligence," vol. i. p. 121.

ways Love. Omnipotence, in itself considered, possesses no moving or determining principle. God does not create the world to reveal his infinite power. Infinite Wisdom devises the best means and methods for the Divine efficiency, but it does not supply the ultimate reason why the world exists. The Love of God is the moving principle of his wisdom and power in that it appoints the *end* to which omnipotence is related as the efficient, and wisdom as the formal cause. Whatever displays of power or of wisdom may be made in the created universe, they are all subordinated and made subservient to the purpose of Love. The highest law of the universe is Love. "The conservation of Love is the loftiest conservation of Force."

The world, then, was created to be a revelation of God, and especially to be a revelation of the perfections of the Divine nature which are grounded in and deducible from Love; and it exists as the self-manifestation and self-communication of God to personal creatures who can know Him and love Him in return. "That which can determine God, absolutely sufficient in Himself, in the production of beings distinct from Himself, is *Love alone;* consequently the creation is nothing else than the free self-communication of God Himself, who could be exclusively in Himself, but wills that others may have being and, in fellowship with Him, eternal life."[1] The world-creating, world-preserving Love of God has this for its ultimate purpose, *that there shall be beings who, in the completeness and perfection of personal existence, shall know and love and resemble God, and have fellowship in his blessedness and joy* (Matt. v. 8; 1 Cor. xiii. 12; 2 Peter i. 4; 1 John iii. 2).

The realization of a perfected humanity in fellowship with God is, then, the final end of creation. We find some

[1] Müller, "Christian Doctrine of Sin," vol. ii. p. 146.

intimations of this grand purpose in the sublime record of creation which is given by Moses. We there learn that every thing was created with a view to man—to "man in the image of God." The inorganic world exists for the vegetable kingdom, the vegetable exists for the animal kingdom, and all exists for man (ch. i. 26–30). All its successive changes were a preparation for the appearance of man.[1] The more comprehensive revelation of the New Testament teaches that man exists for the realization of that perfected humanity of which Christ is the model, and which is attained in and through Christianity. The idea of man is the teleological principle of the world, the idea of Christ is the teleological principle of humanity. All things were created *by* Christ and for Christ. "The good pleasure (εὐδοκία = the benevolent purpose) of the Divine Will" is, in the fullness of time, to gather together in one all things both which are in heaven and which are on earth, even in Christ, that in the final consummation *God may be all in all* (Eph. i. 9, 10; 1 Cor. xv. 28).

This purpose of Divine Love is an "*eternal purpose*," ordained before the foundation of the world, and progressively unfolded in the creation, government, and redemption of the world. Thus the world, as an actual, temporal world, reposes on an eternal ideal world which has always been present to the Divine cognition. The visible creation is but the realization of the Divine ideal in such

[1] That man is the final end of the material creation is a principle recognized by scientific men. "The aim of the Creator in forming the earth, in allowing it to undergo the successive changes which geology has pointed out, and in creating successively all the different types of animals, was to introduce man upon the earth. Man is the end toward which all the animal creation has tended from the appearance of the Palæozoic fishes."—Agassiz and Gould, "Principles of Zoology," p. 238. See Dr. Winchell's "Sketches of Creation," pp. 373, 374; Owen's "Anatomy of the Vertebrates," vol. iii. pp. 796, 808.

modes and under such conditions as shall constitute it a manifestation of God to finite intelligences—the external expression of the mind and character of God, the language of the Deity.

Assuming this as a fundamental principle of Christian theology that Creation is the self-manifestation of God, and that the final cause of this manifestation is the communication of the Divine blessedness to intelligent, personal being, we may logically infer the following intermediate principles as *Laws of this Manifestation.*

1. *This manifestation must be* GRADUAL, *not instantaneous. In other words, it must be unfolded in successive steps or phases, so as to be adapted to the nature and capabilities of the being to whom it is made. The determinations of nature, like those of consciousness, must conform to the law of progressive development.*

Divine omnipotence was, no doubt, adequate to the production of new beings without any pre-existing materials or any prearranged conditions; but creation is not mainly or primarily a revelation of omnipotence. The Deity might have brought the phenomena of the universe into instant being without any succession and independent of all means, but a universe thus instantaneously produced and simultaneously presented would reveal no purpose to, and could not be understood by, a finite mind. Finite consciousness can be developed only under conditions of plurality, difference, and succession, and therefore the objects of cognition must be successively presented. We may be sensible of the external reality by immediate intuition, but we can *understand* only through experience; and experience supposes a gradual process—a succession not simply in our mental states, but a succession of external phenomena.

This experience of succession constitutes our consciousness of *time*. Therefore, in order that the Divine manifestation may be understood, it must have a *history*.[1]

2. *This manifestation must be* CUMULATIVE—*that is, it must afford an increase of knowledge through successive additions; it must be an advancing revelation of new principles and laws in an ascending line of creative acts.*

An evolution which is absolutely continuous, and in which the present is the necessary outcome of the past, and that by degrees infinitely small, may be a manifestation of unconscious force, but can not be a manifestation of living Will. If nature be a manifestation of God—the unfolding of an eternal purpose of Love—this manifestation must ever be open to receive *new* additions, the intercalation of new principles, and the superinduction of new laws working for a nobler end. All limitations from the scientific stand-point are illogical and absurd. This law would determine our conception of the universe as an aggregation of combined evolutions from several intermediate principles or beginnings, rather than an evolution from a single first matter or first force. *The creation of the new*, whether as primordial element, or primary force, or principle of life, or rational soul, is the fundamental idea of the *supernatural*—that is, the production of something which is not a necessary outbirth from pre-existing conditions and laws.[2] Therefore what is commonly, though perhaps incorrectly, styled "miraculous interposition," must itself be a law of the Divine manifestation, and the law of uniformity must be subordinated to the more general law of progressive development, which subordinates the inorganic to the organic, the physical to the moral world.

[1] Argyll, "Reign of Law," p. 213.

[2] See Müller's "Christian Doctrine of Sin," vol. i. p. 237.

3. *This manifestation must be* CONSECUTIVE. *Not only must it be a succession of steps or phases, but the entire series must be so related and concatenated as to present an Order of Thought—an ascending development toward a foreseen and predetermined end.*

If it were not so, every thing would be *isolated* and *disconnected*, and consequently unintelligible. There would be a succession of phenomena, but no manifestation of thought; a series of dissolving views presented to the sense, but no revelation to the understanding. Isolated phenomenal changes might be continued through untold ages, but the past would have no connection with the present, and would be unknown and lost to all the future. A revelation of the Infinite Mind to finite intelligences, made through the manifold and diversified phenomena of nature, must be a connected and related whole, so that from phenomena actually observed we may infer antecedent conditions, and anticipate future evolutions; otherwise it could not be understood. To be intelligible, a process of development must be the product of thought, and it must reveal thought—that is, it must be *consecutive.*[1]

4. *This manifestation must be* HARMONIOUS. *Notwithstanding its multiplicity of parts and manifold stages, it must be a unity—a Cosmos.*

Beings the most varied in endowment, things the most diversified in form and function, events the most remote from each other in time and space, must all be related and connected in virtue of the ultimate and all-embracing purpose for which the universe exists. An external purpose revealed under time-relations must be an *all-harmonious evolution* and an *orderly totality*—a Cosmos.

Let us now turn to the record of creation as given in

[1] Argyll, "Reign of Law," p. 219.

the Sacred Scriptures—the Mosaic Cosmogony—and see how that account conforms to the laws which on logical grounds we have deduced as the Laws of the Divine Manifestation.

The fundamental prerequisite for a right interpretation of the sacred narrative is a clear apprehension, first, of its general purpose, and, secondly, of its special literary characteristics. On these two points, therefore, we offer the following preliminary considerations:

1. *The design of the sacred narrative is to teach Theology and not Science.* A cursory reading of the narrative will convince any one that its purpose is not to enlarge men's views of nature, but to teach them something concerning nature's God. It says nothing about the forces of nature, the laws of nature, the classifications of natural history, or the size, positions, distances, and motions of the heavenly bodies. From first to last, every phenomenon and every law is linked immediately to some act or command of God. It is God who creates, God who commands, God who names, God who approves, and God who blesses. Strike out the allusions to God, and the narrative is meaningless. Clearly, it was never intended to teach science. It has obviously one purpose, to reveal and keep before the minds of men the grand truth *that Jehovah is the sole Creator and Lord of the heavens and the earth;* and it leaves the scientific comprehension of nature to the natural powers with which God has endowed man for that end.

All this is what we might legitimately expect. The narrative was designed primarily and mainly for the instruction of the masses of men who knew nothing or scarcely any thing of science; and if designed for their instruction, it must be couched in language which they could comprehend. A revelation made in the language of science would have been unintelligible to the race for nearly six thousand years of its history, and, practically, would have been no revelation at all. Scientific language, moreover, is subject to modification and change as science advances; but the narrative of Genesis was intended for all time, and therefore needed to be couched in language not liable to change. "The only language which possesses these two requisites of general intelligibility and non-liability to change is the *language of appearances*. The facts set forth must be described as they would have seemed to the eye of man; that is, in a word, phenomenally, or the cosmogony would fail of its purpose. All scrutiny or objection in the matter of unscientific, or scientifically inaccurate language, then, must be put aside as irrelevant."[1]

While earnestly maintaining that the inspired history of creation was given for the instruction of unscientific persons, and is therefore theological and not scientific, we also believe that all truth is one, and that all revelation, whether in Scripture or in nature, must be ultimately harmonious. Science in its last generalization must be Theology. Theology in its proper development must be Science. They are twin children of heaven, vestal virgins which can not be wedded to error. We are, therefore, justified in the expectation that the revelation in Scripture, when rightly interpreted, will contain nothing that is inconsistent with the scientific interpretation of nature. While we hold that there are no untimely anticipations of scientific discovery in Genesis, yet we expect that when the scientific discoveries are made, the congruity and dignity of the moral and religious lesson shall not be defeated

[1] G. Warrington, "The Week of Creation," p. 27.

and marred. Nay, more, we maintain that the Mosaic cosmogony presents the great principles which really lie at the basis of a truly scientific interpretation of nature. It teaches that God is before all things and the Creator of all things—that He alone is unbeginning, and that all things had a beginning in his creative word and will. It presents the universe as one harmonious whole, the product of one designing Mind, the project of his thought, the transcript of his plan—a plan evolved through successive stages toward a foreseen terminus or goal. And, finally, it teaches that man is the end toward which creation was tending, that he is the last and crowning work of God, and that he is the child and charge, not of a blind, impersonal force, but of a living, loving God.

2. *The sacred narrative is poetic, symbolical, and unchronological.* It is a noteworthy fact that the early literature of the most ancient nations was poetic—the natural, spontaneous product of that earliest stage of mental development in which the conceptions of God and of nature were determined by subjective feeling and native sentiment, and not by reflective thought. The "Vedas" of the Hindus, the "Iliad" of the Greeks, the "Eddas" of the ancient Germans, were each the product of an age in which "prose was unknown, as well as the distinction between prose and poetry." The earliest Hebrew compositions are of the same character; and it is reasonable to assume that a primitive revelation to the progenitors of our race would be accommodated to this earliest phase in the development of mind.

The Book of Genesis opens with a *Psalm*—"the inspired Psalm of Creation"[1]—"a grand symbolical Hymn of Creation." "The rhythmical character of the passage,

[1] Rorison, "Creative Week," in Replies to "Essays and Reviews."

its stately style, its parallelisms, its refrains, its unity within itself, all combine to show that it is a *poem*."[1] Here is the same organic unity which marks the 104th Psalm, or the Lord's Prayer, or the parable of the laborers in the vineyard. Or, if we go out of the Bible for illustration, it combines with lyric breadth of treatment and stateliness of movement all the compactness of a "solemn sonnet freighted with a single thought from beginning to end." Analysis of its interior structure exhibits a most artificial synthesis, founded upon well-known sacred numbers. It has, first, an *Exordium*, the proemial part. Then it is articulated into six *Strophes*. Finally there is the *Epode*, or peroration. The six strophes separate naturally into two groups, in which there is a balance and correlation of parts celebrating the first three and the last three concordant steps in the creative movement—the *Strophe* and the *Antistrophe*.

The exordium states briefly the subject of the poem: "In the beginning God created the heavens and the earth."

The first three strophes unfold the creative development of the receptacles:

1. A. The luminiferous ether. 2. B. Waters and the firmament between the waters. 3. C. Dry land above the waters, with plants.	"The heavens and the earth."

The second three strophes (or, more correctly, antistrophes) unfold the creative development of the occupants:

4. A. The light-bearers: sun, moon, and stars. 5. B. Water-animals and birds. 6. C. Land-animals and man.	"And all the hosts of them" (Gen. ii. 1).

The epode, or peroration, fills up the sacred number 7

[1] Dr. Whedon, in *Methodist Quarterly Review*, July, 1862, p. 528.

—the symbol always of permanence and repose. "Thus the heavens and the earth (the receptacles) were finished, and all the host of them (the occupants); and on the seventh day God put period to the work which he created by fashioning," etc.[1]

THE SYMBOLICAL HYMN OF CREATION.

EXORDIUM.

In the beginning God created the heavens and the earth.

FIRST STROPHE.

And the earth was formless and empty;
And darkness was upon the face of the abyss.
And the Spirit of God brooded upon the face of the vapors.[2]
And God said, Let there be light:
And there was light.
REFRAIN—*And God saw the light that it was good.*

And God called the light Day:
And the darkness He called Night.
And there was evening and there was morning: one day.

SECOND STROPHE.

And God said, Let there be an expanse in the midst of the waters,
And let it be a division of waters from vapors.
And God made the expanse,
And divided the waters which were below the expanse from the waters which were above the expanse:[3]
And it was so.
And God called the expanse Heavens.
And there was evening and there was morning: a second day.

THIRD STROPHE.

And God said, Let the waters under the heavens be gathered into one place,
And let the dry ground appear:
And it was so.

[1] See "Creative Week," by Rorison, in Replies to "Essays and Reviews."

[2] "The waters of verse 2 is quite another thing than the water proper of the third creative day: it is the fluid (or gaseous) form of the earth itself in its first condition."—Lange.

[3] "We must beware of thinking of a mass of elementary water. . . . Here is meant the gaseous fluid as it forms a unity with the air."—Lange, p. 168.

And God called the dry ground Land;
And the gathering of the waters He called Seas.

Refrain—*And God saw that it was good.*

And God said, Let the land shoot forth shoots:
Herbs yielding seed, fruit-trees yielding seed-inclosing fruit after their kind upon the land:
And it was so.
And the land brought forth shoots;
Herbs yielding seed after their kind, and trees yielding seed-inclosing fruit after their kind.

Refrain—*And God saw that it was good.*

And there was evening and there was morning: a third day.

FOURTH STROPHE.

And God said, Let there be luminaries in the expanse of the heavens to divide the day from the night;
And let them be for signs and for seasons, and for days and years;
And let them be for light-bearers in the expanse of the heavens, to give light upon the earth:
And it was so.
And God made the two great luminaries;
The greater luminary to rule the day;
The lesser luminary to rule the night.
He made the stars lights also;
And God appointed them in the expanse of the heavens to give light upon the earth,
And to rule over the day and night,
And to divide the light from the darkness.

Refrain—*And God saw that it was good.*

And there was evening and there was morning: a fourth day.

FIFTH STROPHE.

And God said, Let the waters swarm forth swarming things, living souls;[1]
And let birds fly upon the land upon the face of the expanse of the heavens.
And God created great leviathans,
And all living souls that creep, which the waters swarmed forth after their kind;
And all birds of wing after their kind.

Refrain—*And God saw that it was good.*

And God blessed them, saying:

[1] נֶפֶשׁ חַיָּה = soul of life.—Lange.

Be fruitful and multiply, and fill the waters of the sea;
And let the birds multiply in the land.
And there was evening and there was morning: a fifth day.

SIXTH STROPHE.

And God said, Let the land bring forth living souls after their kind:
Cattle, and creeping things, and land-animals after their kind:
And it was so.
And God made land-animals after their kind,
And cattle after their kind,
And all creeping things after their kind.
REFRAIN—*And God saw that it was good.*

And God said, Let us make MAN in our image, after our likeness;
And let him have dominion over the fish of the sea,
And over the birds of the heavens,
And over the cattle,
And over the land,
And over all the creeping things that creep upon the land.
And God created MAN in his own image;
In the image of God created He him:
Male and female created He them.
And God blessed them; and God said unto them,
Be fruitful and multiply, and replenish the earth, and subdue it;
And have dominion over the fishes of the sea,
And over the birds of the heavens,
And over all the animals that creep upon the land.
And God said, Behold, I have given you all herbs seeding seed which are upon the face of all the land,
And every tree which has seed-inclosed fruit:
They shall be unto you for food.
And to all land-animals,
And to all the birds of the heavens,
And to all creeping things upon the land wherein is a living soul,
I have given every green herb for food:
And it was so.
REFRAIN—*And God saw every thing that He had made, and behold it was very good.*
And there was evening and there was morning: the sixth day.

EPODE.

Thus the heavens and the earth were finished,
And all the hosts of them.
And on the seventh day God put period to the work which He had made;
And He rested on the seventh day from all his work which He had made.
And God blessed the seventh day, and hallowed it:
Because that in it He rested from all his works which God by making created.

Who can read this sublime composition without feeling that it is "a solemn sonnet freighted with a single thought from beginning to end?" In our English Bible, broken up into verses, and split across into two chapters, it is like an image reflected in a shattered mirror; all its real beauty is concealed. But he who can look upon it with a clear eye, and grasp its real unity, must recognize it as a Sacred Hymn composed probably by Adam, and chanted in the tents of the patriarchs at their morning and evening devotions for more than two thousand years, to commemorate the fact and keep alive the faith that *the world is the work of the triune God.*

Besides being poetic, the sacred narrative is pre-eminently *symbolical*—must be symbolical, because the Divine reality could never be intuitively known. The facts transcend all the possibilities of human experience. Whatever knowledge the writer had in regard to the creative process must have been obtained in a preternatural way—that is, it must have been revealed by Divine Omniscience. But such a revelation could not have been communicated in mere vocables. Words are themselves but signs—mere arbitrary signs of images and ideas—and can convey no meaning unless the image or the idea be already before the mind. The only natural hypothesis is that the knowledge was conveyed in a symbolic representation—a vision of the past in a succession of scenic representations with accompanying verbal announcements, like the visions of the future in the prophecies of Ezekiel and the apocalypse of John. The original formless nebula—the primeval darkness—the brooding Spirit producing motion—the consequent luminosity—the separation of the aeriform fluid into atmosphere and water—the emergence of the solid land—the shooting forth of grass and plants—the appearance of the heavenly luminaries—the swarming of the waters with living things, and the appearance of birds of wing in the expanse of heaven—the bringing forth of land-animals—and, finally, the creation of man—all pass before his mind in a succession of pictorial representations of the actual progress of creation. "The sights seen, the voices heard, the emotions aroused, are just those adapted to bring out the very words the *seer* actually uses, and in both cases the very best words that could have been used for such a purpose. The description being given from the barely optical rather than from any reflective scientific stand-point more or less advanced, is on this very account the more vivid as well as the more universal. It is a language read and understood by all." The words of the inspired writer are descriptive of the "vision pictures," and these were symbolic representations of the Divine realities.

The language of the sacred record must therefore be regarded as *anthropopathic*—the Divine idea being symbolized under the figure of human acts and affections; and from the analogy between the human and the Divine we may conceive not what God is in Himself, nor yet the manner of the Divine action, but the relation of God to the world. We must, however, guard against substituting the human symbol for the Divine reality, and making the human analogy a measure for the infinite Being. "The Sacred Hymn is no more a *literal* detail of the actual process of creation than the description of the New Jerusalem in Revelation is a *literal* picture of the heavenly state."[1] God is forever above all finite relations. Finite acts and relations may be employed as representative symbols of the Divine, but they can never be adequate repre-

[1] Whedon.

sentations. Divine creating and moving, commanding and naming, seeing and approving, working and resting, must not be narrowed down to the standard of our finite personality, and conceived under human limitations. The conception of the Deity as standing outside of matter, and moving and fashioning it after the manner of a human artificer, as commanding and naming in human language, as being conditioned in his action by the time-measures which He himself appointed, as expending energy and then resting after the manner of a human laborer, is the rudest anthropomorphism. God is eternal; neither his being nor his action are conditioned by finite measures of time. God is absolute immensity, essential omnipresence. He is "in all and through all" as truly as He is "above and before all." He is a Living Power immanent in all matter, as well as transcending all matter, moving it, organizing it, vitalizing it continually—a Living Power working from *within*, rather than a mechanical force acting from *without.*

If the primitive composition standing at the commencement of Genesis be "the Symbolical Hymn of Creation," we are not permitted to regard it as *chronological*—that is, we are not justified in expecting that it shall conform to time-measures which had no existence prior to the creative act, but which were consequent upon and determined by the creative act. This is obvious both from the nature of things and the character of the composition.

The 106th Psalm is an epic poem—that is, it is a narrative in poetic measure, a history in metrical form. Who will be so unreasonable as to demand that this Psalm shall furnish any chronological data, or conform to any time-measures whatever? Psalms are composed to be sung and excite emotion, not to be merely read and criticised. The poet groups his materials for the best moral effect, and arranges his numbers to secure rhythm and harmony. It is simply absurd to demand that there shall be any chronology—nay, it spoils the grand effect to think of chronology in reading the "Symbolical Hymn of Creation." In fact, we are forbidden to think of time at all by the first word of the exordium, which states the subject of the poem. The Hebrew *bereshith*, the Greek *ἐν ἀρχῇ*=in Beginning (not in *the* Beginning, for the article is not used), has *no relation to succession in time.* It denotes *pretemporality*, and is rendered by Meyer, Keil, and others—"before time or in eternity." It is the same thought which is presented in John i. 1: "In the beginning was the Word;" and Tholuck and Dean Alford both read the text, "*Before the world was, or before time was.*" Indeed, the whole poem represents an ideal conception, and not a time-march of phenomena. So assured are we on this point that we confidently affirm that no one who endeavors to think of the creation in its relation to God can ever fall into the anthropomorphic error of saying that "God's ways are like unto our ways," "God's speaking is like unto our speaking," "God's working and resting are like unto our working and resting," and "God's days are like unto our days of twenty-four hours." As Dr. Whedon remarks, "Our traditional unscientific scientific constructions of this chapter are Japhetic interpretations of a Semitic text."

The men who persist in regarding "the day of God" as a natural day of twenty-four hours are involved in numberless inconsistencies when they attempt to carry their rigid preconception throughout the whole Bible. Human or finite measures of time, when applied to any thing God does, can only be accommodated representations to meet our feeble comprehension, and we are constantly guarded, in the Bible itself, against a literal and anthropomorphic conception. "Hast thou eyes of flesh, or seest thou as man seeth? Are thy days as man's days?" (Job x. 4, 5.) To say that God's days of working are like *our days* is just as absurd and as degrading a conception as to say that God's eyes are "eyes of flesh," like ours. Our time-measures can not condition the Divine action. "One day is with the Lord as a thousand years, and a thousand years as one day" (2 Peter iii. 8); which means that time is as nothing with God, that time does not condition the Divine life or the Divine action, but that it is the Divine action which makes and conditions all time. *The beginning of the world is the beginning of time*, and time is the duration of the world measured into equal parts by the equable motion of bodies in space.[1] The attempt to measure the creating work of God by days of twenty-four hours is just as absurd as the attempt to measure immensity by a three-foot rule, or to estimate omnipotence by horse-power.

Let any one test the twenty-four-hour measure on such texts as the following: "Your father Abraham desired to see my *day*." "The *day* of the Son of Man." "I must work the works of him that sent me while it is *day*." "If thou hadst known in this thy *day*." "He shall rise again in the resurrection at the last *day*." "The *day* of salvation." "The *day* of judgment." "The terrible *day* of the Lord." It would be a wholesome and profitable exercise to take up the Concordance and refer to all the texts in which the word "day" stands in any relation to the determina-

[1] Hence *αἰών*, time, or the all of time, is used to express the all of the finite, the universe. See Heb. i. 2, xi. 3, where *αἰῶνες* is equivalent to universe.

tions or doings of God, and it will be found that it is always an indefinite period of longer or shorter duration, and may be twenty-four hundred years, or twenty-four thousand years, just as well as twenty-four hours.

The Hebrew יוֹם (yom), first occurring in Gen. i. 5, is the name of an indefinite period, a cycle of time radically grounded on the primitive conception of division or separation. Light is the first *separation*. It is "divided from the darkness." "And God called the light *day*, and the darkness He called *night*." This is God's own naming, and we must take it as our guide in the interpretation of the subsequent "days." Obviously, it is not the duration, but the phenomenon, the appearing itself which is for the first time called day. Then the term is used for a period, or the whole first cycle of events, with its two great antithetical parts—"And there was an evening, and there was a morning, *one day*." We look into the sacred narrative to see what corresponds to this naming. What was the night? Certainly the *darkness* on the face of the waters. What was the day? Certainly the *light* consequent on the brooding of the Spirit and the commanding word. How long was the day? How long was the night or the darkness? The account tells us nothing about it. There is something on the face of it which seems to forbid such questions. Where are we to get twelve hours for this first night? Where is the point of commencement when darkness began to be on the face of the deep? All is vast, sublime, immeasurable. The time is as formless as the material. It has, indeed, a chronology of some kind, but on a scale vastly different from that afterward appointed (ver. 14) to regulate the history of a completed and habitable world. Whoever thinks seriously on the impossibility of accommodating this first day to the measure of twenty-four hours needs no other argument. The first day is, in this respect, the model of all the rest.[1]

It is equally impossible to reduce the "seventh day" to a chronological standard of twenty-four hours. "And God rested on the seventh day from all his works which He had made." Are we to presume that God "rested" as we rest, because He was weary, and that He needed to rest just twenty-four hours? Is not God "resting" still in the sense in which the word "rest" is here used, viz., *to cease doing* a particular work? Is not all time since the Creation God's grand Sabbath, in which he is not doing works of Origination, but works of Love and Mercy to our race?

It is obvious that the first and the seventh days can not be days of twenty-four hours; and, furthermore, a clear apprehension of the nature of the first day must open to us the true conception of all the rest. The days are *new appearances, new manifestations, new developments* in the Creative Week—the great *day* of God (Gen. ii. 4). According to the analogy of the first day, the evening is the time of a peculiar or partially chaotic condition, like the glacial epoch which closed the Cenozoic and opened the Phrenozoic day. The morning is a *new evolution of a new order of things*, which carries the world-formation to a higher stage. With each creative morning there comes a higher, fairer, richer state of the earth, until it reaches the Sabbath of the world, the day on which God rested or ceased from his world-creating work, that He might educate and recreate and redeem and glorify the human race.

In these antithetical movements of each creative day we are not necessitated to assume a sudden catastrophe, or any return to the chaos of the first day, any more than we now

[1] See Special Introduction by Prof. T. Lewis, in Lange's "Commentary."

conceive of night as a sudden return to darkness, or of day as the sudden return of light. There is a steady progression, an orderly movement in the history of each creative day, just as there is in the history of a single solar day. The light does not break suddenly upon the world—the sun rises gradually upon the earth. And so the creative day was a slow development, a gradual evolution out of a prior order of things, by the direct efficiency of God.

It has been insinuated that this is an interpretation which has been forced upon us by the progress of modern science. Theology, it is said, has been perpetually driven from her positions by science, and is now compelled to take refuge in subterfuge and equivocation. The insinuation is as false as it is foul. This mode of interpretation was propounded ages before the science of Geology was known, and was taught by Jewish doctors and Christian fathers for fifteen hundred years. St. Augustine, the father of Systematic Theology, who was born A.D. 354, asks the question, "What mean these days—these strange sunless days? Does the enumeration of days and nights avail for a distinction between the nature that is not yet formed, and those which are made, so that they shall be called morning *propter speciem* [*i. e.*, in reference to appearing, receiving form or species], and evening *propter privationem* [*i. e.*, in reference to non-appearance, formlessness, and want of sensible quality]?" ("De Genesi ad Literam," lib. ii. ch. 14.) Hence he does not hesitate to call them *naturæ*, natures, births or growths; also *moræ*, delays, or solemn pauses in the Divine work. They are *dies ineffabiles;* their true nature can not be told. Hence they are called days as the best symbol by which the idea could be expressed. They are God-divided days and nights in distinction from sun-divided. Common solar days are mere *vicissitudines cœli*, mere changes in the positions of the heavenly bodies, and not *spatia morarum*, or evolutions in nature belonging to a higher chronology, and marking their epochs by a law of inward change instead of incidental outward measurement. As to how long or how short they were he gives no opinion, but contents himself with maintaining that *day is not a name of duration*, the evenings and the mornings are to be regarded not so much as measuring the passing of time (*temporis prœteritionem*) as marking the boundaries of a periodic work or evolution. This is not the metaphorical, but the real and proper sense of the word *day*, in fact the original sense, inasmuch as it contains the idea of rounded periodicity or self-completed time, without any of the mere accidents that belong to the outwardly measured solar or planetary epochs, be they longer or shorter.[1]

These are not the mere fancies of St. Augustine. This was the doctrine of the ablest Christian fathers—of Irenæus, Origen, Basil, and Gregory of Nazianzen. Nay more, it was the doctrine of many of the doctors of the old Jewish Church. In more recent times we find Calmet, Burnet, Stillingfleet, Henry More, Lord Bacon, Poole, and others, presenting similar views; and this long before Geology existed as a science, and irrespective of any supposed collision with physical induction. Their opinions and interpretations were therefore no shift for the avoidance of difficulties, but conclusions reached independently on sound principles of Biblical exegesis.

Disregarding the chronology of Archbishop Usher printed in the margin of our Bible, and the division into chapters and verses made by Hugh de St. Cher—both modern inventions which are no part of the sacred record—

[1] Lange's "Commentary" on Genesis, Introduction, p. 131.

and purging our minds of those prepossessions which are incident to an uncritical faith, we can now contemplate the Symbolical Hymn of Creation in its simple and original form, as a record of the *self-manifestation of God*, given in such order and under such conditions that it shall be apprehensible and interpretable by the finite mind.

1. *Creation was a gradual process.* God did not create a perfect universe at once, but built it up slowly, step by step. A consistent interpretation of the record forbids us to regard "the Creative Week" as a literal week composed of days of twenty-four hours each. Creation is the work of God, and surely the Divine action can not have been conditioned by time-measures which did not exist before, but were consequent upon the act of God. The great cyclical changes in nature produced by the creative Word are the only measures of time. Therefore the "days" of the Creative Week are *new appearances, new manifestations, new developments* in the creative purpose of God.

The first morning is the appearance of *luminosity* in the aeriform fluid, or nebulous vapor, whatever science may finally determine that to have been. The Hebrew מַיִם (mayim), from the root ים, which denotes *tumultuous, tremulous,* or *undulatory* movement, is used of the waters of the ocean, of the waters above the firmament, of vapor and clouds, because of their susceptibility of tremulous, undulatory motion. The first distinct creative formation was *heat*, or invisible molecular motion, resulting from "the Spirit of God brooding upon the face of the abyss;" and this heat reveals itself in the phenomena of *light.*[1] How closely the ideas of light and heat were

[1] "In a conversation held some years ago by the author (Sir J. Herschel) with his lamented friend, Dr. Hawtrey, Head-Master and late Provost of Eton College, on the subject of Etymology, I happened to remark that the

united in the Hebrew mind is shown by the same word being used for both, with merely a slight difference in pronunciation, אוֹר (ōr) and אוּר (ūr).

The second morning is the appearance of an *expanse* in the midst of the vapors, dividing the vapors which were below the expanse from the vapors which were above the expanse. The Hebrew רָקִיעַ (rakai), from רָקַע (to stretch, to spread out), means properly an extension, an expanse. This is the translation adopted by Benisch, Kalisch, Delitzsch, Keil, and Lange. After heat and light, the next creative formation is an *atmosphere*, with its auroral light and a cloudy canopy.

The third morning is the appearance of *land* and *seas*, and the sprouting forth of *vegetation*, at first in its lowest forms — perhaps as marine plants. The Hebrew אֶרֶץ (eretz) has two significations, "earth" and "land." Whenever it is used in a restricted sense, and especially wherever it is contrasted with "water," the most appropriate rendering is "land." The third creative formation is *gross, ponderable matter*, whether aggregated by molecular attraction, or compounded by elective affinity, or selected and organized by vital force.

The fourth morning is the appearance of *luminaries* or *light-bearers* in the expanse of heaven, which are now "set," or, more correctly, "appointed to give light upon

syllable *Ur* or *Or* must have some very remote origin, having found its way into many languages, conveying the idea of something absolute, solemn, definite, fundamental, or of unknown antiquity, as in the German *Ur-alt* (primeval), *Ur-satz* (a fundamental proposition), *Ur-theil* (a solemn judgment)—in the Latin *Oriri* (to arise), *Origo* (the origin), *Aurora* (the dawn)—in the Greek Ὅρος (a boundary, the extreme limit of our vision, whence our horizon), Ὅρκος (an oath or solemn obligation, etc.). 'You are right,' was his reply, 'it is the oldest word of all words: the first word ever recorded to have been pronounced. It is the Hebrew for *Light*'" (אוֹר, AOR).—"Familiar Lectures on Scientific Subjects," p. 219.

the earth," and to be time-measures in the future world-history. The Hebrew word employed in ver. 14 (מְאֹרֹת), which is unfortunately rendered "lights" in the Authorized Version, is a different word from the "light" (אוֹר) of vers. 3–5. מְאֹרֹת (meoroth) strictly means "light-bearers," or bodies giving light. This distinction is carefully observed in the LXX., DeWette, Benisch, Kalisch, Tuch, Knobel, Delitzsch, and Keil.[1] The fourth creative formation was the establishment of such cosmical conditions or relations as should enable the heavenly bodies to fulfill their light-giving function to the earth. What those conditions were we may not be able to say. The dense clouds and ceaseless showers of the "Age of Rain," which had shut out the light of the heavenly bodies for a geological age, had now passed away, the atmosphere becomes fitted for the transmission of light, and the sun, moon, and stars are visible from the earth. The conditions for a rapid development of vegetable life now exist, and this is regarded as pre-eminently "the Age of Plant-growth."

The fifth morning is the appearance of *animal life*—life moving in the waters and soaring in the air, marine animals, aquatic reptiles, and birds.

The sixth morning is the appearance of a higher order of animal life, *mammals*, chiefly designed for the use of a still higher being—for *Man*, whose appearance is the noontide splendor of the sixth day.

The seventh morning is the commencement of the *Sabbath of God*, which is devoted to the moral and religious instruction of humanity—the New Creation of the moral world.

The following scheme, furnished by Dr. Winchell, presents at one view the order of the Mosaic record, and at

[1] See "Week of Creation," by Geo. Warrington, p. 13.

the same time sets forth the harmony between the *Mosaic* and *Geologic* records:[1]

	Genesis, ch. i.	Brief announcement of chief events in the history:			
	Vers. 1, 2. EXORDIUM.	I. God the Creator of the Substance and Form of the Universe. II. Terrestrial Chaos. III. Darkness on the face of the Deep. IV. Vivification of the Waters.			
DAYS.		GEOLOGY.	GEOLOGICAL AGES.		
I.	Vers. 3–5. Creation of LIGHT.	Igneous Vapor condensing.	Age of FIRE.	ABIOTIC.	AZOIC.
II.	Vers. 6–8. Creation of FIRMAMENT or EXPANSE.	Gathering of Clouds. Descent of Rain. Earliest Sediments.	Age of RAIN.		
III.	Vers. 9–13. Creation of DRY LAND and of PLANTS.	Uplift of Continents. Appearance of Marine Vegetation.	Age of LAND and PLANT-MAKING.	PROTOPHYTIC.	
IV.	Vers. 14–18. Creation (or appointment) of LUMINARIES: sun, moon, and stars.	Dispersion of Clouds. Appearance of Sun, Moon, and Stars.	Age of PLANT-GROWTH.		
V.	Vers. 20–23. Creation of AQUATIC ANIMALS and BIRDS.	Appearance of Marine Animals (mollusks, fishes, etc.), and Aquatic Reptiles and Birds.	Age of MOLLUSKS, FISHES,	PALÆOZOIC.	
			REPTILES, BIRDS.	MESOZOIC.	
VI.	Vers. 24–31. Creation of LAND-ANIMALS and MAN.	Appearance of Mammals and MAN.	Age of MAMMALS.	CÆNOZOIC.	
VII.	Gen. ii. 2, 3. Sabbath of GOD.	Reign of Man. The Sabbath of Creation.	Age of MAN.	PHRENOZOIC.	

[1] The critical reader will discover a slight difference of opinion between Dr. Winchell and myself in regard to how much of chapter i. is to be regarded as the "Exordium" of the Hymn of Creation. Dr. Winchell includes verses 1 and 2; I incline, however, to the opinion that it is embraced in verse 1. The reasons which weigh with me are the following: 1. The chaos or the darkness of verse 2 is clearly recognized as "the *evening*" of the

2. Creation was *cumulative*—that is, it was a succession of beginnings or creative epochs, in which new entities or new forces were inserted into the already existing sphere of nature, carrying it forward toward a nobler end.

This, we think, is the natural impression which the reading of Gen. i. makes on the unbiased mind. Each creative word appears as the dynamical basis of a real *principium*—a beginning of something intrinsically new, and which can not be conceived as the physical result of any pre-existing condition of things.[1] A new entity or a new force was, as it were, inserted in the order of nature; a new impulse was given to matter, or a new direction to existing forces, and from that initial point a new series of developments, which go on in accordance with law—a new succession of births and growths—flows on as a part of the grand totality of effects we call "nature." This is, obviously, the Biblical conception. Here creation does

first day, "And God called the light Day, and the darkness He called Night; and there was evening and morning: one day." I do not see how on a fair interpretation of the sacred poem we can escape the conclusion that the *first* day embraces "the evening and morning"—that is, the primal darkness of verse 2, and the creation of dawning light. This conception furthermore harmonizes with the Hebrew usage, which always regarded the preceding night as part of the one natural day. The Hebrew Sabbath commenced at six o'clock on Friday evening. Thus we read in Leviticus xxiii. 32, "From even to even shall ye celebrate your Sabbath." Hence also the evening—morning=day (νυχθή-μερον)—of Daniel viii. 14. 2. The division I have made is the one which has been followed by the best Hebrew scholars, whose opinion is entitled to the highest deference in this connection. The independent character of the opening sentence of Genesis was affirmed by such judicious and learned men as Calvin, Bishop Patrick, and Dr. D. Jennings. The early fathers of the Church, as St. Gregory of Nazianzen, St. Justin Martyr, Origen, St. Augustine, and others, held that there was a considerable interval between the creation related in the first verse, and that of which an account is given in the third and following verses. See "The Pre-Adamite Earth," by Dr. Harris, p. 281.

[1] Breman Lectures, M. Fuchs "On Miracles," p. 105.

not present itself as a necessary evolution from a first matter or a first force in unbroken continuity, and without any supernatural interposition. Here are clearly defined creative epochs, new beginnings, which have their origin in the creative will and word of God. What these beginnings were is a question of the deepest interest.

A careful study of Gen. i. and ii. has led us to the conclusion that there is something fundamental and radical in the distinction between the creative words with *bara* (בָּרָא) and those with *yetsar* (יָצַר) and *aysah* (עָשָׂה). It is, in reality, the distinction between Origination *de novo* and Formation out of pre-existing materials. There are three instances in which *bara* occurs in Gen. i. We are fully convinced that in each case it denotes the origination of a new entity—a real addition to the sum of existence.

First Origination (Gen. i. 1): "*In the beginning God created* [את = *the substance or essence of*] *the heavens and the earth.*" This is the reading of Parkhurst's Hebrew Grammar (1813), which has since that time been approved by able lexicographers and commentators. Some of these authorities have been already presented to the reader.[1] But even aside from philological considerations, the context forbids us to regard *bara* here as denoting "formation," for the product of that creative act was "*form-less* and *matter-less*;"[2] that is, it was homogeneous, non-differentiated, structureless, and destitute of all sensible quality—an abyss of darkness and death, exhibiting that sole condition of matter, "perhaps its only true indication, namely, *inertia*."[3] The first created element was the single omnipresent fluid *Ether*, out of which all gross matter was built by the action of force. As we

[1] See *ante*, p. 61. [2] Lange, *in loco.* [3] Faraday.

advance in this discussion we shall find that this is an opinion which is entertained by the first physicists of the age, as, for example, Thomson, Tait, Maxwell, Challis, in England, and Norton and Hinrich in America.

SECOND ORIGINATION (Gen. i. 21): "*And God created the great monsters, and every living soul* [נֶפֶשׁ חַיָּה=*soul of life*] *that moveth.*"

The first created animals are here most carefully denoted as "living souls," evidently to distinguish the life now first manifested in nature from the molecular, "bioplasmic" life which organizes the vegetable cell, and builds up the tissues of the animal body. The life here indicated has an *individuality* which separates it from the universal life of nature. There is now an immaterial entity—a soul, which is an individualized and indivisible centre of force, a soul which has sensation, feeling, perception, and memory, none of which are properties of matter or products of organization. The animal soul is not material, neither is it a function or phenomenon of organized matter; it is a creation, and therefore *bara* is here significantly employed to denote the origination of something new; a new power or principle is here inserted into the sphere of existing nature.

The second created entity is animal life—*Soul*—somatic life as distinct and distinguishable from vegetable, molecular, bioplasmic life.

THIRD ORIGINATION (Gen. i. 27): "*And God created man in his own image, in the image of God created He him.*"

The entire paragraph (vers. 26–29) is obviously the record of a supernatural origination. There is a significance even in the change of the *creative* word. In regard to prior and inferior existences the language is, "Let the earth bring forth!" "Let the waters bring forth!" as though there were some parturient power in nature, or as though nature co-operated with and furnished the conditions and means of the Divine efficiency. But when man is to be created the language is, "Let us make man;" thus placing the origin of man outside the chain of physical causation, and ascribing it to the immediate agency of God. Besides, the creation here spoken of is the production of a *spiritual*, not a material entity. "God created man in *his own image*." This creation can not be a formation out of a pre-existent matter, for no form of matter can possibly bear any resemblance to God (Acts xvii. 29). "God is *spirit*," and man can be like God only in so far as he is endowed with a spiritual nature. Spirit alone can bear the image of God. Whatever may be the teaching of Genesis as to the origin of the human body, be it a formation or a development, there is no uncertainty in its language as to the origin of the human spirit. It is an inbreathing from God. It proceeded directly from Him. By no mere figure of speech, but by a Divine reality God is "the Father of spirits," and man is the offspring and the image of God. This likeness of God lifts man out of the sphere of mere nature—it sets him apart in the essential characteristics and endowments of his being as *above* nature, and in some sense *divine*.

The third created entity is *Spirit;* spirit with its reason, its liberty, its conscience, its susceptibility of Divine inspiration, its capacity for endless progression in knowledge and love.

Here, then, are three entities, *matter*, *life*, and *mind* (=body, soul, and spirit), which had their beginning in an act of absolute creation, and are therefore to be regarded as primordial things.[1] Their existence is the necessary

[1] "Three direct acts of the Deity may be recognized, viz., the creation of

condition of all subsequent formative and developing production, inasmuch as all formation supposes a something to be formed, and all evolution a something involved. These primordial entities are the substratum, or ground, of all the mediate architectonic creation which is effected by the moving and informing presence and agency of the Spirit of God.

This leads us to the consideration of those creative words which are *formative*, and which always pre-suppose the existence of real entities as the condition of their efficiency; as, for example, "Let there be light;" "Let there be an expanse in the midst of the waters;" "Let the dry land appear;" "Let there be luminaries in the expanse of heaven." All the dividings, the gatherings, the organizings, the ordainings, and collocations suppose the prior existence of matter.

We have seen that the first act of absolute creation—the beginning of all beginnings—was the origination of that mysterious entity which is the recipient of impulse, or energy, and the physical substratum of all sensible phenomena. From this initial point, the first *formative* act was "the moving or brooding of the Spirit of God upon the face of the abyss." All the qualities which matter presents to the senses, all physical phenomena, are the result of this action of the Deity upon matter—that is, *they are all manifestations of force.*[1] "By various motions of the nature of eddies (vortices) the qualities of cohesion, elasticity, hardness, weight, mass, or other universal properties of matter, are given to small portions of the fluid [ether]

matter, of life, and of mind."—Prof. Hinrich, *American Journal of Science and Arts*, vol. xxxix. p. 57.

[1] See M. Claude Bernard, *Revue des Deux Mondes*, December 15, 1867; Prof. Norton, *American Journal of Science*, July, 1864; Cooke, "Religion and Chemistry," p. 330.

which constitute the *chemical atoms*, and these by modifications in their combination, form, and movement produce all the accidental phenomena of *gross matter;* and the primary fluid by other motions transmits light, radiant heat, magnetism, and gravitation."[1]

The first distinct creative formation was *molecular* and *radiant energy*. "And God said, Let there be light." By this "light" we are not to understand light in its technical sense as distinguished from heat, but rather as including heat, such light, in fact, as we meet with in nature in the light of the sun, the same Hebrew word (אוֹר) being used for both.

The second distinct creative formation was that wonderful mechanical combination of chemical elements we call the *atmosphere*. "And God said, Let there be an expanse in the midst of the vapors, and let it be a division of vapors from vapors." The Creator has endowed the oxygen and nitrogen of the atmosphere with the power of retaining the aeriform condition under all circumstances, while the aqueous vapor is liable to very great fluctuation. Were there no air surrounding the globe, the quantity of vapor would adjust itself almost instantaneously to any variation of temperature, and the maximum amount possible would always be present at any given place; there could then be no clouds and no genial showers of diffusive rain. "An elevation of temperature would be attended by rapid evaporation, and the amount of water required to

[1] *North British Review*, March, 1868, p. 127. This is the doctrine of the first physicists of the age, of Sir William Thomson (see *Nature*, vol. i. p. 551; vol. ii. p. 421; and especially vol. iv. pp. 265–6), of Prof. Maxwell (see *Nature*, vol. ii. p. 421), of Prof. Tait (see *Nature*, vol. iv. p. 271), also of Clausius and Rankine. See also Prof. Hinrich, "On Planetology," in *American Journal of Science*, vol. xxxix. p. 283; and Prof. Norton, "On Molecular and Cosmical Physics," *American Journal of Science*, vol. xlix. pp. 24, 33.

fill the space would suddenly flash into vapor; while, on the other hand, a corresponding depression of temperature would be accompanied by an equally sudden precipitation of the aqueous vapor, not in genial showers, but terrific torrents. . . . The drops, falling without resistance, would be as destructive in their effects as volleys of leaden shot."[1] The presence of a dense medium, such as the atmosphere, retards these sudden changes, and determines the formation of clouds. Thus "the expanse" is admirably adapted to the creative purposes of "*dividing* the waters from the waters."

The third creative formation was the *chemical compounds* and their molar aggregation in land and seas. "And God said, Let the waters below the expanse be gathered together unto one place, and let the dry ground appear." The chemical reactions, crystallizations, precipitations, and sedimentary accumulations involved in the creative formation are admirably sketched in Ch. VI. of Dr. Winchell's "Sketches of Creation." The transmutation of the primary fluid into gross matter was something more than a natural evolution—it was a "*creative* action,"[2] and the exact numerical proportions in which the chemical elements combine must be the result of a distinct creative impulse.

The fourth creative formation was *bioplasm*, or that vitalized germinal matter which is instrumental in building up the tissues and organs of plants (and animals). "And God said, Let the land sprout forth sprouts; herbs seeding seed, fruit-trees producing fruit after their kind wherein is their seed." The vital force which is concern-

[1] Cooke's "Religion and Chemistry," p. 129.

[2] *North British Review*, March, 1868, p. 127; also Prof. Tait, in *Nature*, vol. iv. p. 271.

ed in the formation of bioplasm (vitalized matter) must be regarded as distinct, on the one hand, from the physical forces which are efficient in the combinations and aggregations of non-living matter,[1] and, on the other hand, from that sentient, percipient, self-moving principle which constitutes the animal soul. "The 'life' of a man or an animal is very different from what is termed the 'life' of a white blood, or a mucus, or a pus corpuscle; inasmuch as many hundreds of white blood corpuscles, or elemental units of the tissues, might die in man without affecting the 'life' of the man; moreover the man himself might perish, and some of the corpuscles remain alive. . . . By the *life* of a man (or an animal) something very different is meant from what we understand by the life of each elemental unit of the organism, *and the difference is not merely of degree but of kind.*"[2] Bioplasm, or cell-life, is generic; soul-life is specific, individual, and indivisible. The former we regard as the direct effect of the Divine life, immanent in nature; the latter is an individualized centre of force, "a delegation of Divine power under limits of necessity." The physical forces are the action of God *upon* matter, the vital force is the immanence of God *in* matter. The first is mechanical, the second is vito-dynamical.

The fifth creative formation was the adjustment of the cosmical relations of the heavenly bodies, and the establishment of such atmospheric conditions as rendered the sun and moon the *luminaries*, or light-bearers, to the earth. "And God said, Let there be luminaries in the expanse of heaven to divide the day and night." What these adjustments and collocations were, we are not able to say. The

[1] See Beale, "Protoplasm," pp. 69–71, 88, 108; Carpenter, "Human Physiology," pp. 46, 865–6.

[2] Beale, "Protoplasm," pp. 67–8.

ultimate cause of the sun's luminosity is yet an unsolved problem. No explanation thus far offered has been accepted as adequate by the majority of scientific men. The statement of Genesis, which ascribes "the appointment of the sun and moon to be light-bearers to the earth" to a distinct creative formation of some kind, is not, therefore, invalidated by science.

The sixth creative formation was the *material organisms* of the varied species of "living souls" which people the *waters;* the seventh, of those which people the *air;* the eighth, of those which people the *land.* The final creative formation was the body of man, into which God breathed the breath of *lives,* and in consequence of which he became not merely a living soul, but a spiritual personality, a *spirit-being.*

The question whether the material organisms in which the varied species of "living souls" are embodied were each the product of a special creation, or whether later and higher organisms were derived from prior and lower organisms by "filiation," so that "new species are new births," is of little consequence to the interpretation of Genesis. The essential element of species is a *spiritual* entity. Specific existence is a positive existence, an immaterial existence,[1] "a soul of life." "It is not," says Dr. Winchell, "a primordial organic form: *it is the life embodied within that form*—the principle which rules its existence, moulds its features, determines its instincts, and conserves its specific and individual identity. It is the principle embodied in the ovum—often a mere microscopic organism—which unfailingly holds fast to the specific type, and through all embryonic and immature existence guides the progress of

[1] See Agassiz's "Methods of Study in Natural History," p. 287; also Grindon, "Life, its Nature," etc., pp. 189–190.

development in one direction, toward one end. Here is more than matter: here is a power which controls matter, controls chemistry—manifests its superiority to body, and asserts its dignity as spirit." The establishment of a genetic connection from the lowest to the highest material organism would not decide the question as to "the origin of species." The origin of species lies back of all material organisms. The species is a "spiritual germ," which acts upon and fashions the material elements, and through them expresses its own characteristics. That therefore which constitutes man a distinct species is not to be sought in anatomical peculiarities, but in spiritual attributes. It is the image of God and the inspiration of God which lifts man out of mere animal nature and makes him a *peculiar species*—"one genus, and that genus the only one of the order."[1] Nor would this title be affected by any theory about the mode of the creation of his body. There would be nothing more derogatory to Omnipotence, or even to human nature, in the conjecture that man did not become "a living personal spirit" until he had passed through various stages of animal life, than in the doctrine that he was fashioned immediately out of the dust of the earth. There is as much dignity, or, if the reader please, as much humility of origin in the one case as in the other. The former is an extraordinary birth, consequent on some mysterious action of the Deity on the course of nature; the latter is a miraculous formation. The Hebrew text is as favorable to the one hypothesis as to the other. The preposition "of," or "out of," is not authorized by the original. Dr. Whedon reads the whole passage as follows: "And God developed [וַיִּיצֶר] the man—dust of the earth—and breathed into his nostrils the breath of lives, and the man

[1] Cuvier, "Animal Kingdom," p. 32.

became to a living person."[1] If the body of the second Adam, the Divine Man, was a birth (a miraculous birth), we do not see that any one need be shocked at the suggestion that the body of the first Adam was also an extraordinary or supernatural birth. Science may have free scope to settle the problem on purely inductive grounds.

The following scheme will exhibit our conception of the cumulative character of the creative development:

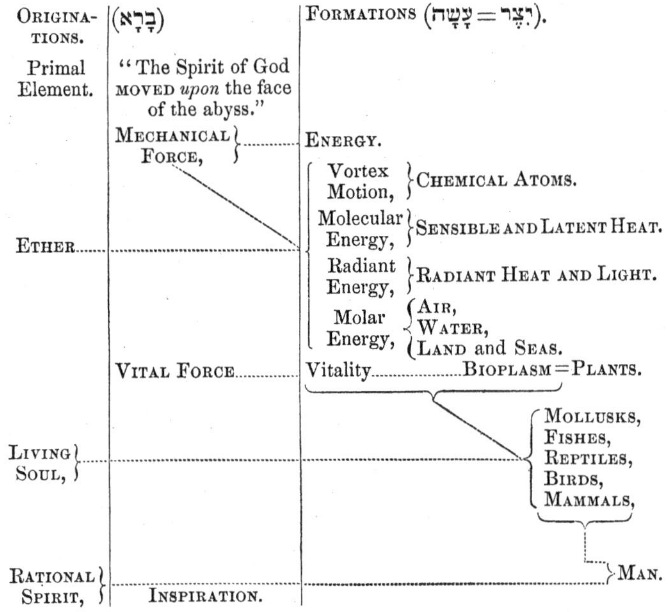

3. *Creation was consecutive.* The creative epochs follow each other in a manifest Order of Thought. The reasons for this order are obvious on the face of the sacred narrative, so that we are constrained to regard the

[1] *Methodist Quarterly Review*, January, 1867, p. 143.

creative process as the realization of a purpose, the development of a foreseen and predetermined plan.

This is clearly manifest from the aptly styled "pauses of contemplation" which occur in the progress of the sacred narrative. At each stage of the creative work the Deity is represented as surveying that already finished, and pronouncing it "*good*" (טוֹב=καλόν, fair and good). This may seem strange when viewed apart from the completed plan. What good, one might ask, is the light when there is no eye to see? What good the expanse of heaven, the land and seas, with none to inhabit them? What good the plants with none to use them? But the Intelligence that foresaw the end toward which the creative process was tending could recognize the fitness and the beauty of each new element of creation as contributing to that completed whole, which, when realized, is pronounced "*very good*." Thus each stage of the advancing work of creation is pronounced "good" in view of its subordination to the ultimate purpose, which is the highest "good." Each is a step upward and onward, and is "good" as a preparation and a means for a better that is yet to come. Thus the reading of the sacred Hymn of Creation leaves the decided impression that a chain of subordination and interdependence runs through the entire organic and inorganic creation, binding the whole together in an ideal unity. All the laws and results of the past are brought forward, and become a prelude and a preparation for the future developments. The earlier stages of the creation furnish the conditions for the later stages, and are in some sense a prophecy of what is to come. The successive stages of creation are thus results, in part, of a "nature"—a constitution and order of things already established, and in part of a new impulse carrying nature forward toward the predestinated goal.

The more extended our acquaintance with the actual economy of nature, the more does the subordination and interdependence of the creative epochs become manifest, and the more are we convinced that " the law of consecution " which reveals itself in the sacred narrative is a real law of the universe.

The existence of radiant energy (heat and light), is the fundamental precondition of all the subsequent creative formations. It is more universal than gravitation, and absolutely co-extensive with the universe,[1] the connecting bond between all worlds. It determines the temperature of space, of the atmosphere, and of the earth, and, in fact, most of the phenomena of meteorology. It is essential to the life and growth of the plant, and ultimately of the animal; without it, indeed, no life could exist upon the earth. Next in importance is the atmosphere, which has peculiar relations to light and heat. It softens the intensity of light, and diffuses it in every direction; it absorbs and retains heat, and, infolding the earth as with a mantle, keeps it warm. It conditions the formation of clouds, and determines the fall of genial showers. It is the medium in which combustion and change, and all the phenomena of life, take place. Its oxygen has been the chief world-builder, and its nitrogen has been aptly styled the *zoögen* or generator of life. The gathering of the waters into lakes and seas, the phenomena of aqueous circulation, the formation of soils through its agency—these were all preconditions of vegetable life. " Reasoning deductively, it is equally presumable that vegetable life preceded animal life in order of appearance. . . .Vegetation is capable of drawing its sustenance from the mineral

[1] Herschel, "Familiar Lectures on Science," p. 218; "Outlines of Astronomy," § 599; *North British Review*, 1868, p. 127.

world, while animals rely exclusively upon organic food. The vegetable stands between the animal and the mineral, performing a sort of commissary function in behalf of the animal. The animal—even the carnivorous animal—implies the vegetable. All things considered, we are led to believe that plant life had a history upon our earth a full epoch before the existence of animals."[1] Finally, all geological preparations and ideas converge in man. "The beneficent provisions of the earth's crust not only prophesy man, but they reach their finality in man. It was only for human uses that the coal was treasured in the recesses of the earth; for human uses alone the mountains have lifted up their burdens of iron; for human uses only the grandest movements of geological history elaborated and distributed the soils. It is only for man that the forests yield their abundant supplies of timber and fuel. For man the edible and medicinal vegetables were provided. For man the natures of the domestic animals were moulded, and their domestic attachments are directed to no other being."[2] Thus through the long ages of geological time the earth was preparing for the dwelling-place of man, and in the earliest forms of animal life his coming was prefigured and foretold.

4. *The completed creation is a Divine harmony.* This is the abiding impression which the sublime Psalm of Creation leaves upon our minds as we close the book. It has taught us this final lesson, that the universe is the manifestation of *one grand creative thought*, as comprehensive in the diversity of its parts as it is complete in the unity of its plan. We learn, not merely that God made all the parts of the universe, but that He made each part for a specific

[1] Dr. Winchell, "Sketches of Creation," pp. 66, 67.

[2] Dr. Winchell, "Sketches of Creation," p. 374.

purpose, and that all the separate and successive parts are chords in nature's music, parts of creation's anthem of perpetual praise. The Symbolical Hymn of Creation, with its striking parallelisms, its balance and correlation of parts, its harmonic numbers (3 and 7 and 10, the symbols of perfection), its pauses and refrains, its rhythm and unity symbolizes the universal prevalence of *Law* in nature; reveals a changeless *Order* in respect to space and time, to number and form; suggests harmonious *relations* between terrestrial conditions and cosmical adjustments, between organic and inorganic existence, and accords with the wonderful rhythm which pervades the Cosmos.

The glorious mansion is first built, then furnished. A triad of days is devoted to its architecture, a triad to its occupants. The former describes a series of *dividings* and *combinings*, the latter portrays a series of *formations* and *vivifications*. "The last day of each era includes one work typical of the era, and another related to it in essential points, but also prophetic of the future. Vegetation, while, for physical reasons, a part of the creation of the third day, was also prophetic of the future Organic era, in which the progress of life was the grand characteristic. The record thus accords with the fundamental principle in history that the characteristic of an age has its beginnings within the age preceding. So, again, man, while like other mammals in structure, even to the homologies of every bone and muscle, was endowed with a spiritual nature which looked forward to another era, that of spiritual existence. The seventh "day," the day of rest from the work of creation, is man's period of preparation for that new existence, and it is to promote this special end that, in strict parallelism, the Sabbath follows man's six days of work."[1]

[1] Dana, "Geology," pp. 745, 746.

The following scheme will exhibit the completeness of the parallelism:

INORGANIC ERA.	ORGANIC ERA.
I. Day....LUMINOSITY.	IV. Day....LUMINARIES.
II. Day.. { WATER, ATMOSPHERE.	V. Day.. { MARINE ANIMALS, REPTILES, BIRDS.
III. Day....DRY LAND.	VI. Day....MAMMALS.
VEGETATION.	MAN.

NOTE.

The Principle of Teleology not affected by the Theory of Evolution.—"It is necessary to remark that there is a wider teleology which is not touched by the doctrine of evolution, but is actually based upon the fundamental proposition of evolution. . . . The teleological and the mechanical views of nature are not necessarily mutually exclusive; on the contrary, the more purely a mechanist the speculator is, the more firmly does he assume a primordial molecular arrangement, of which all the phenomena of the universe are the consequences; and the more completely thereby is he at the mercy of the teleologist, who can always defy him to disprove that this primordial molecular arrangement was not *intended* to evolve the phenomena of the universe." —Prof. Huxley, in *The Academy* for October, 1869, No. 1, p. 13.

CHAPTER VI.

CONSERVATION.—THE RELATION OF GOD TO THE WORLD.

"The relations which unite the creature and the Creator compose a problem obscure and delicate, the two extreme solutions of which are equally false and perilous: on the one hand, a God so passes into the world that He seems to be absorbed in it; on the other hand, a God so separated from the world, that the world has the appearance of going on without Him; on both sides there is equal excess, equal danger, equal error."—Cousin.

In the preceding chapters we have endeavored to present the Christian doctrine concerning God, and concerning the world as the work of God. God is a *person*—the unconditioned Personality, all of whose determinations are from Himself. And creation is the voluntary act of God, who freely chooses to award existence to other beings distinct from Himself. If our scientific conceptions are in harmony with this doctrine, we are safe from the temptations of materialism on the one hand, and proof against the seductions of pantheism on the other. Henceforth we must regard the unconditioned Being as essentially distinct from the material universe. Matter with its phenomena is limited in extent and duration, God is infinite and eternal. Extension is not an attribute of the Divine substance. Succession is not a mode of God's eternity. The Divine life infinitely transcends the dynamical life of the universe.

Still there is some connection, some relation between God and the world. Of this we have the fullest assurance, however incapable we may be of comprehending the mode. The material universe is the product of the Divine efficiency, and therefore the first and most fundamental relation of God to the world is that of *causality*. The universe exists solely through the will of God. It had a beginning, and the beginning of the world was the beginning of time. Prior to that beginning there was no succession, no limitation, no finite existence; only the eternal and infinite One. The creative efficiency was put forth, and matter, as the statical condition necessary to the manifestation of physical phenomena, began to be. The Spirit of God moved upon the formless abyss, and phenomenal change commenced its history. With motion and consequent succession there arose the relations of time. With the differentiation and collocation of matter there arose the relations of space. And the wealth and fullness of inorganic and organic nature sprang up under the directive, formative, and vitalizing energy of the Spirit of God.

But is there no further relation of God to the world, beyond that which is involved in the primary and solitary fact of creative causality? Did the connection of God with his works terminate in an event which belongs to the inapproachable past? Did the Creator, in the beginning, give self-being to the substance of the universe, and endow it with active forces, so that it can exist and act apart from and independent of God? Have the laws of nature a real efficiency, so that the further agency of God is dispensed with, and the universe can pursue a fixed and inevitable path of self-development without his control and oversight? Or is God still immanent in nature, upholding all substance, the power of all force, the life of all life, shaping all forms, and organizing all systems? In a word, has the Divine efficiency remained, since the first creative act, in sublime repose, or does "the Father work hitherto," sustaining, moving, vitalizing, and perfecting the universe—the *Conservator*, as well as the Creator, of all things? This is the living question of our times, whether viewed from the scientific or the theological standpoint. The mental posture we assume in relation to this question must determine our systems of philosophy and religion.

The language of Scripture on this point is direct, and explicit, and unless our interpretation thereof needs to be modified in order to place it in harmony with the general spirit and tenor of Christian teaching, or with the unquestionable facts of nature, which are also a revelation of God, there can be no difficulty in determining the Christian doctrine of God's relation to the world. It teaches us, not only that all things were made by God, but that all things are *sustained* by God. God is still the first and immediate cause of all existence. "He giveth to all life, and breath, and all things" (Acts xvii. 25). The created universe is in complete and ceaseless dependence on the Divine causality; it consists by the same will and the same word by which it was first originated. He who made all things, continues to "uphold all things by the word of his power" (Heb. i. 3). "He is before all things, and by Him all things consist" (Col. i. 17). The universe is not self-existent, nor self-evolved, neither has it any inherent power of self-perpetuation. Notwithstanding the individuality and self-life conceded to the creature, it has no independent existence apart from God, "for of Him, and through Him, and for Him are all things, to whom be glory forever." (Rom. xi. 36.)

The recognition of a real presence of God in nature, and of the immediate agency of God in the production of all natural phenomena, has been a characteristic of the religious consciousness in all ages. This consciousness of the presence of God embracing and sustaining all worldly being is, in fact, an essential content of all vital piety. "It is only a mechanical deism, a barren rationalistic theology, or a piety meagre in the last degree, which has interposed a chasm between God and his creatures." The religious spirit is remarkably developed in the Psalms of David, and here all the operations of nature are spoken of as the operations of Deity. The thunder is "the voice of God." The lightnings are "his arrows." The earthquakes and volcanoes are produced directly by Him. "He looketh on the earth, and it trembleth; He toucheth the hills, and they smoke." "He giveth snow like wool, He scattereth the hoar-frost like ashes, He casteth forth his ice like morsels; who can stand before his cold? He causeth his winds to blow, and the waters flow." "He covereth the heavens with clouds, He prepareth rain for the earth." "He watereth the hills from his chambers, the earth is satisfied with the fruit of his work." "He causeth grass to grow for the cattle, and herb for the service of man." "He giveth to the beast his food, and to the young ravens which cry." "All creatures wait upon Him, and He giveth them their meat in due season. He openeth his hand, they are filled with good. He hideth his face, and they are troubled. He taketh away their breath, they die and return to the dust. *He sendeth forth his Spirit, and they are created;* and He reneweth the face of the earth." To the eye of the inspired writer, the agency of God is concerned in every process and every product of nature. "There are diversities of operations, but *it is the same God who worketh all in all.*" His will and his power are the only real forces in nature.

The interpretation which the Church has given of this teaching of the Sacred Scriptures has been remarkably uniform through the ages. She has always taught that the continuance of the world, no less than its origination, has its ground in the Divine causality; and every theory of the relation of God to the world which has sacrificed the doctrine of the all-embracing, all-sustaining presence of God in the universe, as an immediate and real efficiency, has always been rejected as Pelagian, Rationalistic, or Deistic. The conception of the Divine conservation of the world as the simple, uniform, and universal agency of God sustaining all created substances and powers in every moment of their existence and activity, is the catholic doctrine of Christendom. In attempting the difficult, perhaps impossible task of conceiving the *mode* of this Divine conservation, different theories have been developed. But whatever the conception formed, whether that of the Divine *co-operation* (*concursus Dei generalis*), as taught by St. Augustine and the Schoolmen; or that of a Divine intermediate *impulse* (*impulsus non cogens*), as taught by Luther; or that of the Divine *sustentation* (*sustentatio Dei*), as held by the Arminians; or even that of the *superintendence* and *control* of the Deity, as adopted by some modern religious scientists,[1] they all repose on the ulti-

[1] The theory of "Divine superintendence and control" falls very little, if any thing, short of the ever-present and pervading energy which we advocate. At least, the arguments which would establish such a relation of the Deity to the material universe as amounts to "superintendence and control," would go far to establish the doctrine of a real presence and agency of God pervading and upholding all nature. Superintendence and control imply some agency, some efficiency, and some *intervention* of righteousness or mercy to secure other ends than those secured by the established course of nature, for whoever *overrules* steps on a field beyond his ordinary *rule*. The physical laws are, therefore, simply God's uniform mode of governing the world. This is the conclusion which is reached by Proctor ("Other Worlds than Ours"). In his chapter on "Supervision and Control" (ch. xiii.), he says:

mate truth that whatever is created can have no necessary or independent existence; the same power which called it into being must continue to uphold it in being; and were God to withdraw his conserving efficiency the creature would be immediately annihilated.[1]

St. Augustine, "the father of systematic theology," conceived the Divine conservation of the world as a *continual creation* (*creatio continua*). He taught that the life and activity of the creatures, collectively and individually, are ceaselessly and absolutely dependent on and conditioned by the almighty and omnipresent agency of God. "Were He to withdraw from the world his creative power, it would straightway lapse into nothingness."[2] Thomas Aquinas, "the Angelical Doctor," who is regarded as having brought Scholastic theology to its highest development, held the same views on this subject as Augustine. He taught that "preservation is an ever-renewed creation."[3] All creaturely causes derive their efficiency directly and continually from the First Cause.[4]

Theological writers of more recent times have assented

"Thus we are led to the conclusion that all things happen according to set physical laws; and without, by any means, adopting the view that the Almighty exercises no special control over his universe, we see strong reason to believe that the laws which He has assigned to it are sufficient for the control of all things. Indeed, as far as all things take place in accordance with laws which the Almighty must assuredly have Himself ordained, we may say that *every event which has happened or will happen throughout infinite time is the direct work and indicates the direct purpose and will of Almighty God*" (pp. 329, 332); and further, "*He who made the laws may annul or suspend them at his pleasure*" (p. 333).

[1] St. Augustine's "De Civitate Dei," xii. 25, 26; Neander's "Church History," vol. ii. p. 605; Nitzsch, "System of Christian Doctrine," p. 193; Müller's "Christian Doctrine of Sin," vol. i. p. 248; Harris's "Pre-Adamite Earth," p. 103; Young's "Creator and Creation," pp. 57, 58; Chalmers's "Astronomical Discourses," Dis. iii. pp. 91, 98.

[2] "De Civitate Dei," xii. 25; xiii. 26.

[3] Contra Gentiles, ii. 38.

[4] "Summa Universalis," pt. i. q. 105, art. 5.

to these views with notable uniformity. Dr. Samuel Clarke, the intimate friend of Newton, whose "Lectures on the Being and Attributes of God," and on the "Evidences of Natural and Revealed Religion," secured for him a European renown as a Christian philosopher, states the doctrine of the immediate agency of the Deity with remarkable explicitness. "All things that are done in the world are done either immediately by God Himself, or by created intelligent beings. Matter being evidently not capable of any laws or powers whatsoever, any more than it is capable of intelligence, except only this one negative power, that every part of it will of itself always and necessarily continue in that state, whether of rest or motion, wherein it at present is. So that all those things which we commonly say are the effects of the natural powers of matter and laws of motion, of gravitation, attraction, or the like, are indeed (if we will speak strictly and properly) *the effect of God's acting upon matter continually and every moment*, either immediately by Himself, or mediately by some created intelligent beings. . . . Consequently there is no such thing as what we commonly call the *course of nature*, or the *power of nature*. The course of nature, truly and properly speaking, is nothing else but the will of God, producing certain effects in a continued, regular, constant, and uniform manner."[1]

Dr. Clarke may properly be regarded as the representative of the metaphysico-theological thought of the seventeenth century. No apology is needed at this hour for

[1] "Evidences of Natural and Revealed Religion," Prop. xiv. Dugald Stewart, after quoting the above, adds, "My opinion on this subject coincides with that of Dr. Clarke" ("Philosophy of the Active and Moral Powers of Man," vol. ii. p. 29).

presenting John Wesley as the best representative of the evangelical movement of the eighteenth century which adhered firmly to the *ipsissima verba* of the sacred writers. He expresses the evangelical conception with admirable clearness and force: "God is also the supporter of all the things which He has made. He beareth, upholdeth, sustaineth all created things by the word of his power; by the same powerful word which brought them out of nothing. As this was absolutely necessary for the beginning of their existence, it is equally so for the continuance of it; were his almighty influence withdrawn, they could not subsist a moment longer. . . . He preserves them in their several relations, connections, and dependencies, so as to compose one system of beings, to form one entire universe, according to the counsel of his will. . . . He is the true author of all the motion in the universe. All matter of whatever kind is absolutely and totally *inert.* It does not, can not in any case move itself. . . . Neither the sun, moon, nor stars move themselves. *They are moved every moment by the Almighty hand that made them.*"[1] These views are earnestly maintained by Nitzsch and Müller, Chalmers and Harris, Young and Whedon, Channing and Martineau.

The religious life of the present age, in all its purest and most vigorous manifestations, still clings with passionate ardor to the belief that God is every where present, and that the ceaseless, uniform, and direct agency of God is still upholding, moving, vivifying, and controlling all things. The harp of David is restrung and swept with a firmer hand. It rings with nobler conceptions, and swells into diviner harmonies. God is recognized as "*above* all, *through* all, and *in* all." "In Him we live and move,

[1] "Sermons," vol. ii. pp. 178, 179.

and have our being." The Christian still believes, with a fuller and richer assurance, that God's presence—

> "Warms in the sun, refreshes in the breeze.
> Glows in the stars, and blossoms in the trees."

He still hears the voice of God in the thunder at midnight, and in the rustling of the forest leaves at noonday. He sees the beauty of God in "the silent faces of the clouds," and in the virgin blush of the solitary flower. He sees the life of God in the activities of organic nature, and marks his power and presence in the falling rain and noiseless dew, the flowing river and the restless ocean. The seasons, as they come round to him in their grateful vicissitudes, bring to him fresh tokens of the goodness of God, and inspire him with perennial joy.

> "These as they change, Almighty Father, these
> Are but the varied God. The rolling year
> Is full of Thee. . . . .
> But wandering oft, with brute, unconscious gaze,
> Man marks not Thee, marks not the mighty hand
> That, ever busy, wheels the silent spheres;
> Works in the secret deep; shoots, steaming, thence
> The fair profusion that o'erspreads the spring;
> Flings from the sun direct the flaming day;
> Feeds every creature, hurls the tempest forth;
> And, as on earth this grateful change revolves,
> With transport touches all the springs of life."[1]

A discussion of the Christian doctrine of the relation of God to the world can scarcely be regarded as adequate and complete which keeps not constantly in view the theories of certain "advanced thinkers" that conflict with the views here presented. We do not now refer to the extreme opinions of the Atheists, who deny the existence of God, proclaim the eternity of matter, and regard force as an inherent and essential attribute of matter, by which all the phenomena of nature and humanity are necessarily

[1] Thomson's "Seasons."

evolved; nor of the Pantheists, on the other hand, who deny the personality of God, and represent the Deity as an eternal *natura naturans*, which by a spontaneous and unconscious development is forever emerging as the *natura naturata*. For these thinkers there can be no conceivable Providence. "Science has shown us that we are under the dominion of general laws, and that there is no special Providence. Nature acts with fearful uniformity; stern as fate, absolute as a tyrant, merciless as death; too vast to praise; too inexplicable to worship; too inexorable to propitiate; it has no ear for prayer, no heart for sympathy, no arm to save."[1]

At present we are to deal with the theories of a class of scientists who believe in the existence of God—of a personal God, and who profess the greatest reverence for the Sacred Scriptures, but whose God is clearly not the God the Bible reveals. This general class of thinkers may be subdivided into subordinate schools, as they verge toward one or the other of the extremes above indicated.

1. One school is represented by such writers as Prof. Tyndall, Dr. H. Bence Jones, and Dr. Bastian. Their fundamental principle is "the absolute inseparability of matter and force;" consequently they do not recognize the Divine Will as the sole and immediate cause of the motion and life of the universe. Molecular attractions and repulsions are the primal forces communicated to matter at the Creation, and from "the self-activity of these primary forces" result all the forms of energy in nature, whether organic or inorganic. "Our idea of the grandeur, the unity, and the power of the first cause," writes Dr. H. Bence Jones, "will surely not be lessened if we can show that one law of the union of matter and force

[1] Holyoake, "Discussion with Townley," p. 68.

and of the conservation of energy obtains throughout the organic as well as the inorganic creation."[1] Here we have a close approximation, if not intentionally, yet logically, to the Atheistic extreme. The transition seems easy, if not inevitable, to the recognition of force as an inherent and necessary attribute of matter which *may* be eternal. Then what need of a God, or what place for one, if the forces and laws of matter are adequate to the explanation of all phenomena? As Martineau aptly suggests, "These properties and powers once installed in the cosmic executive are too apt, like mayors of the palace, to set up for themselves," and eject the real Lord and God.

2. Another school is represented by such men as Professors Owen, Huxley, and Baden Powell, who deny the ultimate distinction between matter and force, and regard both as phenomenal manifestations of some "unknown substratum"—a supramaterial PHYSIS (φύσις) which is identical with the Divine substance, the *natura naturans* of Spinoza. To these minds the universe discloses nothing but immutable law, absolute continuity, and necessary development. "The grand principle of the *self-evolving powers of nature*,"[2] and "the grand inductive conclusion of universal and *eternal* order,"[3] are the bases of all rational theology. Here we encounter a phase of thought which verges toward the extreme of Pantheism. The Deity himself is conditioned in his action by the eternal and immutable laws of nature, and can not be conceived as a living Will exercising control over and subordinating these laws to higher moral ideas and ends. This doc-

[1] Croonian Lecture, "On Matter and Force," p. 94. Is it not significant that Dr. Jones must write his "First Cause" without the initial capitals?

[2] Powell, "Essays and Reviews," p. 139.

[3] Powell, "Christianity and Judaism," p. 11.

trine, Prof. Powell admits, "summarily overrides the Mosaic creation, renders miracles irrational, excludes a special providence, and, we may add, dismisses prayer as a useless absurdity."

3. A third and intermediate school assumes the existence of a plastic nature (*vis formativa*) intermediate between the Creator and his work, by which the phenomena of nature are produced. This hypothesis was propounded by Cudworth, and has lately been reproduced by Dr. Laycock and Mr. Murphy under the name of "unconscious organizing intelligence," to explain those facts of organic nature which come under the relation of means and ends, or structure and function. This hypothesis must deflect toward one or other of the extremes indicated, when it attempts to decide in what subject this "unconscious intelligence" inheres. If it be said that it inheres in matter, the tendency must be toward Atheism; that it inheres in spirit, then the tendency is toward Pantheism.

Common to all these hypotheses is the denial of the direct, immediate, and voluntary agency of God in nature as *the only real and efficient force.* They are all attempts to account for the conservation of the world by "the conservation and transformation of energy," that is, by secondary causes, which in reality are only conditions and not real causes. They interpose a chasm between God and the world. The universe is a self-supporting, self-evolving machine, and God is an isolated, incommunicable abstraction.

It is to be deplored that certain Christian writers have deemed it necessary, on what they consider moral grounds, to give countenance to theories which in one form or another ascribe a real efficiency to natural laws, and dispense with the immediate and ceaseless agency of God in the conservation of the world. They imagine that some such hypothesis is needed to vindicate the Divine honor and righteousness. In their imagination, it derogates from the Divine majesty to be ceaselessly concerned and busied with the minute and insignificant operations of nature, or even cognizant of them. His eternal serenity would be disturbed, and his unsullied purity compromised by any connection therewith, and He would become responsible for the disorders and abnormities, the evils and sufferings, which appear in the world. He must, therefore, be released from a constant and direct connection with the universe. He must leave nature to the necessary predestinated course of self-evolution, or, if He interpose at all, it must be in some exceptional, extraordinary, and supernatural way; so that, if there be a providential administration, every act and incident thereof must be a *miracle.*

We respect the motives, but we can not approve the procedure or commend the logic of these theologians. The moral difficulties they would by these hypotheses evade still remain in all their force. "Any hypothesis which essays to relieve these difficulties from pressing against Providence only transfers and leaves them to press with equal force against an original creation."[1] The Supreme Intelligence which originally endowed matter with its properties, and ordained the laws of force, must have foreseen all possible combinations, interactions, and consequences, and, if it be proper to speak of responsibilities in this connection, must be as responsible for these consequences as though they were the direct effect of immediate volition. An agent is accountable not only for his acts, but for all the foreseen consequences of his acts.

[1] Dr. Harris, "Pre-Adamite Earth," p. 104.

The solution of these difficulties must be sought in another field.

Meantime it may be observed that these theologians affect a concern for the Divine honor which even revelation itself does not confess. It teaches that all the operations of nature are the operations of God, and no apologies are offered for consequences which, to short-sighted men, may appear to conflict with righteousness or love. Does the earthquake tear the mountain asunder, and spread devastation and death throughout the surrounding country? it is the Lord who roareth from Zion, and uttereth his voice from Jerusalem; He causeth the habitation of the shepherds to mourn, and the top of Carmel to wither.[1] The people bow their heads with reverence, and in their chastening sorrows see the hand of God. But these philosophic theologians must correct the language of Scripture, and tone it down in harmony with the capricious demands of modern scientists. The language of the ancient Prophet of God is simply the expression of a childlike and subjective conception of nature which modern science has emptied of all its significance. The earthquake was the product of "secondary causes"—of inherent nature-forces which now exist and act independent of the agency and control of God. To maintain the consistency of their hypothesis, they will even affirm that the catastrophe was unforeseen, and did not come within the purview of the creative plan. The exuberance of the Oriental imagination has thrown a haze of unreality over all the descriptions of natural phenomena, and therefore the language of the inspired Psalmist must be amended. When he tells us that God "covereth the heavens with clouds, and prepareth rain for the earth," we must paraphrase after the follow-

[1] Amos i. 2.

ing fashion: "In the beginning God gave to water those properties, and determined those cosmical conditions which, when coincident, result in the formation of clouds and the descent of rain!" This, we are told, is the interpretation which modern science demands. Conservation is simply "the indestructibility of matter and the persistence of force," and Providence is "the uniformity of natural law." We must no longer believe that God is a present, immanent, and diffusive Power and Life in nature. To find the connection between God and nature we must remount by a process of regressive thought to the first, and, indeed, the last act of creation—the primal origination of matter and motion. So that if now piety would stand face to face with its supreme object, it is compelled to fling itself back into the abyss of duration, before the mountains were brought forth, or ever the earth and the world were formed.

Practically, this conception gives us a universe without a God; for the world, once created, and stocked with the necessary forces and adjustments and laws, will henceforth govern itself. It will run its predestinated course in obedience to an original impulse, and realize a perpetual motion without further oversight or care or control. The world is a huge soulless machine, and theology is reduced to Mechanical Deism! But surely no one pretends that this theory satisfies the demands of Scripture language, and fills up the complement of its idea. Practically, it renders the Word of God of no effect.

This theory is equally inadequate to satisfy the cravings of the human heart. "The heart demands a present God—a God who is never far from any one of us; it demands the immediate presence and constant care of a heavenly Father; it demands, when it looks upon nature, to feel that God is there, not in his laws only, but in conscious and perpetual action; not in the sense of a Wisdom and Goodness, embodied in arrangements contrived and perfected long ago, as the mind of an artificer may be said to be present in the work of his hands, but in the sense of a Love co-present to every aspect of nature, and a Will inworking in every event that takes place."[1] "Reacting against the usurpation of secondary causation, wearied of its distance from the Fountain-head, it flings itself back with pathetic repentance into the arms of the Primary Infinitude."

The relation of God to the world, however, is a problem which can not be solved by an appeal to sentiment. The religious consciousness may be the counter-proof, but it can not be the starting-point of a philosophy which aims at the explanation of things—that is, of their origin and continuance—by principles and ideas of the reason. For what is meant by *understanding*, but translation into ideas, and comprehending under necessary principles? Any theory which essays such explanation of things must therefore commend itself to the logical understanding, and be capable of logical construction.

Now the various hypotheses which seek to dispense with the immediate agency of God, and to explain the conservation of the world by "secondary" or natural agencies, when critically examined do not satisfy the understanding. However convenient for the evasion of difficulties, however plausible for their simplicity and manageable clearness, on a closer inspection they are found to be inadequate.

1. *There is the hypothesis of natural law.* The world is governed by general laws which are fixed and immutable. These laws were impressed upon matter at the

[1] Hedge, "Reason and Religion," p. 74.

beginning, and in obedience to them the universe has gradually evolved itself in rigid continuity and necessary order. No room, therefore, is left for special direction or providential control, and if the term "providence" is at all permissible, it is only as a synonym for natural law.

It is affirmed by the advocates of this hypothesis that "the grand principle of the uniformity and constancy of natural causes is *a primary law of belief* so strongly entertained by the truly inductive inquirer that he can not conceive the *possibility* of its failure."[1] As science extends her domain and pushes her discoveries into new regions, cases that once seemed anomalous are found to be conformable to this general rule, and therefore we are justified in assuming the absolute uniformity and inviolability of natural law through all the realms of time and space. Thus we reach "the grand inductive conclusion of the universal and *eternal* order of nature." But an *overruling* providence must step beyond *ordinary rule:* it must control, interrupt, modify, or in some manner give a new direction to the action of nature, and thus become *super*natural—that is, miraculous. So that were we even to concede the phenomenal reality of the miracles recorded in the New Testament, and to accept them as "objects of faith, but not as the evidences of faith," still modern science would forbid us to believe that any supernatural interposition can *now* take place. Not a single instance of counteraction or control of natural law can now be authenticated, and therefore we must regard special providence as incredible and impossible.

The first error, and indeed the fundamental error, of this hypothesis is the assumption that the absolute uniformity and permanence of nature is "*a primary law of*

[1] "Essays and Reviews," p. 102.

belief," and therefore the natural philosopher "must set out with clear ideas of the *possible* and the *impossible*."

Now we grant that had we such *à priori* conviction of the permanence and immutability of nature, then it would be impossible to prove that the order of nature had a beginning, or that there could be any interference with the agencies or laws of nature by a supernatural power. "No evidence adduced in favor of a creation or of Divine interposition could ever be so strong as to overcome the necessary belief in direct opposition to it."[1] But the truth is, we have no such intuitive conviction. Our belief has none of the characteristics of an *à priori* intuition: it is neither self-evident nor universal nor necessary. John Stuart Mill has successfully shown that this belief is the result of experience, that it is entertained only by the cultivated and educated few, and that even among such it has been of slow growth. Therefore he properly concludes that "the uniformity in the succession of events . . . must be received, *not as the law of the universe, but of that portion only which is within the range of our means of observation*, with a reasonable degree of extension to adjacent cases."[2]

Belief in the uniformity of nature is an induction from *experience*, and not a primary intuition. And by the word experience, in this connection, we must understand not the experience of one man only, or of one generation, but the accumulated experience of mankind in all ages as registered in books or transmitted by tradition. But how limited, at best, is human experience—how circumscribed both in time and space! Compared with the vastness and duration of the universe, it is narrowed down to a mere point. All experience, be it that of the individ-

[1] McCosh, "Intuitions," p. 276. [2] "Logic," vol. ii. pp. 117, 118.

ual or of mankind, is only finite. To infer a universal law from a limited number of instances is to violate to the uttermost the fundamental canon of logic that "no conclusion must contain more than was contained in the premises from which it is drawn."[1] Inductive science can only give us the contingent and the relative, it can never attain to the necessary and the absolute. By abstraction, comparison, and generalization it may furnish us with *general* notions, but it can not give us *universal* principles. "Experience can not conduct us to universal and necessary truths — not to universal, because she has not tried all cases; not to necessary, because necessity is not a matter to which experience can testify."[2] The intuitive reason, we doubt not, is furnished with necessary and universal principles which may illuminate the pathway of experience, and give meaning and law to the facts of sensation, so that man may become "the Interpreter of Nature;" but certainly the absolute uniformity of nature is not one of these ideas.

Notwithstanding the boasted mathematical precision of the inductive method, and the rigid exactness of its results, scientific men are not wholly exempt from the common infirmity of hasty generalization. They are perpetually liable to the temptation to draw immense conclusions from premises that are too narrow and inadequate. The history of science is a record of the correction of hasty generalizations by future discoveries, and leads to the final conviction that there are no laws of nature which can lay claim to absolute universality. Since the time of Newton, the law of gravitation has been regarded by many as strictly universal. But now we are

[1] Hamilton's "Lectures on Metaphysics," vol. i. p. 102.
[2] Whewell, "Novum Organon Renovatum," p. 7.

told by Herschel that "our evidence of the existence of gravitation fails us beyond the region of the double stars, or leaves us at best only a *presumption* amounting to moral conviction in its favor." Furthermore, in regard to the luminiferous ether, he tells us, that "we are freed from the necessity of any mental reference to the actual weight or specific gravity of the material, which in this case is the more necessary, as, though we suppose the ethereal molecules to possess inertia, *we can not suppose them affected by the force of gravitation.*" "Beyond all doubt, the widest and most interesting prospect of future discovery . . . is that distinction between *gravitating* and *levitating* matter, that positive and unrefutable demonstration of the existence of a repulsive force . . . enormously more powerful than the attractive force of gravity."[1]

Until recently the presence of free oxygen as the necessary condition of life has been regarded as a universal biological law. "But the latest researches of Pasteur have shown that, so far from oxygen being essential to the life of the simplest living beings, there are certain forms of infusoria which not only pass their lives without oxygen, but are killed by its presence."[2]

Other illustrations might be adduced, but these are sufficient for our purpose. The truth is, there is not a phenomenon known to man that can properly be said to be the result of the action of *one* invariable and universal force, not even the falling of a stone to the earth; for some force must have previously been exerted to raise the stone from the earth, which force is represented by energy of position, or "potential energy."[3] And this poten-

[1] "Familiar Lectures on Science," pp. 218, 284, 140.

[2] "Physiological Anatomy," by Todd, Bowman, and Beale, p. 19; Nicholson's "Biology," p. 14.

[3] Jevons, "Principles of Science," vol. ii. pp. 433, 434.

tial energy is the exact numerical equivalent of the energy of motion which it acquires in falling—*i. e.*, the mass multiplied by the square of the velocity. Every event, every change in nature, is due to "some *variable* combinations of invariable forces."[1] Material causes are always complex. Every law of nature is liable to counteraction and modification by other laws, and the most fundamental fact of the universe is that material forces are adjusted, combined, and modified in endless modes in order to the fulfillment of purposes and ends. The phenomena of life present a vast series of such adjustments and modifications. The mechanical and chemical forces are controlled and subordinated by the vital force, so that life has been defined as "a *resistance* to the physical forces of matter"[2] —a resistance which Liebig regards as in a certain degree invincible. Living matter is the seat of energy, and so long as it is living, can overcome the primary law of the *inertia* of matter, and moves spontaneously.[3] Living matter overcomes the attraction of gravitation, and resists, suspends, and modifies the action of chemical affinity.[4] It is in direct opposition to chemical affinity that organized beings exist.

Thus the various forms of energy are mutually conditioned. The mechanical, chemical, and electrical energies are counteracted by the vital force. And all the forces and energies of nature are controlled and subordinated by a higher force which orders means to ends, and adapts structure to function, viz., an *Intelligent Will*. The conviction finally becomes irresistible that nature is a system

[1] Argyll, "Reign of Law," p. 100.
[2] Laycock, "Mind and Brain," vol. i. p. 225.
[3] Beale, "Protoplasm," pp. 39, 42, 109.
[4] Beale, "Protoplasm," pp. 104, 117; Laycock, "Mind and Brain," vol. i. pp. 222, 224; Liebig, "Organic Chemistry," p. 69.

of things designed to be subject to Mind, and that a law of design is the highest law of the universe.

It must now be obvious that we can reach no definite conclusion in regard to the question under discussion—the uniformity of nature—unless we have a clear and precise conception of the meaning of the term "nature." The word is employed, even by men of science, in a very loose and ambiguous sense. At one time it is used to denote the totality of sensible phenomena; at another, the conditions or causes of phenomena; again, the relations of phenomena; and often, all these collectively. We must endeavor to extricate ourselves from this confusion.

According to its derivation, nature (*natura—nascitur*) means that which is born or produced—*the becoming;* that which has a beginning and an end; that which has not the cause of its existence in itself, and the cause of which must be sought in something antecedent to and beyond itself—that is, nature is *the phenomenal.* This the word itself expresses in the strongest manner. That which begins to be, as the necessary consequence of antecedent conditions, is *natural.* The co-existence, resemblance, and succession of phenomena constitute the *order of nature;* and the uniformity of these relations among phenomena are the *laws of nature.* So much is clear from the standpoint of mere empirical science. Now if law is "the uniformity of relations among phenomena,"[1] then it is equally clear that the phrase "uniformity of natural law" is meaningless, for, by the definition, the uniformity itself is the law, and the expression is simply equivalent to "the uniformity of the uniformity," which is absurd. Furthermore, if "nature" is the phenomenal—the becoming—then the

[1] Spencer, "First Principles," p. 128.

word can not be properly employed to denote the causes of that becoming, unless by causes we understand antecedent conditions, which, as we shall presently see, are not real causes. Nature, or the sum-total of phenomena, is an *effect*—an effect which demands a cause. There can be no phenomena without change, no change without motion, no motion without force, no force without Spirit, for Spirit-force is the only force of which we have any knowledge or consciousness. A rational Will, and not a blind necessity, must stand at the fountain-head of being, and uniformity in nature must be the result of *reason* and *choice*.

But suppose we are permitted to employ the term "nature" to denote the essential properties of matter, and the various forms of energy,[1] potential and kinetic; and suppose we admit that matter is indestructible, and that the amount of energy in the world is unchanged, the sum of the actual and potential energies being a constant quantity; still we are not entitled from these premises to infer the absolute uniformity in the succession of events—that is, the uniformity of the phenomenal. We have already seen that no phenomenon known to man is the result of a single property of matter or a single form of energy. "All issues in nature are the effects produced upon matter by the resultant of component forces." The phenomena of nature are the result of adjustments, combinations, and distributions of matter and of force in endless variety and complexity. Hence we have in nature the variable, the contingent, the particular, as well as the invariable, the

[1] By *Energy* we understand "the power of doing work," or overcoming resistance, which in nature is something perfectly intelligible and measurable, equivalent in all cases to the product of the mass into the square of the velocity. By *Force* we understand "that which originates motion." All the forms of Energy have therefore their origin in Force, and Force has its origin in the Will of the Deity.

uniform, and the general. This is admitted by Comte: "That which engenders this *irregular variability* of the effect is the great number of different agents determining at the same time the same phenomena; and from which it results, in the most complicated phenomena, *that there are no two cases precisely alike.* We have no occasion, in order to find such complexity, to go to the phenomena of living beings. It presents itself in bodies without life, for example, in studying meteorological phenomena.... *Their multiplicity renders the effects as irregularly variable as if every cause had not been subject to any precise condition.*"[1]

Thus we are led by various lines of thought to the same conclusion. It is certain that we can only learn what the uniformities (the laws) of nature are by *experience*, and in order to determine whether all the successions of events have been and now are universally uniform, we must have a *universal* experience. If there have been deviations from general laws under peculiar conditions—if one form of energy has been counteracted and modified by another form of energy, or even by an intelligent Will, so as to give a *particular* result—experience (=observation and testimony) must be just as adequate to attest the reality of that particular deviation as it is to attest the prevalence of general laws.[2] We have no intuitive and necessary conviction of the uniformity of nature, and therefore we can not affirm in an *à priori* manner what is *possible* or *impossible.* Those scientists who adopt the maxim of Faraday, that in the investigation of new and peculiar

[1] Quoted from "Positive Philosophy," by Dr. McCosh, "Divine Government," p. 167.

[2] Science has been defined as the "knowledge of these *deviations* from the great laws of nature formularized in contingent or derivative laws."—Laycock, "Mind and Brain," vol. i. p. 221.

phenomena "we must set out with clear ideas of the possible and the impossible," are doomed to move in a vicious circle. They can not be sure that a fact of experience is a real fact until they have ascertained the laws of nature in the case, and they can not ascertain what the laws of nature are until they have ascertained the facts. They must not profess to have learned any thing until they have ascertained that it is possible, and they can not decide that it is possible until they have learned every thing, because the single item of knowledge they are deficient in may be the very principle which warrants a belief in the possibility of the fact. The maxim is obviously absurd. In its theological bearings it is repudiated even by Professor Tyndall, the pupil and successor of Faraday at the Royal Institution. "You never hear the really philosophical defenders of the doctrine of uniformity speaking of *impossibilities* in nature. They never say . . . that it is impossible for the Builder of the universe to alter his work. Their business is not with the possible, but with the actual."[1]

The hypothesis under discussion is further vitiated by the assumption that laws are *causes* adequate in themselves to the production of all phenomena. So that now Creation by Law (Nomogeny) is the watchword of this school of thinkers. The men who have defined law as "the uniformity of relations among phenomena"—as "an observed order of facts"—now speak of laws as having in themselves a real efficiency; as producing, regulating, and governing powers. Under this high-sounding phrase—"Creation by Law"—there is not only the artful concealment of a difficulty, but there is also the interpolation of a positive error. The *uniformities* of natural phenomena

[1] "Fragments of Science," p. 162.

are the *causes* of phenomena, or, in other words, the order of nature is its own cause, which is not only erroneous but self-contradictory.

Here, again, we encounter the perplexity consequent on the use of ambiguous phraseology. The term "Law" is employed in an equivocal sense, as denoting, indifferently, property and relation, condition and cause, antecedent and consequence. In such an atmosphere of verbal haze it is impossible to see clearly or think correctly. We must feel our way toward a purer light, and find a less wavering stand-point.

The primary and generic conception of law is "*the authoritative expression of Will.*" This is the most natural, the most obvious, and the most legitimate conception. The true notion of Will is the synthesis of Reason and Power. Power exerted in the forms of reason is self-consciousness. Reason manifested in the forms of power is self-determination. Self-consciousness and self-determination are the two elements of personality. More explicitly, we may therefore define law as "*the idea of the Reason enforced by Power.*" The subjects of legislation are:

1. *The actions of Free Beings.* To ascertain the laws in this case is to answer the question, What *ought* to be done?

2. *The processes of Thought.* To ascertain the laws in this case is to answer the questions, Why do we judge or affirm this or that? and, What are the grounds and criteria of certitude?

3. *The facts or events of Nature.* To ascertain the laws in this case is to answer the questions, *What* are the facts in their observed order? *How* or from what causes do they arise? *Why* or for what end do they exist?

It is under the last division that we encounter the secondary and symbolical senses in which the term law has come to be used by scientific men, which have well-nigh supplanted the primary and only legitimate signification.

That which lies nearest to sense — the phenomena of nature—first engages the awakening intellect. If the attention is confined solely to the phenomena of nature, the simple question propounded is, *What* is the observed order of the facts? At this stage science can be no more than a classification of phenomena according to their relations of co-existence, resemblance, and succession, and law must be defined as "*the uniformity of relations among phenomena.*"[1] Here the term is taken *objectively*, and the facts are simply conceived as perceived by the senses.

But the human mind can never rest in the bare knowledge of phenomena. The reason intuitively recognizes the uniformities of nature as the suggestive signs of properties or powers which are not perceptible to sense, and the question arises, *How*—that is, from what adjustment of antecedent conditions and physical agencies—does the order of nature arise? And now the term law comes to indicate more than an observed order of facts; it denotes an order resulting from the coincidence of some permanent properties, qualities, or forces which are conceived as lying back of the phenomena, and pushing them into the objective field. Accordingly, laws are now defined as "*the necessary relations which spring from the [inner] nature of things.*"[2] Here the phrase is taken *subjectively*, as the expression of a mental conception, and not of a sense perception. "It has relation to us as *understanding*, rather than to the materials of which the universe consists as obeying certain rules."[3]

[1] Spencer, "First Principles," p. 128.
[2] Montesquieu, "Spirit of Laws," bk. i. ch. i.
[3] Herschel, "Natural Philosophy," § 27.

Finally, the human mind approaches the question—*Why* have these physical agencies been so collocated or adjusted? What relation does this adjustment bear to *purpose, intention*, or *end?* Law is now *the reason or end for which an orderly arrangement exists.* Here the phrase is taken ideally or *rationally* as a revelation of the intuitive reason, in the light of which the phenomena of nature find their only satisfactory interpretation.

By this route we are led back to the primary and universal conception of law as "*the idea of the Reason enforced by Power.*" All government, human or Divine, is the enforcement of ideas by authority, and "Natural Law" is the actualization of the Divine idea by the Divine efficiency. As Bunsen remarks, "Law is the supreme rule of the universe, and this law is Intellect, is *Reason*, whether viewed in the formation of a planetary system or the organization of a worm."

Laws and ideas are thus correlated. Viewed in respect to the reason as conceiving, originating, and projecting, we speak of the *idea.* Viewed in respect to the sphere of determinate movement and action in which ideas are realized and actualized, we speak of *law.* Hence Plato often calls ideas laws; and Lord Bacon, the British Plato, describes the laws of the material world as ideas: "*Quod in naturâ naturatâ lex, in naturâ naturante idea dicitur.*"

It is obvious, then, that laws are not attributes of matter, but of intelligence. It is equally obvious that laws are not efficient causes, and can not execute themselves. They are the ideas and purposes of reason, and the rules or methods according to which the ideas are actualized. Law, therefore, presupposes a *Lawgiver* and an *Executive.* Law without a lawgiver is the merest abstraction, and law without an agent to realize and execute it is, in fact, not a law, but an idea. To maintain that the universe is governed by laws, without ascending to the superior reason and source of these laws—to talk of laws, and yet not to recognize that every law implies a legislator, and an executor to put it in force—is to hypostatize laws, to make beings of them, and to substitute mythical and fabulous divinities in the place of the one living and true God, the source of all power and all law.

Few men of recent times can claim a larger acquaintance with the history and the philosophy of the Inductive Sciences than the late Professor Whewell, and he may be fairly regarded as expressing the doctrine of the best scientists. "A law supposes an *agent* and a *power:* for it is a mode according to which the power acts. Without the presence of such an agent, of such a power, conscious of the relations on which the law depends, producing the effects which the law prescribes, the law can have no efficiency, no existence. Hence we infer that the intelligence by which the law is ordained, the power by which it is put in action, must be present in all places where the effects of the law occur; that thus the knowledge and agency of the Divine Being pervade every portion of the universe, producing all action and passion, all permanence and change. *The laws of nature are the laws which He in his wisdom prescribes to his own acts;* his universal presence is the necessary condition of any course of events, his universal agency the only origin of any efficient force."[1]

We grant that the term law may, by metonymy, be employed to designate "the uniformity of relations among phenomena," but then it must not be forgotten that here the effect is put for the cause, the consequence of law for

[1] "Astronomy and Physics," p. 224.

the law itself. It may be that this is the only conception of law which is legitimate within the sphere of strictly physical science, and to limit the scientists solely to the knowledge of phenomena and their relations would simply be to take them at their word. The inquiry concerning Causes and First Principles must then, by common consent, be surrendered to pure metaphysics and theology. But if, after this truce, the scientist still persists in speaking of laws as efficient causes, and claiming for them "an eternal and necessary uniformity," thus virtually denying the liberty and personality of God, and the possibility of Creation and Providence, the Christian Theist must be permitted in the name of polemic fairness and logical consistency to protest.

CHAPTER VII.

CONSERVATION.—THE RELATION OF GOD TO THE WORLD.

(*Continued.*)

Of the various hypotheses which seek to dispense with the immediate agency of God, and to explain the conservation of the world by "secondary" or natural agencies, the second is that of *active Force communicated to matter at its creation.* This force being transformable, and at the same time indestructible, is regarded as adequate to the conservation of the universe.

This hypothesis must not be confounded with the Dynamical theory of matter propounded by Leibnitz, and more fully elaborated by Boscovich, which regards matter as a mere phenomenon or function of force; on the contrary, it conceives of matter as a distinct entity moving under the action of a primary impulse communicated by "the Creator's fiat at the beginning." This hypothesis in its fundamental conception and its further elaboration is purely mechanical. It represents the universe as a machine first set in motion by the Deity, and conserved by the actions and reactions of its several parts. All subsequent motions, changes, and configurations are the prolonged results of the original impulse, without any further direct action or control on the part of the Creator.

A more precise and accurate statement would require that the term "Energy" should be substituted for "Force." In the language of modern physics, *Force* is "that which *originates* or tends to originate motion or change," and "is *wholly expended* in the action it produces."[1] All energy has its origin in force, but force can not pass into energy except under conditions in which it is at liberty to act. For instance, the *force* of gravity produces the *energy* of motion of a falling body, but gravity can not produce motion unless there is space through which the body can fall. *Energy*, therefore, is defined as "the power of doing work."[2] The work done is the resistance overcome, and in overcoming resistance the energy is transformed, but not annihilated. In every case in which energy is lost by resistance, heat is generated; and we learn from Joule's investigations that the quantity of heat generated is a perfectly definite equivalent for the energy lost. It is therefore claimed that the total quantity of energy in the universe is constant, and that the material system is dynamically conservative. The universe is a self-acting and self-sustained machine, and perpetual motion is a necessary consequence.

A little reflection, however, ought to convince any one that this conception of the universe—as a machine which is kept in perpetual motion by the reciprocal action of its parts — is a false analogy. And its fallacy is apparent from this, that the moving force of every machine is not inherent in the machine, but some natural primary force distinct from the machine, such as gravity, or the primary atomic forces of attraction and repulsion; and consequently the very idea of mechanism *assumes* the existence of those primary forces of which it is the professed object of a mechanical theory of the universe to give an explanation. A machine "can no more create energy than it can

[1] Thomson and Tait, "Natural Philosophy," vol. i. p. 164; Mayer, "Correlation and Conservation of Forces," p. 335. [2] Stewart's "Physics," p. 103.

create matter;" its sole function is "to transform energy into a kind most convenient for us."[1] "We may with the greatest ease convert mechanical work into heat, but we can not by any means convert all the energy of heat back again into mechanical work. In the steam-engine we do what can be done in this way, but it is a very small portion of the whole energy of the heat that is convertible into work, for a large portion is dissipated, and will continue to be dissipated however perfect our engine may become. Let the greatest care be taken in the construction and working of a steam-engine, yet we shall not succeed in converting one fourth of the whole energy of the heat of the coals into mechanical work."[2] It is impossible to construct a machine that can do work without parting with energy; and when the energy is all parted with, any machine whatever must necessarily cease to do any more work unless a fresh supply of energy be brought in from without. It is impossible to make a water-mill work without a constantly renewed supply of water, or to make a steam-engine work without a constantly renewed supply of fuel. "Every one who understands mechanics knows that any such inexhaustible supply of energy is impossible by means of merely mechanical arrangements; but it is equally true, though not perhaps equally so evident, that it is impossible by means of any arrangement of thermal, electric, or chemical forces."[3]

But we are told that modern science has proved that the law of the Conservation of Energy is an absolute law of the universe, and that though man can not construct a machine which will realize the dream of perpetual motion, the material universe is in reality such a machine.

[1] Stewart's "Physics," pp. 114, 353. [2] Stewart's "Physics," p. 356.
[3] Murphy, "Habit and Intelligence," vol. i. p. 22.

It becomes us to speak with some degree of diffidence in regard to a question which lies outside of our special department of study. Nevertheless we must confess that we have a growing suspicion of all so-called "absolute laws" in the domain of physical nature. And we are confirmed in this mistrust by the fact that physicists themselves are not agreed in regarding this law of conservation of energy as universally true. "That the amount of energy in the world is unchangeable, the sum of the actual or kinetic and potential energies being a constant quantity, has been by some writers overstrained. It may be taken as a postulate, and is probably true, but it is a proposition equally incapable of proof and of disproof."[1] "This principle," says Sir J. Herschel, "so far as it rests upon any scientific basis as a legitimate conclusion from dynamical laws, is no other than the well-known dynamical theorem of the conservation of *vis viva* (or of 'energy,' as some prefer to call it), *supplemented to save the truth of its verbal enunciation* by the introduction of what is called 'potential energy,' a phrase which I can not help regarding as unfortunate, inasmuch as it goes to substitute a truism for the announcement of a dynamical fact. No such conservation, in the sense of an identity of total amount of *vis viva* at all times and in all circumstances, in fact, exists. So far as a system is maintained by the mutual actions and reactions of its constituent elements *at a distance* (*i. e.*, by force), *vis viva* may temporarily disappear, and be subsequently reproduced between certain limits. Collision, indeed, between its ultimate particles or atoms, regarded as absolutely rigid, and therefore inelastic (*for that which can not change its figure can have no resilience*), can not take place without producing

[1] Professor Charles Brooke, in *Nature*, vol. vi. p. 125.

a permanent destruction of it, which there exists no means of repairing. . . . If, indeed, we could be assured *à priori* that the system [of the universe] is one of simple or compound periodicity, in which a certain lapse of time will restore every molecule to identically the same relative situation with respect to all the rest, we should then be sure that in the nature of things there would take place, so to speak, a winding up from a lower to a higher state of potential energy, to be subsequently exchanged for newly created *vis viva*. But, as we can have no such *à priori* assurance, can only assume such restoration to be possible, and can see no means of effecting it, if possible, otherwise than by foresight and prearrangement; the one equally with the other is an unknown function, variable within unknown limits, and susceptible of fluctuation to an unknown extent; nor can we have any, the smallest, right to assert that what is expended in one form *is* necessarily laid up for further use in the other. It would be very difficult, I apprehend, to show whether, in the winding up of a clock or the building of a pyramid, taking into consideration all the various modes in which *vis viva* disappears and reappears in the expenditure of muscular power, the evolution of animal heat, the consumption of the materials of our tissues, the propagation of vibratory motions, and a thousand other modes of transfer, the total *vis viva* of this our planet is increased or diminished. That it should remain absolutely unchanged during the process is in the last degree inconceivable. The amount of *vis viva* latent in the form of heat or molecular motion in the sun and planets in our immediate system may bear, and probably does bear, a by no means inappreciable ratio to that more distinctly patent in the form of bodily motion in the periodic circulation of the planets round the sun, and the sun and planets round their axes. The latter amount fluctuates to and fro according to laws easily calculable, *but the former we have no means whatever of computing, and to what extent, or within what limits, it may be variable, we are altogether ignorant.*"[1]

The two dynamical laws of Conservation of Energy and Transformation of Energy can not therefore be regarded as universal and absolute laws; they are particular and derivative laws subject to limitations which are supplied by the third dynamical law—the Dissipation of Energy. The law of the conservation of energy simply asserts "that the whole amount of energy in the universe, or in any limited system which does not receive energy from without, or part with it to external matter, is invariable;" in other words, that every material system subject to no other forces than actions and reactions between its parts is a dynamically conservative system. But Sir William Thomson has shown that "in nature this hypothetical condition is apparently violated in all circumstances of motion. A material system can never be brought through any returning cycle of motion without spending more work against the mutual forces of its parts than is gained from these forces, because no relative motion can take place without meeting with frictional or other forms of resistance."[2] "There can be but one ultimate result for such a system as that of the sun and planets, if continuing long enough under existing laws, and not disturbed by meeting with other moving masses in space. That result is the falling together of all into one mass, which, although rotating for a time, *must in the end come to rest relatively to the surrounding medium.*"[3]

[1] "Familiar Lectures on Scientific Subjects," pp. 469–472.

[2] "Natural Philosophy," vol. i. pp. 190, 191.

[3] Ibid. p. 194.

The law of the transformation of energy is "the enunciation of the empirical fact that in general any one form of energy may by suitable processes be transformed, wholly or in part, to an equivalent amount in any other given form." This law, however, is subject to limitations which are supplied by the dissipation of energy. "No known natural process is exactly reversible, and whenever an attempt is made to transform and retransform energy by an imperfect process, part of the energy is necessarily transformed into heat and *dissipated*, so as to be incapable of further useful transformation. It therefore follows that, as energy is constantly in a state of transformation, there is a constant *degradation* of energy to the final unavailable form of uniformly diffused heat, and that will go on until the whole energy of the universe has taken this final form."[1] No mechanical work can be done by heat in a state of equilibrium; as a dynamical agent it is *dead*. "Thus the inexorable laws of mechanics indicate that the store of force in our planetary system, which can only suffer loss and not gain, must be finally exhausted."[2]

So far, then, as the conservation of energy has any scientific meaning, it is inadequate to account for the origin or explain the continuance of the existing order of nature. It is true we may conceive that every atom of matter was endowed at the Creation with a certain store of potential energy—"the potential energy of gravitation"[3]—which it has ever since given out; but as every motion which has resulted from its action has been attended with the expenditure of a certain amount of the original endowment, it must have been continually undergoing

[1] *North British Review*, vol. xl. pp. 182, 183.

[2] Helmholtz, "Correlation and Conservation of Forces," p. 245.

[3] This is the hypothesis of Helmholtz, Mayer, and Thomson.

a diminution. There is, says Professor Norton, no escaping this conclusion but by taking the ground that *the primary atomic forces* (as gravitation, and the atomic repulsion and attraction by which atoms are aggregated into bodies of sensible magnitude) are correlated with the *living forces* (or various forms of energy) which are involved in the motions that have resulted from the previous operation of the primary atomic forces. "But," he says, "*no evidence has been obtained of any such correlation.*" The primary force of attraction (if it be regarded as a primary force) may be the cause of motion in bodies which are separated in space, and part of that energy of motion may be transformed into the energy of heat or light or electricity, but the primary force of attraction is not transformed. Energy is convertible into other forms of energy, but heat, light, and electricity are not transformable into primary force. The correlation of force and energy is therefore a scientific heresy.[1]

Modern physicists are agreed that visible motion, heat, electricity, magnetism, and radiance (radiant light and heat) are forms of actual *energy* which are correlated and capable of mutual conversion. Any one form may, by suitable processes, be transformed, wholly or in part, to an equivalent amount of any other form of energy. So much is generally accepted by scientific men.

But in regard to the primary *force* or forces in which these forms of energy have their origin, there is not the same agreement among physicists. Some regard gravitation, cohesion, and chemical affinity as the three primary forces of nature; while others suggest that the last two are related with and probably derived from the first.

[1] Tyndall, "Fragments of Science," p. 31; Murphy, "Habit and Intelligence," vol. i. p. 23.

There is also a respectable school of physicists who teach that atomic attractions and repulsions are the universal cosmic forces which originate all molecular and mechanical motions. Then, again, each of these forms of force have their special advocates. On the one side it is affirmed, as an important generalization, that all primary force is *attractive;* "there is no such thing in nature as a primary repulsive force."[1] Universal attraction is the one world-forming and world-conserving energy. On the other side it is contended that gravitation is not a primary, but a secondary and derivative force, and that the grand primal force is a universal force of *repulsion*.[2]

It is beyond our province to discuss the merits of these conflicting theories. Our position is that no purely physical hypothesis is adequate to account for the conservation of the universe, and therefore it is of little consequence to our argument which of the above theories may find most favor with scientific men. The tendency of modern scientific thought is toward the conception of "one primordial form of matter, and but one primary form of force," as the simplest basis upon which a physical theory of inanimate nature can be erected. The ultimate nature of this one primary force is a question for pure metaphysics. From the stand-point of physical science it can only be thought "as a *pull* or a *push* in a straight line."[3] Universal attraction or universal repulsion must be the ultimate dynamical conception for the pure physicist.

1. Let us consider the first hypothesis. It is claimed that gravitation, or universal attraction, is the great con-

[1] Murphy, "Habit and Intelligence," vol. i. p. 43.

[2] Professor Norton, "On Molecular Physics;" *American Journal of Science and Arts*, vol. iii. 3d Series, pp. 329–331.

[3] Tyndall, "Fragments of Science," p. 76.

serving and sustaining principle of the universe. A stone falls to the earth, a round body rolls along a plane inclined toward the horizon; a liquid mass, as a brook or a large river, flows on the sloping surface which forms its bed. All these phenomena are the varied manifestation of a universal *tendency* in all bodies to fall one toward the other. In virtue of this tendency the great orbs which hang suspended in space gravitate toward one another; the moon and the earth fall toward each other, and they both gravitate toward the sun. All the planets of our solar system continually act one on the other, and on the immense sphere which shines at their common focus. By its enormous mass, the sun keeps all of them in their orbits. If we ask why one body *falls* toward another which is more than ninety millions of miles off, in preference to moving in any other direction, the answer given is that, "Every particle of matter in the universe *attracts* every other particle with a force whose direction is that of the line joining the two, and whose magnitude is directly as the product of their masses, and inversely as the square of their distance from each other." This force of attraction is the universal bond which holds the universe together, and sustains its physical life.

To the superficial thinker, the language of the Newtonian philosophy appears to sanction the materialistic notion that gravitation and attraction are active powers essential to and inherent in matter. Such, however, was by no means the doctrine of Newton, and he was careful to guard his readers against any such misapprehension of his meaning. "The words attraction, repulsion, or tendencies of whatever kind toward a centre, I use indifferently and without distinction for each other, considering these forces not physically but metaphysically. Wherefore let not the reader suppose that by words of this kind I any where mean a species or mode of action, or cause, or physical reason; or that I really and in a physical sense assign forces to centres (which are only mathematical points), even though I may say that centres *attract*, or that *forces belong to centres*."[1]

The history of scientific opinion on the point before us furnishes a striking illustration of the manner in which language reacts on the ideas which it is intended to express, and thus men fall into the habit of talking nonsense without knowing it. The conception of atoms having the property of exerting various forces across a void space seemed to follow as a matter of course from the discovery of the law of gravitation, and from the language in which it is expressed. After Newton a school arose which taught that atoms have the property of *exerting force at a distance*, and that this property must be inherent in the atoms, just as Lucretius taught that hardness and elasticity were original indefeasible properties of the primordial elements, the "semina rerum," or seeds of things. But Newton did not teach this; he stated a fact, but did not devise an hypothesis; he attempted no explanation of the law of gravitation.

"The law of gravitation considered as a *result* is beautifully simple; in a few words it expresses a fact from which most numerous and complex results may be deduced by mere reasoning—results found invariably to agree with the records of observation; but this same law of gravitation looked upon as an axiom or first principle is so astonishingly far removed from all ordinary experience as to be almost incredible. What! every particle in the whole universe is actively attracting *every other particle*

[1] "Principia," Def. viii. p. 8.

[that is, every particle in the universe with the same force, without any expenditure of force], through void, without the aid of any communication by means of matter, or otherwise—each particle, unchecked by distance, unimpeded by obstacles, throws this miraculous influence to infinite distance without the employment of any means![1] No particle interferes with its neighbor, but all these wonderful influences are co-existent in every point in space! The result is apparent at each particle, but the condition of intermediate space is exactly the same as though no such influence were being transmitted across it! Earth attracts Sirius across space, and yet the space between is as if neither Earth nor Sirius existed! Can these things be? We think not; and Newton himself did not affirm this."[2] On the contrary, he earnestly rejects any such hypothesis. "It is inconceivable that inanimate brute matter should, without the mediation of something else *which is not material*, operate upon and affect other matter without mutual contact, as it must do if gravitation, in the sense of Epicurus, be essential to and inherent in matter. . . . That gravitation should be innate, inherent, and essential to matter, so that one body may act upon another at a distance, through a vacuum, without the mediation of any thing else, by and through which their action and force may be conveyed from one to another, is to me so great an absurdity that I believe no man who has in philosophical matters a competent faculty of thinking can ever fall into it. *Gravity must be caused by an agent acting constantly according to certain laws.*"[3]

[1] "Does every grain of salt and pepper in a million salt-cellars and pepper-casters individually and separately pull and actually move the sun and fixed stars?"—De Morgan.

[2] *North British Review*, vol. xlviii. March, 1868, p. 125.

[3] Third Letter to Bentley.

The ancient axiom that "Matter can not act where it is not any more than when it is not," was universally believed till Newton's time, and Newton himself regarded it as a self-evident truth. Some of his disciples asserted that gravitation must be considered as an essential property of matter, and they were under the necessity of assuming that atoms can exert a force upon one another across a void. This to Leibnitz was either miraculous or absurd; and in modern times the doctrine is rejected by the first physicists — by Faraday, Helmholtz, Thomson, Tait, and Maxwell.[1] Sir William Thomson, the Newton of modern physics, says emphatically, "I have no faith whatever in attractions and repulsions *acting at a distance* between centres of force according to various laws."[2] And Clerk Maxwell, in his lecture on "Action at a Distance,"[3] explains how Faraday, by his discovery of magnetic rotation of polarized light, and by his showing how lines of force arise in media, "rudely shook the theory of attraction and repulsion at a distance across a void."

If, now, "direct action at a distance" is rejected by scientific men as inconceivable and absurd, how can it be that the sun *pulls* the earth toward it, and holds the planets in their orbits? The verbal statement of the law of gravitation is no answer to this question. It expresses a fact, but it does not assign a cause. Gravitation is a phenomenon which demands an explanation, and some of the first scientists of the day are engaged in devising a theory which shall afford a rational answer to the question, What is the *cause* of gravity?[4]

[1] *Nature*, vol. iii. p. 51; vol. ii. p. 422.

[2] *Nature*, vol. i. p. 551.

[3] Delivered at the Royal Institution, and reported in *Nature*, vol. vii. Nos. 174, 175.

[4] *North British Review*, vol. xlviii. March, 1868; "Correlation and Conservation of Forces," p. 368; *Amer. Jour. of Science and Arts*, vol. xlix. p. 24.

The first and most fundamental presupposition for any physical hypothesis which seeks to explain the action of gravitation is that some *medium* of communication exists. This is suggested by every physical analogy. Sound is communicated through a medium. The influence which is exerted at a distance by heat, light, electricity, and magnetism is effected through media. The most plausible suggestion yet made is that "a single omnipresent fluid, *ether*, fills the universe," which by various forms or modes of motion transmits light, radiant heat, magnetism, and electricity.[1] May not gravitation, it is asked, be transmitted by the *same* fluid? may it not consist of or result from actual recurring impulses propagated in ethereal waves?

The hypothesis that gravitation is transmitted through the same medium as light, or indeed through any medium, is encumbered with serious if not insuperable difficulties. All transmission of whatever kind—of a letter by the post, a gunshot, a sound, a wave of light, an electro-magnetic disturbance—*occupies time.* It has a velocity—sometimes a very great one, as in the case of light; still it is a measurable velocity. But, according to Herschel, the pull which the sun exerts on the earth is delivered *instantaneously.* Were it not so there would be "a continually progressive increase of the major axis of the earth's orbit, and therefore of the length of the year."[2] Surely it must be obvious to every one that the *instantaneous* transmission of the sun's attractive force to the planet Neptune, three thousand millions of miles distant, through a physical medium like the ether, would be as great a miracle as action at a distance through a perfect void. But the advocates of this hypothesis have not thereby escaped the

[1] *North British Review*, vol. xlviii. p. 127; *Nature*, vol. vii. p. 343.
[2] "Familiar Lectures on Science," p. 90.

difficulties of action at a distance. The majority of physicists regard the luminiferous ether as consisting of "discrete particles"—"elementary molecules of inconceivable minuteness and tenuity." These ultimate particles or atoms of highly attenuated matter must have some magnitude, some extension, however inconceivably minute. If extended, they must have some form, and must occupy separate positions in space. If they are capable of motions—undulatory, rotatory, or spiral motions—they can not be in mutual contact. Conceive, then, two such atoms, and draw around each an imaginary circle. Let these circles touch at the middle point between the two, and ask yourself the question, What exists there? On the hypothesis under consideration you are bound to answer pure, empty space—that is, pure nothing. "But if there is no matter between the atoms, then all their actions, one upon the other, must be exerted across a void—that is, through a medium of nothingness;" in other words, through no medium at all. Now the size of the interval makes no difference in the argument. "Whether that interval be the 92-billionth of an inch, or the 92 millions of miles or thereabouts between the earth and the sun, it is still action at a distance, and no escape."[1]

The physicist who regards the ether as consisting of discrete particles not in bodily or actual contact, and at the same time finds himself logically compelled to reject this "mystical action at a distance," has no alternative but to accept the doctrine of Newton that the action of one particle of matter upon another is mediated by an agent which is not *material*. "If it be true that the conception of *force* as the originator of motion in matter without bodily contact . . . is essential to the right interpretation

[1] Picton, "Mystery of Matter," p. 49.

of phenomena; and if it be equally true, on the other hand, that its exertion makes itself manifest to our personal consciousness by that peculiar sensation of *effort* which is not without its analogue in purely intellectual acts of the mind, it [*i. e.*, force] comes not unnaturally to be regarded as affording a point of contact, a connecting link between these two great departments of being—between mind and matter—the one as the *originator*, the other as the *recipient* of force."[1]

There are distinguished physicists—as Helmholtz, Thomson, Challis, and Maxwell—who seek to escape the difficulties of action at a distance by the assumption that the ether is absolutely continuous (and therefore does not consist of atoms)—a perfectly homogeneous, incompressible, frictionless fluid which fills the universe. This fundamental presupposition as the basis of a physical theory of the universe necessitates the further assumption that "*motion is the very essence of what has been hitherto called matter*."[2] All quantitative and qualitative phenomena, all statical and dynamical phenomena, are due solely to varied modes of motion in the primordial fluid. "By various motions of the nature of eddies [ring-vortices], the qualities of matter—cohesion, elasticity, hardness, weight, mass, or other universal properties of matter—are given to small *portions* of the fluid which constitute the *chemical atom*, and these, by modifications in their combinations, form, and motion, produce the accidental phenomena of *gross matter*. . . . On this view, gross matter would be merely an assemblage of *parts* of the medium moving in a peculiar way, groups of ring-vortices having

[1] Herschel, "Familiar Lectures on Science," p. 467.

[2] Sir William Thomson, "Papers on Electrostatics and Magnetism," p. 419.

inertia. . . . The primary fluid by other motions transmits light, radiant heat, magnetism, and *gravitation*."[1]

It may be regarded as an act of presumption in an obscure critic to offer an opinion on the theories of these great masters in science. We venture, however, to suggest that most men will find a difficulty in conceiving how space absolutely full of matter can be made to contain more, or how a truly continuous substance can be capable of condensation. The most tenuous ether, if it be absolutely continuous, occupies the whole of the space in which it lies—that is, there is no point of the space which is not occupied by a point of matter.[2] But the hardest iron can do no more than this, and, therefore, on this hypothesis it seems impossible to account for its greater density. It is suggested that if molecules are mere assemblages of parts of the ether moving in a peculiar way, then greater density may be due to a modification in the motion of molecules, and not merely to the greater frequency of the eddying molecules in a given space. But how can a truly continuous substance have *parts*, and how can relative motion occur in an absolute plenum? The very notion of particles is quite inconsistent with the continuity of matter; and in a universe absolutely full no motion whatever would be possible. We are told that Sir William Thomson and Professor Tait find no difficulty in all these, to our minds, contradictory conceptions, and therefore we must conclude

[1] *North British Review*, vol. xlviii. p. 127.

[2] We do not by any means assert that two substances can not occupy the same point in space at the same moment in time. We accept the Hegelian maxim that "two substances may occupy the same point in space at the same time *provided their qualities are essentially different*." If the qualities of the ether are essentially different from gross matter, then to call ether "matter" is to confound and mislead the mind. May not ether be a "tertium quid" between matter and mind?

that our intellect is not properly "focussed so as to give definition without prenumbral haze."

Granting, then, the absolute continuity of all matter, and the possibility of motion in an absolute plenum, the question which concerns us most in this essay is, How is motion generated and sustained? One of the greatest lights of this new school tells us that "all we can affirm of matter is that it is the *recipient* of impulse and of energy."[1] They no longer regard the atom "as a mystic point endowed with inertia and the attribute of *attracting* and *repelling* other such centres with forces depending on the intervening distances."[2] They have "no faith whatever in *attractions* and *repulsions* acting at a distance between centres of force."[3] Force, then, is not regarded by these leading physicists as an inherent attribute of matter. The primary fluid, originally inert and motionless, must have been set in motion by some force, by some agency external to and distinct from itself. An "original impetus" *from without*, according to Maxwell,[4] or a "pressure" of the universal ether "from somewhere *outside* the world of stars," according to Challis,[5] must be the source of all motion and all forms of energy in the universe.

It is a fundamental principle of dynamics that "force is wholly expended in the action it produces,"[6] therefore, if all the forms of energy in the universe are the result of pressure, that pressure must be *continuous*; if they are the result of impulses, these impulses must be *incessantly renewed*, and must recur with immeasurable rapidity. On either supposition, "the universe is not even temporarily

[1] Prof. Clerk Maxwell, in *Nature*, vol. ii. p. 421.

[2] Sir William Thomson, in *Nature*, vol. iv. p. 266.

[3] Sir W. Thomson, in *Nature*, vol. i. p. 551. [4] *Nature*, vol. ii. p. 421.

[5] *Philosophical Magazine*, 1868.

[6] Thomson and Tait, "Natural Philosophy," vol. i. p. 164.

automatic, but must be fed from moment to moment by an agency external to itself," and "the preservation of the universe is effected only by the unceasing expenditure of enormous quantities of work;"[1] that is, it is ceaselessly sustained by Divine Omnipotence — "He upholdeth all things by the word of his power."

So much with respect to the first form of this hypothesis which regards atomic *attraction* as the sole world-forming and world-conserving force. We turn now to that form of the hypothesis which considers atomic *repulsion* as the grand primal force in which all the other physical forces, even gravitation itself, have their origin.

This view is presented by Professor W. A. Norton, in his articles "On Cosmical and Molecular Physics" in the *American Journal of Science and Arts.* His theory rests essentially upon the following principles:

1. The doctrine of *inertia* applied to all matter.

2. The existence of a single primary force of *repulsion* exerted by every atom upon every other atom.

3. The existence of but one primary form of *elementary matter*, viz., the universal or luminiferous ether; the atoms, so called, of ordinary matter, and of the electric ether being but different masses of condensed luminiferous ether.

4. The doctrine of the *interception of force* by matter. This is a necessary consequence of the fact that a certain portion of the propagated force is instantly expended in imparting motion to the molecules or atoms which it encounters, and is therefore abstracted from this force.

5. The primary force of repulsion is made up of *impulses recurring with an immeasurable rapidity.* This is no new hypothesis. In all treatises on Mechanics, grav-

[1] *Nature*, vol. viii. p. 280; also Challis, "Principles of Mathematics and Physics," pp. 685–687.

ity and all incessant forces are conceived to consist of an indefinitely great number of impulses taking effect in a finite interval of time.[1] "The ever-recurring pulses of the primary cosmical force, emanating from all the atoms of the one primary form of matter, are directly *consumed* in communicating opposite movements, or virtual movements, to every atom in the universe. It is, as I conceive, because in the existing condition of things the distribution of matter is unequal in different directions round a point, and therefore the partial interception of the impulses of the cosmical force along the different lines of direction is unequal, that an effective gravitating force exists.[2] The entire amount of the cosmical force consumed in any interval of time is the amount intercepted by all the atoms of matter, and is independent of the motions that result from the inequalities just noticed. Gravitation, and molecular and chemical attractions, which originate in the gravitation of electric ether toward atoms of ordinary matter, are then *derivative* forces incidental to the direct actions exerted by the cosmical force upon the atoms."[3]

In a communication from Professor Norton to the author, he furnishes the following further exposition of his theory: "If, as I conceive, the primary atomic force is of the nature of a perpetual emanation from each atom, and is expended in the act of producing motion, we must thence infer that the atom is an entity through which a stream of force is *perpetually flowing from the Infinite Source of all power and all existence.* That the primary force is a force of repulsion, and that the immediate source

[1] *American Journal of Science and Arts*, vol. xlix. pp. 32, 33.

[2] How gravitation may result from the interception of the Cosmic Force of Repulsion is explained by Prof. Norton at pp. 26–28, and still more fully in vol. iii. 3d Series, May, 1872, pp. 332, 336.

[3] *American Journal of Science and Arts*, vol. xlix. p. 34.

of all the forces that are known to take effect upon ordinary matter is the action of recurring repulsive impulses upon the atoms of the universal ether, and their subsequent propagation and partial interception by the atoms which they encounter, I infer from the fact that this conception furnishes a rational explanation of all the known forces and phenomena of inanimate nature."

It will thus be seen that the theory of Professor Norton gives no countenance to the materialistic tendencies of the physical science of the age. He is decidedly of the opinion that "force is *not* an inherent and essential attribute of matter," and he "devoutly acknowledges that in following the chain of cause and effect into the precincts of that most deeply hidden of all mysteries, the origin of force, *we have come into the presence of the Infinite Spirit who puts forth unceasingly, from every point in the realms of space, his creative and sustaining power upon the subtile matter that fills all space, and is the essential substance of all worlds.*"[1]

3. The third hypothesis is that of a *plastic nature*, intermediate between God and the material universe, by which all the phenomena of visible nature are produced.

This hypothesis was first presented (at least in modern times) by Ralph Cudworth, in his "True Intellectual System of the Universe."[2] In opposition to Democritus, who explained all phenomena by means of matter and motion; and also in opposition to Strato, who taught that matter is the only substance, but at the same time a living and active force, Cudworth maintains that there is a *plastic nature*—a vital and spiritual, but unconscious energy, dis-

[1] *American Journal of Science and Arts*, vol. xlix. p. 33.
[2] See vol. i. pp. 217–284.

tinct from and created by the Deity, which "doth drudgingly execute that part of his providence which consisteth in the regular and orderly motion of matter,"[1] and in the organization and development of plants and animals, "according to laws prescribed for it by a perfect intellect, and impressed upon it."[2] This *plastic nature* is an "inferior kind of life or soul," destitute of all consciousness,[3] which, though it "acts for the sake of ends," does "not know the reason of what it does," and therefore operates "fatally and sympathetically."[4]

The arguments urged by Cudworth in support of this hypothesis are mainly of a negative character. On the one hand he endeavors to show that force and vitality are not essential attributes of matter, and on the other hand that the motion and life of the universe can not be properly regarded as the direct action of the Deity upon matter. It is with this latter part of the argument that we are here immediately concerned. He urges (1) that if every thing in nature were done immediately by God, it would render Divine Providence "operose, solicitous, and distractious;" and, furthermore, it would be unbecoming the Divine Majesty, and "indecorous," for God "immediately to do all the meanest and triflingest things Himself drudgingly." He maintains (2) that if God do all things immediately, then he does them "*miraculously*"—that is, "forcibly and violently." And (3) that the immediate agency of God is inconsistent with that slow and gradual development of things we see in nature, which would seem to be a "trifling formality" if the agent were omnipotent, and especially inconsistent with "those errors and bunglings which are committed when the matter is

[1] "Intellectual System of the Universe," vol. i. p. 224.
[2] Ibid. p. 271.
[3] Ibid. p. 244.
[4] Ibid. p. 271.

inept and contumacious." "Wherefore it may be concluded that there is a plastic nature under God which, as an inferior agent, doth drudgingly execute that part of his providence which consists in the regular and orderly motion of matter, yet so that there is also a higher providence, which, *presiding* over it, doth often supply the defects of it, and sometimes *overrule* it; forasmuch as the plastic nature can not act electively nor with discretion." So that, after all, as Plato says, God "is the beginning and end and middle of all things," and therefore their being is "*as much to be ascribed to his causality as if Himself had done all things immediately* without the concurrent instrumentality of any subordinate natural cause."[1]

There is nothing original in this hypothesis of a plastic nature except perhaps the name. It is the old *anima mundi* of the Platonic physics, a vital soul of the world, distinct from but created by the Supreme God. It has reappeared under various names in the history of natural science, especially in that department which is now comprehended under the general name of Biology. The "*motus tonico-vitalis*" of Stahl, the "animating principle" of Harvey, the "*materia vitæ*" of John Hunter, the "organic force" of Müller, and the "organic agent" of Dr. Prout, are all but separate names "for an imaginary principle, or entity, possessing powers and properties which (however men may try to impress themselves with a contrary notion) would entitle it to rank as an intelligent agent. It is true that, according to most of the advocates of this doctrine, this power is supposed to be superintended and controlled by the Deity himself, and by this supposition they have screened themselves against the accu-

[1] "Intellectual System of the Universe," vol. i. pp. 223–4.

sation of attributing to a creature the powers of the Creator."[1]

Cudworth's hypothesis of a plastic nature has been recently reproduced, without the slightest recognition of its paternity, by Joseph John Murphy, under the name of "*unconscious intelligence*"—"a power transcending the ordinary properties of matter and adapting means to purposes, presiding over all vital actions, whether formative, motor, or mental, directing each action to its specific end."[2] Mr. Murphy is very solicitous that we should not understand him to teach that "the formative intelligence" which in nature adapts structure to function is Divine. "I believe," he says, "that the Creator has not separately organized every structure, but has endowed vitalized matter with intelligence, under the guidance of which it organizes itself."[3] This "unconscious intelligence," which builds the tissues and fashions the organs of plants and animals, becomes conscious of itself in the deliberate thought of man.[4]

It is worthy of note that this hypothesis commends itself to the mind of Murphy by considerations akin to those which are urged by Cudworth; and especially because it is supposed to relieve certain moral difficulties connected with the belief of a Divine purpose in creation—as, for example, the existence of parasitic worms which inflict pain and disease on beings endowed with sensation and consciousness, and the presence of "immoral instincts" in higher forms of animal life.[5]

We readily grant that the relation of God to the existing order and economy of the world is mysterious; and we believe that no conceivable hypothesis can deprive it

[1] Todd, Bowman, and Beale, "Physiological Anatomy and Physiology of Man," p. 25.

[2] "Habit and Intelligence," vol. ii. p. 5.

[3] Ibid. p. 8.

[4] Ibid. p. 5.

[5] Ibid. pp. 6, 7.

of this mysteriousness. There are numerous difficulties which arise from the imperfection of our knowledge and the limited range of our powers. We see through an obscure medium, and we know only in part. There are also difficulties peculiar to individual minds—intellectual, ethical, emotional difficulties—which are the products of a peculiar culture, or the offspring of certain theoretical prepossessions. Some of these difficulties may be relieved by the hypothesis of "unconscious intelligence," but on a further examination it will be found that this hypothesis is embarrassed with still greater difficulties and open to more serious objections both intellectual and moral.

First, there is the difficulty of forming any conception of "*unconscious* intelligence." This has been felt by the ablest minds. "The hypothesis," says Wallace, "has the double disadvantage of being both unintelligible and incapable of any kind of proof."[1] Mivart observes that the phrase will "to many minds appear to be little less than a contradiction in terms; the very first condition of an intelligence being that, if it know any thing, it should at least know its own existence."[2] Mr. Murphy tells us that this unconscious intelligence "adapts means to ends," "it presides over all vital actions, directing each action to its specific end."[3] But an intelligence adapting means to ends without any knowledge (consciousness) of either the ends to be secured or the means to be employed to secure the end surpasses all comprehension and all belief. We can readily believe, with Hamilton, that the human mind "exerts energies and is the subject of modifications" of which it is not immediately conscious, the combined results of which are manifested in the complex fact of consciousness. But

[1] "On Natural Selection," p. 360. [2] "Genesis of Species," p. 294.
[3] "Habit and Intelligence," vol. ii. p. 5.

to call that *intelligence* which never had a perception, a thought, an emotion; which has no knowledge of self or of any thing else; in short, which is not and never was conscious, is to reduce philosophic terminology to chaos, and tantalize thought by meaningless words. An intelligent agent is one who *understands*, who distinguishes between subject and object, who knows things in their relations, who can unite the terms of a relation in thought, and judge of their congruity or incongruity, all of which are conscious operations. Intelligence is consciousness (conscientia = relational knowledge); unconscious intelligence is unconscious consciousness, unintelligent intelligence, which is a contradiction and an absurdity.

Secondly, in endeavoring to find the mental stand-point of Mr. Murphy, in order that we may fairly estimate his hypothesis, we encounter the still more serious difficulty of conceiving how unconscious intelligence can exist apart from some *subject* or substratum in which it inheres.

We are aware that "the tendency of modern thought" is to hypostatize force and intelligence, and conceive them as entities. We have conscientiously made the attempt again and again to realize this conception, but we must confess we can only conceive of force and intelligence as properties or attributes of some subject. It is beyond our ability, and we imagine it is beyond the ability of Mr. Murphy, to conceive of force without something that exerts force, of intelligence without a being who is intelligent. Indeed, Mr. Murphy concedes that "where there are properties there must be a *substance*,"[1] and by substance, he says, he understands "*underlying reality*."[2] Unconscious intelligence, if there be such a thing, must be

[1] "Habit and Intelligence," vol. ii. p. 160.
[2] "Scientific Basis of Faith," p. 43.

an attribute or quality inherent in some underlying substance. But Mr. Murphy asserts "there is no scientific basis for the old belief in a distinct *mental substance*"[1] —that is, if we understand him aright, so far as finite mind is concerned. On the other hand, he distinctly affirms that this unconscious intelligence is not Divine intelligence. The power and intelligence which work in the world of matter and mind "are not the Divine power and intelligence."[2] Unconscious intelligence, then, must be an "endowment of vitalized matter;"[3] and life has its origin in no secondary cause, but in the direct action of creative power."[4] Now the question arises, What is matter? On this point we must be careful not to misunderstand or misrepresent Mr. Murphy. "Matter, whether viewed from a metaphysical or from an inductive point of view, is known only as a function of force, and can be described only in terms of force. In other words, *the universe is nothing but a manifestation of force.*" And now we ask, Of what force? "Force," says Mr. Murphy, "is known to us by immediate consciousness as a function of our own mind and will; that is to say, the mind, acting in will, is conscious of itself as a force—and we are able to conceive of force in no other way; the only conception of force which we are able to frame is that of voluntary force, or the exertion of will. *Either the force manifested in the universe is the force of a Creative Will, or we are able to form no conception of it whatever.*"[5] Can there be any possibility of misunderstanding this language? Matter itself is not an entity, not a *substance;* it is a phenomenon, not a reality. Matter is "a function

[1] "Scientific Basis of Faith," p. 14.
[2] "Habit and Intelligence," vol. ii. pp. 4, 7.
[3] Ibid. p. 8.
[4] Ibid. vol. i. p. 89.
[5] "Scientific Basis of Faith," pp. 351, 352.

of force." Force is a "fact of mind, and therefore spiritual." Consequently "matter can only be conceived as *spiritual*."[1] And now let us recall the statement of Mr. Murphy that there is no finite, created, underlying reality for the phenomena of mind and will—"*no distinct mental substance*." If we hold to this doctrine, then we must say with Mr. Murphy again that "the powers of matter and mind alike are the result and expression of a Living Will —and if a Living Will, then also an Intelligent Will."[2] The final and only conclusion is that God, "the Self-existent Being," is the one only underlying reality or *substance* in the universe; all the force in the universe is "the force of the Creative Will," and all the intelligence in the universe a modification of the Divine Thought.

This, however, is Pantheism, even according to that very defective definition of Pantheism given by Mr. Murphy: "Pantheism is the identification of the Divine power and intelligence with the powers and intelligences that work in the world of matter and mind."[3] Still, Mr. Murphy declares, "I am not a Pantheist;" and we are bound to accept his disclaimer—"the power and intelligence which work in nature are not identical with the Divine power and intelligence." Be it so; then there is power, and there is intelligence in nature, which are not attributes of any reality, and which do not inhere in any substance; and we come round to the original difficulty of conceiving of an attribute apart from a subject.

[1] "Scientific Basis of Faith," pp. 46, 47. [2] Ibid. pp. 51, 52.

[3] "Habit and Intelligence," vol. ii. p. 7. "Pantheism asserts the absolute UNITY and permanence of SUBSTANCE with its two attributes of *matter* and *force* (= extension and thought), and their innumerable modifications which go to form all the phenomena of the universe."—Dr. Cohn. Under this definition, Mr. Murphy must be ranked a Pantheist. He knows but of ONE SUBSTANCE underlying all phenomena.

The reader can not have failed to see that Mr. Murphy has been leading us round a vicious circle. "Force is a function of matter, and matter is a function of force."[1] "Matter is only explicable as a function of force, force only explicable as a function of conscious mind,"[2] and mind is "one of the functions of matter."[3] "It is perfectly certain," says Mr. Murphy, "that inductive psychology gives no hint of any mental *substance* as distinguished from the material substance of the brain."[4] But the material substance of the brain after all is not material; "matter can only be conceived as *spiritual*"[5]—that is, as *force*. There is no underlying reality which men call "matter," and there is no underlying reality which men call "spirit." Matter is spirit, spirit is matter; but in reality neither the one nor the other has any substantial reality. If all finite existences are but modes of the Infinite Being, we have a consistent Pantheism at any rate. But if all finite existences are simply phenomena without any underlying reality, then "perception is a dream, and my existence the dream of that dream."

Thirdly, the hypothesis of an "*unconscious intelligence*," distinct from the Supreme Intelligence, which does "the drudgery of Providence," and to which the defects and disorders and "immoralities" of nature are ascribed, is neither adequate nor satisfactory.

The conceit of Cudworth that it is unbecoming the Divine Majesty to be immediately concerned in every thing that takes place in nature is scarcely worthy of consideration: "If it were not congruous in respect of the state and majesty of Xerxes, the king of Persia, that he should condescend to do all the meanest offices himself,

[1] "Scientific Basis of Faith," p. 29.
[2] Ibid. p. 14.
[3] Ibid. p. 36.
[4] Ibid. p. 35.
[5] Ibid. p. 47.

much less can this be thought decorous in respect of God."[1]

Human conceptions of what is great or small, dignified or indecorous, are merely relative conceptions which vary with our knowledge, culture, and taste; but—

> "There is no great and no small
> To the soul that maketh all."—*Emerson.*

For the Creator of all things an atom is an ample field in which to display the resources of his omnipotence. The more the microscope and spectroscope reveal of the "infinitely little," the more do we see of the greatness and glory of God. So of men's conceptions of what is dignified or indecorous; it may be that, in a land and an age where labor is held in contempt, it becomes the state of an Eastern monarch that he should live in voluptuous ease, but the followers of Him who said, "My Father worketh hitherto, and I work," have learned to believe in the dignity of labor, and to regard all true work as divine. An imperfect human ruler can not do every thing, therefore he must employ agents and ministers; the Omnipotent Ruler of the universe can do all things, and needs no subordinate ministry. A finite mind can not know every thing, and often staggers beneath the burden of its limited acquisitions; the Infinite Mind *must* know all things, and can not be perplexed amid the boundless profusion of its own creations. It is only a childish impotence or a barbaric vanity which sees the need of supplementary agencies to add to the splendor and efficiency of the Divine government of the world. "Are not two sparrows sold for a farthing? and one of them shall not fall on the ground without your Father." "The very hairs of your head are all numbered." Such views exalt rather than diminish

[1] "Intellectual System of the Universe," vol. i. p. 223.

our reverence for the majesty of God. But there is neither congruity nor dignity in the hypothesis that God has associated with Himself an agent which is "*unconscious*," whose action He must direct,[1] and whose "shortcomings and defects" He must supply.[2] Dr. Mosheim, the annotator of Cudworth's "Intellectual System," pertinently remarks: "That master has enough to do who must continually take care that the servants he employs, unskillful and devoid of reason, do not err; who must preside over the actions of his agents, and continually remedy the defects and mischiefs they occasion. . . . That master is the happier man who possesses the power of conducting his own affairs, who can do all things himself, and needs no servants whatever." But if subordinate agents are needed, or if it please the Supreme Being to employ them, the presumption is certainly in favor of rational conscious agents, rather than blind unconscious forces which can neither conceive a purpose nor adapt means to secure it. If we must have formative agents, we prefer the "junior divinities" of Plato or the "higher intelligences" of Mr. Wallace.[3]

But even admitting there are "defects, deformities, and superfluities" in nature, we are at a loss to conceive how the hypothesis of an "unconscious intelligence," working necessarily, removes the blame (if there be any blame) from the Author of nature. Does not every theist believe that the Creator of matter "saw and knew every purpose which every particle and atom of matter should subserve in all suns and systems, and through all coming æons of time?" Must not that Intelligent Will, which is the fount-

[1] "Scientific Basis of Faith," p. 52.
[2] "Intellectual System," vol. i. p. 224.
[3] "On Natural Selection," p. 372.

ain-head of all the force that sweeps like a tide of life through the universe, have known every form of energy which could result therefrom, and foreseen all the possible effects which would arise from the composition of any and all systems of forces? Did not He who created this supposed "organizing force," who ordained all its laws, and who directs and controls all its actions, know with mathematical precision every consequence which could possibly arise from its prearranged and necessitated adaptations? If God is the creator of this unconscious, necessitated "plastic nature," if He always observes what it does, if He directs and overrules it, if He supplies some of its defects and corrects most of its mistakes, must not He be regarded as the real cause of all things which, in popular language, are said to be done by nature? If we believe with Mr. Murphy that

> "Nature is but the name for an effect
> Whose cause is God,"

we shall find no relief from the difficulties and mysteries of Divine providence by interposing between the first creative volition and the last phenomenal result a series of secondary causes which are themselves only effects of the primal creative act. It were better far to leave the mystery untouched, and take refuge in faith; better to confess the difficulties are insoluble, and

> "Still trust that God is love indeed,
> And love Creation's final law;
> Though nature, red in tooth and claw
> With ravin, shrieks against our creed."

We are brought finally to the question whether, in reality, there is any thing defective or any thing superfluous in the normal products of organic nature? or, in other words, whether the Author of nature has made any thing inadequate to its purpose, or which fulfills no purpose whatever? We venture to suggest that inductive science is not in possession either of the facts or the principles which are necessary to a correct judgment. To be competent to deal with this question, science should not only know all the purposes which may be fulfilled by a single organism, but also the ultimate purpose which is subserved by the wondrous play of all the means and relative ends which constitute the entire cosmos. Far be it from us to depreciate the achievements or dare to set limits to the possibilities of inductive science. But, assuredly, the most enthusiastic scientist will admit that, compared with the vastness and complexity of natural phenomena, human knowledge is exceedingly limited and very imperfect. As to the final purpose of creation—the ultimate end of the Creator in the existence of the universe—modern science does not even claim to have an opinion.[1] With no knowledge of the ultimate purpose of creation, with a limited acquaintance with the general plan of the universe, with an imperfect knowledge of the reasons and ends of individual existences, it seems little less than impertinence for science to sit in judgment on the works of God, and unceremoniously condemn this as defective and that as unnecessary. As Baden Powell observes, "How can we undertake to affirm, amid all the possibilities of things of which we confessedly know so little, that a thousand ends and purposes may not be answered, because we can trace none, or even imagine none, which seem to our short-sighted faculties to be answered."[2] In view of the fact that hitherto the belief in "purpose" or "final cause" has been the guiding light of science, and the further fact that sci-

[1] Tyndall, "Fragments of Science," p. 104.
[2] "Unity of Worlds," p. 230.

ence is every day making new discoveries as to the utility of existences and organs of which before we were ignorant, scientific men might learn a profitable lesson, and manifest less "audacity."[1] Meantime we shall be content with the assurances of Scripture that "the works of God are *perfect*," and that "He hath made nothing *in vain*."

We may now gather up the several threads of thought which run through this essay, and state our final conclusions:

1. Matter is the merely passive or statical condition for the action of force.[2] The most fundamental condition or characteristic of matter, "perhaps its only true indication, is *inertia*."[3] "All that we can affirm of it is that it is the *recipient* of impulse and of Energy."[4] All the attempts which have been made to reduce matter to a function or phenomenon of force have ended in failure. Motion necessarily implies a *something* which is moved by the action of force. Even that most wonderful and subtile of all "modes of motion"—light—necessarily implies an entity which is moved. "The magnetic rotation of the plane of polarized light, discovered by Faraday, implies an *actual* rotatory motion of something." "The seeing intellect," says Mr. Tyndall, "when properly focused, must realize this conception at last." Matter must consist of ultimate continuous atoms or molecules possessing inertia and capable of being moved in space. By virtue of its extension and inertia it

[1] Tyndall.

[2] By the statical properties of matter we understand extension, limit, position, impenetrability, and *inertia*. We have no idea that there is a *vis inertiæ* in matter. Vis inertiæ is a *forceless force*, which is an absurdity. Inertness in matter is not a force, but the opposite of a force—a passivity which requires a force in order to change.

[3] Faraday, "Correlation and Conservation of Forces," p. 368.

[4] Clerk Maxwell, in *Nature*, vol. ii. p. 421; Herschel, "Familiar Lectures on Science," p. 467.

can intercept force, transform force into energy, and transmit energy. The various forms of energy (heat, light, electricity, magnetism, etc.) are transformations of force resulting directly or indirectly from the interception of force by inert matter, and "all the phenomena of material nature result from the action of force *upon* matter."[1] "Matter," says M. Claude Bernard, "does not generate the phenomena which it manifests. It is only the substratum, and does absolutely nothing but give to phenomena the conditions of its manifestation."[2]

2. Force is that which originates or tends to originate motion, or changes or tends to change the state of a body with regard to motion. It is not and can not be a property of matter. The doctrine that force is an attribute of matter is disproved by the fact of inertia. Inert matter can have no spontaneous power—it can not change its own state of motion or rest. Neither is motion capable *per se* of producing motion. It is a fundamental axiom of natural philosophy that motion can not be generated by motion itself, any more than by the negation of motion. Inertness and exertion, passivity and activity, are contradictory attributes, and can not be affirmed of the same subject. To say that matter is inert, and at the same time that it can exert force, is to violate the law of non-contradiction to the uttermost.

Force is an attribute of mind or spirit, and of mind or spirit alone. Spirit-force is the only force in the universe. It is a doctrine as old as the hills that mind is the first cause of motion. Νοῦς μὲν ἀρχὴν κινησέως.[3] It is a doc-

[1] Professor Norton, in the *American Journal of Science and Arts*, July, 1864, p. 64; Herschel, "Familiar Lectures on Science," p. 467; Dr. Carpenter, "Human Physiology," p. 542.

[2] *Revue des Deux Mondes*, 1867.

[3] Anaxagoras.

trine toward which all modern science tends with remarkable unanimity that all motion is the product of mind; and, though continued and transformed and transmitted through various means, it never commences except in a volition either of the Supreme Mind or of a created mind. "The deep-seated instincts of humanity and the profoundest researches of philosophy alike point to *Mind as the one and only source of power*."[1] "The conception of force as the originator of motion in matter, without bodily contact or the intervention of any intermedium, is essential to the right interpretation of physical phenomena; . . . its exertion makes itself manifest to our personal consciousness by the peculiar sensation of *effort;* . . . and it [force] affords a point of contact, a connecting link between the two great departments of being—between mind and matter—the one as its *originator*, the other as its *recipient*.[2]

3. All the forms of energy manifested in the universe are only transformations of the one omnipresent force issuing from the one fountain-head of power—*the Divine Will*. The final disclosure of modern science is the convertibility and homogeneity of all forms of physical energy —"a dynamical self-identification masked by transmigration." Of this wonderful transformation of energy many striking illustrations may be given; we select the following from the "Lecture Notes" of Dr. A. F. Mayer (p. 64): "The heat developed by the 'falling force' of a weight striking the terminals of a compound thermal battery (formed by pieces of iron and German-silver wire twisted together at alternate ends) caused a current of electricity through the wire which, being conducted through a helix, magnetized a needle (which then attracted iron particles),

[1] Dr. Carpenter, in *Nature*, vol. vi. p. 312.

[2] Herschel, "Familiar Lectures on Science," p. 467.

caused light to appear in a portion of the circuit formed of Wollaston's fine wire, decomposed iodide of potassium, and finally moved the needles of a galvanometer."[1] Here we have visible kinetic energy transformed into sensible heat, then absorbed heat converted into electricity, then electricity transformed into magnetism, also into light, and still further into the energy of chemical separation, while some portion of it returns to the form of visible energy of motion. Of course, some of the energy is dissipated in the form of radiance (radiant light and heat), but no energy is either created or destroyed. All the various forms of energy are thus reducible to *unity;* they are one force transformed by mechanical arrangements. "Electricity and magnetism, heat and light, muscular energy and chemical action, motion and mechanical work, are only different forms of one and the same power. . . . Moreover, chemical union of the elements of matter, the attraction of gravitation in all the bodies of the universe, are but varied forms of this universal motive force."[2] If it be asked, What is that one form of force which is to be taken as the type of all the rest? the explicit answer of the first scientists of the age is, "Force must be regarded as the direct expression of that mental state which we call *Will.* All force is of one type, and that type is mind."[3] This is conceded even by Herbert Spencer: "The force by which we ourselves produce changes, and which serves to symbolize the cause of changes in general, is the final disclosure of analy-

[1] For other illustrations, see Cooke's "Religion of Chemistry," pp. 326-8; Grove, "Correlation and Conservation of Forces," pp. 116, 117.

[2] Dr. Cohn, of the University of Breslau, in *Nature*, vol. vii. p. 137.

[3] Carpenter, "Human Physiology," p. 542; Herschel, "Outlines of Astronomy," pp. 233, 234; Wallace, "On Natural Selection," p. 368; Murphy, "Scientific Basis of Faith," p. 51; Laycock, "Mind and Brain," vol. i. pp. 225, 258-9, 304.

sis."[1] The whole conception is summed up in one comprehensive statement by Professor Norton, of Yale College: "I regard the primary force of repulsion as incessantly outstreaming in every direction from every ethereal atom (which is incessantly renewed), and as it spreads outward ever tending toward evanescence on each radiating line by the mere result of its own expansion—*a perpetual stream of force flowing from the Infinite Source of all power*, vanishing ultimately by diffusion in the infinite expanse of the universe. It breaks incessantly against the atoms of bodies, and so furnishes the secondary streams of force that maintain the constitution and determine the phenomena of the material universe."[2] Force, then, is the act of the immanent Deity, who puts forth unceasingly from every point in the realm of space his creative and sustaining power.

4. All the phenomena of molecular life (bioplasmic phenomena) are the result of the immediate presence and direct agency of God.[3]

This is the doctrine which must finally be accepted, whether vitality be regarded as a mode of energy—a transformation of chemico-physical forces—or as a distinct and special force. Dr. Carpenter has long held that the physical and vital forces are mutually convertible, but he regards both as the result of the direct action of the Deity. "Believing that all force which does not emanate from the will of created sentient beings *directly and immediately proceeds from the will of the Omnipotent and Omnipresent Creator;* and looking on the (what we are accustomed

[1] "First Principles," p. 235. [2] Letter to the author.

[3] The distinction made by Dr. Carpenter between *molecular* (bioplasmic) and *somatic* (individual) life is important: molecular life is a cosmic force, somatic life is an individualized force; the former is the direct action of Deity, the second is the indwelling of a created but yet dependent spiritual entity in a vitalized organism.

to call) physical forces as so many *modi operandi* of one and the same agency, the creative and sustaining will of the Deity, I do not feel the validity of the objections urged against the idea of the absolute metamorphosis or conversion of forces."[1] Inasmuch, however, as the advocates of this theory have failed to establish either a *quantitative* or a *qualitative* relation between the vital and physical forces, but, on the contrary, the most exact and careful biological researches show them to be inconvertible and antagonistic, we are constrained still to hold the doctrine maintained by Dr. Beale.

The ancient doctrine that "Life is the cause, and not the consequence of organization,"[2] still maintains its ground against all assaults. Harvey's famous maxim, *Omne vivum ex ovo*—as amended by Charles Robin, *Omne vivum ex vivo*—stands yet unrefuted; and, as Sir William Thomson remarked in his inaugural address before the British Association of Science, "This seems to me as sure a teaching of science as the law of gravitation. I confess to being deeply impressed by the evidence put before us by Professor Huxley, and I am ready to adopt it as an article of scientific faith—true through all space and all time—that *life proceeds from life, and nothing but life*."[3] Life has its origin in no secondary cause, but in the immediate presence and direct action of the Deity. God is the author and giver of Life—the constant sustainer of all vitality; "in Him we live and move and are."

The final conclusion to be drawn from these propositions is that God is not simply the *transitive* but the *immanent*

[1] "On the Mutual Relation of the Vital and Physical Forces," *Philosophical Transactions*, 1850, p. 730. See also Laycock, "Mind and Brain," vol. i. p. 304; Wallace, in *Nature*, vol. vi. p. 285.

[2] Huxley, "Introduction to the Classification of Animals."

[3] *Nature*, vol. iv. p. 269.

cause of the universe. He is in nature, not merely as a *regulative* principle impressing laws upon matter, but as a *constitutive* principle, the ever-present source and ever-operating cause of all its phenomena. If by the term nature we understand the totality of necessary and uniform phenomena, God is the immediate cause of all uniform and necessary phenomena. If by nature we understand the varied forms of energy which underlie the phenomena, and are manifested in the phenomena, these forms of energy are but various modes in which the omnipresent power of God reveals itself. God is immanent in matter, and his ceaseless energy produces all the phenomena of nature. Nature is more than matter: it is matter swayed by Divine power, and organized and animated by the Divine life.

But the question may be here raised, Is not this identification of the dynamical life of the universe with God, Pantheism? We answer in the language of James Martineau: "It certainly would be so if we also turned the proposition round and identified God with no more than the life of the universe, and treated the two terms as for all purposes interchangeable. If in affirming the Divine *immanency* in nature we deny the Divine *transcendency* beyond nature, and pay our worship to the aggregate of all its powers, the law of its laws, the unity of its organism, . . . then undoubtedly we do pass from part to whole, and rest in a dream of future science instead of emerging into immediate religion."[1] The theory which represents the Deity as the transitive cause of the universe—a Δημιουργός mechanically fashioning the materials supplied to his hands, and then leaving it to the working of its own inherent forces—is rank Deism. The hypothesis which regards the

[1] "God in Nature," in *Old and New*, 1872, p. 163.

Deity as *no more* than the dynamical life of the universe—an informing and organizing soul associated with matter—is naked Hylozoism. The theory that reduces all existence, material and mental, to phenomenal manifestations of one eternal self-existent substance which evolves itself according to an inward law of necessity, and which is elusively called God, is Pantheism. But the doctrine which embraces the two conceptions of *transcendence* and *immanence*, and while it teaches the immanence of God in matter, proclaims the infinite distinctness in essence between matter and God, and the infinite omnipresence of a personal God above and beyond the limitations of matter, is Christian Theism.[1]

And now, in conclusion, may we not say that this dictum of faith that the universe exists only in virtue of the continued Will of its Creator, is coming more and more to be recognized as a scientific fact. The will of God is the one primal force which streams forth in ever-recurring impulses with an immeasurable rapidity at every point in space—an incessant pulse-beat of the Infinite Life.[2] The disposition and collocations of matter are simply the conditions necessary to the manifestation of this primal force. The chemical atom, "already quite a complex little world,"[3] is a mechanism for the interception, transformation, and transmission of force. All the varied forms of energy are but secondary and derivative streams of force—forms of energy which are conceivable only as effects, and which by mere accommodation we may be permitted to call "causes," yet with this specific reservation that "they

[1] *Methodist Quarterly Review*, July, 1871, p. 499.

[2] "All atomic forces are incessant forces that are made up of impulses which are renewed every instant."—Professor Norton, in the *American Journal of Science and Arts*, vol. iii. 3d Series, p. 331.

[3] Sir W. Thomson, in *Nature*, vol. iv. p. 266.

are not vicegerents outside of the Divine Will, but are held within the Divine Will." "The word '*cause*' may be used in a secondary and concrete sense as meaning antecedent forces, yet in an abstract sense it is totally inapplicable; we can not predicate of any physical agent that it is abstractedly the cause of another; and if, for the sake of convenience, the language of secondary causation be permissible, it should only be with reference to the special phenomena referred to, as it can never be generalized." "The common error, if I am right in supposing it to be such, consists in the abstraction of cause, and in supposing in each case a general secondary cause—a something which is not the First Cause, but which, if we examine it carefully, *must have all the attributes of a first cause, and an existence independent of and dominant over matter.*" "CAUSATION IS THE WILL OF GOD."[1] The Divine conservation of the world is the *simple, universal, uniform efficiency of God.*

[1] Grove, "Correlation and Conservation of Forces," pp. 15, 18, 199. See also the words of Dr. Mayer in the same volume, p. 341.

CHAPTER VIII.

THE PROVIDENCE OF GOD IN HUMAN HISTORY.

"He hath made of one blood all the nations of mankind to dwell upon the face of the whole earth, and ordained to each the appointed seasons of their existence and the bounds of their habitation, that they should seek God."—St. Paul.

"Divine providence, which conducts all things marvelously, rules the series of human generations from Adam to the end of the world *like one man*, who, from his infancy to his old age, furnishes forth his career in time in passing through all its ages."—St. Augustine.

"The right education of the human race, so far as concerns the people of God, like that of a single man, advances through certain divisions of time, as that of the individual through the consecutive ages of human life."—St. Augustine.

"Les nations sont régies par les mêmes lois que les individus."—Laurent.

From the central and fundamental truth that God is the Creator and Conservator of the universe, Christian theology advances to the still more practical truth that He determines and presides over the development of the human race, leading it toward a foreseen and predestinated goal.

This is the natural and logical order of thought. If nature and man were created and are still conserved by an intelligent power, there must be some reason or end for which they exist; for intelligent power can only be conceived as a power which works toward ends. The existence of the world and of man being given, the question concerning the purpose or end for which they exist becomes unavoidable and necessary; and though physical science may proclaim "its inability to disclose the final purpose of creation," and speak contemptuously of all such inquiries, it does not by any means follow that Christian doctrine can furnish no satisfactory answer to this inevitable question. As the reference of the dependent universe to the efficient ground of its existence gives the concepts of *Creation* and *Conservation* with which the idea of power is pre-eminently associated, so the reference of the same to the ultimate reason of its existence gives the concepts of *Providence* and *Moral Government* with which the idea of all-wise love is immediately correlated.

The Christian doctrine of Providence in human history is succinctly stated in the words of St. Paul: "God hath made of one blood all the nations of mankind to dwell upon the face of the whole earth, and ordained to each the appointed times of their existence and the bounds of their habitation, that they should seek after, and indeed feel after, and find the Lord." He has endowed man with intelligence and freedom by which he may achieve the conquest of nature, and be able to maintain his existence and ascendency in every part of the habitable globe. A new and subtile force appears in the arena of nature, which is superior to nature, which can control and regulate its action, and subordinate the forces of nature to the higher purposes and needs of spiritual and moral being. By travel and observation, by reasoning and invention, by interchange of ideas and products, man may continually enlarge the sphere of his knowledge, and multiply the means of improvement and happiness.[1] God has also "determined beforehand the *time* of each nation's exist-

[1] Mr. Wallace, the author of the theory of natural selection, denies its applicability to man. Man is "a being apart," a "being superior to nature." "He has not only escaped 'natural selection' himself, but he is actually able

ence, and the geographical *boundaries* of their habitation." Divine providence has decreed and presided over the dispersions and migrations of the human race, and in the plan of history fixed the time when and the people by which each continent and island shall be inhabited. And the ultimate purpose of this providential arrangement and supervision is that men "may seek God, and feel after and really find Him," who for all dependent rational existence is the chief good.

This, then, is the explicit teaching of Christian theology: The appearance of rational existence on the earth constitutes a distinct creative epoch; the final cause of all rational existence is to know God, consciously to feel after and find Him; and the whole of God's action upon humanity has been an inspiration, guidance, and education toward this end. *The progress of the human race, the course of human history, is therefore a revelation of the Providence of God.*

"The consideration of nature," says Niebuhr, "shows an inherent intelligence, which may be also considered as coherent in nature; so does history, on a hundred occasions, show an intelligence distinct from nature which conducts and determines those things which may seem to us accidental; and it is not true that history weakens our belief in Divine providence. History is, of all kinds of knowledge, the one which tends most decidedly to that belief."[1] "History," observes Richter, "has, like nature, the highest value (if studied philosophically) in so far as we by means of it, as by means of nature, can divine

to take away some of that power from nature which, before his appearance, she universally exercised" ("On Natural Selection," pp. 325, 326). See also Lubbock's "Prehistoric Times," last chapter.

[1] "Lectures on the History of Rome," vol. ii. p. 59.

and read the Infinite Spirit who, with nature and history as with letters, legibly writes to us. He who finds a God in the physical world will also find one in the moral world —which is history. Nature forces on our hearts a Creator; history, a Providence." To the student of history it becomes apparent that the hand of God has been guiding humanity toward the fulfillment of its destiny. God has presided over the development of human society and government. Throughout the ages He has been the Educator of the race—leading, instructing, chastening, and blessing the nations. "Man holds relations to God not merely at the moment of creation; he does not cease to be in connection with his Creator through the endless duration of his existence. The incessant action of God on man is grace; the incessant action of God on humanity is providential government."[1] "History is the manifestation of God's supervision of humanity, and the judgments of history are the judgments of God."[2]

If we have here the true conception of history, if it is a manifestation of Divine supervision, direction, and discipline, then the question is at once legitimate and practical, What is the end of this discipline? what is the foreseen and predestinated goal toward which, through conflict and pain and travail, Divine providence is leading the human race?

It must be conceded on all hands that the adequate and final answer can only be given by that Divine prescience which "sees the end from the beginning." The study of the past and of the present moral and religious phenomena of the world may afford to the philosophic mind some prevision of the future, but it is obvious that revelation alone can supply the principles which must con-

[1] Laurent, "Études sur l'Histoire de l'Humanité," vol. v. p. 14.
[2] Cousin, "History of Philosophy," vol. i. p. 160.

stitute the light of history—the light in which even its darkest chapters may be interpreted, and its true philosophy evolved.

The general answer which speculative thought has furnished to this question is that the goal of history is *the highest perfection of humanity.* Aristotle clearly recognizes that there must be an end or final cause of human existence and action—a τέλειον τέλος (*summum bonum*), or chief end.[1] He therefore addresses himself to the inquiry, What is the chief good, or highest end of man? The conclusion which he reaches is, that it is the absolute satisfaction of his whole nature—that which men have agreed to call *happiness.* This happiness, however, is not mere sensual pleasure. The brute shares this in common with man, therefore it can not constitute the happiness of man. Human happiness must express the *completeness* of rational existence, or, as he expresses it, "a perfect practical activity in a perfect life."[2] This "complete and perfect life" is the complete satisfaction of our rational nature. It is the realization of the Divine in man, and constitutes the absolute and all-sufficient good.[3] A good action is thus "an end in itself," inasmuch as it tends to secure the *perfection* of our nature.

The human mind can not, however, rest in the general and vague idea of perfection; we are therefore pressed with the further question, In what does the highest perfection of humanity consist? by what standard are we to judge of this perfection? what is the *ideal* toward which the progress of humanity may be presumed to tend, and which we hope it will ultimately attain? The following considerations may furnish the answer:

[1] "Nichomachean Ethics," bk. i. ch. ii. [2] Ibid. bk. i. ch. x.
[3] Ibid. bk. x. ch. viii.

1. That ideal must be the same for the race as for the individual, the same for the nation as for the man. For, on the one hand, society exists for the sake of the individual, and it is only in society that individual existences can be preserved, developed, and perfected; on the other hand, national character is but the expression of the collective or average character of the individual citizens.

In seeking for the ideal of individual perfection, we must take account of all the capacities, powers, and relations of man. We must have in view, not simply his physical and intellectual, but also his moral and religious nature. We must think of the relation in which he stands to his fellow-beings and to his God, as well as the relation in which he stands to himself—that is, to the liberty and intelligence which are in him, and which he must develop. Now no man can be said to be complete, to be *perfect*, no man can be said to have reached his τέλος, or end, until he has developed in his thought and realized in his life the idea of the useful, the true, the just, the good, the pure, the Divine. Loyalty to God and the truth, justice and charity toward men, self-control and purity of mind, intellectual discipline and cultivated taste—these are the characteristics of the perfect man. Judged from the Christian stand-point, he is the perfect man who has attained to that ideal of moral and spiritual excellence which was exhibited in the human life of Christ, that grand embodiment of all that is "pure and true and just and lovely and of good report." The realization of this ideal in the collective life of humanity must be the goal of history.

2. Further light is shed upon this problem by the consideration of the Christian idea of God. The gravitating point of Christian theology is found in the Divine declaration, "*God is Love*" (1 John iv. 8, 16). This is the

most fundamental revelation of the Divine nature, so that nothing can pertain to his perfections or his works which is not ultimately resolvable into love. "If ever the idea of Divine justice shall obtain consistency [in our systems of theology], it must be in general through the relation of infinite holy love to the spontaneous and self-determining capacity of the personal being, or the relation of Divine perfection to the existence of the economy in the universe."[1] The fact that God creates worlds and gives birth to personal existences is not grounded in his omnipotence, but in his love. Divine love is the determinative principle of Divine efficiency—the final cause or ultimate reason of all existence. Creation must therefore be conceived as the free self-communication of God, who is Himself eternally self-complete and self-sufficient, but who, from love alone, wills that other intelligences shall have existence who can "know God," and in fellowship with Him attain that fullness and fruition of being which is called "Eternal Life."[2] If, then, the Divine mind has always had this end in view—the perfection and blessedness of personal being in fellowship with Himself—it must be regarded by us as the consummation toward which his providence is leading humanity.

3. The explicit declarations of Scripture are in perfect accord with these inferences drawn from the nature of man and the idea of God. We learn from the words of St. Paul that the aim of Divine providence is to lead the race to the practical recognition of the personal dignity of man as "the offspring of God;" to the practical recognition of the universal brotherhood of man, as "of one blood," with equal rights to place, provision, and free self-

[1] Nitzsch, "System of Christian Doctrine," p. 172.
[2] Müller, "Christian Doctrine of Sin," vol. ii. p. 146.

development in "every part of the earth;" finally, to the practical recognition of our relation to God as his dependent creatures, in fellowship with whom we have eternal life.[1] God's great end in the whole course and discipline of providence is to unite all men in bonds of mutual affection and aid, and to unite the race to Himself in bonds of loyalty and love. Then "whatsoever things are true and pure and honest and lovely and of good report" will be revered and practiced among the nations of the earth.

These views of Divine providence can scarcely be said to have had any place or any recognition in the ancient schools of philosophy. The Stoics taught that an invincible necessity rules in the realm of history as well as in the field of nature, to which God and man are equally subject. "God is the reason of the world (τοῦ παντὸς τοῦ λόγου); the laws of the world are as necessary as the laws of eternal reason. This necessity is at once *fate* (εἱμαρμένη), and the *providence* (πρόνοια) which governs all things."[2] The Epicureans reduced all existence to the plane of mere physical nature, and represented humanity as a development from the lower forms of life by the agency of blind, unconscious force. If they recognized the existence of any god or gods, they removed them far away from all intercourse with humanity, and all supervision of or concern in human affairs. "They admitted their existence in words," says Cicero, "but denied it in act." These two forms of error are combined by the modern deniers of

[1] Acts xvii. 25–28.

[2] Laurent, "Études sur l'Histoire de l'Humanité," vol. v. p. 12. Not all the Stoics seem to have understood this "necessity" in so rigorous a sense. Cleanthes would exempt the evil actions of men from necessity: "Nothing takes place without Thee, O Deity, except that which bad men do through their own want of reason; but even that which is evil is overruled by Thee for good, and is made to harmonize with the plan of the world."—*Hymn to Zeus.*

providence. Human society, languages, laws, institutions, arts, sciences, are all the products of matter and force. The succession of events, the progress of civilization, and the religious phenomena of the world, have not been determined by an intelligent Will, or presided over by a conscious Personality. In the last analysis, matter is resolved into a function of force, and a process of necessary evolution, which has no design and no final purpose, is substituted for Divine providence. The ultimate destination of the world and humanity is unknown, or, if conjecture is permissible, is chaos and death.

In opposition to these cold and cheerless speculations Christianity affirms the doctrine of Divine providence in human history.[1]

By Providence we understand intelligent *forethought* and timely *provision* for all contingencies. The term supposes a precognized *plan*, a constant supervision of its development, and the control and subordination of all finite powers and agencies in order to its completion. From nature, strictly considered as the empire of mechanical necessity, nothing can proceed but that which is posited in it by the immediate act of God; and consequently, considered apart from man, there can be no contingency; and, properly speaking, no providence in this sphere. The existence of mere nature, however, can not be regarded as an end in itself. The whole interest and significance of nature is found in the conception that it exists as a means for a higher end. As matter is simply the condition for the manifestation of force, as the physical forces are subordinated to the vital force, and the vital is subordinated to the mental, so is it a legitimate assumption, which we shall justify in the sequel, that all these are

[1] Laurent, "Études sur l'Histoire de l'Humanité," vol. v. p. 12.

subordinated to the *moral* and *spiritual.* It is only in the sphere of spiritual being—that is, of self-conscious and self-determined being—and in the *relation of nature to spiritual being,* that contingency can arise and providence find place.

The uniform teaching of Scripture is that human history is the special field of Divine providence. In fact, the historic portions of the Bible are nothing else than a record of the control and direction and subordination of human agencies, and of external physical conditions in their relation to personal beings, by the hand of God. This primitive revelation throws light upon the cradle of human civilization. It points to a period when man, at his departure from the hand of God, received those intellectual, moral, and spiritual endowments which raise him in the scale of being immeasurably above the animal creation, and fit him for a progress, a development to which no conceivable limits can be assigned.[1] The Bible

[1] The statement of the text will remain unaffected by any theory as to the derivation of the material organism of the primitive man. If the hypothesis be true that "man is the descendant of some pre-existent generic type, the which, if it were now living, we would probably call an ape," this can only be affirmed of the body of man, and the statement is still correct that "God formed man of the dust of the earth." The body of the ape and the body of man are formed of the same materials. But, as Prof. Cope, a thorough-going Evolutionist, remarks, this material nature can not bear or be "the image of God," for "God is a spirit," and "a spirit hath not flesh and bones" (Luke xxiv. 39). The image of God must inhere in that spiritual nature which was inbreathed by God, and consists in reason, conscience, and moral liberty. (See Cope, "On the Hypothesis of Evolution," pp. 33, 34.) This theory as to the descent of man's material organism from some pre-existent generic type does not by any means involve the conclusion of Sir J. Lubbock that "the primitive condition of mankind was one of *utter barbarism.*" We may grant that the primitive condition of man was one of childhood ignorance and inexperience, a state in which his intellectual and moral nature was undeveloped; but this is not "Savagism." Barbarism is the lapse and deterioration of man. Even if it could be shown that primeval man was destitute of the industrious arts, "it would not afford the slightest

is the history of Divine providence from that signal commencement to the planting of the Christian Church, where we can clearly see all the lines along which the race advanced, converging upon "the Kingdom of God." It is a history of Divine interposition in human affairs, and of supernatural guidance toward a higher development and a nobler destiny. Indeed, to the eye of the observant and conscientious student of all history, whether secular or ecclesiastical, there are undeniable evidences of the presence of Intelligence, disposing and collocating the conditions of human progress, and directing humanity toward a nobler civilization.

Considering the earth in its relation to man, we must recognize the providence of God in the physical universe. The earth was unquestionably made for man. It was created, and has been especially adapted to be the theatre of human history. This is the doctrine of Scripture (Gen. i. 28–31; Psa. cxv. 16)—I believe it is also the doctrine of science. The geological changes through which the earth has passed indicate "a process of preparation" for the inhabitation of man. This process of preparation is fully recognized by Agassiz. "There has been," he says, "a manifest progress in the succession of beings on the surface of the globe. This progress consists in an increasing similarity to the living fauna, and, among the vertebrates especially, in the increasing resemblance to man. But this connection is not the consequence of a direct

presumption that he was also ignorant of duty or ignorant of God" ("Primeval Man," by the Duke of Argyll, p. 132). "Whenever we can trace back a religion to its first beginnings, we find it free from many blemishes that affect it in its later stages" (Max Müller, "Chips from a German Workshop," vol. i., preface). The most ancient form of religion was the Monotheistic (Grimm, "Deutsche Mythologie," p. xliv. 3d ed.). See also "Les Origines Indo-Européennes," vol. ii. p. 720, by M. Adolphe Pictet.

lineage between the faunas of different ages. The fishes of the Palæozoic are in no respect the ancestors of the reptiles of the Secondary age, nor does man descend from the mammals of the Tertiary age. The link by which they are connected is of an immaterial nature, and their connection is to be sought in the thought of the Creator Himself, whose *aim* in forming the earth, in allowing it to pass through the successive changes which Geology has pointed out, and in creating successively all the different types of animals which have passed away, was to introduce man upon the surface of the globe. Man is the end toward which all the animal creation has tended."[1] The language of Prof. Owen is equally explicit: "The recognition of an ideal exemplar in the vertebrated animals proves that the knowledge of such a being as man existed before man appeared; for the Divine Mind which planned the archetype also foresaw all its modifications. The archetype idea was manifested in the flesh long prior to the existence of those animal species that actually exemplify it."[2] "Of the nature of the creative acts by which the successive races of animals were called into being, we are ignorant. But this we know, that as the evidence of unity of plan testifies to the oneness of the Creator, so the modifications of the plan for different modes of existence illustrate the benevolence of the Designer. Those structures, moreover, which are at present incomprehensible as adaptations to a special end, are made comprehensible on a higher principle, and a *final purpose* is gained in relation to human intelligence."[3] That these views are still held by Prof. Owen is evident from his remarks in the fortieth chapter of his "Anatomy of the Vertebrates:"

[1] "Agassiz and Gould's "Zoology," p. 238. [2] "On Limbs," p. 88.
[3] "On the Skeleton and Teeth," p. 228.

"Of all the quadrupedal servants of man, none have proved of more value to him, in peace or war, than the horse; none have co-operated with the advanced races more influentially in man's destined mastery over the earth and its lower denizens. . . . I believe the horse to have been predestinated and prepared for man. It may be a weakness; but, if so, it is a glorious one, to discern, however dimly, across our finite prison-wall, evidence of 'the Divinity that shapes our ends,' abuse the means as we may."[1]

Long before the appearance of man upon the earth, the providence of God laid up in its strata those vast treasures of granite, sandstone, lime, marble, coal, salt, petroleum, and the various metals, the product of a long succession of ages and revolutions, thus making an inexhaustible provision for the necessities of man, and furnishing ample resources for the development of his genius and skill.[2] In the vegetable life which appeared on the globe immediately prior to and contemporaneous with the advent of man, we can recognize a providential arrangement made for man. In the flora of the Palæozoic and Secondary periods we can not fail to observe the absence of all those plants which are adapted for human food. Even in the Tertiary epoch, which immediately precedes the Adamic or human period, so far as Geology reveals, there were few or no plants yielding the appropriate supplies for the sustentation of man. There are few indications of any of those vegetables from which man may derive food and valuable fibre, and, in a word, of species which support and clothe by far the larger portion of the human race. "Scarcely any grasses appear in the list of extinct vegetation, and there

[1] "Anatomy of the Vertebrates," vol. iii. p. 796.

[2] "The Harmonies of Nature," by Dr. C. Hartwig, pp. 46, 47.

is reason to believe that the principal cereals which are characteristic of the human period—as barley, wheat, oats, rye, millet, Indian corn, and rice"—had no existence.[1] When the fullness of time was come, and all things were ready for the reception of man, then God called him into being, and invested him with dominion over nature.

Physical geography also indicates, not only a state of preparation for man, but also a special adaptation of the fixed forms of the earth's surface for securing the perfect development of man according to the Divine ideal. And as the land which man inhabits, the food he eats, the air he breathes, the mountains and rivers and seas which are his neighbors, the skies that overshadow him, the diversities of climate to which he is subject, and indeed all physical conditions, exert a powerful influence upon his tastes, pursuits, habits, and character—we may presume that not only are all these conditions predetermined by God, but continually under his control and supervision.

The distribution of terrestrial areas—the continents, islands, and seas; the disposition of the climate, soil, and vegetation, apparently accidental, have played an important part in the moral history of our race. There is a close relation between nature and history, between the earth and man. The soul of man is distinct from, but not totally independent of the body and of external physical conditions. To deny this would be to reject all the lessons of experience. The relation of man to nature is not, however, a relation of cause and effect, but, as Cousin remarks, "Man and nature are two great effects which, coming from the *same* cause, bear the same characteristics, so that the earth and he who inhabits it, man and nature,

[1] "Typical Forms and Special Ends," R. McCosh and Dr. Dickie, p. 352.

are in perfect harmony."[1] "A living God," says Ritter, "is at the head of the physical and moral world."[2] The earth was created for man, not simply to be a dwelling-place, but a *school-house*[3]—made to be a theatre for the education, the development, and the perfection of the human race. And as the moral and intellectual culture of the child is materially affected by the physical conditions with which he is surrounded, and as these are consequently the subject of care and forethought on the part of the intelligent and prudent parent and teacher, so the external physical conditions of a nation exert a powerful influence on its intellectual and moral development, and therefore must be presumed to be the subject of forethought and providence on the part of God, "the Father of the families of all the earth." God has superintended the peopling of the earth, the dispersions and migrations of nations, guiding the footsteps of the "covenant, educating, and missionary nations" to those countries best adapted to their highest development. In a word, He has ordained the progress of empire and the course of civilization.

Thus nature and history are the two great factors of Divine providence; in their relations and harmonies we have a revelation of the purposes and plans of God.[4]

That geographical conditions do exert a powerful influence on the character of nations can not be denied. "The bodily constitution of a people, their temperament, modes of life, habitations, customs, languages, and even religious opinions have been formed or modified under the influence of that magic circle of nature which surrounds them, and

[1] "History of Philosophy," vol. i. p. 169.

[2] "Geographical Studies," p. 34.

[3] "Ritter, "Geographical Studies," p. 314; Guyot, "Earth and Man," p. 34.

[4] Ritter, "Geographical Studies," p. 34; Guyot, "Earth and Man," p. 35.

which so powerfully affects what is individual in national character." So that, could we fully grasp all the characteristics of a country—its position, configuration, climate, scenery, and natural products—we could, with tolerable accuracy, determine what are the characteristics of the people who inhabit it. We have discussed this topic at some length in "Christianity and Greek Philosophy," and shall here simply recall such of the general facts and principles as may be needed for a clear understanding of the present discussion.

1. *The habits and characteristics of the dwellers in the Temperate Zone differ widely from those of the dwellers in the Torrid Zone.* This is an obvious fact; and the causes of this difference are equally obvious to the observant mind. In the tropical regions the powers of vegetable and animal life are stimulated to the highest degree, and here nature displays her fullest energy, her greatest variety, and her richest splendors. Excessive heat enfeebles and enervates man. It induces lassitude, dreaminess, effeminacy, and tempts to quietude and indolence. Where nature pours her fullness into the lap of ease, forethought and providence are little needed. Here is none of that struggle for existence which awakens sagacity and develops industry. Nothing calls man to that effort for the conquest of nature by which the intellect is aroused and the reasoning faculties are developed. Consequently the mere life of the body, the powers of the physical nature of man, overmaster the faculties of the mind. The instincts predominate over the reason. Simple spontaneity of thought is manifested, but little or no analytic reflection. Feeling, imagination, sentiment, predominate over intellect, reason, and science. In a temperate climate all is reversed. The alternations of heat and cold render man more vigor-

ous, and impart more physical tone. Where there is less profusion and lavishment of nature's gifts, there is more room and motive for industry. The change of seasons, and an annual period of dormancy, demand forethought and prudence. The preservation of life demands, not merely physical toil, but some degree of contrivance, and, indeed, the vigorous exertion of the intellectual powers. And here, though nature is not prodigal of her gifts, she grants to industry and skill something more than the bare necessities of life. She allows man to lay up a store for the future, and furnishes some leisure for the culture of the mind. The active powers of man, his reason and judgment, rule his instincts, and control, more or less, his appetites and emotions. Here man becomes a careful observer of events; he treasures up the results of experience, compares one fact with another, notes their relations, and makes new experiments to test his conclusions. Thus science has its birth in the Temperate Zone.[1]

2. *There is a marked difference between the mental habits and modes of thought of the peoples who dwell in the interior of an immense continent and those who dwell on the margin of the sea.* Vast continents, unbroken by lakes and inland seas, and extended plains where broad deserts and high mountain ranges separate the populations, are the seats of immobility. The inhabitants are isolated from the rest of the world, and excluded from a stimulating and profitable intercourse with the nations of the earth. They have comparatively no navigation, their commerce is limited to the bare necessities of life, and there are no inducements to movement, to travel, and to enterprise. Society is therefore stationary, as in China; the habits, manners, and usages of social and civil life remain as they

[1] See Guyot, "Earth and Man," pp. 268–270.

were two thousand years ago. Infolded and imprisoned within the overwhelming vastness and illimitable sway of nature, man is almost unconscious of his freedom and personality. He surrenders himself to the disposal of a mysterious "fate," and yields readily to the absolute control of rulers who are regarded as of supernatural origin and endowed with superhuman powers. The forms of government remain unchanged from age to age, and the state is the reign of fixed and inexorable laws—"The laws of the Medes and Persians are unalterable." The rights of the person are scarcely recognized, and the individual is lost in the mass.

Extended border-lands on the margin of great rivers and inland seas are, on the contrary, the theatre of movement, activity, and life. Here man is set free from the bondage imposed by the overpowering magnitude and vastness of continental and oceanic forms. Here industry is not stationary, but progressive; and commerce thrives because the rivers and inland seas furnish the means of easy transit, and the opportunity for a free interchange of commodities. Along with the exchange of commodities there will be an exchange of ideas, because ideas flow along the channels of commerce. Here also the arts will be cultivated, first for purposes of gain, and subsequently for the gratification of taste. And, where there is freedom of movement, where there is creative industry, where nature is subjugated by man, the idea of personal liberty will be developed, and the rights of the individual will be regarded. These ideas of personal liberty and rights will become incorporated with the laws and institutions of society, and the government will tend toward a democracy. Finally, this freedom of movement and action will engender freedom of thought. Reflection will commence, the speculative and critical spirit will arise, and philosophy will be born.[1]

3. *There is also an acknowledged difference between the mental character of the inhabitants of a bright and sunny climate who breathe an elastic atmosphere, and are surrounded by the most inspiring scenery, and that of the people who dwell under a gray and sombre sky, and daily look upon the more stern and rugged aspects of nature.* The dwellers in the former climate are ardent, vivacious, and mercurial; the inhabitants of the latter are slow, deliberate, persistent, and conservative. One nation will be speculative, enamored of plausible hypotheses, and prone to hasty and brilliant generalization; the other will be practical, intolerant of hypotheses, and clamorous for facts and logical inferences from facts. In the former climate the fine arts will be enthusiastically cultivated, and elegance and taste, and all that is graceful in sentiment and action, will find a congenial home; in the latter, the exact sciences and the useful arts will be cultivated with persistence and zeal. Under the former conditions, a religion of poetry, of sentiment, of artistic display and imposing ceremonial, will sway the popular mind; under the latter, a religion of personal duty and purity, of social righteousness, of active beneficence, and of universal charity, will command respect.

These principles constitute what may be designated the *statics* of history—the more or less stable and permanent *conditions* under which the living forces of humanity are developed.

The *dynamics* of history are the fundamental powers and rational ideas of human nature. There are certain primary ideas of the reason which are revealed in the uni-

[1] Cousin, "History of Philosophy," vol. i. pp. 169–170.

versal consciousness of our race under the conditions of experience—the exterior conditions of physical nature and sensational life. Such are the ideas of substance and cause, of unity and infinity, which govern all the processes of discursive thought, and lead us to the recognition of the uncreated and unconditioned Being; such the ideas of right, of duty, of accountability, and of retribution which regulate all the conceptions we form of our relations to other moral beings, and constitute *morality;* such the ideas of order, proportion, and harmony which preside in the realm of art, and constitute the beau-ideal of *æsthetics;* such the ideas of God, the soul, and immortality which rule in the domain of *religion*, and constitute man a religious being. In addition to these, there are the powers of observation, of abstraction, of generalization, of inference, the capacity of symbolic conception and expression, the faculty of creative imagination, the powers of invention, of foresight, and of scientific prevision. These are the living forces of humanity, fundamentally the same under all circumstances, but modified in their intensity and development by geographical, climatal, and scenic conditions. The providential adjustment and harmonious relation of the exterior conditions with the inherent powers of humanity is the problem of history.

Before attempting to trace the hand of Divine providence in the original location and subsequent migrations of the historic races, let us briefly reproduce the sentences which express the *conditions* most favorable to the development and perfection of humanity. 1. While the tropical climate of Southern Asia, of Africa, and of South America is unfavorable to the highest intellectual and moral development, the temperate climate of Western Asia, of Europe, and of North America is peculiarly adapted to minister to the advancement and perfection of the human race. 2. The massive, unbroken continents of the South, shut in by immense oceans and impassable mountain ranges, are the seats of immobility and the home of despotic power; but the deeply indented and elaborately articulated continents of the North, with their inland seas and large navigable rivers, are the theatre of activity, of progress, and of liberty. 3. The sunny skies and glowing landscapes and inspiring scenery of the south of Europe are most congenial to poetry and music, and painting and sculpture, and all that is graceful in expression and action; the deeper tone and sterner features of the northern portion of Europe, "whose skies are sombre, and whose mountains are rugged and gray," determine it to be the home of practical industry and useful arts, of benevolent enterprises and philanthropic deeds. Bearing in mind these principles, we turn to history in the belief that we shall find that Divine providence has at successive periods placed the historic races in such geographical relations and amid such physical conditions as have been most favorable to their intellectual and moral development.

1. The first historic fact to which we would now direct attention is *that the human race really commenced its history in the midst of the continents of the Temperate Zone.* Western Asia was unquestionably the cradle of the human race, the grand centre whence the different families or races commenced their migrations.

Whatever views may be entertained of the doctrine supposed to be taught in Gen. i.–iv. that the whole human race originally descended from a single pair, or whatever method of interpretation in regard to that ancient document may finally prevail—even should we adopt the theory of Dr. McCausland[1] that the Biblical account is concerned

[1] "Adam and the Adamites."

only with the origin of a covenant and redemptive race (the Adamite or Edenic race), which was to be the instructor and benefactor of the pre-Adamite races—there can be no question that the sacred historian traces the source of the great historic nations to the family of Noah (Gen. ix. 19). Whatever difficulties there may be in determining the site of Eden — and they are confessedly great, if not insurmountable—there is no difficulty in locating the second geographical centre from whence the great historic races departed to overspread the earth. Ararat is, no doubt, in its Biblical import, the Armenian highlands, the lofty plateau which overlooks the plains of the Araxes on the north and Mesopotamia on the south. This "Armenian plateau stands equidistant from the Euxine and the Caspian seas on the north, and between the Persian Gulf and the Mediterranean Sea on the south. With the first it is connected by the Acampsis, with the second by the Araxes, with the third by the Tigris and the Euphrates, the latter of which serves as an outlet toward the countries on the Mediterranean coast. These seas were the highways of primitive colonization, and the plains watered by these rivers were the seats of the most powerful nations of antiquity — the Assyrians, the Babylonians, the Medes, and the Colchians. Viewed with reference to the dispersion of the nations, Armenia is the true ὀμφαλος—the middle part—of the earth; and it is a significant fact that at the present day Ararat is the great boundary-stone between the empires of Russia, Turkey, and Persia."[1]

The Scripture account, which certainly authorizes us to fix upon the highlands of Armenia as the new centre whence the descendants of Noah went forth to people the

[1] Article "Ararat," in Smith's Dictionary.

earth, is confirmed by the most ancient traditions and the most reliable historic records. Josephus tells us there was in Armenia a city which was called Ἀποβατήριον — the Place of Descent[1]—"for the ark being saved in that place, its remains are shown by the inhabitants to this day."[2] He further adds that "all the writers of the barbarian histories make mention of the flood, and of this ark, among whom is Berosus, the Chaldæan,[3] who, when he goes on to describe the circumstances of the flood, remarks, 'it is said there is still some part of this ship in Armenia, at the mountain of the Cordyæans;' Hieronymus, the Egyptian, who wrote the Phœnician antiquities, and Manases, and indeed a great many others, also make mention of the same. Nay, Nicholas of Damascus, in his ninety-sixth book, hath a particular relation about them, where he speaks thus: 'There is a great mountain in Armenia, over Minyas, called Baris, upon which, it is reported, . . . that one who was carried in an ark came on shore upon the top of it, and that the remains of the timber were a great while preserved.'"[4]

This concurrent testimony of sacred and profane history, which designates Western Asia as the cradle of the historic nations, has received additional confirmation from

[1] It is called in Ptolemy *Naxuana*, and by Moses Chorenensis, the Armenian historian, *Idsheuan*, but at the place itself *Nachidsheuan*, which signifies "the first place of descent." See Whiston's note on p. 87, vol. i. of Josephus.

[2] "Antiquities," bk. i. chap. iii. § 5.

[3] Ibid. bk. i. chap. iii. § 6. Scaliger was the first to draw the attention of scholars to the writings of Berosus. In his work "De Emendatione Temporum" he has collected his fragments, and vindicated their authenticity. Berosus is always quoted with respect by English divines, and Niebuhr has sustained his claims to be regarded as a reliable authority. In more than one place he speaks of Armenia as the resting-place of the ark. See Rawlinson's "Historical Evidences," p. 63, and note liii.

[4] "Antiquities," bk. i. chap. iii. § 6.

the researches of modern ethnologists and philologists. In the tenth chapter of Genesis, the sacred historian sketches the nations of the earth at his time of writing, indicates their ethnic affinities, and marks to some extent their geographical positions. The professor of ancient history in the University of Oxford, George Rawlinson, remarks that "the *Toldoth Beni Noah* (the Generations of Noah) has excited the admiration of modern ethnologists, who continually find in it the anticipations of their greatest discoveries."[1] Sir Henry Rawlinson assures us that "the Toldoth Beni Noah is undoubtedly the *most authentic* record we possess of the affiliations of the human race which sprang from the triple stock of the Noachidæ."[2] The same distinguished Oriental scholar in an essay "On the Ethnic Affinities of the Nations of Western Asia," fur-

[1] "For instance, in the very second verse, the great discovery of Schlegel, which the word Indo-European embodies—the affinity of the principal nations of Europe with the Ayran or Indo-Persic stock—is sufficiently indicated by the conjunction of the Madai or Medes (whose native name is Mada) with Gomer of the Cymry, and Javan of the Ionians. Again, one of the most recent and unexpected results of modern linguistic inquiry is the proof which it has furnished of an ethnic connection between the Ethiopians or Cushites, who adjoined on Egypt, and the primitive inhabitants of Babylonia; a connection which was positively denied by an eminent ethnologist only a few years ago, but which has now been sufficiently established from the cuneiform monuments. In the tenth chapter of Genesis (vers. 8–10) we find this truth thus briefly stated: 'And Cush begat Nimrod,' the 'beginning of whose kingdom was Babel' (ver. 11). So we have had it recently made evident from the same monuments that 'out of that land went forth Asshur, and builded Nineveh'—or that the Semitic Assyrians proceeded from Babylonia and founded Nineveh long after the Cushite foundation of Babylon. Again, the Hamitic descent of the early inhabitants of Canaan, which had often been called in question, has recently come to be looked upon as almost certain, apart from the evidence of Scripture; and the double mention of Sheba, both among the sons of Ham, and also among those of Shem (vers. 7 and 28), has been illustrated by the discovery that there are two races of Arabs—one (the Joktanian) Semitic, the other (the Himyaric) Cushite or Ethiopic."—Rawlinson's "Historical Evidences," pp. 71, 72.

[2] *Asiatic Society's Journal*, vol. xv.

ther remarks: "In Western Asia, the cradle of the human race, the several ethnic branches of the human family were more closely intermingled and more evenly balanced than in any other portion of the ancient world. Semitic, Indo-European, and Tâtar or Turanian races not only divided among them this portion of the earth's surface, but lay interspersed and confused upon it in a most remarkable entanglement. It is symptomatic of this curious intermixture that the Persian monarchs, when they wished to communicate to their Asiatic subjects in such a way that it should be generally intelligible, had to put it out not only in three different languages, but in three languages belonging to the *three principal divisions of human speech.* Hence the trilingual inscriptions of Behistun, Persepolis, etc., which consist of an Indo-European, a Tâtar, and a Semitic column."[1]

Thus do all the varied lines of evidence proceeding from history, ethnology, and philology converge upon Western Asia as the cradle of the human race—the centre from which the families of mankind departed to people the earth; and we are constrained to regard the early populations of that region as furnishing the *typical* standard or average sample of our species.

Proceeding from a purely zoological stand-point, we should be led to an opposite conclusion. Looking to the general phenomena of the geographical distribution of animals, and the natural rather than the artificial conditions of human existence, and arguing solely on naturalistic grounds, we should be constrained to place the centre of our race in the tropics; and of the intertropical regions those which are the habitat of the anthropoid (or anthropomorphic) ape, as Western Africa and the southern ex-

[1] Rawlinson's "Herodotus," vol. i. p. 523.

tremity of Asia. In the protoplasts of his species the mere zoologist sees but so many naked bipeds, with the capabilities, indeed, of working out for their future behoof the essentials of clothing, the use of fire, and the like, but in the first instance unfit for any climate except the mildest, and incapable of sustenance on any soil except the most luxuriant. He consequently fixes upon the tropics as the cradle of our race; and those who assume the lineal descent of the human species from the quadrumana fix upon those intertropical points which are the habitats of the anthropomorphic apes.

The law which governs the distribution and development of vegetable and animal life would also lead us to fix upon the tropical regions as the geographical centre of our race. That law may be thus stated: *The degree of perfection of the types of life, and the diversity and number of species, are proportional to the intensity of heat.* In this progress, as Humboldt has remarked, we find organic life and vigor gradually augmenting with the increase of temperature. And the number of species increases as we approach the equator, and decreases as we retire from it.[1]

In the Frigid Zone life seems almost extinguished during the greater part of the year by the rigors of an almost perpetual winter. The vegetation of the polar regions is stunted, dull, and monotonous in color, and inadequate to sustain animal life. The plains are covered with mosses and lichens, and here and there a few herbs and shrubs (saxifrages, gentians, papaver, etc.), but no stately forest trees. In short, the general characteristic of these cold regions is the preponderance of cryptogamous plants. In the Temperate Zone we have a marked superiority in vegetable life. Here we have grassy pastures, cerealia,

[1] "Cosmos," vol. i. p. 348.

and dicotyledonous trees—the oak, ash, beech, maple, chestnut, walnut, the apple, pear, plum, etc. The number of genera and species is greatly increased, and the superior types acquire a fuller development. The preponderance of phanerogamous plants, the richer coloring, and the appearance of evergreen trees, are the signs of an immense progress. But the soft tints, the medium forms, and the wintry sleep extending through half the year, clearly indicate that the perfection of physical nature is not attained.[1] It is in the heat of the Torrid Zone where nature puts forth all her energy, and displays her greatest resources. "The cryptogamous plants attain, in arborescent forms, the proportions of our forest trees. The grasses which we know in our climates only under the humble forms they put on in our fields, rise, in the elegant and majestic bamboo, to the height of sixty or seventy feet. A single tree is a garden, wherein a hundred different plants intertwine their branches, and display their brilliant flowers on a ground of verdure, where their varied hues and forms of leaves are richly blended." And here the perfection of vegetable life is attained in the graceful palms which stand at the head and crown the vegetable kingdom. This is the region of a perpetual summer, where nature makes ample provision for the support of animal life, and the date, the cocoa-nut, the banana, the plantain, the sugar-cane, the pine-apple, supply all the wants of uncivilized man.

The same gradation is marked in the animal kingdom. The most characteristic feature of the arctic fauna is its dull uniformity. The species are few in number, their forms are regular, and their tints are dusky as the north-

[1] Article "Botany," *Encyclopædia Britannica*, vol. v.; also "Geographical Botany;" and Guyot, "Earth and Man," p. 251.

ern heavens. The most conspicuous animals are the reindeer, the white bear, and the various seals; but the most important are the whales, which rank lowest of all the mammals. The preponderance of marine animals clearly indicates an inferior development. The faunas of the temperate regions are much more varied than in the Arctic Zone. Instead of consisting mainly of aquatic tribes, we have a considerable number of terrestrial animals of graceful form, animated appearance, and varied coloring, though less brilliant than those found in tropical regions. It is in the tropics that animal life attains its highest development. The boundless variety of species, the richness of the colors, the diversity of forms, the size and strength of the great pachyderms that people the forests and rivers, the fleetness and vigor of the ferocious denizens of the jungle and the plain, all attest that this is the privileged zone. And here only are found the quadrumanæ, which stand at the head of the animal kingdom.

Such, then, is clearly the law of the physical world. "Nature goes on adding perfection to perfection from the polar regions to the Temperate Zone, and from the Temperate Zone to the region of the greatest heat." Animal life increases in strength and development; the types are improved; intelligence enlarges; the form approaches nearer the human figure; the ourang-outang occasionally stands erect; and the presence of the mastoid and styloid processes, the development of the heel-bone, and the form of the pelvis, together with the shape of the ears and a higher frontal development, give the gorilla a startling resemblance to man. Following, then, the ascending series (especially if man be regarded as the lineal descendant of the anthropomorphic apes), we might reasonably suppose that here would be found the proper home and habitat of man, and that the tropical man would be the highest type of humanity, and, physically speaking, the most beautiful of the species.

But this, as every one knows, is not the case. While all the types of plants and of animals go on increasing in perfection from the polar to the equatorial regions in proportion to the increase of temperature, "man presents to our view his purest, his most perfect type at the very centre of the temperate continents, at the centre of Asia-Europe, in the region of Iran, of Armenia, and of the Caucasus; and, departing from this geographical centre in the three grand directions of the lands, the types gradually lose the beauty of their forms in proportion to their distance, even to the extreme points of the southern continents, where we find the most deformed and [physically] degenerated races, and the lowest in the scale of humanity."[1]

The distribution of the human race over the face of the earth has thus been governed by a different law from that which has governed the distribution of plants and animals.

In the latter case, the degree of perfection of the types is exactly proportional to the intensity of heat and other material conditions favorable to the development of physical life. *This is the law of a physical order.*

In the former case, in man, the degree of perfection of the types is in proportion to the degree of intellectual and moral improvement, and to the physical conditions favorable to intellectual and moral development. *This is the law of a moral order.*

This difference between the two laws has its ground and reason in the essential difference between the nature and

[1] Guyot, "Earth and Man," p. 255.

destination of these different orders of being. The plant and the animal are not destined to become a different thing from what they already are. The end of their existence is already attained. The development of each individual is bound to an immutable necessity of nature. Therefore vegetable life and organization are ceaselessly uniform; there are always the same cellular structures and the same morphological forms. Unreasoning and instinctive life never leaves its sphere. The beaver builds its dam, lives, and dies, just as it did six thousand years ago. The bee builds the same hexagonal cell she built before the flood. There is an all-pervading order in the physical world. But with man it is quite otherwise. Man, created in the image of God, is a free moral being. He is not solely under the dominion of mere nature-conditions, and he is therefore a progressive being. The physical man is not the true man; the body is not an end, but a means. There is another man—the intellectual, the moral, the spiritual man—which grows up with the body, and to which the physical man is a servant and minister. The unfolding, the development, the perfection of this spiritual nature is the grand end of man. This development can only take place under freedom; this nature be unfolded only by education; the maturity and the perfection of man secured only by the exercise and discipline of his spiritual powers.[1]

Who does not see a plan, a purpose, a Providence in this fact that the cradle of the human race was placed in the midst of the continents of the north and not at the centre of the tropical regions? The balmy but enervating atmosphere of the equatorial regions would have lulled

[1] Guyot, "Earth and Man," pp. 264, 265; Wallace, "On Natural Selection," pp. 324–6; Martineau, "Essays," 1st Series, p. 126.

S

man to sleep, and he would have made no progress. With an abundant supply for his natural wants, there would have been no motive to industry, to enterprise, and to the development of his intellectual powers. Unable to endure the rigors of a colder climate, and to live on a less luxuriant soil, he could not have been induced to migrate to less favorable regions, and, crowded on a narrow area, the race must have been finally exterminated. But planted in the Temperate Zone, in the midst of the continents of the North, so well adapted by their forms, their highly articulated peninsulas, and their climate to stimulate the active powers of man, to promote enterprise, to favor commerce, and hasten individual development and social organization, he was surrounded by conditions most favorable to the fulfillment of his destiny.

It is also worthy of being noted that Western Asia was not only the geographical centre of the human race, but also the grand centre of religious light — the cradle of man's spiritual nature. It was here in the midst of the six great nations of antiquity—the Babylonians, the Assyrians, Medes, Persians, Phœnicians, and Egyptians — that for ages "the living oracles" proclaimed the "Truth of God," and patriarchs and prophets and seers were received into intercourse with the higher world. And it was in Palestine, the centre of the three continents of the Old World, and near five great seas—the highways of the world's travel and commerce—that Jesus of Nazareth taught "the glad tidings of great joy" for the nations, and sent forth his apostles "into all the world to preach that Gospel to every creature."

2. Another important fact which history enables us very

distinctly to recognize is *that those epochs of civilization which represent the highest degree of culture attained by man at different periods in his history have not succeeded one another in the same place, but have passed from one country to another.*

It is an undoubted historic fact, as we have already seen, that Asia was the cradle of the human race. Western Asia is the theatre of the earliest civilization of which we have any historic records. Then a newer and higher form appears on the peninsula of Greece. The centre of civilization again changes place, and Rome embraces and improves upon that of the ancient world. Then passing the Alps, still further to the west, it spreads over France and Germany and the British Isles, and assumes a nobler form; and finally it crosses the Atlantic Ocean, and develops its highest type in the New World. This order may be called the geographical march of civilization.

In the principle we enounced at the opening of this chapter, that the earth is the school-house of man — its highest function being to aid in his intellectual and moral training, and furnish the conditions in which he may fulfill his noble destiny—we can recognize at once the reason and the law of this remarkable progression. And as no single continent furnishes all the conditions necessary to the complete development of man, and each of the three northern continents, by virtue of its structure and climate and physical conditions, has a special function to fulfill in the education of mankind, so God, in his providence, has led the human family from east to west, over the continents of the Temperate Zone, in order to secure the education, the moral advancement, and the final perfection of our race.

The education of the race has, no doubt, proceeded very much in the same manner as the education of the individual. The general law observable in the development of one human mind may be traced in the development of humanity as a whole. That which takes place on the limited field of individual consciousness may also be found upon the larger field of universal consciousness, which is the theatre of history; and as one epoch succeeds another in the progress of the individual, so must it be in the progress of nations. What, then, are the clear and obvious stages in the development of the human mind? Do we not clearly recognize the following order?

1. *The period of submission to absolute authority.* This is the first condition of infancy. The child is controlled absolutely by the will of the parent. It is almost passive amid surrounding conditions, and parental authority is its only law of movement and action.

2. *The discipline of the conscience.* This is the era of childhood. The ideas of the right and the good are developed in the mind. An internal law of duty begins to reveal itself. The child begins to discriminate between what he ought and ought not to do. And in the education of the child the object of a wise and virtuous parent is to strengthen this tendency by urging him to act upon these ideas.

3. *The development of personal liberty*—that is, of independent thought and self-originated action. This is the period of youth. The youth passes from the control of his parents and teachers, and begins to think and act for himself.

4. *The training and discipline of the will under social law*—that is, the voluntary obedience to laws imposed by society, submission to regulations imposed for the public

good. This is the period of manhood. The young man passes into society, he becomes a member of the body politic, and freely acts, not simply as an individual, but as a member of a corporation and of a state.

5. *The development of active philanthropy.* The man advances beyond the claims of social law, and acts from the promptings of love and good-will toward all men. Passing through all the varied stages in the progressive development of human character, and retaining the results of each, he becomes the perfect man.

And now it will be promptly recognized that this has been the order of progress in humanity as a whole—that is, the progress of history and of civilization. The first corresponds with *Oriental*, the second with *Hebrew*, the third with *Greek*, the fourth with *Roman*, and the last with *Christian* civilization.

It will also be observed that each epoch in the development of the individual has demanded new conditions, and has taken place in a new sphere. The first stage in the development of individual character is infoldment in the arms of the parent. He is still held, as it were, within the circle of maternal life. He is bewildered by the vastness and variety of external nature, and he sinks back into his mother's arms. The second sphere is in the bosom of the family and amid the scenes of domestic life, where he recognizes relations and becomes conscious of duties. The third is in the school and the outer world, where thought awakens, and, enjoying more freedom of movement, he becomes more conscious of his personal liberty. The fourth is in society, the state, the arena of political life, where his movements must be regulated by law; and the pursuit of his own pleasure or aggrandizement must not interfere with the rights of his fellow-man. The fifth and last is in the church, the home of religious life, where he is called to ascend from the region of mere law to that of holy love. So also each epoch in the development of humanity has had its separate sphere and its new conditions, first in Asia proper, next in Palestine, on the borders of the Mediterranean Sea, then on the peninsula of Greece, then in Italy, and lastly in Continental Europe, England, and America.

1. Asia, as we have seen, was the cradle of the race. Here, in the infancy of humanity, Oriental Civilization dawns. Amid the extended plains and lofty mountains of Asia, those stupendous and massive forms of Oriental nature, man felt himself absolutely dependent. To the river he looked as the fertilizer of the soil; to the animal which roamed in the desert, and the almost spontaneous vegetation of the earth, for his food; to the sun, as the fountain of light and heat, the giver of life and death.[1] He was environed and overpowered by nature. Almost unconscious of his own freedom, he lay in her bosom, as the child reposes in the arms of its mother. Underlying all the massive forms of Oriental nature he recognized an invisible Power and Presence, and he worshiped nature as an impersonation of God. Every thing inspired him with the sense of the Infinite, the consciousness of dependence on an absolute Will. The patriarchal government, imposed by nature, restrained his personal liberty. His property and life were at the disposal of his chief—an absolute autocrat, who exercised over him an unlimited power. Oriental civilization unquestionably represents the *infancy* of man.

2. In Hebrew civilization we have, as an especial feature, the discipline of the conscience. The child-man

[1] Guyot, "Earth and Man," p. 304.

comes more directly under the power of moral culture. The government and discipline to which he is now subjected aim to develop in his mind the idea of the just, the right, the pure. He is receiving instruction in what he ought and ought not to do. His conceptions of the moral character of God are to be enlarged, the idea especially of the holiness of God is to be developed in his mind through the medium of material symbols and religious rites. The call of Abraham sets forth at once the central lesson of faith in an unseen personal God. The history of the patriarchs brings into clearer light the sovereignty of God as opposed to the mere dominion of nature and fate. A nation grows up in presence of Egyptian culture, and after the purpose of God in the discipline of Egypt is accomplished, they are led into the wilderness, and God now reveals Himself as a Lawgiver and Judge, and a ritual is given which teaches at once the holiness of God and the exceeding sinfulness of sin.[1]

For the achievement of this object a new sphere is demanded—the seclusion and isolation of family life. Accordingly Abraham was called to leave Chaldæa, the scene of Oriental civilization, and led into Canaan, that he might become the father of a great nation, and the source of a new and better civilization. The mountainous region of Palestine was admirably fitted to be the theatre of this new civilization. No other land on the globe was so peculiarly fitted to fulfill this office. The northern half of Syria was not so favorable a locality; for traversed as it was by the great highway from Asia Minor to Assyria, it was subject to the influence of foreign travel from the earliest times. But Palestine lay surrounded by populous

[1] See Article "Philosophy," in Smith's "Dictionary of the Bible." See also Shairp, "Culture and Religion," pp. 40–46.

countries, and yet isolated from them. In the midst of the six great nations of antiquity—the Babylonians, the Assyrians, the Medes, Persians, Phœnicians, and Egyptians—it was separated from them all.[1] Thus secluded and isolated from the rest of mankind, the Hebrews dwelt alone as one great *family*. The first form of government was a patriarchy—the father of the family and of the tribe being the ruler. The second was a theocracy, in which God, the Father of the families of all the earth, becomes the immediate ruler. The third was a monarchy—the government of a man appointed and sustained in his authority by God. And the history of this nation is little else than one of instruction, discipline, and chastisement—a tutelage in which the people were under law and not under grace. The Hebrew civilization represents the *childhood* of humanity.

And the lessons here taught were not lost to the race. They were carried to Assyria and Babylonia during the period of the two captivities; and in the colonies which were founded in Asia Minor, Rome, and Alexandria the influence exerted by Judaism was considerably greater than that which was exerted upon it. The union of Judaism and Platonism is fully represented in Philo the Alexandrian Jew.

3. In Grecian civilization we have the development of personal freedom of thought and action. The Divine discipline of the Jews, as we have seen, was essentially a moral discipline—a discipline of the conscience. This,

[1] "Palestine was from the beginning an isolated land, as Israel was an isolated people, and therefore for thousands of years both have been unintelligible to the world at large. No great highway led through Palestine from people to people; all passed *by* it, and not *over* it; all its coast was without favorable harbors. No one of the pagan states of antiquity could come into close geographical, mercantile, political, and religious relations with a people existing under the sway of Jehovah."—Ritter, "Geographical Studies," p. 43.

however, was not a complete discipline of our whole nature. The reason demands culture as well as the conscience. The process and the issue in the two cases were widely different, but they were in some sense complementary; and the one succeeds the other in the order of time. The Divine kingdom of the Jews was just overthrown when free speculation arose in the Ionian colonies of Asia; and the teaching of the last prophet nearly synchronizes with the death of Socrates.[1]

This new civilization could not be achieved on the continent of Asia, and therefore a new theatre is prepared. "Europe may be called a continuation of Central Asia. It surpasses its Oriental neighbor in the advantage of having no internal mountain barrier to divide its north and south. Thus Europe has been able to develop itself more independently and freely in consequence of the number of its peninsular forms. . . . The three characteristic features in the formation of Europe that are the physical grounds of the development of its nations are its large extent of seaboard, its peninsular forms, and the number of its islands."[2] On the peninsula of Greece, on the shores of the Ægean and Ionian seas, there was freedom of movement, facility of intercourse with the surrounding nations, and inducements to maritime enterprise. These conditions were undoubtedly favorable to a higher development. "The inland sea, the magnificent river," says Cousin, "is the natural symbol of *movement*." These represent the activity of nature, and they become natural centres of progress. The sea is the highway of commerce, and commerce is the grand channel of ideas, the medium through which the knowledge acquired by one people can

[1] Article "Philosophy," in Smith's "Dictionary of the Bible."
[2] Ritter, "Geographical Studies," pp. 342, 343.

flow readily into other lands. Amid such conditions the mind awakes to activity, and the *period of youth* commences. Awakening thought is first directed to the outer world, and attempts an explanation of its phenomena. Greek philosophy thus becomes, at its first appearance, a philosophy of nature, and the Ionian school was a school of physicists. Here the great names which appear at the dawn of mental activity are Thales, Anaximander, Anaximenes, Heraclites, and Diogenes. From the study of nature the human race advances to the study of man. The new school is a school of moral and mental philosophy, or, more correctly, of psychology and ethics, adorned by such immortal names as Socrates, Plato, and Aristotle. In Greece, philosophy, poetry, eloquence, the fine arts, were extensively cultivated. As this was an age of great activity of thought, so it was also an age of great political freedom. The government was in many respects a government of the people, a democracy. "Every thing, in fact, in Greece bears evidence of the preponderance of human personality, and the energy of individual character."[1] Grecian civilization represents the *youth* of humanity.

The results of this culture were carried to other lands by the conquests of Alexander, and subsequently by the conquering Romans. The poets, the architects, the sculptors, the historians, the philosophers of Greece, are still the guides and models of the men of thought and taste in all cultivated nations. The Greek is still, in a peculiar sense, the teacher of the world.

4. In Roman civilization we have the discipline of the will under social and civil law, the more perfect organization of society and of government, the development of the science of jurisprudence.

[1] Guyot, "Earth and Man," p. 307.

This social and political organization was a new work, a higher civilization, and it demanded a new and, in fact, a larger sphere. The centre of the civilized world now changes place, and, moving westward, establishes itself in the peninsula of Italy. By successive conquests its circumference enlarges, and finally it embraces at once the South and the East and the West. The place which Rome occupied, in the very middle of the basin of the Mediterranean Sea, seemed to foreshadow that she was destined to become the metropolis of all the civilized nations who dwelt upon its shores. Rome extended its conquests to Spain, Gaul, Britain, Illyria, Greece, Asia Minor, Egypt, Africa, and the islands of the Mediterranean—over, in fact, six hundred thousand square leagues of the most fertile country; and all but realized the dream of the world's great conquerors—a universal empire. It was defended by a regular army of five hundred thousand men, ranged in the order of the famous legions, which constituted the most effective military organization known. The government of an empire of such vast proportions and diversity of populations demanded the greatest political skill. To establish durable ties between these diverse peoples, and to combine in the same social network all the civilized nations of the world, demanded the highest legislative talent, and gave birth to the science of jurisprudence, which, next to that of theology, is the most important and useful to man. The inability of the Greek to achieve this great work is clearly evinced by the terrible Peloponnesian War and the lamentable history of the empire of Alexander and his successors. Greece represents individuality; Rome, association, unity, and, in some degree, the equality of all races of men.

This was unquestionably a marvelous development: "In

public law, the extension, step by step, through many a civil commotion, of the full rights of citizenship from the narrow circle of a few score of favored families to the entire sphere of the free subjects of the empire; in private law, the equal communication among various classes of the rights of property and dominion over the national soil; the abolition of territorial privileges; the readjustment, by gradual and peaceful manipulation, of the cadastral map of the empire; the relaxation, by slow and experimental process, of the patriarchal authority of the head of the family; of the father over the son, whom at first he might punish, sell, or slay; of the husband over the wife, whom at first he received from her parents as the spoil of his own spear, and ruled as the chattel he had plundered;[1] of the master over the slave, absolute at first, final and irresponsible to law, custom, or conscience; the gradual replacement of the strictly national and tribal ideas on these subjects by views of right, justice, and virtue to mankind in general; the slow but constant growth of principles of natural and universal law, and their application, searchingly and thoroughly, to every subject of jurisprudence, and to all the dealings of man with man."[2]

This vast Roman Empire combined all the elements of civilization characteristic of former periods. The philosopher, the lawyer, and the statesman were united in the person of her great men, as Cicero and Cato, and sometimes also the warrior, as in the case of the first of the Cæsars. The days of the Roman Republic present the most brilliant social and political epoch in the history of the ancient world. The life of a Roman citizen was emphatically a public life.

[1] "The conjugal tie was held sacred, and polygamy prohibited."—De Pressensé, "Religions before Christ," p. 160.

[2] Merivale, "Conversion of the Roman Empire," p. 92.

The love of country was carried to the highest pitch, and was paramount to every other consideration. The laws and jurisprudence of Ancient Rome have furnished models for the whole civilized world. "The world-wide elastic system of jurisprudence by which the great Roman Empire, with all its boundless variety of races, creeds, and manners, was for ages harmoniously and equitably governed; which was accepted and ratified as an eternal possession by the same empire when it became Christian; and has been proved to satisfy the principles of law and justice announced by a religion which alone proclaimed the unity and equality of man; . . . finally, a jurisprudence which has been incorporated into the particular legal systems of, I suppose, every modern nation in Christendom," marks a high degree of civilization, and justifies us in regarding Roman civilization as representing the *manhood* of our race.

5. And now comes, last of all, the Christian civilization, or the age of philanthropy. When the Roman Empire had attained its zenith, and all civilized nations were brought under one government; and the world was at peace; and the philosophy of Greece and the jurisprudence of Rome had prepared the way for a higher and a nobler civilization, then, "in the fullness of time"—the ripeness and maturity of the ages or dispensations—"God sent his Son, made under the law, to redeem them that are under the law, that we might receive the *adoption of sons.*" He came to exhibit completely the truth which had been partially revealed to Plato, that "*God is Love*"—that "Love is creation's final law"—and that the completeness and perfection of humanity is "*resemblance to God.*"[1] He came to announce and enforce the brother-

[1] "God," said Plato, "is supremely good" ("Republic," book ii. ch. 18); and "virtue is likeness or assimilation to God" ("Theætetus," § 384).

hood of mankind, and the equality of all classes and races in the sight of God. He proclaimed the equal worth of all human souls in the estimation of the heavenly Father; and to prove that all men are alike the objects of Divine care and solicitude, He laid down his life as "a propitiation for the sins of the whole world." For the reception of this gospel of universal brotherhood and equal rights the Grecian and Roman civilizations had prepared the way. And now He gives to the race the "new commandment," which is the fundamental law of the Kingdom of God, and is finally to become the universal law for all nations, that "*Men should love one another, as He loved all men, and laid down his life for them.*" The whole spirit and tendency of this crowning form of civilization can not be misapprehended. Its sympathies are all with the poor, the suffering, and the oppressed; it can not fail to overthrow castes and aristocracies, to destroy tyranny, oppression, and slavery, and at last to unite all men in bonds of love to each other and to God.

And now to what people shall be committed the office of diffusing and perpetuating this noblest and highest civilization? Not to the Jewish nation, for it was exclusive and selfish; not to the Greek, for it had become effete; not to the Roman, for it had become corrupt. Christianity, it is true, was born on Jewish soil, but it was soon transferred to a more favorable clime. The Church was early planted in Rome, but achieved its grandest conquests among another people. The fierce Germanic tribes of the North conquer the Roman Empire, and are conquered by its Christianity. Already the Germans had the conception of an illimitable Deity, toward whom they looked with solemn and reverential awe.[1] Having penetrated into the midst of the Roman Empire, they came fully into the presence and under

[1] Milman, "Latin Christianity," vol. i. p. 357.

the influence of Christianity. Their conversion was speedy and comparatively complete. The constant intercourse now maintained between Rome and Central and Northern Europe in a short time carried this new civilization across the Alps; the circle rapidly widens, and embraces all Europe in a common faith.

All the rich treasures of the past are appropriated by Christianity—the moral culture of the Hebrew, the poetry and philosophy of Greece, the jurisprudence of Ancient Rome. All these—in so far as they are pure and good—are absorbed by Christianity, and ennobled and baptized by the Christian spirit. In Christian Europe poetry, philosophy, science flourished as they had never flourished in any preceding age, and they lay their richest tribute at the feet of Christ, the Divine King of the world. Nature, also, herself becomes more and more subject to man, and to the religion of the God-man. Science multiplies the means of diffusing knowledge and the facilities of intercourse among the nations of the earth. The discovery of the art of printing opens the Book of Life to the millions of our race. Space has been annihilated by railroads; by the help of steam continents are united; the electric telegraph is binding the nations in one. And now the genius of Christianity begins more signally to reveal itself as a power acting on the social life of man. The forms and conditions of his earthly lot are being wonderfully transformed and improved. Science is emancipating labor, and constantly overcoming the sources of human suffering. Hygienic science is preserving life and extending the term of human existence. Mankind is rising above the sphere of mere law, into the sphere of noble love. Philanthropic institutions are being daily multiplied, humanitarian and Christian enterprises most vigorously prosecuted, and a noble benevolence is rapidly supplanting the ignoble selfishness of former ages. Chalmers, Howard, Wilberforce, Hitchcock, Amos Lawrence, Elizabeth Fry, Florence Nightingale, Mrs. Gladstone, are representative men and women of the new age.

Christian civilization is no longer the property of any one nation alone. Now it embraces in its purposes and plans the evangelization of all the nations of the earth. The world is now its field. The accumulated waves of light and power from Hebrew and Grecian and Roman civilizations, to which Christianity has added a new life and force, are destined to roll back a tide of blessing upon the remnants of those ancient nations, and sweep northward and southward—

> "Till like a sea of glory,
> It spreads from pole to pole."

The crowning achievement of a Christian civilization will be the political regeneration of the nations—the establishment of all human governments on the principles of human equality, natural rights, and the brotherhood of man. The glory of this achievement, in all its fullness, is not, however, the work of Europe. She inherits too positively the martial spirit of Ancient Rome. Ancient customs and prescriptions, hereditary castes, aristocracies, and kings, and an ecclesiastical polity moulded by these, stand in the way of a Christianity of equality, of freedom, and of universal brotherhood. Europe has her roots too deeply infixed in the past to adapt herself, fully and readily, to the enlarged principles of a thoroughly Christian civilization. A new country is therefore needed, a *New World*, where Christianity can remodel human society, and reconstruct human governments upon her own principles, and the human race can enter upon the last stage in its progress toward the now visible portals of its final goal. "The East," says Ritter, "represents *hope*, the West, *fulfillment*." That new continent was discovered just at the proper hour. Had North America been discovered earlier, it would have been peopled by Catholic nations, and the noble civilization which Christianity was designed to achieve would have been cramped and fettered by the hand of an ecclesiastical hierarchy. The New World reposed quietly in the bosom of a yet untraversed ocean awaiting the advent of the Protestant Reformation. Luther drew the Bible from its concealment in the library of the University of Erfurt at the same time (1502) that Columbus discovered the American continent.[1]

The first settlers in New England were eminently Protestant. They were men who loved the Word of God, and they sought to organize society in this new country upon its holy principles. This new colonization had its birth amid the agonizing throes of martyrdom. The "Pilgrim Fathers" had been persecuted and driven from home for Christ's sake. They sought the desert that they might have freedom to worship God according to the dictates of their own consciences; and they braved the dangers of the almost untraveled deep, and the perils of an inhospitable shore in mid-winter, to lay the foundations of a new empire which should be the home of liberty, and the sanctuary of piety for themselves and their children. The Puritan love of freedom and reverence for religion has left its impress on the mind and character of the American people, upon their modes of thought, and upon the institutions of their country. The ideas of universal liberty and equal justice are interwoven in her Constitution, and, in general, the spirit of her legislation has been in accord-

[1] Guyot, "Earth and Man," p. 322.

ance therewith. A relic of barbarism landed at Jamestown, in Virginia, which after a fierce struggle of years was finally conquered, and the rank offense was expiated by tears and blood. God has destroyed slavery in America by "the breath of his mouth," and its death-knell has sounded all over the globe. The cause of freedom is stronger in Europe as the reflex of her triumphs here.

Finally, a remarkable characteristic of the civilization of the New World is the emancipation of man from the dominion of nature. By an amazing fertility of mechanical contrivance man is here rapidly "subduing the earth." Released from merely local and hereditary ties, he spreads freely over the vast territory, and rapidly multiplies the means of easy locomotion. The soil is being extensively cultivated; the climate, even, modified; the physiognomy of nature changed by the intelligence of man; and a regenerated earth is to be, at last, the consequence of a regenerated race. Physical nature sympathizes with the intellectual and moral condition of man. Science is anticipating the time "when the earth will only produce cultivated plants and domestic animals; when man's selection shall have supplanted 'natural selection;' and when the ocean alone will be the only domain in which that power can be exerted which for countless cycles of ages ruled supreme over the earth."[1] "The whole creation has groaned and travailed together in pain until now, . . . waiting for the manifestation of the sons of God."

"Verily there is a God" that not only judges in the earth, but guides and instructs the nations, and who in the development of the earth and of history "worketh all things according to his eternal counsel and purpose," that for the rational creation "God may be all in all."

[1] Wallace, "On Natural Selection," p. 326.

CHAPTER IX.

SPECIAL PROVIDENCE AND PRAYER.

"England's thinkers are again beginning to see, what they had only temporarily forgotten, that the difficulties of metaphysics lie at the root of all science."—J. S. MILL.

THE most sharply defined issue between Science and Religion—in fact, the only real issue at the present time—is in regard to the doctrine of Special Providence and the efficacy of Prayer.

These are not in reality two distinct questions: they are but opposite phases of one and the same question. The doctrine of special providence is the *theoretic* aspect, and the doctrine of the efficacy of prayer is the *practical* aspect of the Christian doctrine of the relation of God to nature and man. We can not, therefore, discuss the practical question apart from the theoretic; neither can we reach any decisive conclusions in regard to either unless we start with clear and well-defined conceptions of the fundamental relations between God and nature, and between God and man.

We shall assume the existence of God as the common postulate of all religion and of all philosophy. If this be denied, then all discussion of the present question is useless, because we have no common starting-point. But it will not be denied, we think, that the vast majority of scientific men are agreed that the idea of God is the necessary presupposition of all those branches of science which concern themselves with "genetic problems"—that is, with problems of origin; and which, strictly speaking, are not problems of science, but of philosophy. These scientists may not all choose to employ the term "God," but they will all recognize, with Mr. Spencer, the existence of "an unconditioned Cause" as "the ultimate of all ultimates," and they will admit with him that the First Cause must be infinite, absolute, and perfect, "including within itself all power and transcending all law."[1] Mr. Spencer calls this idea of a First Cause "a datum of consciousness;" and he asserts that this "inexpugnable consciousness, in which religion and philosophy are at one with common-sense, is likewise that on which all exact science is founded."[2]

Taking this fundamental presupposition as generally conceded—namely, the existence of a Power which is unoriginated and independent; a Power which is conscious of itself and determines itself; a Power which transcends all law and is the source of all law—the question at issue may be thus stated—*Have our prayers any influence with this Power?* Can they in any way affect the Divine feeling and action toward us? Do they have any indirect influence upon that succession of events in nature and history which is effectuated and determined by that Supreme Power? This is the real question at issue between science and religion.

Nothing need be said to deepen our sense of the importance of this issue. We all regard it as one of the vital questions of the hour, the most vital question for religious men, yea, the most vital question for scientific men, inasmuch as there are moments of sadness and sorrow, of doubt and mystery, when man feels that his only refuge

[1] "First Principles," p. 38. [2] Ibid. p. 496.

is in prayer, and, science or no science, he must pray. But if there is no living God to sympathize with us in our sorrow and help us in our deepest need, or, which amounts to the same thing, if God is so completely environed by laws which He has Himself enacted, and so imprisoned in his own works that He can do nothing to aid us, then prayer is an illusion, and instead of being in any way beneficial to us, it inflicts a deep and irreparable injury upon our intellectual and moral life. If there is nothing in the universe but mechanical force and necessary law; if there is no freedom and no moral purpose, then prayer for help and succor and guidance is a conscious or unconscious deception practiced by the soul upon itself, and the sooner we are undeceived the better; for of all deception the most pernicious and depraving is that which a man practices upon himself. We could not even accept the cold apology for prayer which was made by David Hume, that it may have a wholesome reflex influence upon the mind of the worshiper, and be a good way of preaching to ourselves.[1] There can be nothing useful or helpful in the belief and practice of a lie. No accession of moral force or moral purity can come from doing any thing in which we do not believe. If there is any moral value and any real helpfulness in prayer, it must be based upon a *rational* belief that the Divine mind is accessible to the supplication of his creature, and that the Divine will is moved thereby. "He that cometh to God must believe that He is, and that He is a rewarder of them that diligently seek Him."

Humbly professing this belief without any reservation, and regarding it as a perfectly rational belief, we proceed to defend it against certain so-called scientific objections,

[1] Buchanan, "Modern Atheism," p. 285.

and to consider certain difficulties which present themselves to the minds of scientific men.

We have said that there is a *real* issue between science and religion as to the efficacy of prayer. The statement is not strictly correct, and we amend it by saying that the issue is not between science and religion, but between certain men who study and teach science and certain men who study and teach religion. For, as Mr. Murphy observes, "The antagonism between science and religion themselves is purely imaginary. The antagonism between the men who study and teach science and the men who study and teach religion is unfortunately sometimes real, though it is the fashion [just now] to exaggerate it; but so far as it is real it is an accident of the present time, which will disappear, and indeed is already visibly disappearing."[1]

No man is in a position to affirm that there is an antagonism between science and religion until he has first clearly determined the sphere and function of each, and can say distinctly *what science is and what religion is.* He may have utterly misconceived the nature of religion, or he may have misapprehended the function of science, and therefore the supposed antagonism may be purely imaginary. For example, Herbert Spencer says, "Every religion may be defined as an *à priori* theory of the universe."[2] If this definition were correct, we could easily conceive how religion and modern science might come into collision, because the tendency of science at the present time is to occupy itself with "questions of origin"—that is, with "theories of the origin of things," instead of being, as Spencer defines it, "a systematic collection of facts, ascertained with precision, and so classified and gen-

[1] "Scientific Basis of Faith," p. 6. [2] "First Principles," p. 43.

eralized as to reveal the uniform relations of co-existence and succession among phenomena, and thus give *prevision*." This is the legitimate sphere of all that science which can lay any claim to be regarded as "exact science." When it transcends this limit it ceases to be science and becomes philosophy—a philosophy which will be more or less valid and legitimate as it recognizes the authority and submits to the guidance of *à priori* ideas of the reason.

But is Mr. Spencer's definition of religion correct? We think not. Indeed, it would be difficult to give a definition of religion wider from the mark. He might with just as much propriety have said that religion is an *à priori* theory of the origin of language, of government, of trade, or of music. Either Mr. Spencer must have made this definition for an unworthy purpose, or he must be in utter darkness as to the nature of religion. One needs only to cast a hasty glance over the history of ancient religions, or to consider with an unprejudiced mind any of the contemporaneous forms of religion, to be convinced that religion is, and always has been, a mode of life determined by the sense of dependence upon a Supreme Power.[1] Religion has always been a matter of practical interest and personal concernment, and has no more to do with "theories of the universe" than with theories of light, or theories of electricity, or theories of political economy.

The separate spheres of religion and science have been admirably defined by James Martineau in a few words—

[1] Without referring to the writings of theologians, we may take any definition of religion which incidentally occurs in general literature. For example, Froude defines religion as "the attitude of reverence in which noble-minded men instinctively place themselves toward the Unknown Power which made man and his dwelling-place. It is the natural accompaniment of their lives, the sanctification of their actions and their acquirements. It is what gives to man in the midst of the rest of Creation his special elevation and dignity" ("History of England," vol. xii. p. 560).

"Science discloses the *Method* of the world but not its cause; religion [or theology] discloses the *Cause* of the world but not its method. There is no conflict between them except when either forgets its ignorance of what the other alone can know."[1] This is well said, and directly to the point. Religion, or more properly theology (for theology is the objective correlate and piety the subjective correlate of religion), teaches *what God is*, what are his attributes, what are the moral and spiritual relations which subsist between God and man, and what are the duties which arise out of these relations. Science teaches *what nature is*, and what are the relations and laws of natural phenomena. Science is the co-ordination of phenomena. Here no conflict can arise. The truths which are taught by each rest on their own appropriate evidence, and they are capable of verification by direct or indirect reduction to experience—the facts of science to external experience, and the facts of religion to internal experience. These experiences can not, in the nature of the case, be contradictory, because religion deals with one class of facts and science with another. Such being the case, the scientist may be as certain of the reality of religion as of the reality of science—that is, he may be directly and immediately conscious of the same feeling of reverence, the same sense of dependence, the same feeling of obligation, and the same loyalty of soul toward the unseen "Power which makes for righteousness,"[2] which is experienced by the unscientific believer. This is frankly avowed by Dr. Tyndall. He says, "The facts of religious feeling are to me as certain as the facts of phys-

[1] "Essays," 1st Series, p. 178.

[2] Preface to the seventh edition of the Address before the British Association of Science at Belfast.

ics;" and he refers with evident emotion to a period in his earlier years when he "prized the conscious strength and pleasure derived from moral and religious feeling." "Give me," he says, "their health, and there is no spiritual experience of those earlier years, no resolve of duty or work of mercy, no act of self-denial, no solemnity of thought, no joy in the life and aspect of nature which would not still be mine."[1] We doubt not that there are thousands of scientific men who to-day might bear the same testimony.

Here the question will suggest itself, How, then, comes it to pass that there exists any antagonism between the teachers of science and the teachers of religion? We answer, the antagonism has arisen on that debatable ground which lies between the two, where speculative thought, whether from the stand-point of religion or the stand-point of science, seeks to form definite conceptions of the relation between God and nature, to bring our outer and inner experiences into a higher unity of reason, and to construct "*à priori* theories of the origin of things."

We do not presume to say that these metaphysical speculations are either futile or improper. But what we do insist upon, and beg the reader distinctly to note, is that these speculations are neither *scientific* nor *religious*, and that neither true science nor true religion is responsible for them. They are not religious, even though indulged in by theologians; because religion is solely concerned with the personal consciousness of our relation to God, and the discharge of our personal duty to God, and not in the remotest sense with any theory as to the method of causation in the world around us. It is equally certain that

[1] Preface to the seventh edition of the Address before the British Association of Science at Belfast.

these speculations are not scientific, even though indulged in by scientists; because science deals only with phenomena, and the laws of phenomena; and it is a fundamental canon of all scientific induction that no problem is to be mooted unless it can be presented in terms of experience, and no principles are to be admitted which can not be verified by experiment. But the modern speculations respecting the *origin* of motion, of life, and of mind can not be presented in terms of sensible experience, and can not be verified by actual experiment. So far as sensible experience goes, every case of physical motion is a transformation of energy, and every new physiological unit or aggregation of units is derived from pre-existent bioplasm. And so Dr. Tyndall, in the speculations in which he indulges, in the now celebrated "Inaugural Address" delivered at Belfast, particularly in regard to the origin of life, admits that he "*oversteps the boundary of the experimental evidence*;" therefore, by his own admission, these speculations are *unscientific*.[1] These discussions are inevitable, and even valuable. We would protest as earnestly as Dr. Tyndall against the attempt of any man to set limits to human thought, but we would equally protest against the attempt to pass off the results of speculative thinking in any direction as "exact science." True science is itself dishonored and discredited by all such attempts.

[1] Dr. Tyndall subsequently defends his course by saying, "The kingdom of science cometh not by observation and experiment alone, but is completed by fixing the roots of observation and experiment in *a region inaccessible to both*, and in dealing with which we are forced to fall back upon the picturing power of the mind" — "*Einbildungskraft*" — the force of imagination (Preface to seventh edition). Are we then to believe that the imagination is the source of scientific principles, that it has ány "power of intuition, or can in any way create its own objects?" Why does he not fall back on his "*Anschauungsgabe*," or faculty of rational intuition, and admit that he is in the region of the metaphysical? See "Fragments of Science," p. 130.

We have said that it is solely within the field of speculative thought that all controversy has arisen concerning the doctrine of special providence and the efficacy of prayer. This will be apparent from the consideration of the fact that from the dawn of speculative thought to the present hour two radically opposite theories of the origin of things have prevailed—one *mechanical*, the other *vital*.

The vital theory regards nature as the product and the continued work of an ever-living and ever-creating Spirit, who is the immediate fountain of all force, and the immanent life of all that lives. It looks upon the universe "as the manifestation and the abode of a Free Mind like our own," who realizes his thoughts in its collocations and adjustments, embodies his ideals in its typical forms, and by his free volition subordinates nature to the higher purposes of intellectual and moral life — the formation of noble human characters. In a world so constituted prayer is a real power, and human character is a free development through the power of prayer which influences that ever-present Will that sustains our life.

The mechanical theory regards the world as a huge machine supplied with motor power in the primal act of creation, and then left to make its own history according to rigid laws of mechanics and "the multiplication table." There is no "Power which makes for righteousness," and no purpose of love mingling in the necessary order of things. Evolution is the only law of creation; there is nothing spontaneous, nothing free. All the processes of nature, all the forms of life, all the facts of consciousness, all the sympathies, sacrifices, joys, and sorrows of social life, and all the noble or ignoble deeds of history, are only mechanical functions which can be weighed or measured, and catalogued in tables of statistics. Inflexible necessity, inexorable law, absolute uniformity, unbroken continuity tell the story of the universe. In such a world there is no place for prayer, or at most it is but the cry of anguish wrung from the lips of those who are being mangled and crushed by the ponderous mechanism, which floats away into the infinite spaces, and never finds a living ear or touches a compassionate heart. Then, as Dr. Hedge puts the melancholy case, "We must rough it as best we can with driving-wheel and fly-wheel, and trust that the power may not fail and the gearing foul in our short day."

This is the position of some, but by no means of the majority of the scientists of our time. We venture the assertion that it is no part of the doctrine of modern science, neither does it follow as a logical consequence from any of the accepted principles of modern science, nor does it reflect the real feeling of the best exponents of modern science.

Dr. Tyndall stands as one of the most popular exponents of scientific knowledge, and may be regarded as a fair representative of the feelings of many scientific men. And in his estimation "the problem of problems of our day is to find a legitimate satisfaction for the religious emotions." He admits that these religious emotions are inexpugnable facts of human nature, as certain and as incontestable as the facts of physics. Now what is meant by a *legitimate* satisfaction of the religious emotions? Does it not mean that human reverence must have a *real* and a worthy Object? that for human duty there must be an imperative ground of obligation? that for true loyalty of soul to truth and right there must be an eternal reason? and that the instinctive trust of the soul in everlasting righteousness and everlasting love must have a rational vindication? Where shall we look for this object? "May we look upward and onward, or have we nothing to do but yield to the pressure from behind and below?" What conception are we to form of that mysterious Power or Principle which stands in necessary correlation with the religious nature of man? Dr. Tyndall permits us "to fashion this conception as we will"—with that "he has nothing to do;" only he demands that in doing so we observe two conditions: 1. "Be careful that your conception is not an unworthy one;" "invest it with your highest and holiest thoughts." 2. Allow "no intrusion of purely creative power into any series of phenomena," no arbitrary interference with the order of nature "for special purposes." The first condition would be violated by our conceiving that Power as purely *mechanical*, for then the sublimest interests of our moral and spiritual life would be surrendered to the action of the same force as that which draws a stone to the earth. The conception of unconscious and unmoral force is not our highest and holiest thought—it can not inspire reverence and loyalty and love. The second condition would be violated by our regarding that Power as *arbitrary*—that is, as following no law; for that would be opposed to all the inductions of modern science, and would invalidate all conclusions based on the assumed permanence of natural laws. The problem, then, is to steer between the Scylla and Charybdis of mechanism and arbitrariness, and find the open sea where freedom may move in harmony with law, and where, in the grand hierarchy of laws the physical order of the world may be coordinated with, perhaps subordinated to, the higher reign of righteousness and love.

The solution of this problem can only be reached through

the discussion of the following questions: 1. What are "the facts of religious feeling" involved in this problem, and what are the necessary correlatives of these facts? 2. What are the facts concerning the order of nature involved in the problem, and what are the logical inferences from these facts? 3. How can the conception of the *Force* which is manifested in the phenomena of nature be brought into harmony with the idea of *God* as revealed in the religious consciousness?

1. First, then, what are the facts of religious feeling which "as experiences of consciousness are perfectly beyond the assaults of logic," and what are the necessary correlatives of these facts?

We present first of all the incontestable fact that *prayer is natural to* man. Like our instinctive belief in the being of God, the accountability of man, and the immortality of the soul, we have also an instinctive prompting to pray, and an instinctive belief in the efficacy of prayer. This is an essentially human characteristic; it is common to all men. Man has been defined in many ways, as "a rational animal," "a social animal," "a tool-using animal," "a language-speaking animal;" with more justice may he be called "a *praying* animal," for prayer is a universal characteristic and fundamental differentia of man. Never has the traveler yet found a people which did not pray. Tribes of men have been found without houses, without raiment, without letters, without science, but never without prayer any more than without speech. This was remarked by Plutarch eighteen centuries ago,[1] and the researches and explorations of modern travelers and ethnologists have added confirmation to its truth. The flow of prayer from human lips is just as natural as the flow of speech. Is

[1] "Πρὸς Κολώτην," xxxi.

man in danger or in sorrow, his most natural and spontaneous refuge is in prayer. The suffering, bewildered, terror-stricken soul that knows not where to fly, flies to God. There are few men, probably no men, who in moments of extreme peril or intense anguish can resist the impulse to pray. Nature is stronger than all our logic; and, science or no science, the cry for help will rise from the lips of even skeptical men.[1]

We ask that these facts may be fully considered and fairly estimated. The instinctive tendency to pray is a universal fact of human nature, as valid and as significant as any fact in physics. It presents as rightful a claim to be taken account of in our theories of the ultimate constitution of the universe as the First Law of Motion or the Conservation of Energy. If we disregard it, our *Systema Mundi* will be one-sided and partial, and, instead of being a philosophy, will be only a caricature.

We do not claim that the presence in man of this in-

[1] This is admitted even by those who regard prayer for physical change, as, for example, the averting of disease or the fall of rain, to be "irrational and unconsciously irreverent." "I repeat that no theory of the universe, no philosophy of human nature, and no conclusion of science can ever lay an arrest upon the instincts of the universal heart in the presence of calamity, and with the prospect of its increase. Let men philosophize as they will, and let science march where it will (conquering realm after realm, and reducing all under the rigor of law), the human spirit will always 'cry unto God' in times of crisis, and will find immeasurable solace in 'committing its causes' unto Him; for the instinct to pray for relief in times of anxiety or of peril is one which can never be exorcised from the heart of man. But it does not follow that it will always (or that it ought ever) to imagine that by so doing it can deflect the order of nature or induce God to alter his prearrangements. The relief obtained is in the act of *submission* and of filial trust, not in the notion of being able to persuade an infinitely powerful and sympathetic Listener" ("Prayer: 'The Two Spheres:' They *are* Two," by the Rev. William Knight, *Contemporary Review*, December, 1873, p. 35). Of course we have no reason to expect that Dr. Tyndall should yield his judgment to the authority of Scripture, but we may legitimately expect the Rev. William Knight, of the Free Church of Scotland, to defer in some measure to James v. 13–18.

stinctive tendency to pray proves the efficacy of prayer—that is, proves the existence of a living God and Father who hears and answers prayer. But it does establish a strong presumption in favor of the doctrine; for how comes it to pass that the sentiment is so perennial and so universal? Either it was originally implanted in the soul of man by the Creator, or there exists something in the constitution of nature—the "relation between the organism and its environment"—which determines this feeling in man, and in either case it must be regarded as normal, and as essential to humanity. If nature teaches us to pray, and, as it were, compels us to pray, then we are justified in the assumption that there is nothing in the ultimate constitution of nature which can contradict her own ordinances and render prayer an absurdity.

The next fact to which we desire to direct attention is that *prayer is an essential element of life*—we do not mean physical life, but that which gives significance and value and completeness to human existence—namely, ethical and spiritual life. That religion is deeply seated in the nature of man, and, in fact, ineradicable, is conceded by Dr. Tyndall. "No atheistical reasoning," he says, "can dislodge religion from the heart of man. Logic can not deprive us of life, and religion is life to the religious. As an experience of consciousness, it is perfectly beyond the assaults of logic."[1] This general admission that man has a religious nature, a religious consciousness, is important. The bearing of this upon our argument will be obvious when we have considered more particularly the nature and content of this "religious consciousness." In what does it consist? Into what elements is it resolvable by psychological analysis? We answer, religious consciousness is a conscious-

[1] Preface to the seventh edition of Dr. Tyndall's "Address."

ness conditioned by the idea of God, and involves a sense of dependence; a feeling of reverence; a sense of obligation; a sentiment of loyalty; a conscious community of nature; and a longing for a deeper fellowship with the *Divine.*

Every thing around us and every thing within us makes us conscious of limitation and dependence. We know that our own existence is not self-originated or self-sustained. We have the sense of an immanent all-pervading Life which sustains and conditions our life. We have the sentiment of an overshadowing Power and Presence which compasses us behind and before, and lays its hand upon us, and we are constrained to bow in reverence and awe before that Power which controls our destiny. With the sense of dependence is associated the feeling of obligation to conform our conduct to the will of this Supreme Being, and to subordinate the ruling purpose of our life to the Divine purpose of creation so far as that purpose can be known. There is also more or less loyalty of soul to what is just and true, a natural and constitutional sympathy of reason with the law of God—"it delights in that law," and "consents that it is good." Finally, there is the consciousness of some community of nature between God and man, and some living susceptibility to the influences and inspirations of the higher world which authorizes the belief that there may be a communion of thought, a relation of conscience, and an approach of affection between the Divine and human that shall purify and elevate our nature, and lift us up into a resemblance to God.

The bearing of all that we have just said on the necessity of prayer will have already suggested itself to the reader. The feeling of dependence, the sense of feebleness will prompt man to pray. Man is not sufficient for himself. He is not fit to be his own all in all. He has not resources within himself to supply his own spiritual wants. He needs some external succor, some support to the will, some inspiration from without. And he can become a strong man and a noble man only by aspiring and striving after something beyond and above himself—

> "Unless above himself he can
> Erect himself, how mean a thing is man!"

When his affections and cares and thoughts all centre upon himself, his soul shrivels down to a dreary selfishness, and becomes a dry microscopic point, or else a mass of putrid sensuality. Man needs a lofty object above himself, after which he may aspire and upon which he may lay hold and lift himself into a nobler form of life. That lofty object is the ideal of a *perfect, noble human character.* "The formation of noble human character," says Mr. Murphy, "is the highest work that man or, so far as we know, that God can be engaged in."[1] The thoughtful mind recognizes that there is a purpose to be fulfilled in life which is nobler than mere enjoyment. Who has dared to say that our highest duty is to be happy? But every one must feel that it is our highest duty to form a nobler character and let the happiness take care of itself.

And now is it not a fact of experience that the more a man strives after a pure and noble life, the more does he become conscious of the need of superhuman strength and grace? He finds that he has to wage an uncompromising, sometimes even agonizing warfare against hereditary "taints of blood," against morbid instincts and low passions, against inherent selfishness and meanness, against tyrant habits engendered in the recklessness of youth, against the temptations of designing men and abandoned

[1] "Scientific Basis of Faith," p. 39.

women, and the false sentiment, despotic opinion, and arbitrary customs of modern fashionable society. In the presence of these giants of evil with their fetters of iron he stands appalled, and against himself, against his temptations and sins, even against society itself, he feels he must *call upon God for help.* Through Divine strength he may conquer; without it—never. There are those who hope to conquer evil through a certain inherent force of nature, or a certain self-caused and self-attained culture. We do not dare to say that they will utterly fail, or that what they achieve is utterly valueless. But we do say that the character they develop is not the highest style of excellence. There is in it a boldness bordering on audacity, a self-sufficiency akin to haughtiness, and an arbitrariness which is repulsive. The very basis of a noble character, the very essence of that prophetic power which has exerted the mightiest influence on the destinies of man, is humility. The loftiest and finest minds have been eminently trustful—men of heroic confidence who derived their inspiration and confessed their dependence on the light and strength which come from above. These are the men who really shape the history of the world,[1] these are the men who command the esteem and win the reverence even of unbelievers. We can not illustrate this point better than by quoting the words of Dr. Tyndall in regard to Michael Faraday. Faraday, it is well known, was one of the greatest of modern scientists — it ought also to be as widely known that he was a devout Christian. Tyndall dined with Faraday, and on that occasion Faraday "said grace."

[1] "When ten men are so in earnest on one side that they will sooner be killed than give way, and twenty are earnest enough on the other to cast their votes for it but will not risk their skins, the ten will give the law to the twenty in virtue of the robuster faith, and of the strength that goes along with it." —Froude, "History of England," vol. xii. p. 562.

Tyndall writes: "I am almost ashamed to call his prayer a 'saying' of grace. In the language of Scripture, it might be described as the petition of a son into whose heart God had sent the Spirit of his Son, and who, with absolute trust, asked a blessing from his father. We dined on roast beef, Yorkshire pudding, and potatoes; drank sherry, talked of research and its requirements, and of his habit of keeping himself free from the distractions of society. He was bright and joyful—boylike, in fact—though he is now sixty-two. His work excites my admiration, but contact with him warms my heart. Here surely is a *strong* man. I love strength, but let me not forget the example of its union with *modesty*, *tenderness*, and *sweetness* in the character of Faraday."[1]

This, then, is the point we desire to emphasize. It is a fact of experience that prayer can give calmness, purity, and strength of soul. It can lighten perplexity and sorrow. It can empower us to resist temptation, and enable us to overcome sin. It can give "modesty, tenderness, and sweetness" to character. In a word, it can aid us materially in the formation of a noble human character.

Noble character can only be formed under two conditions. First, it can only be formed under the condition of *freedom*. The unfree is the unmoral.[2] There can be no dignity and no moral worth in action which results from mere mechanical force. Personality alone has responsibility, dignity, and worth. If, then, moral personality has true freedom and self-determination, we are free to pray, and God is free to answer prayer. We may believe that the physical world is held in iron bands of necessary

[1] "Fragments of Science," p. 350.

[2] "Only in the domain of Freedom can there exist the moral."—Martensen, "Christian Ethics," p. 1.

causation, but we can not believe that the moral world is so bound. The human will is free, and the Divine will is free. "The First Cause," says Mr. Spencer, "includes within itself all power"—therefore alternative power—"and transcends all law"—therefore it can not be necessitated. We can not doubt that Mr. Tyndall would freely accord this position. He might hesitate, he would unquestionably refuse to unite in "prayer for rain," for example, because he holds that the fall of rain is governed by changeless physical laws, and "no act of humiliation, individual or national, could call one shower from heaven;" this would be a miracle, and "the age of miracles is past."[1] But we do not see how he could refuse to unite in the prayers of the National Church for the forgiveness of sins, for strength to overcome sin, for fortitude to endure, and for consolation under the afflictions and sorrows incident to human life.

The second condition necessary to the development of noble character is that man shall be capable of receiving inspiration from the great source of all life, especially of all spiritual life. The universal belief of our race that there is a community of nature between God and man, expressed alike in the words of Aratus, the Asiatic poet, Cleanthes, the Stoic philosopher, and Paul, the Christian teacher—"*We are the offspring of God*"—justifies the further expectation and hope that there may be a real communion between the human and the Divine. Of course this is fundamentally "a question between Theism and Atheism, between a God and no God," between a conscious Being and an unconscious Force. If there is a personal God, then He may communicate with our souls which dwell, as it were, within the ocean of his immensity, and are surrounded and

[1] "Fragments of Science," p. 39.

interpenetrated by his living presence. Then there may be a real sympathy, a loving fellowship, and a sanctifying communion. Even should science forbid the Author of nature to interpose in the slightest degree in the procession of phenomena or modify in the least the action of the so-called natural forces, surely it will not be so "audacious"[1] as to forbid that He shall come near to human souls, and interpose in the moral order of the world to deliver man from sin and purify and elevate human society. Here at any rate science is out of its place. It is guilty of that very presumption with which it is evermore charging the theology of the Middle Ages, viz., the attempt to monopolize the whole field of human knowledge and experience. If the good man does feel that God is with him and in him, if he knows by experience that prayer is an act of Divine communion—that it opens to him an unfailing fountain of refreshment, solace, and strength; if he is conscious that it does lift him up to a larger and more blessed life, then even science, which boasts its rigid adherence to the inductive method, and its unswerving loyalty to fact and experience, must obey the Divine injunction—"Be still, and know that I am God." "I dwell with him that is of a contrite and humble spirit, to revive the spirit of the humble, and to revive the heart of the contrite."

2. We come now to the consideration of the second question, What are the facts concerning the order of nature which have been placed beyond controversy by the inductions of science, and what are the logical inferences from these facts?

The facts concerning the order of nature which it is

[1] "Questions such as these derive their present interest in great part from their *audacity*."—Tyndall.

claimed are placed beyond controversy may be stated in the following words: Now of all the results of science, none is more universal and more emphatic than this: that there is no arbitrariness in the series of events which constitute our experience; but that a perfect order or uniformity prevails through them all, an order which our intellect can apprehend under the form of cause and effect, or *permanent* force and *necessary* phenomena, or, better, a constant persistency of amount both of matter and force in the universe.[1] This statement of the scientist is accepted by many theologians (of the Calvinistic school), who say with Rev. William Knight, "The doctrine of the persistence of physical force and the invariability of natural law, is a physical truth of which the theological phase or corollary is the uniformity of Divine operation and the inviolableness of Divine love. 'The permanence of the order of nature' is the scientific equivalent of the Divine constancy—'the same yesterday, to-day, and forever.'"[2] How far and in what sense we accept this doctrine will be seen as we advance in the discussion.

At the beginning of this chapter we remarked that if the Christian doctrine of the efficacy of prayer is disputed, whether on *theoretical* or *experiential* grounds, an adequate and complete defense can only be made by falling back upon the fundamental conception of God, and the relation of God to nature and humanity presented in the preceding chapters of this volume. Is there a God in the proper and commonly accepted sense of the term—a conscious, free, personal First Cause, the Creator of the world and man? Is He the immanent Conservator of the universe—is his omnipotence the *force*, his reason the *law*,

[1] See "Fragments of Science," pp. 38 and 64–65.

[2] *Contemporary Review*, December, 1873, p. 30.

and his omnipresence the *life* of all nature? These are the questions which must be settled before we can successfully deal with the problem of the efficacy of prayer. If we are not agreed on these points, the debate must be adjourned until we have settled the first principles which underlie the discussion. This will be obvious to all who are acquainted with the history of the controversy. If it can be proved that there is no conscious, free, personal God, the creator and conservator of the universe, the question is settled; then prayer can be of no avail, and must "be abandoned to the domain of recognized superstitions." But if it be admitted that there is a God, in the proper import of that term, then the question may be debated whether the Christian doctrine of the efficacy of prayer is consistent with the scientific conception of material nature as "the living garment of God."[1]

Dr. Tyndall is the fairest and ablest representative of that class of scientific men who to-day are denying the efficacy of prayer—that is, of such prayer the answer to which would seem to involve the interference of personal volition in the economy of nature; and he believes in the existence of a God. He has again and again repelled with feeling the imputation of atheism which the English theologians have inconsiderately and unfairly cast upon him. He is a frank, outspoken man, and he admits that in "his hours of weakness and doubt" he has temptations to material atheism. "But," he says, "I have noticed that it is not in hours of clearness and vigor that this doctrine commends itself to my mind, and that in presence of stronger and healthier thoughts it ever disappears as offering no solution of the mystery in which we dwell and of which we

[1] Tyndall, "Fragments of Science," p. 160.

form a part."[1] He also expresses his conviction that "the Power which works for righteousness is *intelligent* as well as ethical."[2] And furthermore he asserts that "it is no departure from scientific method to place behind natural phenomena *a universal Father* who, in answer to the prayers of his children, alters the currents of those phenomena. Thus far theology and science go hand in hand."[3] Let it, then, be distinctly remembered that we are arguing with men who believe in the existence of God.

In an article which appeared in the *Fortnightly Review* for August, 1872, entitled "Statistical Inquiries into the Efficacy of Prayer," by Francis Galton, a species of guerrilla warfare is opened on this doctrine from the standpoint of experience.

Mr. Galton assumes that "the efficacy of prayer is a perfectly appropriate and legitimate subject of scientific inquiry." It must be assumed to be subject to unvarying laws, and, like all physical problems, may be brought to the test of rigid mathematics. By the marshaling of very incomplete and partial statistics, drawn chiefly from Chalmers's "Biographical Dictionary," he endeavors to show that praying men, especially clergymen, are no healthier, recover from sickness no better, and do not live any longer than the men who do not pray. Insurance companies make no distinction between the prayerful and the prayerless; they regard them as equal risks. Furthermore, praying men do not make any better statesmen, any more successful men of business, or any better physicians and lawyers than prayerless men. On the contrary, "it is a common week-day opinion of the world that praying men are

[1] Preface to the Address before the British Association of Science at Belfast.

[2] Preface to the seventh edition.

[3] *Contemporary Review.*

not practical." Finally, the children of praying parents are no better endowed intellectually, and do not turn out any better morally than the rest of mankind. His gentle impeachment is that they are somewhat below the common average. By this "scientific method," as he is pleased to call it, the writer flatters himself that he has routed the army of believers in the efficacy of prayer, and that the practice of prayer will soon become "obsolete;" "just as the Water of Jealousy and the Urim and Thummin of the Mosaic law did in the times of the later Jewish kings."

But Mr. Galton's fusillade did not produce the effect he expected. True, it made some noise, and for a brief season commanded attention; but it was soon discovered to be a mere discharge of rhetorical blank-cartridge which hit nothing. His parade of argument was found to be utterly inconsequential. The dullest mind could perceive that the attempt to solve moral problems by statistical averages was a practical folly, because it began by unceremoniously assuming the very point it ought to prove, namely, that *the determinations of will, whether Divine or human, are governed by necessary laws* as surely as the revolution of planets and the vibration of molecules. It is precisely because personal acts are *not* reducible to any fixed laws, or capable of representation by any numerical calculations, that statistical averages acquire any value as substitutes. "No one dreams of applying statistical averages to calculate the period of the earth's rotation, by showing that four and twenty hours is the exact medium of time, comparing one month's or one year's revolutions with another's. It is only where the individual movements are irregular that it is necessary to aim at a proximate regularity by calculating in masses."[1] The com-

[1] Mansel, "Prolegomena Logica," p. 280.

parison of large averages may approach equality and furnish a basis of probability as to the future, but the contingency of each individual case remains still a contingency.

In no department of human inquiry is there so much temptation and so much opportunity for plausible sophistry as in the now somewhat popular application of statistics to ethological problems. By a skillful manipulation of figures, Mr. Buckle[1] flatters himself that he has made it apparent that "individual felons only carry into effect the necessary consequences of preceding circumstances;" that marriages are regulated by the price of wheat; and that the number of suicides is determined by the rise and fall of the barometer; in a word, that the whole of man's social and moral life is part and parcel of nature, and subject to the same necessary mechanical laws.

The logic of statistics, or rather the sophistry of statistics by which Mr. Galton proves the uselessness of prayer, would, if skillfully managed, be equally efficacious in proving that sobriety and integrity, honor and honesty, are unprofitable and useless virtues—at least so far as this life is concerned; and we might say of each of them what Shakespeare's "Murderer" says of conscience: "It fills one full of obstacles. . . . It beggars any man that keeps it. It is turned out of all towns and cities for a dangerous thing; and every man that means to live well endeavors to trust himself, and live without it." Dishonest men are as healthy, recover as well from sickness, and live as long as honest men. Wicked men prosper in the world, they succeed in business and increase in riches better, it may be, than good and godly men. Dishonorable and unprincipled politicians climb into place and power with more facility than men of honor and integrity. Distinguished lawyers

[1] "History of Civilization."

and skillful physicians have not been strictly temperate; and statistical tables may be easily produced which show that the longest-lived men have been such as did not go to bed sober for the last fifty years of their lives. Therefore sobriety, honesty, integrity, veracity are not profitable virtues, and, weighed in the same scales and by the same standards as are used by Mr. Galton to test the weight and worth of prayer, they are practically valueless and do not pay.

Simultaneous with Mr. Galton's article, there appeared a communication in the *Contemporary Review* entitled "The Prayer for the Sick: Hints toward a serious attempt to estimate its value," with the indorsement of Dr. Tyndall. The proposal contained in this communication came to be generally known in newspaper slang as "Tyndall's Prayer-gauge," though Tyndall was not its author. The proposition was that "One single ward or hospital under the care of first-rate physicians or surgeons, containing a number of patients afflicted with those diseases which have been best studied, and of which the mortality rates are best known, should be, during a period of not less than three to five years, made the subject of special prayer by the whole body of the faithful, and that at the end of that period the mortality rates should be compared with the past rates, and also with those of other leading hospitals similarly well managed during the same periods." This experiment, the writer thinks, offers "to the faithful an occasion of demonstrating to the faithless an imperishable record of the power of prayer."

There was a tone of moderation and candor in this proposition which for a moment beguiled the popular mind, and there were Christian ministers so injudicious as to admit that the proposal should be entertained and the experiment tried. But its superficial fairness was delusive, and its plausibility concealed a snare. The writer must have been sufficiently conversant with the Christian doctrine concerning prayer to know that the acceptance of his challenge would be a theological blunder; for there are no unconditional assurances in the Word of God that prayers for health and long life shall always be answered. We presume also that he must have been sufficiently acquainted with medical science to perceive that the acceptance of his challenge would be a scientific blunder, for there are elements in the problem which can not be scientifically appreciated, measured, and recorded. Such, for example, are the temperament, idiosyncrasy, hereditary diathesis, previous habits of life, and mental characteristics of the patients; such the variety in skill, care, sympathy, and almost inspiration among physicians and nurses; such also the differences of climatal, sanitary, and hospital conditions; all these elements, whose varied degrees of potency are incapable of being estimated, enter into the problem and affect the results. The multiplicity and complexity of these elements render the effects as irregularly variable as if each cause had not been subject to any previous conditions.[1] The problem is not even capable of being scientifically presented in terms of experience, and until that is done it can not be subjected to experiment. Suppose the experiment to be tried in the manner proposed by the writer, and the mortality rates to be in favor of the hospital for which prayer had been offered, it would still be open for the scientific skeptic to affirm that the causes of the difference are to be found in those elements whose varying values had not been enumerated in the statement of the problem, and not in any Divine interpo-

[1] Comte, "Positive Philosophy," vol. i. p. 45.

sition in answer to prayer.[1] He might claim that the patients were not all of the same age or temperament, the physicians were not all of equal skill, the nurses were not all alike attentive, the climatal and sanitary conditions were not equal, and the question would be left in precisely the same condition as before.

Whatever may be the award of a thoughtless derision, we do not hesitate in saying that the proposition is an improper one, and can not be entertained. Especially because there is one party concerned in this matter for whom no human being is authorized to make any engagements, and that is "the Hearer and Answerer of Prayer." There is only one class of blessings for which He has given us any warrant to pray unconditionally, and these are *spiritual* blessings. For strength to resist temptation, to endure affliction, and perform well our appointed work in life; for grace to purify our nature, elevate our aims, conquer our selfishness and pride, and help us to form a noble character, God has authorized and commanded us to pray. But for the blessings of this life, for deliverance from danger and suffering, for restoration from sickness and for long life, we are taught to pray in submission to that highest wisdom which knows what is best for us, and to append to every supplication, however ardent our desire and intense our solicitude, "Nevertheless, not as I will, but as Thou wilt." This submission is the loftiest attitude of prayer.

At the same time we shrink not from the distinct avowal of the Christian doctrine that it is reasonable and prop-

[1] "No record of *coincidences* can prove a causal connection, or even suggest it—unless the instances are exceptionally numerous, and unless other causes leading to the result are excluded by the rigid methods of verification." —"Prayer: 'The Two Spheres:' They *are* Two," *Contemporary Review*, Dec., 1873, p. 39.

er to offer prayer for recovery from sickness, and that such prayer, offered in submission to the Divine will, may be answered. We are not ashamed of the good old faith—"the Aberglaube," or superstition, as some are pleased to call it—that "*the prayer of faith shall save the sick.*" The calmness and serenity of mind which the prayer of faith supplies is favorable to recovery. In fact, as "the systematic excitation of a definite expectation and hope," it has a legitimate place in psycho-therapeutics, as Feuchtersleben has shown, and even as Dr. Tuke concedes in his work on the "Influence of the Mind on the Body."[1] This "definite expectation and hope" is not a mere illusion. We have the assurance of Scripture that there is a Divine blessing which "giveth wisdom to the wise and knowledge to men of understanding," and which may descend upon the head and the heart of the most skillful physician in answer to prayer. Furthermore, it is generally admitted by medical men that "as in health certain mental states may induce disease, so in disease certain mental states may restore health."[2] Now these "mental states" may be the subject of Divine influence. Science has not dared to shut out the Spirit of God from the realm of mind, and therefore restoration to health may be given, in this manner at least, in answer to prayer. But no man would propose to make the prevalence of such prayer the subject of statistical averages. Prayer for the sick can not always result in their recovery, for then they would never die. Our lives are in the hands of God, and we shall live until our work is done, or until we have clearly shown that we will not do our work, and our life is a failure and a defeat.

[1] See pp. 386–7.

[2] Dr. Tuke, "Influence of the Mind on the Body in Health and Disease," p. 351.

Finally, in the name of our holy religion, we repel with scorn the attempt of certain scientists to test the value of prayer, and with it also the value of a life of self-denial, purity, and piety, by merely temporal, secular, and visible results which may be weighed and measured and set down in statistical tables. Christianity teaches that the present life is a probationary scene. It is a state of trial and discipline with a view to the formation of moral character. Therefore our principles and our virtues must be put to the test. Temptation tries our fortitude; affliction ascertains our submission; suffering purifies our souls; doubt and mystery give energy to our faith. Amid the good and the evil of the present our character has to be developed and perfected. There is much to be encountered, much to be endured. But as Richard Winter Hamilton has said, "This discipline is salutary. The furnace heat purifies the gold by its rigorous assay. The vine prunes until it bleeds that it may bear its richer clusters. A theatre is raised for lofty struggle and celestial dint." The end of all is to make us pure and noble and heroic souls.

The scientists of this age, who are so enamored of inert matter and insensate force, may have no eye to see, no heart to sympathize with, and no competent faculty by which to estimate the value of this blessed vintage; but there are souls to whom honor is dearer than life, and wisdom more precious than rubies, and purity more desirable than fine gold, who will continue to pray—"Cleanse the thoughts of our hearts by the inspiration of thy Holy Spirit, that we may perfectly love Thee and worthily magnify thy holy name."

So much for the argument against the efficacy of prayer from the experiential stand-point. We are compelled to pronounce it a failure. There seems good reason to believe that Dr. Tyndall regards it as a failure, for we do not find that he any where denies the efficacy of prayer for spiritual blessings. But, like a second Ajax Telemon, he makes haste to interpose his ample shield for the defense of his unfortunate friends; he is careful, however, to change the entire mode of warfare, and he opens the attack on the efficacy of prayer from the *theoretical* stand-point.

Dr. Tyndall begins by observing that "the idea of direct personal volition mixing itself in the economy of nature is retreating more and more" in presence of advancing science, and among educated and scientific communities there is a growing conviction that "nature is absolutely uniform," and that her laws are changeless and permanent. He takes the ground that all prayer for Divine interposition "to produce changes in external nature," such, for example, as "prayer for rain or for fair weather," is irrational, because the answer to such prayer would be "a violation of the order of nature," "a manifest contradiction to natural laws," and in fact "a *miracle.*" "The dispersion of the slightest mist by the special volition of the Eternal would be as great a miracle . . . as the stoppage of an eclipse or the rolling of the St. Lawrence up the Falls of Niagara. No act of humiliation, individual or national, could call one shower from heaven or deflect toward us a single beam of the sun."[1]

We have characterized this attack of Dr. Tyndall's as an attack on the efficacy of prayer from the *theoretical* standpoint: 1. Because he does not claim that the belief in the changeless uniformity of nature is a *self-evident* truth—a direct intuition, either of sense or of reason, which needs no proof. 2. Because he does not assert that the absolute

[1] "Fragments of Science," pp. 36–39.

uniformity of nature has been *inductively* proved, or is even capable of verification by experience, since all experience, whether of the individual or the race, is necessarily limited, and can not, therefore, give a universal truth. All that he can say of it is that it is "an *assumption*"—an assumption which all carefully conducted experiments have justified, and upon which all successful scientific research has been based. The majestic fabric of modern science has been reared upon this foundation.

But mark, it is still "*an assumption*,"[1] and the central question around which the battle must be fought is, *What ground have we for the assumption that the order of nature is so absolutely persistent and changeless that it never has been and never can be interfered with by an act of intelligent volition?*

Dr. Tyndall has attempted an answer to this question. We shall endeavor, first, clearly to comprehend his answer, and, secondly, to estimate its logical validity.

1. He tells us that the belief in a changeless order of nature "is a kind of inspiration." "The passage from facts to principles (that is, the passage from our limited experience of uniformity to the affirmation of universal and permanent order) is called induction, which in its highest form is inspiration."[2] This, however, is poetry, and not science. This inductive inference embraces vastly more in the conclusion than is contained in the premises; the antecedent is limited, the consequent is unlimited; and the only warrant that Dr. Tyndall has for the violation of the most fundamental logical canon is "inspiration." But, whatever Dr. Tyndall may understand by this ambiguous phrase, it is certain that his own mind is not satisfied, and so he tries again.

[1] "Fragments of Science," p. 40: "The *assumed* permanence of natural laws."

[2] Ibid., p. 60.

2. He tells us that this belief rests upon the long-continued observations, registered experiences, and experimental verifications of a succession of scientific men, as Galileo, Torricelli, Pascal, Kepler, and Newton. But here again the experiences are limited, and do not justify a universal conclusion; and Dr. Tyndall himself is not satisfied. He says, "The scientific mind can find no repose in the mere registration of sequences in nature. The further question obtrudes itself with resistless might, *Whence come the sequences?* What is it that binds the consequent with the antecedent in nature?" What is it, we ask with redoubled earnestness and emphasis, which authorizes our drawing a universal conclusion from particular premises? "The truly scientific intellect never can attain rest until it reaches the FORCES by which the observed succession is produced. . . . Not until the relation between the forces and the phenomena has been established is the *law of the reason* rendered concentric with the *law of nature*, and not until this is effected does the mind of the scientific philosopher rest in peace."[1] Here we have "the law of the reason" substituted for "the highest form of inspiration," and we are curious to learn what this "law of the reason" is. Is it the principle or law of causality—namely, that "all phenomena present themselves to us as the expression of *power*, and refer us to a causal ground?" But this law of the reason says nothing about uniformity. The same power may produce a diversity of effects. "Infinitely numerous and various universes might have been fashioned by the various distribution of the original nebulous matter, although the particles of matter should obey the one law of gravity."[2]

[1] "Fragments of Science," p. 64.
[2] Jevons, "Principles of Science," vol. ii. p. 434.

3. And, finally, Dr. Tyndall tells us that "The expectation of likeness [*i. e.*, uniformity] in the procession of phenomena is not that on which the scientific mind founds its belief in the order of nature. If the force is *permanent*, the phenomena are *necessary* whether they resemble or do not resemble any thing that has gone before. Hence in judging of the order of nature our inquiry eventually relates to the permanence of force,"[1] or, as he elsewhere styles it, "the conservation of energy," which means "that no power can make its appearance in nature without an equivalent expenditure of some other power; that natural agents are so related as to be mutually convertible, but that no new agency is created."[2] Whether this is or is not a correct statement of the principle of the conservation of energy we shall see by and by. And now, after having hunted the game through many tortuous passages to its final burrow, what have we found? That the ultimate principle which justifies the belief or "assumption" that the laws of nature are so rigidly inflexible and the order of nature is so absolutely uniform that "personal volition can not mingle in or interfere with the economy of nature" *is the principle of the conservation of energy.*

The answer of Dr. Tyndall is now fully and clearly before our mental view, and we are prepared for the consideration of its logical validity. This answer may be conveniently divided into two propositions. First, personal volition, human or Divine, can not intermingle or in any way interfere with the economy of nature because her laws are inflexible and her order is uniform. Second, the ultimate principle which justifies the assumption that the laws of nature are absolutely inflexible and the order

[1] "Fragments of Science," p. 64.
[2] Ibid. p. 38.

of nature is absolutely uniform is the principle of the conservation of energy. We shall consider this latter proposition first.

There are in this proposition three ambiguous terms, which have hitherto been the source of serious misapprehension; and unless we can attain to clearer and more definite conceptions, which shall be mutually accepted, the controversy will be interminable. These are the terms "nature," "laws of nature," and "uniformity of the order of nature." We have made the attempt in a previous chapter[1] to give precision and definiteness to the concepts which these terms should connote. Referring the reader to the chapter indicated, we shall here simply restate our results.

1. *Nature* is the aggregate or totality of all material or physical phenomena.[2] "Nature (*nascor*, to be born) means that which is produced or born."[3]

2. *A Law of Nature* is the statement of a certain uniformity observed in the relations among phenomena.[4] The laws of nature are "simply expressions of phenomenal uniformities, having no *coercive* power whatever."[5]

3. *The Uniformity of the Order of Nature* may mean either "uniformity of co-existence" or "uniformity of succession." "Uniformity of co-existence" means that the same substances must always have the same essential properties[6] and the same permanent relations to other sub-

[1] "On the Relation of God to the World," pp. 187–201.

[2] See Coleridge, "Works," vol. i. pp. 152, 263; Hamilton, "Metaphysics," vol. i. p. 40.

[3] Fleming, "Vocabulary of Philosophy," *in loco.*

[4] See Jevons, "Principles of Science," vol. ii. p. 440; Spencer, "First Principles," p. 128.

[5] Carpenter, "Mental Physiology," p. 692; see Lewes, "Problems of Life and Mind," vol. i. p. 336.

[6] Essential properties "are those which admit neither of intension nor re-

stances, as, for example, every molecule of hydrogen must have the same properties, the same definite mass, the same periodic vibrations, and the same chemical affinities. If these were to be altered in the least, it would no longer be a molecule of hydrogen.[1] This is uniformity in the ultimate *constitution* of nature. "Uniformity of succession" means that the same or similar consequents will always be found to follow similar antecedents, or "the same causes will always be followed by the same effects,[2] as, for example, the combination of carbon and oxygen will always be followed by the evolution of heat, and heat will always melt ice." This is uniformity in the *course* of nature or the procession of phenomena. Belief in the constancy of the course of nature or the uniformity of causation is the general expectation that "the future will resemble the past."[3]

With a clearer apprehension of the terms, we may now discuss the first proposition with more precision, and hope to reach a logical conclusion. We approach the discussion by remarking—

1. The constancy of the *course* of nature or the uniformity of causation is not a self-evident and necessary truth. In so far as it is a scientific truth it is purely an induction from experience, an experience which is necessarily limited, and therefore does not warrant a universal conclu-

mission of degrees."—Newton, *Regula Tertia Philosophandi*, "Principia," lib. iii.

[1] Maxwell, "Theory of Heat," p. 310; and also in *Nature*, vol. ii. p. 421.

[2] By "causes" is here meant nothing more than all the antecedent conditions. The statement makes no real distinction between "causes" and "conditions." "We can not predicate of any physical agency that it is abstractedly the cause of another." "*Causation is the will of God.*"—Grove, "Correlation and Conservation of Forces," pp. 15, 199.

[3] See Murphy, "Habit and Intelligence," vol. ii. p. 157; "Scientific Basis of Faith," pp. 75, 76; J. S. Mill, "Logic," vol. ii. ch. xxii. § 1.

sion. There is no rational *à priori* ground for the assumption that the same or similar causes (even if we understand by physical causes all antecedent conditions) shall necessarily produce the same effects. In other words, there is no authority for the assertion that the course of nature or the procession of phenomena must be absolutely uniform. Science has succeeded in establishing a strong probability, but it is beyond her power to demonstrate an absolute certainty. This is generally conceded, alike by physicists and metaphysicians. J. S. Mill says, "The uniformity in the course of events . . . must be received, not as a law of the universe, but of that portion of it which is within the range of our means of observation, with a reasonable degree of extension to adjacent cases."[1] "The uniformity of causation," says Murphy, "is not a truth of the reason, it is known by experience only; and the truth of a conclusion from experience can never be free from all possibility of limitation or exception."[2] And Professor Jevons asserts, "The conclusions of scientific inference appear to be always of a hypothetical and purely provisional nature. Given certain experience, the theory of probability yields us the true interpretation of that experience, and is the surest guide open to us. But the best calculated results which it can give us are never absolute probabilities: they are purely relative to the extent of our information. It seems to be impossible for us to judge how far our experience gives us adequate information of the universe as a whole, and of all the forces and phenomena which can have place therein."[3]

2. It is an immediate fact of consciousness that the will

[1] "Logic," bk. iii. ch. xvi. See also McCosh, "Intuitions," pp. 275–7.
[2] "Scientific Basis of Faith," p. 79.
[3] "Principles of Science," vol. ii. p. 465.

is a cause which is adequate to the production of a diversity of effects. Whatever may be true of the world of matter, it is certain that within the sphere of our conscious personality the relation of cause and effect is not a relation of invariable and necessary sequence. Further, it is certain that a self-determining agent exists. "Every event in the universe of matter is determined by the events which precede it, but physical reasonings make it certain that the chain of causes and effects can not have been of absolutely endless length through past time. There must have been a first link of the chain; there must have been a first act of causation; and this act must have been determined, not by any previous act of causation when as yet there was none, but by the free self-determining power of the agent. The first act of causation we call Creation; the freely self-determining agent we call God."[1]

3. Physical science itself does not teach that the course of nature is absolutely uniform; on the contrary, all the conclusions of science lead to the conviction "that the universe is ever changing, and that, notwithstanding secular recurrences which would *primâ facie* seem to replace matter in its original position, nothing in fact ever returns or can return to a state of existence *identical* with a previous state."[2] Every theory of the origin of things is compelled to assume that an innate tendency to *variability* is a fundamental fact of nature. This is made apparent by the reasoning in Spencer's chapters on "The Instability of the Homogeneous" and "The Multiplication of Effects."[3] The advocates of Natural Selection are very

[1] Murphy, "Scientific Basis of Faith," pp. 80 and 49–51; Jevons, "Principles of Science," vol. ii. p. 438.

[2] Grove, "Correlation and Conservation of Forces," p. 193.

[3] "First Principles," chs. xiii. and xiv.

emphatic in the assertion of this "Law of Variation," as the cardinal fact upon which turns their doctrine of the origin of species, and the whole system on which organic life has been developed from the lowest to the highest forms.[1] "There is," says Comte, "an irregular variability of effect engendered by the great number of different agents determining at the same time the same phenomena [meteorological, social, and vital], from which it results in the most complicated phenomena that *there are not two cases precisely alike*." "The multiplicity [of the agents] renders the effects as irregularly variable as if every cause had not been subjected to any previous conditions."[2] Dr. Tyndall himself is in fact compelled to surrender the doctrine of uniformity in the succession of phenomena. He says "if the force be permanent, the phenomena are necessary whether they *resemble* or do not resemble any thing that has gone before."[3] But if the phenomena do not resemble any thing that has gone before, how can there be "uniformity" in the succession of phenomena?

4. The uniformity of the *constitution* of material nature, or the principle that the same substances must always have the same essential properties, is undoubtedly a self-evident and necessary truth, an *à priori*, rational intuition. It is simply a statement in concrete form of the principle or law of identity (A = A, or A is not equal to non-A). As we have already observed, a substance which ceases to have the same essential properties ceases to be the same substance; for substances are only known to us through their properties. But this "uniformity of co-existence" is

[1] Wallace, "On Natural Selection," p. 266.
[2] "Positive Philosophy," vol. i. pp. 153–156.
[3] "Fragments of Science," p. 64.

distinct from "uniformity of succession," and we can not infer the latter from the former. Admitting that the same substance must always have the same properties, we can not affirm that the same substances will always be collocated in the same manner, or distributed in space with the same uniformity. In fact, "we can discover nothing regular in the distribution of matter through space; we can reduce it to no uniformity, to no law."[1] Matter is never replaced in its original position; "nothing repeats itself, because nothing can be placed in the same conditions; the past is irrevocable."[2]

Even should we say with Sir William Thomson that "motion constitutes the very essence of what is commonly called matter," still we know with infallible certainty that there must be a *something* that moves, and that this something which moves must have ultimately a definite *mass* (inertia) and a measurable *velocity*, and that the *energy of motion* to which the power of doing work is due is proportionate to the mass multiplied into the square of the velocity. Matter, then, is something more than motion.[3] We know further that there are different "modes of motion"—transitive, rotatory, vibratory, pulsatory, gyratory — and that these are undergoing perpetual transformation or conversion one into the other. And, finally, we know that the quantities of visible molar energy, and of invisible molecular energy (as heat, light, electricity, magnetism), are not uniform; on the contrary, the quantity of mechanical energy is being continually dissipated—that is, transformed into radiant heat, "which may be compared to the waste-

[1] Jevons, "Principles of Science," vol. ii. p. 434.

[2] Grove, "Correlation and Conservation of Forces," p. 24.

[3] "There is one wonderful condition of matter, perhaps its only true indication, namely, inertia."—Faraday, "Correlation and Conservation of Forces," p. 368; Maxwell, "Theory of Heat," p. 86.

heap of the universe,"[1] and uniformly diffused heat will not yield a single unit of work.

The principle of the conservation of energy is therefore subject to limitations which are supplied by the principle of the dissipation of energy. It simply asserts that, so far as our observation extends, the whole amount of potential and kinetic energy in the universe is invariable, but it can not determine whether the amount of vital force, or of psychic force, is invariable; and it is certainly incompetent to fix a limitation to the exercise of Creative Power. "It is nothing more than an intelligent and well-supported denial of the chimera of perpetual motion, and that a machine can no more create work than it can create matter."[2] In the words of Grove, we can not conceive of the production of any new force in the universe "*without the interposition of Creative Power.*"[3]

Dr. Tyndall, in his solicitude to exclude all Divine interposition in the economy of nature, has stated the law of the conservation of energy in a form quite different from that of his scientific brethren. He says, "The principle of conservation is, *no creation* but infinite conversion;"[4] and he seems desirous to convey the impression that any interposition of God to answer prayer would be a creation of physical force, and as much a miracle as the rolling of the waters of the St. Lawrence up the Falls of Niagara. Dr. Tyndall does not here display his usual fairness and candor. Surely he would not assert that the qualitative and quantitative combination of the different natural agents —such as light, heat, electricity, elasticity of vapors, and aerial currents—which determine the fall of a shower of

[1] Stewart, "Physics," p. 357.
[2] Ibid. p. 355.
[3] "Correlation and Conservation of Forces," p. 195.
[4] "Fragments of Science," p. 39.

rain, would be a *creation* of energy; or that the disposition of the meteorological, physical, chemical, vital, and psychical conditions which result in the cure of the sick, would be as much a miracle as "the stoppage of an eclipse;" for these natural agents are more or less under the control of man. But suppose it were granted that all interposition of God in the economy of nature must be regarded as *miraculous*, would he deny the possibility of miracles even if they should involve a creation of energy? Because we can not by any of our mechanical arrangements create energy, does it therefore follow that God can not create energy? Dr. Tyndall will not say this. "If you ask who is to limit the outgoings of Almighty power, my answer is—not I."[1]

It will be seen presently that Dr. Tyndall admits that the interference of personal volition in the economy of nature is not forbidden by the law of the conservation of energy. The point we now insist upon is that he has not succeeded in showing that this principle is an absolute and universal law of nature. We have already seen that it is limited and conditioned by the law of the dissipation of energy, and that in reality "it is merely a kind of *movable equilibrium* between supply and destruction."[2] By no experimental evidence has it been shown that it holds true in the realm of vital dynamics and psycho-dynamics. There are able scientific men who question its absolute certainty even in the realm of physics. Professor Brooke says that "the amount of energy in the world is unchanged, the sum of the actual or kinetic and potential energies being a constant quantity has been by some writers overstrained. It may be taken as a postulate, and is probably true; but it is a proposition equally incapable of

[1] "Fragments of Science," p. 420.

[2] *Nature*, vol. viii. p. 280.

proof and of disproof."[1] To the same effect are the words of Sir John Herschel,[2] and still more recently of Professor Jevons.[3]

"Nature," says Dr. Cohn, of Breslau, "is an equation with very many unknown quantities. It is the work of natural science to determine the value of these quantities. Some believe it never will be possible to solve the equation, since in it factors occur which can not be determined." Until this is done, it is simply presumptuous for Dr. Tyndall to pretend to know all the antecedents which determine the complex phenomena of nature, and dogmatically to affirm that "no new agency is created," and no "interference of Divine agency" can be permitted. "Our knowledge of things is finite, while our ignorance is infinite; and we must consequently regard all known lines of causation as being liable to be cut through by unknown ones." For aught we know to the contrary one of the unknown factors in the equation may be "personal volition," may be the ceaseless energy of the Divine Will sustaining and carrying nature forward through successive stages toward a predestinated goal. The foremost physicists do not deny that there may possibly be forms of energy which are neither potential nor kinetic.[4] We venture to assert with Prof. Challis that will, or personal energy, is neither the one nor the other, but the source of both. Mind is the originator, and matter is the recipient of force.[5]

We sum up what has been said in the preceding paragraphs on the uniformity of nature in the following words:

[1] *Nature*, vol. vi. p. 125.

[2] "Familiar Lectures on Science," p. 469.

[3] "Principles of Science," vol. ii. p. 83.

[4] Maxwell, "Theory of Heat," p. 92.

[5] Challis's "Mathematical Principles of Physics," p. 107; Herschel, "Familiar Lectures on Science," p. 467.

We admit that the uniformity of the *constitution* of nature is a self-evident and necessary truth. We admit also that, so far as our experience extends, the uniformity of the *course* of nature must be admitted as a scientific truth, for to deny this would be to deny the possibility of all science, inasmuch as all science is *prevision*. But at the same time we maintain that the conclusions of scientific inference must always be of a hypothetical and purely provisional character, because it is impossible for us to judge with absolute certainty how far our experience gives us adequate information of the universe as a whole, and of all the forces and phenomena which can have place therein.[1] The conservation of energy, for example, is a very probable hypothesis which accords satisfactorily with the experiments of scientific men during a few years past, but it would be a gross misconception of the nature of scientific inference to suppose that it is certain in the same sense that a proposition in geometry is certain, or that any fact of immediate consciousness is certain.[2]

Admitting the principle of the uniformity of nature as a hypothetical inference from a limited experience, we advance to the main position of Dr. Tyndall, namely, *that personal volition can not mingle in or interfere with the procession of phenomena in nature.*

Dr. Tyndall admits the reality of "personal volition." We have not discovered in his writings any indications of

[1] "It is pretty much the same to the greater number even of the instructed hearers whether a man of science say 'I know' or 'I suppose;' they only ask after the result and the authority by which it is supported, not the grounds of the *doubts*. It is thus not to be wondered at if earnest investigators *do not willingly shock the confidence of their readers in what the former may think true and demonstrable by the enumeration of ideas of the correctness of which they do not feel themselves quite secure.*"—Helmholtz, "On John Tyndall," in *Nature*, vol. x. p. 301.

[2] Jevons, "Principles of Science," vol. ii. p. 466.

the tendency manifested by some of his scientific associates to reduce volition to a form of physical energy. He grants "the power of free-will in man,"[1] but he seems unwilling to admit that free-will can exert any controlling, modifying, or determining influence on the procession of phenomena. "Assuming the efficacy of prayer to produce changes in external nature, it necessarily follows that natural laws are more or less at the mercy of man's volition, and no conclusion founded on the assumed permanence of those laws would be worthy of confidence."[2] But are not natural laws more or less subject to man's volition? Does he not act *upon* the chain of cause and effect in nature, and *alter* the procession of phenomena on earth? Certainly he can and does control and direct the forces of nature. He can so collocate and adjust the properties and forces of matter as to accomplish the purposes of his intelligence, and bring about *new* results which would not otherwise have been produced. That man has materially modified the physical geography of the globe can not be denied. He has altered the climatal condition of whole tracts of country, and changed the physiognomy of the globe. The rain-fall has been changed by the felling of timber or the planting of trees.[3] He has extended or circumscribed the geographical boundaries of plants and animals. He has learned to control the mechanical, chemical, and electric forces. When he lifts a stone from the earth and suspends it in the air, or locks it in the arch that spans the river, the law of gravitation is subordinated to the higher law of intelligent purpose. By the collocation and adjustment of mechanical forces

[1] "Fragments of Science," p. 40.

[2] Ibid. p. 40.

[3] Marsh, "Man and Nature," chs. i. and iii.; Lyell, "Principles of Geology," pp. 713–717.

he overcomes the resistance of winds and tides, and guides his vessel across the trackless deep. He seizes the lightning in the clouds and guides it harmless to the earth, and sends the electric current along the telegraphic wire to chronicle his deeds and report his thoughts at the ends of the earth. He loosens the most intricate combinations of elementary substances, and recomposes them in new forms of the highest value in medicine and the fine arts. He solidifies carbonic acid; freezes water at the tropics, and even in red-hot crucibles in the Temperate Zone. He also modifies and changes the development of vegetable life, obliterating thorns and spines, altering the color and size of flowers, and the flavor and nutritive character of fruits. And, finally, he has wrought marvelous changes in the form, size, habits, and instincts of the animal creation.[1] Thus in numberless ways does man control, modify, and subordinate nature to accomplish the purposes of his intelligence; but we can not see with Dr. Tyndall how this renders scientific "conclusions founded on the assumed permanence of natural law unworthy of confidence."

There is a vacillation in Dr. Tyndall's treatment of this aspect of the subject which renders it difficult to fix his exact position. Does he intend to assert that "personal volition" can not in the slightest degree change the succession of phenomena? Will he say that man does not, and that God can not control and modify and subordinate natural forces so as to bring about *new* and *special* results? Unless he is prepared to assert this in the most unequivocal manner, the whole superstructure of his argument falls to the ground. If it is granted that human volition can

[1] Wallace, "On Natural Selection," pp. 324–326; Lyell, "Principles of Geology," pp. 681-688, 579–590.

change the procession of phenomena, and "alter within certain limits the current of events," then *à fortiori* we may conclude that Divine volition may also interfere in the economy of nature to answer prayer. At one time Dr. Tyndall insinuates that "our notion" (that is, the Christian's conception) "of the Power which rules the universe" is a "mere fanciful or ignorant enlargement of human power, . . . a *mythologic imagination* which pictures a being able and willing to do any and every conceivable thing."[1] At another time he admits that "the theory that the system of nature is under the control of a Being who changes phenomena in compliance with the prayers of men is, in my opinion, a perfectly legitimate one. . . . It is a matter of experience that an earthly father, who is at the same time both wise and tender, listens to the requests of his children, and if they do not ask amiss, takes pleasure in granting their requests. We know also that this compliance extends to the alteration, within certain limits, of the current of events on earth. With this suggestion offered by our experience, it is no departure from scientific method to place behind natural phenomena a universal Father, who in answer to the prayers of his children alters the currents of phenomena. Thus far theology and science go hand in hand. The conception of an ether, for example, trembling with the waves of light, is suggested by the ordinary phenomena of wave-motion in water and in air; and in like manner the conception of personal volition in nature is suggested by the ordinary action of man upon earth. I therefore urge no *impossibilities*, though you constantly charge me with doing so. I do not even urge inconsistency, but, on the contrary, frankly admit that you have as good a right to place

[1] "Fragments of Science," p. 421.

your conception at the root of phenomena as I have to place mine."[1]

If this concession is made in good faith, and really means any thing at all, it covers the whole ground. It is neither unscientific nor irrational to place behind natural phenomena a universal Father who alters the current of phenomena in answer to prayer. But this is not the conception which Dr. Tyndall places behind the phenomena of nature. His conception is that of a *permanent force*, which is "under the circumstances *necessary*," producing "an unerring order which in our experience knows no exception." This brings us to the third and last question.

3. How can the scientific conception of the *force* which is manifested in the phenomena of nature be brought into harmony with the idea of *God* as revealed in the religious consciousness?

We are now in the very heart of what we have characterized as the debatable ground which lies between science and religion, where questions are mooted concerning the relation between God and nature.

On the one side we have the facts of external sensible experience—the *statical* phenomena of nature as mass, extension, position, and distance—conditions essential to the action or manifestation of force; then the *dynamical* phenomena of nature as rotatory, vibratory, pulsatory, gyratory, and transitive motion, which to our reason, not to our senses, are manifestations of force. Science observes the uniformity of relations among these phenomena—uniformities of resemblance, co-existence, and succession, and calls these uniformities *laws of nature*. This is all that science can do, all that men of exact science claim to be able to do.

[1] *Contemporary Review*, July, 1872.

On the other side we have the facts of internal experience—the consciousness of effort, the sense of power and freedom, the idea of right and wrong, the feeling of dependence, of duty, and of obligation, the consciousness of moral responsibility and of moral desert, and the anticipation of a future retribution. These to our reason are the revelation of a righteous Lawgiver and Ruler who is over us; by whom we are obliged, and to whom we must account. This is the theoretic basis and necessary presupposition of all religion.

And now speculative philosophy steps in and endeavors to reduce these concepts of science and religion to an ultimate unity. It endeavors to construe in thought the nature of that relation between the force manifested in nature and the moral Ruler revealed in conscience. Therefore it asks the questions, What is force? What is life? What is mind?

If we say that force is as inherent and essential to matter as extension and inertia are, and that life and mind are but modes of force, we are on the high-road to mechanical Deism, if not *material Atheism.* If we say that matter is itself only a function of force, and that force is the ultimate of all ultimates, then the distinction between finite existence and the infinite Being is a merely verbal distinction, and we must yield to the seductions of *Pantheism*, which under this aspect of it is but another name for Atheism. But if we say that Spirit is the originator and matter the recipient of force, or "the recipient of impulse and energy," and that the immanent God is the life of all nature, we are pure *Theists.* We have now a "workable theory" by which we can satisfactorily interpret the universe.

This, however, is not the conception of Dr. Tyndall. The

power which he sees in nature is a force which is inherent and essential to matter, and "in that matter he sees the promise and the potency of all *terrestrial* life," but not of all life, for "religion is life." The Power which is revealed as the object of the "religious emotions" is a Power which works for "righteousness," and is "intelligent" as well as "ethical." This Power he seems to regard as distinct from the force which produces the necessary phenomena of nature. But whence does he obtain this conception of force? He writes as though he had seen force, or cognized force, by some one of the senses. We claim that force is "a subtile mental conception, and not a sensuous perception or phenomenon;"[1] it is a metaphysical idea, "a postulate of reason applied to nature." We venture the assertion that the physicist has not the remotest conception of force except as a datum of consciousness. The senses give us only phenomena. All we perceive is motion, change, succession. "All we know or see is the effect; we do not see force."[2] So say all physicists as well as all metaphysicians. "Experiences of force are not derived from any thing else, . . . and the force by which we ourselves produce changes, and which serves to symbolize the cause of changes in general, is the final disclosure of all analysis."[3] Whenever, therefore, Dr. Tyndall attempts to account for motion and change in external nature by assuming the existence of invisible, imponderable forces, he is interpreting nature in terms of consciousness—we mean that consciousness of personal causation which we have when we put forth *effort* with an *intention* thereby to accomplish an end. Force is known to

[1] Grove, "Correlation and Conservation of Forces," p. 20.
[2] Ibid.
[3] Spencer, "First Principles," pp. 235, 252.

us by immediate consciousness as a function of our own mind—that is, mind acting in will is conscious of itself as a force. We are able to conceive of force in no other way. "Force dissociated from personality and will must be forever incomprehensible by us, because it would be something contradictory to our consciousness."[1] If we may not regard will-force as "the type of all the force in nature," then the physicist knows nothing about it, does not know there is any force, and the only consistent course is to unite with Comte in eradicating the word from the vocabulary of science.

In the only case in which we are admitted into any immediate personal knowledge of the origin of force, we find it connected with volition, with will, with motion, with intellect, and with all the attributes of mind in which personality consists.[2] We must, therefore, conclude that all force is mind-force, is spirit-force, and that the forces which animate nature are spiritual. Either the force manifested in the universe is the force of a self-existent and self-determining Intelligent Will, or we can form no conception of it whatever.

When we have once arrived at the conception of force as an expression of will, which we derive from our experience of its production, "the universal and constantly sustaining agency of the Deity is recognized in every phenomenon of the universe."[3] "The laws of nature are the laws which God in his wisdom prescribes to his own acts. His universal presence is the necessary condition of any course of events. His universal agency the only origin of all efficient force."[4] The persistence

[1] Challis, "Mathematical Principles of Physics," p. 681.

[2] Herschel, "Familiar Lectures on Science," p. 461.

[3] Carpenter, "Mental Physiology," p. 703.

[4] Whewell, "Astronomy and Physics," p. 224.

of force is the permanence of the Divine agency, and the deepest ground of our faith in the uniformity and changelessness of natural laws is the immutability of God.

We come, then, at last, to this, that the Power which is manifested in nature is the God who is revealed in consciousness, and that He is at once a God of power, of righteousness, and of love. In prayer, the intelligent believer does not invoke a different Power from that which is manifested in all the forms of physical energy which were manifested in nature; he does but invoke the *same* Power and the *only* Power which is the source of all causation and produces all the processions of phenomena.

The perpetual immanence and ceaseless action of God in nature is the source of all *force* and all *law*. There is no force and no law besides and apart from this. All our conceptions of necessity and uniformity, of special providence and miracle, are merely relative conceptions which result from our imperfect vision. These are all swallowed up and lost in the Divine Immensity. God is Power. God is Law. God is Love. Love is the motive, Law is the method, and Power is the hand manifested in all the changes of the universe. "The devout feel that wherever God's hand is, *there* is miracle; and it is simply an undevoutness which imagines that only where miracle is can there be the hand of God."

Let us say with Goethe, "Nature is the living garment of God," which at once reveals and conceals his mysterious splendors. In our days of darkness and sorrow and danger there are vouchsafed to us clearer gleamings of the Creative Spirit through the veil of nature in answer to prayer. These we may call "special providences," and even "miracles," if we please, but let us not fall into the error of supposing that we have seen more of God than in the budding of the leaf or the blooming of the flower in the time of spring. "There are diversities of operations, but it is the *same* God which worketh all in all."[1]

[1] 1 Cor. xii. 6.

CHAPTER X.

MORAL GOVERNMENT.

I. ITS GROUND.—THE CORRELATION BETWEEN GOD AND MAN.

"That they may seek the Lord, and truly feel after Him and find Him, though He is not far from any one of us, for in Him we live and move and are; as certain of your own poets have said, '*For we are his offspring.*'" —St. Paul.

"Jove's presence fills all space, upholds this ball;
All need his aid, his power sustains us all—
For we his offspring are."—Aratus.

"Thou art able to enforce obedience from all frail mortals,
Because we are all thine offspring."—Cleanthes.

From the fundamental truth that God is the Creator and Conservator of the universe, and that his providence presides over and directs the historic development of humanity, Christian doctrine advances, in a natural and logical order, to the recognition of the more direct and personal relations between God and each individual human soul. "He is not far from *any one* of us, for in Him we live and move and are." God is intimately near to the human soul. God is the immanent ground of men's spiritual being. God is the Father of the human spirit. Therefore God is manifested *in* man—in the constitution of his moral nature, and in the susceptibilities, the aspirations, the longings, the hopes and fears of his spiritual being; and God manifests Himself *to* man by an inward illumination—"the true *light* which lighteth every man that cometh into the world." Contemplate these relations on the Divine side, and you have the foundation of all moral government; study them on the human side, and you have the foundation of all religion, for religion is a mode of thought, of feeling, and of action determined by the consciousness of our relations to God.

All Christian teaching proceeds upon the assumption that there exist in all men the elements of a *religious consciousness.* The recognition of some relation to an unseen moral Personality is a universal fact of human nature. The feeling of dependence, the sense of obligation, the sentiment of reverence, the tendency to worship, the apprehension of a future reward or punishment—these are the common characteristics of man. The untutored savage, the half-civilized pagan, the ancient philosopher, the modern scientist, all alike betray the consciousness of some mysterious bond which holds them fast to the unseen Power which controls the destinies of men. With this sentiment of the Divine there is associated in all human minds an instinctive yearning after the Invisible, a conscious susceptibility of our spiritual nature to the influences of the higher world, and a reaching out of the human spirit toward the Infinite, which prompt man to seek for a fuller knowledge and a deeper communion. Christianity assures us that this religious consciousness may, by a loving reception of the truth and a loyal allegiance to duty, be raised into a living *koinonia* — a living fellowship with and a conscious participation of the Divine life. Man may know God, not simply by verbal instruction, not merely through the symbolism of nature, or the providential unfoldings of human history, or even the moral attributes of his own spiritual being, but by an exalted and immediate consciousness. "The pure in heart shall *see* God" by an inward vision of wondrous power and glory, in which they shall know God, and be as fully assured of his personal love and guidance as of the love and guidance of any human friend.

Now there is a natural order in which the knowledge of God is clearly differentiated and fully developed in the human mind; and this order is distinctly recognized and noted in the words of St. Paul—"That they may *seek* God, and truly *feel* God, and actually *find* God."

1. There is an earnest *inquiry* (ζητεῖν)—a search after God. This is the effort of reflective thought to attain a more exact and definite conception of that Power and Intelligence which the spontaneous consciousness of man immediately and instinctively affirms as the ground and cause and law of the created universe.

2. There is a real *feeling* (ψηλαφᾶν) of God—an awakening consciousness of some near relation to God, excited by the voice of conscience and the spiritual affinities and yearnings of the soul. There is, as it were, a "*touching*" of the living God[1]—the sense of a living bond which holds man to God, not merely by a consciousness of dependence and obligation, but a spiritual nexus, a real filiation, which enables man to articulate the wondrous words, "*We are the offspring of God.*"

3. There is an actual *finding* (εὑρίσκειν) of God—that higher religious consciousness in which the pure and earnest soul attains a personal knowledge, and enters into a beatifying communion with "the Father of the human spirit." This direct "manifestation of God" in its highest form is the peculiar glory of that new and divine life of the soul communicated through Christian faith, for which all antecedent knowledges and experiences, whether of the individual mind or of collective humanity, are a preparation and a discipline.

[1] "ἄραγε ψηλαφήσειαν αὐτόν"=truly feel or touch Him.

This inspired statement of the order in which the conception of God as a determinate mode of thought is evolved in the human mind is exactly verified by the history of reflective thought as presented in Greek philosophy. Reflective thought began with Thales in Asia Minor and Pythagoras in Lower Italy. The Ionian and Italian schools commenced most naturally with the objective phenomena of nature, and sought for the ἀρχή—the first principle and cause of all that appears. Their question was not, *Is* there a first principle and cause? but *What* is the first principle and cause? The orderly phenomena of the universe presented themselves to their minds as the expression of *power* and *thought* as certainly as they do to ours; and their endeavor was to construe this intuition in logical form and give it articulate expression. It is true their method was at first defective, and the results attained were consequently often erroneous. Still their mental effort must have been unconsciously governed by those fixed laws of cognition which constrain all minds to regard all phenomena as the expression of power, and all orderly arrangement as the utterance of thought. If in the realm of objective things they fixed upon a single element as that out of which all things else were evolved, that first seed of things was either a living, potential energy, or it was associated with and animated by a living soul.[1] Or if guided by analogy, they conceived the universe as a living organism,

> "Whose body nature is, and God the soul."

The informing principle was still an *intelligent* Power. So that at the end of this period of inquiry we find that Anaxagoras distinctly articulates the word which his coun-

[1] See Ritter, "History of Philosophy," vol. i. p. 200.

trymen had half unconsciously recognized, "the ἀρχή, or first principle, is mind, intellect, νοῦς."

From this point we date a new era in philosophy. The Socratic school turned from the contemplation of external nature, and commenced the study of mind. Man finds his rational nature in changeless correlation to a moral law. There are within his spiritual nature the ideas of justice, of truth, of purity, and of goodness. These ideas of the human reason reflect the character of its Author and Source, and we can not refrain from ascribing these attributes in their most perfect form to the Maker of the human soul. God is now regarded as the Moral Ruler of the world. Man becomes conscious of obligation to a personal Lawgiver, and of accountability to a personal Judge. He feels that he has spiritual susceptibilities and longings for a Divine inspiration. He believes that man "may become conscious of the wisdom and the love of the Deity," and that there are "Divine secrets which may not be penetrated by man, but which are imparted to those who consult, who adore, and who obey God."[1] Yielding to these spiritual affinities of the soul, he seeks God in prayer.[2] He desires to come near to God, to feel his presence and inspiration, and to become "assimilated to God," by "becoming holy, just, and wise."[3]

Whether any of the ancient philosophers attained to that high religious consciousness in which God is actually "found," so that He becomes the object of a real love and confidence, and a refuge amid the storms and adversities of life, is a question we may not be competent to answer.

[1] "Memorabilia," bk. i. ch. iv.

[2] "Timæus," ch. viii.; also "Second Alcibiades," which is a discourse on prayer.

[3] "Laws," bk. v. ch. i.; bk. x. ch. xii.; "Theætetes," § 83.

To attempt an answer may be deemed presumptuous. If the Divine declaration that "*every one* that asketh receiveth, and he that seeketh findeth, and to him that knocketh it shall be opened," is of universal application, then it may, at least, be hoped that the prayer of Socrates was answered, and the desire of Plato was fulfilled, and the aspiration of Epictetus was satisfied in some degree. Socrates certainly expressed the belief that "he was moved by a certain Divine and spiritual impulse."[1] Plato held that the highest form of philosophy is the love of the Supreme Good—that is, God; and that "a man who is just and pious and entirely good is loved of God."[2] And Epictetus taught that "if we always remember that in all we do God stands by as a witness, we shall not err in our prayers and actions, and *we shall have God dwelling with us.*" Do not these utterances remind us vividly of the Saviour's promise—"If *a man* love me, he will keep my words, and my Father will love him, and we will come unto him, and make our abode with him?" Can we doubt that these words express the Divine feeling and the Divine procedure toward the heathen world? Was not God their Father as well as ours? Was not Christ their Saviour as well as our Saviour? May we not hope that the redeeming Word enlightened their minds, and the sanctifying Spirit touched their hearts?

It will be obvious to the thoughtful reader that this order, in which the definite knowledge of God is attained, is the reverse of that in which the idea of God is manifested in the spontaneous consciousness of the individual and the race. The former is analytical, the latter is synthetical. The *idea* of God as the ground and cause and reason of all existence is immediately given in spontaneous thought.

[1] "Apology," § 19.

[2] "Philebus," § 84.

The *conception* of God as pure Spirit, as the eternal Reason, the righteous Will, the supreme Good, the omnipresent Ruler of the universe, and the Father of humanity, is gradually developed in reflective thought. The first is a metaphysical *datum*, standing at the commencement of all inquiry, the second is a logical *quæsitum* which is reached at the end of a process of rational inquiry. Spontaneous consciousness begins with an indeterminate feeling, a mysterious presentiment of the Divine; it proceeds through simple intuition, and ends with affirmative thought. Reflective consciousness begins by questioning our primitive beliefs, and asking for their logical grounds; it proceeds by analytic and inductive reasoning, and may result in the union of logical convictions, with determinate affections—an intelligent reverence and an appreciating love. Spontaneous thought is involuntary, and must necessarily result in faith. Reflective thought is voluntary, and may result in error, doubt, and skepticism. Therefore the method by which we attain to a clear and determinate knowledge of God—by which we really *feel*, and actually *find* God—may be defeated, interrupted, and marred by sin. Unholy passion and a perverted will may materially vitiate the process by which the human reason reaches a logical conviction of the being of a God. The ungodly man may desire that the First Cause shall have no moral attributes. The sinner may imagine that the Deity is "altogether such an one as himself." The fool may say in his heart, "There is no God." While the idea of God presents itself naturally and necessarily in spontaneous thought, there may be an "unwillingness to retain God in the knowledge." And even where God is known, He may not be honored and gratefully recognized; and, as a consequence, the "understanding may be darkened." Swallowed up of uncleanness and lust, the abandoned man may "barter the truth of God for lies," and eventually "worship and serve the creature *more* than the Creator." Still man can not utterly relegate himself from all sense of obligation, and all feeling of dependence upon God. He can not sever the link which binds him to his Maker. He can not wholly extinguish in his heart the sense of the Divine, nor eradicate from his reason the ideas which, in their spontaneous, unimpeded development, reveal to him the personal Lawgiver and Judge. Where there is any rectitude of purpose, any sincere love for truth, there will be, in a proportionate measure, the true knowledge of God. And the pure mind may assuredly rise to that higher religious consciousness in which doubt and uncertainty are swallowed up in an inward vision of his glory.

Here, then, we have the rational foundation for moral government, and the ultimate ground of all religion. The possibility of knowing God, the obligation to reverence and obey God, the power to do the will of God, the susceptibility of the human heart for Divine inspiration and Divine communing, are all grounded upon the *correlations between God and man.* "God is not far from any one of us, for in Him we live and move and are; as certain of your own poets have said, '*For we are his offspring.*'"

1. *The relation between God and man is a relation of contiguity.* God is perpetually near to man. "He is not far from any one of us." The sacred Scriptures not only teach the ubiquity of God, but they emphasize the immediateness of the Divine presence in relation to man. "Whither shall I go from thy Spirit? or whither shall I flee from thy presence? If I ascend up into heaven, Thou

art there; if I make my bed in hell, behold, Thou art there. If I take the wings of the morning, and dwell in the uttermost parts of the sea, even there shall thy hand lead me, and thy right hand shall hold me. Thou hast beset me behind and before, and laid thine hand upon me." No man can escape from God. We may retire to the remotest parts of the earth, and take up our abode in the most solitary isle; we may press our way into the deepest recesses of the primeval forest, to spots where the foot of man has never trod, and on which the light of heaven has never shone, and where solitude has held its undisturbed reign ever since the morning of creation, and the conviction that "God is in this place" will relieve the loneliness, and hold us fast within the grasp of his government and laws. Let human thought take to itself the wings of imagination and pierce the heavens, let it travel on through the immensity of space until it has reached the confines of the universe, let it alight on one of the outermost stars which seem to stand as sentinels at the very outposts of creation, and looking out upon the depths of space, there shall be heard the voice of God toning on throughout the fathomless abyss, "Can any hide himself in secret places that I shall not see?" "Do not I fill heaven and earth? saith the Lord." God is not far from any one of us. He is the "*Ever Near*." Nearer to us than the air we breathe, nearer than the light which reveals surrounding objects, nearer than our body, the living vesture of the soul, is God. In the words of the Persian oracle, "God is nearer to thee than thou art unto thyself." As the Infinite Mind is present to all rational beings, so are they all present to Him. God is omniscient. The thoughts, feelings, and actions of all men are immediately and directly known by Him. "O Lord, thou hast searched me and known me. Thou knowest my downsitting and mine uprising, Thou understandest my thought afar off. Thou compassest my path and my lying down, and art acquainted with all my ways. For there is not a word in my tongue, but lo, O Lord, Thou knowest it altogether." The first condition of a moral government is found in the nearness, the contiguity of God to every human soul, and the immediate and infallible knowledge which He consequently must possess of every human thought and act.

2. *The relation between God and man is a relation of immanency.* "In Him we live and move and are" (ἐσμέν, = have conscious being). Our life, our power, our consciousness are *from* God, *through* God, and *in* God. This relation is manifestly something more immediate than the relation of contiguity. It is the present, instant, ceaseless relation of Divine *efficiency.* This is involved in the very idea of the creature. If man is the creature of God, he has not only his beginning, but his continuance of existence by a real and immediate causality. God alone possesses true life—"life in Himself"—He alone is really self-existent, our life and our being are continually derived from Him. If we were without God, and entirely isolated from Him, we could not live or move or even exist. God is every where, not virtually but actually. He pervades and interpenetrates all existences without displacing them in space or disturbing their operations. His infinite essence underlies all the principles and powers of all created existences; they all move within the range of his presence, and act within the sphere of his energy. And God is not only present immediately to man, but his mighty will sustains man in existence every moment, vitalizing his organism, endowing him with power, illuminating his reason, and inspiring him with knowledge. God is immanent

in man, and man is immanent in God. "To us there is but one God, the Father, of whom are all things, and we *in* Him."[1]—"One God and Father of all, who is above all, and *through* all, and *in* you all."[2]—"The same God who worketh *all* in *all*."[3] Our life is from God and in God. Our power to energize is from God and constantly sustained by God. We consciously know in and through God, who so illuminates our reason that we can interpret the symbolism of nature. "God teacheth man knowledge." "He giveth wisdom to the wise and prudence to men of understanding." "There is a spirit in man, and the inspiration of the Almighty giveth him understanding." The reason of man is a beam of the eternal reason. "The spirit of a man is the candle of the Lord." All good desires, all noble impulses, all power to resist temptation and perform heroic acts of endurance and suffering, are from God. "Every good and every perfect gift cometh down from above, from the Father of Lights."[4]

The constant, ceaseless dependence of all rational existence on God for vitality, for power, and for consciousness must be maintained, if we would be faithful to the plain language of Scripture. We are aware that fears of a pantheistic perversion has led some men, without reason, to refine upon the language of Scripture. By the expression "*in* Him" (ἐν αὐτῷ), we are, they say, to understand "*with* Him." But ἐν αὐτῷ does not mean "*with* Him" or "*through* Him." The most natural grammatical construc-

[1] 1 Cor. viii. 6. [2] Eph. iv. 6. [3] 1 Cor. xii. 6.

[4] "Without God there is no great man. It is He who inspires us with great ideas and exalted designs. When you see a man superior to his passions, happy in adversity, calm amid surrounding storms, can you forbear to confess that these qualities are too exalted to have their origin in the little individual whom they ornament? A god inhabits every virtuous man, and without God there is no virtue."—Seneca, "Epistles," 41, 73.

tion is "*in* Him," and this suits best the logical connection. The Uncreated is the only self-existent being. All other existences are derived and dependent, and therefore can not be self-existent. The Supreme can not communicate the attribute of self-existence any more than the attribute of infinity. A finite existence can not be at once dependent and independent. Of mind, as well as of matter, it is equally true that the sole ground of its continuing to be, as well as its beginning to be, is in the Almighty will and power directly and ceaselessly put forth. The direct agency of God sustaining conscious life is a universal, constant, profound *reality.*[1]

It may be objected that in maintaining these views we are in danger of sacrificing the personality of man. It may be asked, How can we sustain the antithesis between the I and Thou of a commandment or of a prayer? How can we reconcile human self-determination with absolute dependence upon God? How can we conceive the possibility of sin—the possibility of a creature dependent every moment on God for power, acting in opposition to the mind and will of God?

These are questions of profound significance; they are also questions of extreme difficulty. Our reason staggers under their weight. We tremble in the presence of the mystery of evil. It is obvious that these questions involve the deeper question as to the causal connection of God with his creation, which all men confess is an insoluble and impenetrable mystery. The feeling of dependence on the one hand, as well as the sense of personal power and freedom on the other, are primitive facts of consciousness. That we live and move and have our being in God, and that we have a real determinate self-

[1] See "Creator and the Creation," by Dr. Young, pp. 57, 58.

hood, a finite personality, a responsible spirit-life, are both affirmed in Scripture. That a holy God made the world, and still actually upholds it; and that sin, as lawlessness (ἀνομία), as a real antagonism to the will and nature of God, exists in his world, can not be denied by Christian men. These are equally truths. To our conception, they may appear antithetical, if not contradictory. But truth is often of a dual character; like the magnet, it may have opposite poles. And many of the differences which agitate the world are often to be traced to the exclusiveness with which different parties affirm one half of the duality in forgetfulness of the other half. We must accept both aspects of the truth, even though we can not at present effect their real conciliation in thought, and wait for further light.

A profound faith in the unity of all truth will inspire the hope that reason may yet attain to ultimate principles in which shall be found the harmony of facts and subordinate principles that to-day seem irreconcilable. Underlying the above apparently antithetical truths we can even now dimly discern still more fundamental principles which prophesy a solution. If Divine Love will that there shall be other existences who shall resemble God, and be capable of fellowship with Him in knowledge and in love—in other words, shall be *perfect* so far as is consistent with the notion of dependent existence—these beings must have a real selfhood, a conscious personality, a conditioned freedom. For impersonal being, even though it may by its absolute dependence reveal the eternal power, and in some degree reflect the thought of God, can not in any sense be the *image* of God, who is absolute Personality. Above all, that which can not know itself, can not know God, and can not love God. That which can not freely determine itself, can not obey God or resemble God. The highest form of spirit-life "is the conscious return, by a free identification, of every delegated power into harmony with its source." Real being and real life in God must therefore involve, not only a consciousness of dependence and obligation, but also self-consciousness and self-determination. Resemblance to God and fellowship with God are possible only through these fundamental elements of personality. Moral union requires dynamical separation. And because God wills this highest unity, He creates the highest individuality, and gives being to a will under concessions of freedom.

We conceive of the Divine conservation of the world and man as "the simple, universal, uniform efficiency of God which sustains the created powers in every moment of their activity, and thereby keeps them bound to Himself. As such it makes itself the basis of all individual efficiencies in the life and movement of the world, *without indeed itself, as such, giving to the efficiency of creaturely powers any particular direction.*" The conserving activity of God moves in pre-arranged lines, and according to laws and measures determined by the infinite wisdom of God, and conserves, therefore, all individual existence only within the boundaries which are fixed by these arrangements, and through the relations of the powers of the world. Thus as the world-conserving activity of God leaves all creatures just as it finds them, and equally embraces irrational as well as rational beings, "the evil as well as the good" (Matt. v. 45), it can in nowise remove the answerableness of man for his sins, or in any way taking part in the same. The world-conserving efficiency of God sustains man every moment in being, and conditions the activity of his moral powers even when they are exerted in an evil choice, just as it sustains the universe according to a predetermined plan and in harmony with fixed laws; but it does not thereby give to the activity of the moral creature any determinate direction whatever, either good or evil. The general power to will and do is received immediately and constantly from God, but it is a delegation of power under concessions of freedom and conditions of accountability. The specific determinations of that power are from man himself. He may give an evil direction to his derived and dependent activities, and thus commit sin. The responsibility for that evil determination rests upon himself alone, even though he is every moment pervaded and sustained by the conserving efficiency of God. Alternative power is a talent loaned out by God to man. But it is a talent which still belongs to God, for the proper or improper use of which man is accountable.

It has been urged by the captious critic, who would fain cast upon God all responsibility for the presence of evil in the world, that "if God does not actually determine the evil, He delegates to man the power to actualize evil; let Him only refuse his conserving efficiency to the will of man, and thus prevent the evil!" The reckless objector knoweth not what he saith. In order to render evil impossible, it is demanded that God shall rob man of his personality, and degrade him to the level of impersonal nature; for the possibility of evil is inseparable from the notion of free, self-determined existence. "The momentary withdrawment of the conserving activity of God from the moral creature were the immediate annihilation of its existence."[1] Liberty is not only a good, but it is the necessary condition of all goodness. It is the sphere of all great virtues, noble deeds, and heroic acts. There can be no

[1] See Müller, "Christian Doctrine of Sin," vol. i. pp. 248, 249.

virtue, no praiseworthiness, no godlikeness, no real felicity, where there is no freedom. Shall we reproach God for having made us free personalities? Shall we complain because God has honored us by committing to us a sacred trust, and placed our happiness and well-being largely under our own control? Who would surrender his conscious power and freedom, and sacrifice the infinite possibilities of good which lie before him, to escape the possibility of failure and suffering and defeat? Will any rational man exchange his position for that of the ant or the beaver? "What," exclaims Rousseau, "to render man incapable of evil, would we have him lowered to mere brute instinct? No! God of my soul, I will not reproach Thee for having made me in thine image, so that I might be good and free and happy like Thyself."

The ceaseless dependence of man on the conserving efficiency of God imposes upon him the obligation to determine himself, and to regulate his action in conformity with the will of God. Here, then, we have found a still deeper ground for moral government.

3. *The relation of God to man is a relation of paternity; the relation of man to God is a relation of childship.* "We are his offspring;" and as the offspring of God we must have a kindred nature, and, in some sense, "resemble God."

God is "the Father of the human spirit" by no mere figure of speech, but by a Divine reality; and man, in virtue of that rational and spiritual nature inbreathed and, as it were, begotten within him by the "Eternal Word of God," is "the likeness and image of God." It is one of the changeless laws of all derived and dependent existence that the offspring shall resemble the parent. And just as every seed must produce its own kind, just as every offspring must be of the same species as its parent, so must man bear the image of God.[1] This image of God can have no reference to the body of man, nor to any qualities or attributes which belong to matter. Spirit is the only thing which does bear or is capable of bearing any resemblance to God. The all-pervading personality of God is mirrored in the finite personality of man. The four grand elements of personality are *intelligence*, *will*, *affection*, and *conscience*, and these in man reflect the character of God. Elevated to absolute perfection, they become the august attributes of Omniscience, Omnipotence, All-lovingness, and All-holiness. "One God," says Cousin, "is doubtless the author of the world, and as his workmanship it must reflect, in some measure, his perfections. But He is especially the Father of humanity. His intelligence and his personality are therefore of the same kind with our intelligence and our personality, to which we add infinity by a necessary law of thought." So that our knowledge, our freedom, our charity, our justice, give us the idea of Divine wisdom, Divine freedom, Divine justice, and Divine charity.[2] These conclusions of philosophy are in striking harmony with the positive statements of Scripture. Here we are taught that the image of God in man consists in *power*, *knowledge*, *righteousness*, and *benevolence* (ὁσιότης)[3]—ὅσιος, from חָסִיד = kind, merciful, benevolent.

Inasmuch, then, as man is the "offspring of God," he may know *that* God is, and he may, in some measure at

[1] Some theologians affirm that this "image of God" was utterly and totally lost in the fall. Such an unqualified statement does not, however, seem warranted by Scripture. After the fall, the sanctity of human life is still grounded upon the fact that man is "made in the *image* of God" (Gen. ix. 6), and Paul affirms of man, as man, that he is "the *image* and glory of God" (1 Cor. xi. 7).

[2] "History of Philosophy," vol. i. p. 115.

[3] See Psa. viii. 6; 1 Cor. xi. 7; Col. iii. 10; Eph. iv. 24.

least, know *what* God is, and what are the duties which he owes to God. Selfhood or personality in man is the primordial germ of the idea of God. The self-consciousness, the intelligence, the free activity, the potential righteousness and charity of man must have their origin in a cause which is itself a full and adequate explanation. We accept the ancient philosophic maxim "*ex nihilo nihil*," and apply it rigorously to the case in hand. "That which is can not have arisen out of that which is not." "Out of nothing nothing can arise." Consciousness can not arise out of unconsciousness. Reason can not arise out of unreason. Self-activity can not arise out of absolute passivity and eternal rest. Justice, righteousness, charity, can not be generated from brute matter, or born in the abyss of nothingness. The Creator of man, of the reason that is in man, of the moral liberty of man, of the ideas of justice and benevolence which dwell in the conscience of man, must Himself be intelligent, free, just, and good. Such is the logic of Scripture and of common-sense. "He that planted the ear, shall He not hear? He that formed the eye, shall He not see? He that chastiseth the heathen, shall not He correct? He that teacheth man knowledge, shall not He know?" He that made man a sentient, percipient, self-conscious personality, shall not He be percipient and self-conscious? He that hath given man reason, is He not the Eternal Reason? He that hath planted in the hearts of men the principles of justice, must not He be a righteous Being? He that inspires man with compassion, must not his nature be Love? "If the First Cause be destitute of these qualities, then for us, at least, He is as though He were not." He is a thousand times inferior to us—inferior even in his infinity and his eternity to one hour of our finite existence, if during that fugitive hour we can *know* and *think* and *love.* A finite moral personality, even though it be the most perfect form of *dependent* existence, points, with an infallible logic, to a being beyond and above itself, and suggests an Infinite Personality who is absolute perfection—that is, a Being of perfect knowledge, perfect freedom, perfect righteousness, and perfect love.

This community of nature between man and God is not only the ground and condition of our knowing God, but it is also the living, everlasting bond which holds man to God, even in his sins. It involves much more than obligation—obligation to an omnipotent Master, and submission to an omnipresent Lord. Such sense of obligation may be developed within the sphere of instinctive and unreasoning life. But the kinship of souls to God brings man within the sphere of *moral* life, with its eternal and immutable laws. It endows man with the power and imposes upon him the duty to reverence, adore, and love the heavenly Father. Wonderful and awful, this idea of the paternity of God and the childship of human souls! This paternity of God is suggestive at once of the highest form of authority and the most sacred form of duty that can be conceived by the human mind. "The power of a sovereign, however extensive it may be, is, after all, only conventional; it admits of being circumscribed or suspended. . . . All earthly forms of authority, which belong to the political, civil, or social relation of men, are accidental and official, created by men for their own purposes, and may be modified or abolished by the power that created them. But the authority of a father over his child is founded in *nature* and established by God. This is not a voluntary arrangement among men themselves, which they are at liberty to continue or to terminate as they please; but, on the contrary, it is a Divine constitution. Such authority as a father possesses over his child—so natural, so real, so Divine—no human being besides can possess over another. This, accordingly, is the selected type of the supreme rights of God, and of the essential sovereignty which belongs to the Father of minds. No other explains, as this does, the *foundation* and *nature* of Divine authority. There are, indeed, other terms which indicate the mere fact of sovereignty in God, and do so more pointedly and directly than this. For example: He is compared to a *king*—a name which belongs to the highest secular office and the highest secular authority on earth. 'The Lord is king forever.' His creatures are his subjects; He gives them wise and righteous laws, and they must answer to Him for obedience and disobedience. The comparison is obviously just up to a certain limit; but it is obvious that in many essential respects it entirely fails. The king and his people are connected together only by one bond—that of authority and corresponding subjection." The relation is purely a contingent relation, and may be maintained by arbitrary power. But the relation between God and his rational creatures is a natural and a necessary relation. All that is denoted by the word *king*—authority, power, law—is really contained in the word *father;* but there is much more conveyed in the word *father* than can be possibly expressed by the word *king.* God is a king, but He is a Father-king; his subjects are his own children, and his government of them—in its origin, its spirit, its laws, and even its penalties—is strictly paternal. God's kingship is a *figure,* his fatherhood is the profoundest *reality.*[1]

This correlation between the spirit of man and the spirit of God is the living indissoluble bond which has

[1] See Dr. Young's "Christ of History," pp. 136–138.

ever held, and shall forever hold the hearts of men to the living God. Humanity has not been enchained to the throne of God by servile fear, and held in subjection to his government by the dread of future punishment. Fear never made men virtuous, never can insure virtue. Man has been held to God by spiritual affinities and a conscious kinship. Men have always felt that the Ruler of the world is merciful and just, and that his claim upon their allegiance and loyal obedience is reasonable and right. Therefore they have in all ages hoped in his mercy, and confided in the righteousness of his administration. This has been the consolation of the wise and good in seasons of danger and adversity. To this Being innocence and weakness under oppression and wrong have made their proud appeal, like that of Prometheus to the elements, to the witnessing world, to coming ages, to the just ear of Heaven. When, therefore, Paul at Athens announced that "God is not far from any one of us, for in Him we live and move and are," he touched a chord which vibrated in every heart. For in every age men have had a presentiment of some nearer relation to God than the rest of creation—a relation not of dependence only, but of kinship and sonship. In moments of deep feeling the poets, who are the best interpreters of nature, have given oracular utterance to the native feeling of the human heart:

> "We are all thine offspring,
> The image and the echo of thy eternal voice."—CLEANTHES.

> "All need his aid, his power sustains us all—
> For we his offspring are."—ARATUS.

Finally, as the spiritual nature of man is derived from and correlated to God, he may become inwardly conscious of the Divine favor, or may be sensible of the Divine displeasure. These are the sanctions of the moral law—the reward and the penalty awarded to men. The smile of God is heaven, the frown of God is hell. Here we have found the deepest ground of a Divine government—the paternity of God.

CHAPTER XI.

MORAL GOVERNMENT.

II. ITS NATURE, CONDITIONS, METHOD, AND END.

"The times of this ignorance God overlooked, but now commandeth all men every where to repent; because He hath appointed a day in the which He will judge the world in righteousness."—ST. PAUL.

THE relations existing between God and man, especially the correlations of paternity and filiation, constitute the ultimate foundations of Moral Government. This is the conclusion of the preceding discussion. If God is intimately near to man—if He is immanent in man, and man is immanent in God—if God is "the Father of the human spirit," and man "the offspring of God," then man must bear some resemblance to God—he must have a spiritual and immortal nature, must be a free personality, must be capable of knowing and loving God, and therefore must be under solemn responsibility to God, and within the sphere of the eternal and immutable laws of moral life; in a word, he must be the subject of *moral* government.

We proceed now to consider, more especially, the *nature*, the *conditions*, the *methods*, and the *ends* of moral government.

I. *The nature of moral government.*—Government, in general, is control—control with a view to the maintenance of order. This may be effected by direct coaction or forceful compulsion; or by the reaction of natural consequences; or by the pervasive influence of moral motives. The first is constraint, the second is restraint, the third is authoritative direction. We must, therefore, distinguish between physical, natural, and moral government.

The *physical* government of God is the absolute control which He exercises over the material creation. He is the Fountain-head of all the forces, and the Author of all the laws according to which passive, unconscious matter is resistlessly impelled; and because his power and wisdom are infinite, and his purposes are immutable, therefore material nature is uniform, and there is an all-pervading order in the physical world.

The *natural* government of God is that constitution of nature, and of man in so far as he is a part of nature, by which the sensations of pleasure and pain result directly and necessarily from the actions of man; and inasmuch as he is able by an induction from experience to foresee these consequences, and to determine his own conduct in view of them, they are not improperly called rewards and punishments. Thus it is found by experience that disease and suffering result from acts of intemperance and licentiousness, and men are restrained from the commission of these acts by the fear of their foreseen results. This is control by the reaction of natural consequences in that intermediate sphere which we may designate the physico-moral order of the world.

The *moral* government of God is that kind of control which a wise and virtuous parent exercises over his family, or a just and equitable magistrate over his subjects.[1] It is a government by laws or rules addressed to the reason, by moral motives which appeal to the conscience, and by moral sanctions which appeal to the emotions. It is a

[1] Butler's "Analogy," pt. i. ch. iii.

constitution in which God has declared his will to man, and taught him, prior to the experience of retributive consequences, what is right and what is wrong; a constitution under which man is endowed with the capacity of perceiving the inherent righteousness of the Divine law, of feeling the imperative claims of duty, and of apprehending a future retribution, and also a real causative power of self-determination and choice. Finally, it is an economy in which ample scope is afforded for the development of responsible character. It is a probation in which there are tests and temptations, in which forbearance is exercised and consequences are delayed, in which remedial agencies are plied and opportunities are afforded for repentance and reformation, and in the final consummation of which virtuous character shall receive its meet reward, and sinful character its merited punishment. This is the ideal order of moral life.

This twofold distinction between the *physical* and the *spiritual*, and between the *natural* and the *moral*, runs through the entire domain of existence and action, of being and becoming.

The terms *physical* and *spiritual* are employed as collective terms to connote the essential, changeless, and permanent attributes of certain entities or realities which are regarded as ultimate, viz., matter and spirit. The attributes of matter are extension, divisibility, absolute incompressibility, and inertia; the attributes of spirit are sensitivity, reason, power, spontaneity, and memory. The term physical is further employed to denote certain "affections of matter"—that is, mechanical effects which are the result of the action of force upon matter. It is true we often speak of "physical forces," as though force were an essential attribute of matter. But this is one of the many ambiguities of language. All that we mean by physical force is a force which acts upon matter, and produces in the motions and collocations of matter its appropriate effects.[1] Spirit-force is the only force in the universe; all that our physical science deals with is "forms of energy which have their origin in force." "Mind," says Dr. Carpenter, "is the one and only source of power."[2]

The terms *natural* and *moral* are employed to denote opposite modes of action and classes of effects. In the one case the mode of action is fixed and uniform, and the effect is necessary; in the other case the mode of action is free and volitional, and the effect is contingent and variable. The first is the order of nature where force reigns, the second is the order of moral life where freedom prevails. "Whatever is comprised in the chain and mechanism of cause and effect, of course necessitated, and having its necessity in some other thing antecedent or concurrent, this is said to be *natural*, and the aggregate and system of all such things is nature."[3] While, on the contrary, that which lies within the agent's power, and to which he determines himself by an act of free choice; and especially that which the agent knows he *ought* to do, and in choosing which he is conscious of power to put forth, in the same unchanged circumstances, a different volition instead, is called *moral*.

Thus does morality commence with "the sacred distinction" between *thing* and *person*. "On this distinction all legislation, human and Divine, proceeds." That which fundamentally distinguishes a person from a mere thing of nature is *free causality*—that is, "the power or immu-

[1] "Reign of Law," by the Duke of Argyll, p. 121.
[2] *Nature*, vol. vi. p. 312.
[3] Coleridge's Works, vol. i. p. 152.

nity to put forth in the same circumstances either of several volitions." A thing is unconscious, involuntary, and powerless, and consequently limited to one sole possible eventuation. A thing has no responsibility for its movements, which it has not willed, and of the nature and consequences of which it is ignorant. A person alone is responsible, because he is intelligent and free; that is, he can foresee the consequences of his action, and freely determines himself to its performance. A thing has no dignity; dignity attaches only to personality. Personality is inalienable, sacred, and inviolable; it can not be abrogated, surrendered, or transferred, and it demands to be respected. In a word, it has both duties and rights, while things have neither.[1]

Thus do we find that all dignity, all sacredness, all responsibility, all morality belong to and are predicable only of the personal being, because intelligence and freedom are the essential moments of personality.

Furthermore, the sphere of the *moral* is to be determined by another important limitation. Not all the actions of men are personal and responsible acts. Sensation is not a voluntary operation. When the external object is brought into proper relation with the animated organism, perception necessarily occurs. The intuitive apperceptions of the reason are impersonal; when a change transpires, the reason necessarily affirms the existence of a cause. Reflex nervous action is involuntary. Many muscular movements are spontaneous, but not volitional. A responsible action is an *intentional* action—that is, an act performed to realize an end which lies within the agent's contemplation. Spontaneity or self-determination only thereby becomes *will.* A moral act is consequently a premeditated, in-

[1] Cousin, "True, Beautiful, and Good," pp. 287–289.

tentional, voluntary act, and the merit or demerit of an agent is as his actual intention.

The last and most important limitation of the moral sphere is to those voluntary actions which have relation to personality, human and Divine. "The peculiar distinction of moral actions, moral character, moral principles, moral habits, as contrasted with the intellectual and other parts of man's nature, lies in this, that they always imply a relation between two persons."[1] Morality is the relation of person to person.

We sum up what has been said in the preceding paragraphs in these words: The moral government of God is a *legislation* which has respect to personality, especially the relations of person to person; and it is an *administration* under which the subjects have power to resist and violate its requirements, but which is provided with ample means to vindicate its authority, and maintain the moral order of the universe.

II. *The subjective conditions of moral government.*—It will be apparent from what has been already said that the following conditions are essential to moral government:

(1.) The subject of moral government must be *intelligent.* He must be able to understand the Divine requirements, to perceive their inherent rightness, and to feel the sense of obligation to comply therewith. He must also be susceptible of certain pleasurable or painful *emotions* which follow as the direct consequences of his actions, and secure an adequate retribution. In a word, he must have a moral consciousness, or, briefly, a *conscience.*

(2.) The subject of moral government must be a *free power.* He must be the efficient cause of his own action,

[1] Sewell's "Christian Morals," p. 339.

and he must be conscious of this power of self-determination—that is, he must be conscious of power to put forth, in the same unchanged circumstances, either of several volitions. In short, he must have a *free will.*

These, then, are the essential conditions of moral agency—the possession of a *conscience,* and the *power to obey or disobey* the requirements of moral law. Both these conditions of accountability exist in man. By virtue of his constitution as a spiritual being made in the image of God, he is capable of perceiving what is inherently right, just, and good. His reason intuitively apprehends the good, and affirms the imperative obligation to choose the good. His judgment pronounces upon the relation of human conduct to the law of right, affirming man has or has not done right. And his emotive nature yields him complacence and joy as the reward of well-doing, or inflicts pain and remorse as the punishment of wrong-doing. In the words of Chalmers, "he is endowed with a conscience which performs within his bosom all the offices of a lawgiver and a judge."

The possession of this faculty necessarily supposes the existence of power in the agent to comply or not to comply with its behests. A moral law is designed only for the government of a free being, and nothing is moral or immoral which is not voluntary. If there is no self-determination, there is no proper personality to which the law of reason can attach. Remorse, on the one hand, satisfaction on the other, are emotions which are inconceivable and impossible in a being who is not consciously free.

The nature and authority of conscience is a question which is earnestly discussed. Among philosophers and theologians there are diverse and conflicting opinions. It has been variously characterized as a *witness* of our past actions; as a *judgment* passed upon our actions; or as a *feeling* arising in view of our actions. By one, conscience is regarded as an *appetite* — a craving for the right, but not a faculty intuitively perceiving the right. Another defines it "as a *capacity* and a *tendency* to inquire into duty, but not as supplying a law of duty."[1] While a third regards it as a state of the *sensibility*—" a simple feeling, emotion, or vivid sentiment which arises immediately in the mind in presence of certain actions, and to which we give the name of moral approbation."[2]

These definitions of conscience may all be regarded as containing some truth. They are all defective, however, in this one respect—*they fail to recognize an internal law which constitutes a subjective standard of right*, and an intuitive perception of moral distinctions and qualities in human action.

As an essay toward a clearer apprehension of the nature of conscience, we present the following propositions:

1. *Conscience is not a distinct faculty of the mind.* Conscience (*conscientia*=joint or double knowledge) is the knowledge of self in relation to a known law of right and wrong. Conscience and consciousness may therefore be regarded as, in some respects, identical. The terms in their etymology and their general import are synonymous. There is, however, a technical distinction to be made. Consciousness expresses self-knowledge in general. Conscience expresses self-knowledge relative to responsibility. Consciousness is the recognition by the thinking subject of its own states and affections. Conscience is the knowledge of an act or an affection as having some moral quality—as being right or wrong.

2. *Conscience is, like consciousness, a complex phenom-*

[1] R. W. Hamilton. [2] Dr. Thomas Brown.

enon, the result of the simultaneous action of the primary powers of the mind. The simplest fact of consciousness is a synthesis of sensation and reason in a primitive psychological judgment. Sensation alone is not knowledge, and it becomes consciousness only as it is illuminated and informed by the reason. And so a mere state of the sensibility—a mere feeling of approbation or disapprobation—does not constitute conscience until it is informed by the reason. Conscience is the unity of feeling and reason in a judgment which has respect to voluntary action.

3. *Conscience is the common field in which is revealed the result of the operation of all our faculties in their especial relation to moral law.* As consciousness is the common field in which the results of the operation of all our faculties come to light, so conscience is that department of the same field in which is revealed the action of the mind in relation to the unchangeable principles of order and right which dwell in the bosom of the Infinite. Conscience is pre-eminently the Godward side of our mental being, which reflects the moral character of God, and brings us into relationship with Him. It is that which carries us *per saltum* to the immediate recognition of a God, the Lawgiver and the Judge who is over man, and which holds him in mysterious but indissoluble bonds of obligation. Conscience is therefore,

(1.) The *reason* intuitively apprehending universal moral ideas and laws. It furnishes *the idea of the good.* It affirms that the good is universally *obligatory.* It asserts that the good has *desert*, worthiness, and dignity. And it demands for the good an appropriate recognition and a just reward.

(2.) The *understanding* apprehending the relations in which we stand to God, to our fellow-beings, and to self as a moral personality endowed with reason and freedom.

(3.) The *judgment* comparing the acts of a voluntary agent existing in certain relations with the immutable ideas and laws of the reason, and affirming this is *right* and worthy of praise and reward, or that is *wrong* and deserving of blame and punishment.

(4.) A particular state of the *sensibility*—the painful or pleasurable emotions which spontaneously arise in presence of right or wrong in our own actions or in the actions of our fellow-men.

Thus conscience is, as it were, the focal point at which are united and blended the varied acts and states of the soul in its immediate relation to the moral law. It is the synthesis of moral ideas, cognitions, and feelings in a moral judgment.

The co-operation of these powers and susceptibilities of the soul in their relation to the *good* has a parallel and an illustration in their operation in relation to the *beautiful.*

The ideas of order, proportion, harmony, fitness, and unity in variety are unquestionably fundamental and necessary ideas of the *reason.* In the Divine reason these ideas have always existed as the laws in accordance with which He fashioned the material universe. And inasmuch as the human reason is configured to the Divine, these ideas must also exist in the human mind. Like statuary in the inner palaces of the soul, they are the models by which we recognize and the standards according to which we judge the forms of beauty in the external world. The correspondence between these external forms and the inner ideals of the reason is recognized by the *judgment.* And the delight we experience in presence of the beautiful in nature and art is a particular direction of the *sensibility*.

This is not, however, the chronological order in which the idea of the beautiful is developed in the mind. The *sense* of beauty first reveals itself in the spontaneous consciousness in presence of the order and harmony and fitness which pervade the universe. We experience delight without being able to specialize the precise causes of our pleasure. But the reflective consciousness, which is pre-eminently analytic, brings out into clear light the fundamental ideas of order, harmony, fitness, and unity, which had a prior existence in the reason, and have now recognized themselves as mirrored in the universe. The repeated observation of the forms of beauty around us, and the comparison of these with the standard ideas of the reason, will result in the beau-ideal of a pure and correct taste—true αἰσθητικόν.

So in relation to the idea of the *good*. It does not stand forth to the eye of consciousness, in the first instance, as an abstract conception. The *moral sense*—the affection of the sensibility in presence of voluntary and responsible action—is first revealed in the spontaneous consciousness. When we behold an act of justice, of kindness, of beneficence, we experience the fullest satisfaction. We admire and esteem the actor. We feel that his conduct is praiseworthy, and that he is deserving of honor and reward. These sentiments spring up spontaneously and involuntarily in our bosoms long before we have defined their reason and law. The reflective consciousness subsequently elicits the rational ideas which underlie these emotions—the ideas of the useful, the just, the beneficent, the noble, and the perfect, all which are finally embraced in the idea of the *good*. And the repeated comparison of the conduct of voluntary agents existing under certain relations, with the fundamental ideas of the reason, these standards of right erected in the soul, will result in an ideal of moral excellence—a true ἠθικόν.

If this doctrine of conscience be the product of a true psychological method, it will enable us to account for the apparent want of uniformity in its suffrages in individual cases, and the varied phenomena presented in different men.

Conscience, like consciousness, has its gradual development. Though natural and necessary to every human soul whose powers are normally developed, it is not exercised at the beginning of its existence, but only after certain conditions of growth and stages of growth have been attained. This development may be arrested or it may be perverted. The absence of proper conditions, the lack of suitable discipline and culture in any one of the faculties whose operation enters into the concrete phenomena, will modify the general result. An excess of *sensibility* will give a morbid conscience; the lack of sensibility, a slumbering conscience. A defective apprehension of the relations in which we stand to God and to our fellow-men will prevent our seeing our specific duties. Inattention to the character of our own motives, or ignorance of the real intentions of other men, may mislead the *judgment* in discriminating between the quality of actions. There are also natural differences in the soundness and accuracy of the judgments of individual men. We meet those who with a limited acquaintance with particular facts and abstract notions are nevertheless endowed with sound practical judgment; while others, with a larger knowledge of facts and general principles, are strangely defective in judgment. Finally, unless men accustom themselves to reflection, to analysis, the ideas of the just, the right, the good, do not come clearly into the light of consciousness. Hence the different manifestations of conscience in individual men.

We claim, however, that the moral ideas of the reason are in all men *identical;* that they exist and operate, even though unconsciously, in all minds, determining their moral judgments; and that *when the same relations of personality are clearly before the mind the moral judgments of men are uniform.*

In spite of all the topical moralities to which factitious circumstances may have given birth, there is unquestionably *a universal and immutable morality.* In every nation under heaven, veracity, justice, and beneficence are separated by a clear, unmistakable line from falsehood, injustice, and cruelty; nor can all the casuistry and sophistry in the universe transpose or confound them. Custom, prescription, conventions of human opinion, factitious circumstances, can never blur over and obliterate these lines which separate right and wrong. Beneath all these apparent differences, the conscience will make her voice heard in the depth of the soul, in the common sentiments of mankind, and in the statutes of universal jurisprudence. The great ideas of justice and right were prominent and well defined among the nations of antiquity. "Nemesis and Themis were not only their abstractions and deities—they were embodied in their systems of jurisprudence. Law secured property and sanctified life. Law guarded every relation and ordered every act. Law was the theme of their philosophy and the burden of their song. We are not unacquainted with the jealousies and disputes of their schools of philosophy. They placed the good of man and the reason of morality in the most incongruous things, but *they never differed concerning the conduct which was right.* Epicurus and Zeno knew no divergence here."[1] Indeed, they asserted the immutability of moral law for all times and places—

> "The unwritten laws of God that know not change;
> They are not of to-day nor yesterday,
> But live for ever."[2]

"There is," says Cicero, "one true and original law, conformable to nature and reason, diffused over all, invariable, eternal, which calls to the fulfillment of duty and to abstinence from injustice, and which calls with that irresistible voice which is felt in all its authority wherever it is heard. This law can not be curtailed or abolished, nor affected in its sanctions by any law of man. A whole senate, a whole people, can not dispense with its paramount obligation. It requires no commentator to render it distinctly intelligible, nor is it different at Rome, at Athens, now and in ages before and after, but in all ages and all nations it is and has been and will be one and everlasting—one as that God, its author and promulgator, who is the common Sovereign of all mankind, is Himself one. Man is truly man as he yields himself to this Divine influence. He can not resist it but by flying, as it were, from his own bosom, and laying aside the general feelings of humanity, by which very act he must already have inflicted on himself the severest of punishments, even though he were to avoid what is usually accounted punishment."[3]

Among the most savage tribes, as among the most refined and polished nations, are also to be found the same common principles of morality. Theft, murder, adultery are offenses condemned and punished by every nation un-

[1] R. W. Hamilton. [2] Sophocles, "Antigone," v. 450–460.
[3] Quoted by Dr. Brown from "Lucani Pharsalia," bk. ix.

der heaven. The high qualities of virtue are the things which win esteem and command respect in every country, however rude. Were proof demanded, we might bring it at once from the darkest corners of the earth. The savage Fijian regards theft, adultery, abduction, incendiarism, and treason as serious crimes.[1] And Dr. Livingstone tells us that, "On questioning intelligent men among the Backwains as to their former knowledge of good and evil, of God, and of a future state, they have scouted the idea of any of them ever having been without a tolerably clear conception on all these subjects. Respecting their sense of right and wrong, they profess that nothing we indicate as sin ever appeared to them as otherwise, except the statement that it was wrong to have more wives than one."[2]

We conclude that the universal consciousness of our race, as revealed in human history, languages, legislations, and sentiments, bears testimony to the fact that the ideas of right, duty, accountability, and moral desert are native to the human mind; and consequently the existence of the first condition of moral government—namely, the possession by its subject of a *conscience*—is an unquestionable fact.

The *second* condition of moral government is the existence, in the subject, *of free self-determining power:* the agent must be the real cause and the sole cause of his own actions; he must have freedom both *to* and *from* the act.

Under a reign of necessity there can be no moral government and no just retribution. It is, at best, a mere physical or natural government; for moral government must be of beings who are free and self-determined, and not of mere machines. To blame a necessitated thing is

[1] "Fiji and the Fijians," by Williams and Calvert, p. 22.

[2] "Missionary Travels and Researches in South Africa," p. 153.

irrational, to punish it is a cruelty and an injustice. The necessitarian himself is unable to conceal his conscious embarrassment in presence of these difficulties, and to save his theory he becomes reckless in assertions. He affirms that "the whole system of morality—its duties and responsibilities; the whole scheme of moral government, with its rewards and punishments—remains, on his theory, as entire and stable as ever."[1] This affirmation runs athwart all the dictates of common-sense, and collides with the universal conviction of humanity. He is the only consistent necessitarian who rejects the Christian doctrine of sin, denies all accountability and retribution, and reduces the government of God to mere physical impulsion and the management of a universal mechanism. The necessitarian dogma can not be made to quadrate with our primitive convictions; it is out of harmony with all our instinctive beliefs. The innate idea of right, the native sense of duty and accountability, the consciousness of sin, our faith in the justice of God, our religious hopes and fears, all impel us onward to find a rational and valid basis for human responsibility and moral government in the freedom of the will.

That man does possess an alternative power of self-determination and choice is evident:

1. *From the direct testimony of consciousness.* We *know* that any doing of ours might have been reserved—we *feel*, by that same direct consciousness which certifies our existence and our reason, that we have the fullest power of choice. No subtlety, no abstraction of argument, can convince us that we are otherwise than free. "Men are not conscious of compulsion of any kind, not conscious of certain mental states, called choices, which

[1] Chalmers's "Institutes of Theology," vol. ii. p. 294.

are either wholly or partially independent of their free agency; but they are perfectly and distinctly conscious of entire liberty, and of complete inward power to choose."[1]

That we have a direct consciousness of freedom is the doctrine of most of the writers on moral science. Cousin is emphatic in the assertion of this doctrine: "I am conscious of this sovereign power of the will. I feel in myself, before its determination, the force that can determine itself in such a manner or in such another. At the same time that I will this or that I am equally conscious of the power to will the opposite; I am conscious of being master of my resolution, of the ability to arrest it, continue it, repress it."[2] The distinguished Professor of Moral Philosophy in the University of Edinburgh, Dr. Calderwood, teaches the same doctrine: "It is in our consciousness of self-control for the determination of activity that we obtain our only knowledge of causation. Every one knows himself as the cause of his own actions. In the external world we continue ignorant of causes, and are able only to trace uniform sequence, as Hume and Comte have insisted. But in consciousness we distinguish between sequence and causality. We are conscious of our own causal energy by knowing the origin of our activity in self-determination."[3]

The direct consciousness of freedom is denied by Sir

[1] "The Creator and the Creation," by John Young, LL.D., pp. 101–2. See also "Man Primeval," by Dr. Harris, p. 109; Hamilton's "Revealed Doctrine of Rewards and Punishments," p. 67.

[2] "True, Beautiful, and Good," p. 286.

[3] "Hand-book of Moral Philosophy," p. 184. See also Cairns's "Treatise on Moral Freedom," p. 222; and Hazard on "Causation and Freedom in Willing," p. 7; Dr. Alexander, "Outlines of Moral Science," p. 125; Sir John Herschel's "Familiar Lectures on Science," p. 461; Carpenter's "Human Physiology," p. 543; Wallace, "On Natural Selection," p. 367; Beale's "Protoplasm," p. 121.

William Hamilton. This denial is a necessary consequence of his doctrine of relativity. If we are not conscious of self as a reality, but only of certain modes or affections, then, of course, we can not be conscious of self as a free power. But as Mansel has forcibly replied: "Does it not rather appear a flat contradiction to maintain that I am not immediately conscious of myself, but only of my sensations or volitions? Who, then, is the *I* that is conscious; and how can *I* be conscious of such states as *mine?* In this case it would surely be more accurate to say, not that I am conscious of my sensations, but that the sensation is conscious of itself; but, thus worded, the glaring absurdity of the theory would carry with it its own refutation. . . . Self-personality is revealed to us with all the clearness of an original intuition."[1] With an inconsistency which shows the fallacy of Sir William Hamilton's whole theory of relativity, he admits that, "As clearly as I am conscious of existing, so clearly am I conscious at every moment of my existence that the conscious Ego is not itself a mere modification, nor a series of modifications of any other subject, but that it is itself something different from all its own modifications, and a *self-subsistent entity.*"[2]

If, then, we admit, as we must admit, the existence of an immediate consciousness, not merely of the phenomena of mind, but of the personal self as actively and passively related to them, we must also admit the direct testimony of conscience to the fact of liberty. "I am conscious not merely of the phenomenon of volition, *but of myself as producing it, and as producing it by choice, with a power to choose the opposite alternative.*"

[1] "Prolegomena Logica," p. 122.

[2] "Lectures on Metaphysics," vol. i. p. 373; also Porter's "Human Intellect," p. 95.

The necessitarians are all compelled to concede that the universal conviction of our race is, and always has been, that man is free. They have, however, asserted that this dictate of common-sense is not to be accepted as philosophically true. Lord Kames admits the natural conviction of freedom from necessity, though he declares it to be an illusion:

> "Man fondly dreams that he is free to act;
> Naught is he but the powerless, worthless plaything
> Of the blind force that in his will itself
> Works out for him a dread necessity."

And Hommel, certainly one of the ablest and most decided of fatalists, says, "I must believe that I have a feeling of liberty, at the very moment I am writing against liberty, upon grounds which I regard as incontestable. Zeno was a fatalist only in theory; he did not act in conformity with his convictions."[1]

The possession of alternative power is a fact of consciousness as clear and indubitable as the fact of personal existence. It is admitted by the necessitarians that all men have "a natural conviction of freedom;" they believe themselves to be free beings, and they act upon this belief in all the relations of life. If this fact of consciousness is an illusion, then our existence is also an illusion, for that same intuition which certifies to me that I exist certifies also that I am free. If the testimony of consciousness is invalidated, there is no criterion for truth. If one of its deliverances is found to be false, how can we vindicate the veracity of any? "Our faculties are bestowed upon us as the instruments of deception; the root of our nature is a lie, and universal skepticism is the only goal."

2. *The idea of moral obligation necessarily presupposes*

[1] Quoted by Hamilton in "Notes on Reid," p. 616.

the freedom of the will. This is a principle so obvious that it needs no elucidation. If man have duties, he must possess the power of fulfilling them. He ought to be free if he ought to obey law, or human nature is in contradiction with itself. The direct certainty of obligation implies the corresponding certainty of freedom. Hence Kant's well-known canon, "*I ought, therefore I can.*" Though denying the direct consciousness of freedom, Kant maintained with earnestness that the fact of liberty is guaranteed by the existence of the moral law, whose categorical imperative *thou shalt* necessarily implies a corresponding *thou canst.* To the same effect are the words of Sir William Hamilton: "The fact that we are free is given to us in the consciousness of an uncompromising law of duty. ... Our consciousness of the moral law, which without a moral liberty in man would be a mendacious imperative, gives a decided preponderance to the doctrine of freedom over the doctrine of fate."[1] Physical causation and moral obligation can not co-exist side by side. In proportion as we extend the domain of necessity we must diminish that of duty.

3. *The sense of responsibility presupposes the freedom of the will.* This sense of responsibility is native to the human mind. Every man feels himself to be accountable for his own conduct, not only at the bar of his own conscience, but before the moral judgment-seat of his fellowmen. Every where he recognizes the right of his fellowmen to inquire into his character, to sit in judgment upon his conduct, and to esteem and treat him accordingly. We necessarily impute blame when an unjust action is performed by another; we feel conscious of guilt and unworthiness when a wrong is done by ourselves. These

[1] "Discussions," p. 587.

are facts of universal consciousness. But these sentiments are irrational and absurd if man is a mere machine impelled by natural causes, and has no self-determining power.[1] Whatever disasters may overtake us in the course of nature, however we may suffer by the wild tornado or the blighting mildew, how much soever of our property may be swallowed up by the ocean tempest or the devouring flame, we impute no blame; and we experience here emotions essentially different from those which we experience when a wrong is intentionally inflicted upon us by our fellow-men. "Suppose yourself to have been the victim of some act of injustice and villainy by which you were reduced to penury, and your family to want and indigence. By what philosophy can you eradicate the sense of wrong or cease to impute blame to the man whose perfidy has despoiled your life? You may forgive him, and follow him with your prayers to the last hour of your life, but you will still pray for him as a guilty man whose crime has been the burden of your life." Now what is this radical and fundamental difference between the events of the material universe and the actions of men? and what is the rational basis for the different feelings we experience and the diverse judgments we pass in regard to them?

There is only one answer to this question. The ultimate ground-difference is found in the fact that one class of events is *necessary*—there is no adequate power in the thing to be or do otherwise; the other class of actions is *free*—they need not have been performed, the actor had full power for a contrary choice. In the world of nature *force* reigns; in the world of moral life *liberty* prevails. The fundamental principle of difference is the *freedom of the will.*

[1] "The feeling of responsibility is unmeaning unless it presupposes the reality of freedom."—Murphy, "Scientific Basis of Faith," p. 85.

This second condition of moral government—namely, the possession of *free alternative power* on the part of the subject to comply, or refuse to comply, with the requirements of moral law—is thus established, first, by the direct testimony of consciousness, from which there can be no appeal, and, secondly, by necessary inference from collateral facts of consciousness, which can not be invalidated by counter-proofs.

Unhappily, the restlessness of speculative minds, the necessities of false theories in philosophy, or the unwarrantable assumptions of dogmatic theologians, have led to the disregard of the affirmations of universal consciousness. Men have asked, How can freedom be possible in a dependent creature? How can it be consistent with our belief in the principle of universal causation? How can it be harmonized with the fact that man always acts under the influence of motives? How can it be reconciled with the omnipotence and absolute prescience of God?

We shall now address ourselves to the consideration of the arguments against the doctrine of the freedom of the will which are suggested by these queries.

1. The first is the *Metaphysical or Causational Argument.* The rational intuition that "every event must have a cause" is a universal and necessary truth. It must therefore be rigorously applied to all mental as well as to all physical phenomena. Every volition must have a cause, and if caused it can not be *free.* This is the grand argument upon which the necessitarian mainly relies, and it is urged with eloquence and force by Edwards, Chalmers, and McCosh.

Now that "every event must have a cause" is an *à priori* truth, which is as readily accorded by the freedomist as it is vehemently insisted upon by the necessitarian. No philosophic writers have more ably and clearly enounced this law of causality than the freedomists Reid, Stewart, and Cousin. They rely upon it as one of the main pillars of the Theistic argument. And they apply it, in all its integrity, to mental as well as to physical phenomena. They hesitate not to say that "*every volition must have a cause.*" That cause is the efficient creative power which resides in a free, spiritual personality. And that power is not, like a material or physical cause, shut up to one sole mode of effectuation: it is an *alternative* power, a pluri-efficient cause. Where, then, is the discrepancy between the universal principle of causality and the doctrine of alternative causation? Is the infinite First Cause confined to one solely possible mode of effectuation? If so, how will you account for the endlessly varied effects which appear in the physical universe? God is the Eternal *One;* whence the plurality and diversity of his creative acts if He be not an equi-potent cause? And yet, of all the events which have transpired in the universe, whether natural or supernatural, we affirm "every event must have had a cause."[1] The endless diversity of effects which originate in the alternative causation of God is in perfect harmony with this universal law of causality.

But on a closer examination it will be found that when the necessitarian attempts to invalidate our consciousness of alternative power by the application of the causational argument he adroitly shifts his ground. He assumes another proposition, which is neither equivalent to the above axiom, nor in itself axiomatic and self-evident, nor justifiably

[1] "The miraculous interpositions recorded in the Scriptures are not inconsistent with this fundamental axiom, for they are effects of the will of God as the *cause.*"—McCosh, "Divine Government," p. 113.

assumed without proof. McCosh says "the doctrine of necessity is founded on the intellectual intuitions of man's mind, which lead us, in mental as in material phenomena, to anticipate the *same* effects to follow the *same* causes"[1] —that is, every cause is inalternative or unipotent; one effect, and only one can follow.

Now that a given phenomenon must have *a* cause is one assertion; that the *same* cause will again and forever produce the *same* effect is another. The first is an axiom, the second is an induction. That "every event must have a cause" is a rational intuition. That "like causes will produce always like effects" is a generalization from our limited experience, and on a further analysis will be found to apply only to our cognitions of the *material* universe. It is grounded simply on what we know empirically of the uniformity of nature. Now we have no *à priori* intuitive conviction of the uniformity of nature. As the result of maturer thought, McCosh admits this in his work on the "Intuitions of the Mind:" "It is vain to speak of the belief in the uniformity of nature as a self-evident, a necessary, or a universal truth" (page 276). It is perfectly conceivable that the world might have been so constituted that there should have been no regularity in the succession of events. The causes of all the events in nature might have been *supernatural*, and consisted in the immediate free volitions of the Deity, or subordinate angelic agencies.[2] They might have been all "miraculous," and yet the true law of causality would not have been violated, or in any way invalidated. And so when man, in the exercise of his free alternative power, produces a new suc-

[1] "Divine Government," p. 541.

[2] See McCosh's "Divine Government," p. 113, and Mill's "Logic," p. 114, vol. ii., English edition.

cession of events in physical nature, or moves disorder and *ανομιά* into the moral sphere, this is no way inconsistent with the axiom that "every event has a cause."

"In our very definition of freedom of will we assume in the volitional sphere the inapplicability of the maxim that 'like causes ever and always produce like effects.' We assume that *either* one of several effects is legitimate from the *same* cause. And while we admit that in non-volitional causation the law that 'every event must have a cause' means that every event must have its own peculiar cause, adequate for itself alone, in volitional causation an event may have a cause adequate either for it or for other event; and whichever event exists, the *demands of the laws of causation are completely satisfied*."[1]

Driven from this boasted stronghold, the necessitarian resorts to his favorite dialectic strategy. He demands the explanation of equipotent causation, how one cause can be adequate to several effects. He asks, *What causes the will to put forth one particular volition rather than another?*

Now when we have shown that, as a fact of consciousness and experience, a personal, *spiritual* cause is adequate to several results, we are entitled in reason and justice to protest against any attempt to push the inquiry a step farther. We have attained an ultimate fact, and we have no right to cast doubt upon its authority by raising perplexing questions as to the *how* or *why* of that which *is*. This is precisely the method by which the atheist Holyoake would invalidate the argument for the existence of the infinite First Cause. He subjects the Deity to this universal law of causality, and asks, What caused the Creator to create? "The atheist holds that the universe is an endless series of

[1] Whedon, "Freedom of the Will," p. 87.

causes and effects *ad infinitum*, and therefore the idea of a *first* cause is an absurdity and a contradiction." The "infinite series" of Edwards and of Holyoake are constructed on the same principle. They both ask *a* cause for *the* cause.

When, therefore, it is asked, What causes the will to effect one volition rather than another? our answer is, *Nothing whatever!*

"Of its own effect, WILL, in its proper conditions, is not a partial, but a full and adequate cause. Put your finger upon any effect (volition) and ask, What caused this result exclusively of the others? and the reply is, The will, or the agent in willing. Ask then what caused the will in its conditions to cause the volition, and the reply is, NOTHING. Nay, you are a bad philosopher in asking; for for its own effect will or the willing agent is a complete cause: as complete a cause as any cause whatever; *and every complete cause produces its effect* UNCAUSEDLY. The volition, like every other effect, is completely accounted for when a complete cause is assigned. To ask what caused the complete cause to produce the effect is to ask the cause of causation."[1]

But such an "alternative" power, the necessitarian affirms, is incomprehensible and inexplicable. To which we need only reply in the language of Hamilton, "The scheme of freedom is not more incomprehensible than the scheme of necessity."[2] "*Omnia exeunt in mysterium*"—there is nothing the absolute ground of which is not a mystery. In saying so much, however, we by no means grant the

[1] Whedon, "Freedom of the Will," p. 92. "Every intelligent effort is an exercise of *originating creative power* which makes the future different from what it would have been but for the exercise of this power."—Hazard, "On Causation," p. 87.

[2] "Philosophy," p. 511.

affirmation of Hamilton that "we are unable to conceive an absolute commencement [of being or motion]; we can not therefore conceive a free volition."[1] This is not admitted by Mansel, the disciple and annotator of Hamilton, as flowing even from his mental "law of the conditioned." "It may be true, as a fact, that no material atom has been added to the world since the first creation; but the assertion, however true, is certainly not *necessary*. The Power which created once must be conceived as able to create again, whether that ability is actually exercised or not. The same conclusion is still more evident when we proceed from the consideration of matter to that of mind. Of matter we maintain that the creation of new portions is perfectly conceivable, as a result, if not as a process. Every man who comes into the world comes into it as a distinct individual, having a personality and consciousness of his own; and that personality is a distinct accession to the number of persons previously existing. . . . I believe that every new person that comes into the world is, as a person, a new existence."[2] So a volition is a *new* existence, an absolute origination, "a beginning of motion" which has its source in the primordial power of the human spirit as spirit. The *fact* is undeniable, the *mode* is inexplicable. But the inconceivability of the mode in which the will creates a volition no more renders the fact doubtful than the impossibility of conceiving how a new and distinct self-conscious personality comes into existence invalidates the fact that "I exist, and know myself as a distinctly existing being."

2. *The Psychological Argument.*—This may be briefly stated in the following terms:

It is a fact of observation and experience that *motives* do

[1] "Philosophy," p. 508. [2] "Prolegomena Logica," App., note C.

stand to the will in the relation of *causes* which necessitate volition. They have an exact mathematical commensurability, and their prevalence is in the precise ratio of their antecedent intrinsic *strength.* If motives are wanting, there can be no choice; but when the same motives are presented to the same mind, it obeys them with such remarkable *uniformity* that human actions may be reduced to statistical tables as reliable and as accurate as tables of mortality.

We might here at once, and with justice, enter our caveat against the attempt to invalidate a primitive datum of consciousness by alleged deductions from the exterior phenomena of human life and history. A primitive datum of consciousness is unquestionable and infallible. A process of induction is liable to the interpolations of error. The latter is therefore a lesser authority than the former, and a merely derivative assurance can not be argued against an ultimate fact. We must regard it as a philosophic canon that an experience cognition can not conflict with an intuitive belief. The exterior phenomena of life and history, properly interpreted, must harmonize with the interior facts and laws of the human mind, for what is *history* but the development, under the conditions and relations of time, of the primitive powers, ideas, and laws of humanity? If, then, consciousness attests the presence in man's spiritual nature of a power, in the same circumstances, to choose either of several ways, we may confidently expect that the phenomena of the moral world will not belie that testimony. Now it is a palpable fact that an unbroken law of continuity and uniformity pervades the material universe. It is locked up in an unchangeable status. There is no deviation and no progression. All things remain as they were since the beginning. The fundamental fact lying at the basis of this undeviating uniformity of nature is that material causes are unipotent, and shut up to one solely possible mode of effectuation.[1] And it is equally palpable that the phenomena of the moral world, the sphere of human life and history, reveal contingency, diversity, alteriety, and progression. Humanity has not revolved in cycles, neither has it run in the inflexible grooves of an anterior causation, nor remained in the dead-lock of an unchangeable status. History is not an inflexible frame-work in which all events have been shaped by necessity; it is a development of the inherent powers and capabilities of humanity, and it teaches us that new trains of causes have been originated, and new conditions have been superinduced by man. The ground-fact which underlies all the diversity, contingency, and progress which appear in the moral world is that volitional causes are equipotent and efficient for any one of the several results.[2] In moral development the progressive principle is just the freedom of the will. The facts of the inner and outer world are therefore in harmony.

The theory of the necessitarian assumes that the will is a mere passivity, a simple conductor of the impulse which motive power exerts, a mere transition-point where ideal force is transformed into physical force, and desires, inclinations, moral convictions, divine influences become necessary acts. Motives thus prevail by their antecedent intrinsic power just as physical forces prevail in mechanical and vital dynamics. And, proceeding upon this assumption, he labors to construct a science of Ethology in which he would anticipate human action by statistics, and show how individual character *must* be in accordance with physical and mental causation. Whereas consciousness

[1] Whedon, "Freedom of the Will," p. 32. [2] Ibid., p. 56.

asserts that the will "is not a bleak mechanical thing." It is a free alternative power. It is a full, complete, adequate cause. It is *spirit*, not matter.

Now it is freely granted that the mind acts in view of motives, acts in accordance with motives, acts in a certain qualified sense under the influence of motives; *but the freedomist emphatically denies that the will is necessitated to action by motives.* Motives may be reason *for* action, conditions under which will acts, but they are not causes *of* action. They may solicit, invite, urge to action, but they can not constrain, compel, and force action.[1]

Motives have no fixed correlation to the will. They address themselves to the feelings, the judgment, the conscience, and not directly and immediately to the will. They may awaken desire, fear, inclination, preference, a sense of obligation; but these are all states of the intellect and sensibility, and may coexist in the same mind with a state of indetermination and non-differentiation in the will. That which is desirable may appeal to the feelings, that which is eligible to the judgment, that which is obligatory to the conscience, and these may excite the mind in different degrees of intensity; but none of them have power to move the will. We may be able intellectually to perceive that some motives are intrinsically "higher" than others, that some have a prevolition power to excite all minds more intensely than others; but they do not prevail and secure action in any ratio with their supposed *à priori* strength. They can only become real motives for the will by its voluntary placing its interest in them and making them objects of its choice.[2] All the actual strength which a motive has is derived from the action

[1] See Calderwood's "Hand-book of Moral Philosophy," pp. 196, 197.

[2] Müller's "Christian Doctrine of Sin," vol. ii. p. 56.

of the will. On this subject we offer the following propositions:

(1.) *The so-called strength of a motive is the degree of probability that the will will act in accordance with or on account of it.* "And it is most important to remark that the *result* is not always, nor in most cases, necessarily as the *highest probability.* The will may choose for the higher or for the lower. And as the will may choose for a lower rather than a higher probability, so the will may choose on account of what is called antecedently a *weaker* over a *stronger* motive. And hereby is once for all established the difference between mechanical force and motive influence—that whereas in the former, by necessity, the greater effect results from the greater force, in the latter the less is possible from the greater, the greater from the less."[1] That result is not as the highest probability Dr. Whedon has shown most conclusively from the doctrine of Contingencies or Probabilities. And on this he grounds his doctrine of *contingent motive probability.* "This contingent character of motive influence is correspondent with the alternative character of that which is its sole possible object—will. An alternative will and a contingent motive influence are correlatives. They mutually explain and sustain each other. To admit either is to admit both. And so a unipotent will and a necessary motive influence are correlatives. He who is compelled to admit one is compelled to admit the other. It will be a mere controversy about a word to say that an influence which does not produce effect is no influence. That may legitimately be called an influence, it is important to add, which is conceived as *possessing an intrinsic probability for result, though the higher probability be a contingency*

[1] Whedon, "Freedom of the Will," p. 130.

for which there exists power of *failure*. If so, then the doctrine of contingent motive influence is established, and the doctrine of volitional necessity is at an end. The relation between physical force and effect is *necessity*. The relation between motive and volition is *contingency*."[1]

(2.) *The so-called strength of a motive is the comparative prevalence which the will assigns to it by its own action.* It is impossible to erect any standard by which the intrinsic "strength" of motives can be determined previous to volition. "A cold intellection is not intrinsically commensurable with a deep emotion, nor a sentiment of taste with a feeling of obligation, nor a physical appetite with a sense of honor." Now by what standard can the comparative force of these influences be determined? There is no more commensurability between them than between "the brightness of day and the force of magnetic attractions." Or if we could possibly determine, by some rational *à priori* method, that a feeling of obligation is intrinsically stronger than a physical appetite, or that the love of life is stronger *per se* than a sense of duty, we can not affirm that the one or the other shall therefore uniformly and necessarily prevail. These influences derive all their prevalency, and consequently their comparative strength of motive, *from the will alone*. The will places its interest in the one or the other. It decides the mental position. "It settles the question of preferences between alternatives, dismisses the counter-motive from view, and closes the debate."[2]

The "strength" of a motive, in its relation to the will, can only be known by the test of *prevalency*. This is unwittingly conceded by the necessitarian. He says "the strongest motive prevails because that is the strongest

[1] Whedon, "Freedom of the Will," p. 135. [2] Ibid., p. 193.

which the will chooses." This really concedes the position assumed by Dr. Whedon, that "the strength of a motive is the comparative prevalence which the will, in its own action, assigns to it, or the nearness to which the will comes to acting on account of it." Men do not always choose that which is most *desirable*, nor that which is most *eligible*, nor that which appears most *obligatory*. But from whatever motive men may choose to act, however base and unworthy, the necessitarian affirms it was intrinsically the strongest motive *because* it was chosen; which simply amounts to this—the strongest motive is always chosen because the motive chosen is always the strongest motive.

The attempts of the necessitarian to fix upon some standard by which to estimate the antecedent strength of motives have all signally failed. The most plausible is that of Edwards. He asserts that the volition is always as the greatest *apparent* good. But by what standard is that good estimated, by which faculty is it recognized and pronounced *good?* by the reason, the conscience, the judgment, or the appetites? Can that be pronounced *good* which is chosen in obedience to passion and lust? Does the man who inflicts a premeditated injury upon his neighbor choose the greatest apparent good? Does the murderer believe that in taking away the life of his fellow-man "the volition is as the greatest apparent good?" Certainly not. "Never," says Bushnell, "was there a case of wrong, a sinful choice, in which the agent believed he was choosing for the strongest, weightiest, or most valuable motives." The great mass of sinful men are conscious of choosing sinful indulgence against their "highest good."

(3.) *Motives are the conditions, but not the causes of volition.* "Of volition the cause, the sole cause, is will. Motives are collateral conditions . . . for the volition to be; with which there is adequate power for the volition not to be. . . . The motive is only the *occasion*, and all its acts of excitement amount to no more than this, that they stand as *probable conditions* opening the way toward which the will thereby acquires opportunity to act with full adequate power of not acting."[1] The relation between motive and volition is not a necessary but a contingent relation. The will is the controlling conscious self in the exercise of direct causative power in producing volition.

Some modern writers of the necessitarian school, McCosh for example, admit the existence of "self-activity" in the will. But what can be the meaning of "self-activity" if the will have not the power of either resisting or yielding to motives presented, and in the same unchanged circumstances of choosing a different alternative? To be moved absolutely by motives is not *self*-movement. A power to move in only one given direction is a mere nature-force; it can not be self-activity. The distinguished writer above named also admits that "*causation in the will is entirely different from causation in other actions.*"[2] If he mean that motives act upon the will in a manner "entirely different" from that by which physical causes secure action or change in the material world, what right has he to call it *causation* at all? And if he mean that volitional causation is "alternative," and not, like physical causation, "unipotent," then the controversy is at an end.

(4.) *We have no such experience of "uniformities of volition" as shall enable us to generalize a universal law of volitional causation.* The facts of uniformity which present themselves in the continuous life of some men who were absorbed in one great life-purpose, as also in

[1] Whedon, "Freedom of the Will," p. 158. [2] "Intuition," etc., p. 472.

the conduct of aggregate masses of men, are not denied. We affirm that the correct definition of a free will supposes that it may choose in a generally uniform manner. Much of the uniformity in the life of an individual may be accounted for by corporeal nature—disposition, standard purpose, and habit. "Upon a basis of corporeal, psychological, and mental nature are overlaid a primary stratum of dispositions blending the natural and the volitional, and a secondary formation of generic purposes wholly volitional, and formed by repetition into a tertiary of habits; and thus we have, in his mingled constitution of necessitation and freedom, an agent prepared for daily free responsible action."[1]

Now it may be readily granted that character forms a basis of reliable *probability* as to how in given circumstances a man will act. We may be able to judge, with some degree of accuracy, how a man will work in his freedom; but we can never calculate with absolute certainty, because we have numberless examples of men acting strangely "out of character," and disappointing our most confident expectations.

"There is often the action, great or small, which reverses the record of a life or a protracted course of action. He who well watches his neighbor, however blind he may be to his own practical self-contradictions, is sure to find, even in the life most uniform in its great outline, plenty of minor inconsistencies. Or as Müller, in his 'Doctrine of Sin,' well says, that both our observation and our subject's temptation may occur just at the moment of one of his great volitional turning-points. From the apostasy of the first angels and the fall of man, through the whole course of human history, we have innumerable instances of revo-

[1] Whedon, "Freedom of the Will," p. 171.

lutionary volitions, not only *out of the previous character*, but shaping a *new* character. The one disastrous sin of Moses, the one great complicated crime of David, the apostasy of Solomon, the wisest of men, are all proofs how, not only in contrasted traits, but in revolutionary acts, a man may be

'The wisest, brightest, meanest of mankind.'"[1]

Statistics are cited by Buckle, in his "History of Civilization in England," showing that crimes, suicides, marriages, etc., occur with remarkable uniformity, as the result of general conditions of human society; and he thence infers that all the actions of men are governed by a uniform law of causation. This uniformity may, however, be as easily accounted for on the doctrine of freedom as on the doctrine of necessity. In the calculations of contingencies, while results of compared large aggregates in the same conditions may approach equality, the *contingency of each individual case remains still a contingency.* The actuary of an insurance company can assert with accuracy the average duration of human life in different countries; but were he to attempt to predict the duration of any one individual life he had insured, he would certainly fail. The insured may falsify his predictions by a voluntary act of suicide. So though large aggregations of free volitions, surrounded by the same motives, may approach equality, the *freedom of the individual will remains.*[2]

And as Mansel very justly remarks, "it is precisely because individual actions are not reducible to any fixed law, or capable of representation by any numerical calculation,

[1] Whedon, "Freedom of the Will," p. 173.

[2] "So long as there are fluctuations at all, even though they be of infinitesimal magnitude as compared with the total, statistical regularity does not exclude all room for freedom."—Murphy, "Scientific Basis of Faith," p. 84.

that the statistical averages acquire their value as substitutes. No one dreams of applying statistical averages to calculate the period of the earth's rotation by showing that four-and-twenty hours is the exact medium of time, comparing one month's or one year's revolution with another's. It is only when individual movements are irregular that it is necessary to aim at a proximate regularity by calculating in mass."[1]

3. *The Theological Argument.* —The main points of the theological argument may be thus presented: Freedom in a created being is incompatible with the absolute sovereignty and prescience of God. To suppose a being capable of acting either of several ways is to suppose a being out of the control of God. And a free agent can not possess power to do otherwise than God foreknows he will do.

In regard to the first of these supposed incompatibilities, we need only remark that if the Deity, in order to the existence of an equitable moral government, and the consequent possibility of free responsible action by the creature, shall please to subject his omnipotence to conditional limitations, the necessitarian has no business to object.[2] We need feel no solicitude about the Divine sovereignty. God will take care of his own honor and defend his own high and holy prerogatives. Such self-limiting laws prescribed by Divine wisdom and love do not place man beyond Divine control. The necessitarian will not deny that such self-limitation is essential to the very existence of the kingdom of nature. God has established an order

[1] "Prolegomena Logica," p. 280.

[2] On self-limitation of the Divine will, see Müller, "Christian Doctrine of Sin," vol. ii. pp. 208–212.

in nature, a uniformity of antecedence and sequence, with which Omnipotence shall not interfere. "Such a Divine law of non-usance of power is still more necessary in the kingdom of living agents, and most of all in the realm of responsible agents; it being observable that the more close the Divine self-restraint, and the larger the amount of powers in the agent left untouched, the more the creative system rises in dignity, and the higher God appears as a sovereign. Even in the system of living *necessitated* agents, as necessitarians must admit, God forbids Himself to disturb the agent's uniform and perpetual acting according to strongest motive."

The second of these incompatibilities is really predicated upon our ignorance, and not upon our knowledge. We can not understand *how* the Divine Intelligence foreknows all future events. To enable us to understand the exact manner in which an Infinite Intelligence contemplates succession in time, it would be necessary that we should be infinite also. The *fact* that God foreknows all future events is all that is revealed to us; the *manner* of it He has left in darkness, and we can throw no light upon it by our verbal speculations.

Of one thing we may rest assured, that as perception precedes volition in the finite intelligence, so knowledge must precede determination in the Divine Mind. God can not will or act in absolute darkness. Divine predestination must be conditioned on Divine foreknowledge.[1] His foreknowledge does not depend upon his will, or on the adjustment of motives to make us will thus and thus; but He foreknows every thing first conditionally, in the world of possibility, before He creates, or determines any thing to

[1] This is unquestionably the doctrine of Scripture, "Whom He *foreknew*, them also He did predestinate."

be, in the world of fact. Otherwise, all his purposes would be grounded in ignorance, not in wisdom, and his knowledge would consist in following after his will, to learn what it had blindly determined.[1]

Another important principle clearly and vigorously maintained by Dr. Whedon is "that the freeness of an act is not affected by the consideration of its being foreknown." First, because the Divine knowledge must always correspond to the reality. A free action must be known as *free*. "If there be in the free agent, ascertainable by psychology, or required by intuition, or supposably seen by the Divine eye, the power of putting forth the volition with full power of alteriety, then God knows that power."[2] Secondly, the occurrence of an event or act may be *certain* to Divine foreknowledge, and yet perfectly *contingent* in itself. Foreknowledge renders nothing *necessary; it is the consequence, not the cause of events.*

If there be a necessity at all in the case, "the necessity lies not upon the free act, but upon the foreknowledge. The foreknowledge must see to its own accuracy. Pure knowledge, temporal or eternal, must conform itself to the fact, not the fact to the knowledge."[3] The real difficulty is, not how an act can be a free act and yet be foreknown (for the act of knowledge can not change the object of knowledge), but how God can possibly know with certainty a future contingency which may or may not happen.

It is a clear and immediate revelation of consciousness that man has a free power of self-determination. No revelation can contradict this revelation. This fact of con-

[1] Bushnell, "Nature and the Supernatural," p. 50.

[2] Whedon, "Freedom of the Will," p. 273; Müller, "Christian Doctrine of Sin," vol. ii. pp. 236–247.

[3] Whedon, "Freedom of the Will," p. 283.

sciousness can not be invalidated by any conceptions of the logical understanding in regard to the omnipotence or prescience of God, for these by their very nature transcend all human comprehension.

III. *The method of moral government.*—We have seen that government, in general, is control exercised with a view to the maintenance of order. In the material world, order is secured by the direct compulsion of omnipotent force. The things of nature are inertly passive under the hand of God. They can offer no resistance to the Divine control, and consequently, in the sphere of nature, there can be no real disorder. But in the realm of self-determining powers there is the possibility of collision, because there is the power to resist the will of God. And, as a matter of fact, we know there is opposition, lawlessness, and sin. In that sphere, where above all others the demand of the reason is for order, there is the presence of *disorder*—that is, there is disconformity to law and consequent suffering.

And now the question arises, By what *method* is order to be maintained in the sphere of freedom? How are beings that have the power to determine for themselves what they will choose and do, to be brought to act in harmony with the eternal laws of righteousness and love?

There are inconsiderate souls who dream that this may be achieved by force. God, say they, is omnipotent; if He will the non-extension of evil, He is able to destroy it; if He desire the maintenance of moral order, He can compel it. Such reckless declaimers know not what they say.

Had it so pleased God, He could have made beings in human form without any sense of moral right and wrong, and without any power to commit sin; but they would not have been *rational* beings, would not have been *free* beings, would not have been *moral* beings; neither could they, in any high and proper sense, be *happy* beings, because they could experience no sense of rectitude, no approval of conscience, no delight in moral excellence, no blessedness in duty and sacrifice. God, indeed, has made many such creatures that can not sin. The bee, the ant, the swine, the ape—these can not sin; but they are mere things, not free powers; they have no sense of dignity and moral worth, no approving conscience, no joy of sacrifice, and no immortal hopes. Lived there ever a sane man who would change his lot with one of these, even though in being a man he has the fearful power to sin, and in sinning, the fearful susceptibility to suffer—yea, to suffer eternally? Is there any thing on earth whose value does not fade away when compared with the priceless value of being capable of duty, of virtue, of devotion, and of sacrifice? In the eyes of God, the humblest of moral beings is worth more than all the firmament of stars, and all the teeming myriads of brutal forms of sense that dwell upon the earth. Because God preferred to rule over free powers, and not mere things—free powers that could be governed by truth and reason and love; because He loves moral character, and cares for it more than all the things "that can be piled in the infinitude of space, even though they were diamonds," therefore He bestowed on man this high capacity of character—the capacity to know, to choose, to love, to enjoy, and in a conscious communion with God to be blessed forever.

But when God thus determines to create a rational and free being—to make "man in his own image"—He determines to make a being who in acting freely may act in opposition to the mind of God, and in violation of his holy law. In creating a free self-determined being who shall be the cause of his own action, God puts his own omnipotence under conditional limitations, and renders it morally impossible for Him, by mere force, to constrain the will of man. The notion of a free will, which is an efficient cause, being governed by force, is a contradiction. Omnipotence may, if it please, annihilate man, but it can not control man in the sphere of his freedom. "Powers governed by the absolute force or fiat of omnipotence would in that fact be uncreate and cease."[1]

The moral government of God must deal with man *as man*, must treat him as intelligent and free, and must govern him solely by moral influences. He must be controlled by the voice of reason and the sense of duty, by persuasion and sympathy, by hope and fear; in short, by motives addressed to the judgment, the conscience, and the heart. A self-determined being can be brought into harmony with the Divine order only by "the schooling of his consent." He can be perfected—that is, fully established in harmony with the character and will of God—by the discipline of the will. He must, therefore, be placed in such circumstances as invite consent, and at the same time permit resistance. He is to be trained, furnished, and perfected, and to this end he must be carried through just such experiences, changes, and trials as will best help the formation of a noble human character, and will best prepare man for the plenitude and blessedness of that life for which the present is a course of education and discipline.[2]

Furthermore, God's moral government of the world must deal with the *actual man*—that is, with man as he exists in society with certain hereditary taints that are not his fault, and under certain unfavorable conditions in

[1] Bushnell, "Nature and the Supernatural," p. 83. [2] Ibid., p. 99.

which he has been placed without his consent. With reverence, we affirm that God Himself is under moral obligation to treat man equitably, to take account of the weakness which he inherits, the perverted education that has been given him, and the depraved associations that surround him, and graduate his responsibility on the scale of his available light. Finally, the moral government of God must deal with *the man that will be*—with that fixed character which may be formed by man in the exercise of his free power of self-determination, amid the circumstances of his earthly probation. This character must contain within itself the elements of a blessed or a wretched futurition, and thus a retribution be secured by fixed nature, and inflicted by an inflexible necessity.

That the moral government of God is a probationary economy, in which ample scope is afforded for the development of character, and in which we are in the act of being *proved*, is evident,

(1.) From the fact *that all our future interests are dependent upon our present conduct.* God has endowed us with some degree of foresight, and has thus made us provident beings. We have a native tendency to take account of and forecast the future. By the aid of reason we can, in some measure, foresee the tendencies of our actions; we can lay our plans for the future, and anticipate events which are yet remote. We can also bring to our aid the lessons of experience, and from this also we can learn that our present action will have a powerful influence upon our future condition. We know that the circumstances which surround us to-day have been in a large degree created or moulded by ourselves, and that many of our misadventures and our miseries may be easily traced back to particular acts of imprudence and folly on our own part as the cause. So that there is no truth we more certainly know than this, that our future happiness of the next moment, and of every succeeding stage of our living, is dependent upon our present conduct.

(2.) This is further evident from the fact *that the present scene is filled with moral tests and temptations.* There is in the present life an admixture of *good* and *evil.* On the one hand there are numerous solicitations to evil; on the other there are motives and inducements to virtue, the plain intention of which is to prove us. In the words of Bishop Butler, "We have here free scope and opportunity for that good or evil conduct which God will reward or punish hereafter." This is necessary to moral government, because moral government can not exist without freedom of choice, and consequently the existence of those circumstances in which that freedom can be exercised. That we have freedom of choice we know; and our every-day experience of the temptations to wrong-doing, and of the difficulties in the way of a uniform adherence to virtue, teaches us that we are in a state of trial, where our principles are being continually put to the test.

(3.) That our present life is a probation for a future life is evident from the fact *that in the present life punishment is deferred, consequences are delayed, to give play to the exercise of moral motives.*

By "moral motives" we mean regard for what is right and just, *because it is right and just,* respect for the voice of conscience, and reverence for the will and requirements of God. If the consequences of our moral conduct were to follow immediately on the heels of the act, if reward or punishment were instantly to ensue, then moral motives could have no exercise. If there were no delay—no interval between sin and its punishment, moral government would cease, and a merely natural government would remain, such as prevails over irrational creatures. Man would then be influenced purely by motives of personal interest or safety or enjoyment, and his obedience would not be the result of moral motives, consequently neither virtuous nor vicious. God has, therefore, put the consequences of much of our conduct into the future, that we may have room for free deliberate choice, while just so much of consequence is permitted to appear as will clearly indicate that we are under moral government, and awaken the anticipation that *all* our conduct will be brought into judgment.

(4.) That our present life is a probation for a future life is more fully proved by the fact *that as a moral economy the present life is incomplete.* The present is a sphere too contracted for the equitable administration of rewards and punishments, because some of the *last* actions of men's lives, some of their *best* actions or some of their *basest* actions, would come under neither. The blood of the martyrs who died for the faith, or of the patriot who bled for his country, would cry alike in vain for vengeance or reward. The man who first took away his brother's life, and then his own, has evaded justice, and escaped punishment. The hand of violence has robbed the virtuous man of his present reward; and the suicide, by breaking in upon the sanctuary of his own life, has defied and defeated the government of God, if there be no future life.

In the present life retribution fails in uniformity. It is a proposition which the reason of every man must approve —that the government of God must be perfectly equitable, and that under it every man must receive his just due. But men do not receive their requital in this life, consequently we are bound to affirm that in the present life the

Divine administration is *incomplete.* We can not conceal from ourselves the fact that events occur in the present life which we can not conceive as benevolently or righteously consummated. These events lift the tyrant to power, and trample down the patriot and the freeman. The orphan eats the bitter bread of misery, while the man who has robbed him of the paternal inheritance revels in luxury. The ungodly prosper in the world, "their eyes stand out with fatness, they have more than heart could wish," while the righteous suffer affliction, and are in need. And if there is no future life in which God will balance accounts with the universe, and render to every man according to his works, then moral government is incomplete, injustice has triumphed, wrong has prevailed. An imperfect retribution and an unequal providence demand a future life for their vindication—a future life both for the good and the bad, so that God may reckon with all of them—and teach most convincingly that the present life is a probation. The experiences, changes, conflicts, trials of a probationary economy, are all intended to prove men, to test their principles and make manifest their real character.

The government of God is a *moral discipline* by which men are trained in the practice and confirmed in the habits of virtue, and thus brought, by the "schooling of their own consent," into harmony with the Divine order.

It is a question which may be properly entertained, whether a free self-determined being can be made perfect in moral character in any other manner than by the discipline of the will. There certainly can be no created moral desert. Responsible character must be the product of free choice. A man can no more become virtuous without the discipline of the will than he can become intelligent without the discipline of the understanding. For wherein consists the virtue of a self-determined being? Is it not in his free choice of what is right and good, his resistance to temptation, his voluntary submission to the Divine will? Is it not in his integrity, his patience, his fortitude, and his resignation? But how can these virtues exist, how can they be exercised, and how brought to maturity, except in the midst of difficulties and hinderances? Where can patience and resignation and fortitude and sympathy have a place, if there are no sufferings to be endured? How can firmness and diligence and courage be developed, if there are no difficulties and hinderances to the practice of virtue?

Therefore, in order that men may be trained and educated and perfected, they are placed amid such scenes, experiences, and trials as shall draw out the moral powers of the soul, shall strengthen and confirm the will in goodness, and establish them in the law of their being, so that their moral future is secure. "Life, thus ordered, is a magnificent scheme to bring out the value of law, and teach the necessity of right as the only conserving principle of order and happiness; teaching the more powerfully, if so it must, by disorder and sorrow." Suffering is a chastisement which is wholesome: it teaches the blessedness of purity and the sinfulness of sin; and it may develop into "a godly sorrow" which shall heal and purify the soul.

The moral government of God is an equitable administration, in which responsibility is graduated on the scale of available light and opportunity. "This is the condemnation that *light* is come into the world." Light is the symbol of knowledge, because it *reveals* the right and clearly manifests what duty is. Light is consequently the exact measure of responsibility. Our knowledge of what we ought to do, or ought not to do, determines the degree of our accountability. An absolute and involuntary ignorance would be the most perfect plea of innocence. The imputation of sin in such a case would be made void, but thereby the completeness of human nature be destroyed. That which would relegate man from the sphere of responsibility would also banish him from the sphere of rationality.

St. Paul distinctly recognizes an alleviation of responsibility and guilt in the "ignorance" of heathen life, and speaks of a Divine " overlooking of the times of that ignorance"—a non-imputation of sins committed in ignorance. But he does not by any means account the sinning heathen as free from *all* guilt. He shows that they were not in utter ignorance, and that much of their ignorance was voluntary. He refers to the original consciousness of God, and to the fact that this consciousness is kept alive by the revelation of God in nature; and he shows that the disorder of their religious and moral life resulted from the voluntary suppression of this consciousness—" When they knew God, they glorified Him not as God, neither were thankful; but became vain in their imaginations, and their foolish heart was darkened." He also appeals to the no less definite power of conscience in the heart of the heathen, "which shows the works required by the law to be written on their hearts, their consciences also bearing witness to this law, and their thoughts approving or condemning each other," and their civil laws "adjudging their crimes as worthy of death." So far as their ignorance was involuntary it was an alleviation of guilt, though not an excuse for all sin. Whatever light they had, be it little or much, it was the standard and measure of their accountability.

The Founder of Christianity distinctly recognized this

principle of moral government. "If I had not come and spoken unto them, *they had not had sin*, but now they have no cloak for their sin"—clearly teaching that ignorance would be a negation of guilt, and knowledge an aggravation of guilt. Not that we are to suppose that the Jews, without the light which Christ supplied, were absolutely guiltless; their ignorance was a mitigation of their guilt. Christ lays it down as a universal principle that knowledge of the Divine law or ignorance of the Divine law by the person who violates it is the ground of a distinction in the different degrees of culpability. "That servant which *knew* his lord's will, and prepared not himself, neither did according to his will, shall be beaten with *many* stripes. But he that *knew not*, and did commit things worthy of stripes, shall be beaten with *few* stripes."[1] This is the uniform rule of the Divine government among all nations.

Increase of light and knowledge necessarily enhances human responsibility. "To whomsoever much is given, of him shall be much required." More is expected of the man than of the child. More is demanded at the hands of the man who has been blessed with the advantages of a Christian civilization than from the untutored savage. The man who has been favored with a liberal education is held to a more rigid account than the man who has been cradled in ignorance and schooled in vice. And when the kingdom of God comes nigh to men, human responsibility must be enlarged in commensuration with its blessings. There is a holier, richer trust, and consequently a deeper obligation. There is a greater light and a greater condemnation.

"Woe unto thee, Chorazin! woe unto thee, Bethsaida!

[1] Luke xii. 47, 48.

for if the mighty works which were done in you had been done in Tyre and Sidon, they would have repented long ago in sackcloth and ashes. But I say unto you, It shall be more tolerable for Tyre and Sidon at the day of judgment than for you. And thou, Capernaum, which art exalted unto heaven, shalt be brought down to hell: for if the mighty works which have been done in thee had been done in Sodom, it would have remained until this day. But I say unto you, That it shall be more tolerable for the land of Sodom in the day of judgment than for thee."[1]

This aspect of the Divine government, which Dr. Whedon has felicitously styled "the equation of probational advantages," relieves our sadness in view of the moral condition of the world. "The Judge of all the earth will do right" in the case of every human soul that has passed through this probationary scene. His omniscient eye can take in at one view all the influences and circumstances, favorable or unfavorable, which have surrounded each individual, and fix the precise amount of responsibility. He will "overlook" the "defect of doubt and taints of blood," the faults of education and sins of ignorance, and He will make a due allowance for the power of temptation, the trammels of evil associations, and an enfeebled and perverted nature. "He is full of compassion, and his tender mercies are over all his works." "He knows our frame, and He remembers that we are dust." We may safely conjecture that a negro hamlet in Central Africa, however inferior in its temporal moral aspects, may, in its prospect for an eternal destiny, be superior to many an American village. And in the dregs of our large cities there are numbers who are excluded as effectually from the knowledge of the truth as the heathen, and are scarcely developed to the level of

[1] Matt. xi. 21–24.

responsibility. These may be the least in the kingdom of heaven, but by the law of moral equation they can not be excluded.[1] In every nation under heaven, he that has feared God and wrought righteousness, according to his knowledge and ability, will be "*accepted of God.*"

The moral government of God secures an infallible and equitable retribution by binding *character* and *consequence* in indissoluble bonds, and evolving a reward or a punishment out of that permanent moral state of the soul which has been induced by the free self-determination of man.

"Character," says Novalis, "is a completely fashioned will (*vollkommen gebildeter Wille*). It is that ultimate stress and determination of the soul which results from the coherence and complexure of habits, and habit is the result of repeated acts of voluntary choice. From the persistence of habit a fixed disposition and cast of the inner man is evolved which constitutes his *moral individuality.*"

Even in this formative process we can discern the workings of the law of retribution. One good deed handsels a second, and renders its performance more easy and pleasurable. The man who obeys his conscience feels that he can respect himself. He has a consciousness of growing power; a sense of dignity and moral worth. The moral law is for him "a law of liberty." On the other hand, one sinful deed involves a second, and drags it after it. One lie demands another to maintain its consistency. One act of injustice emboldens to the next. Self-respect is broken down by license, and the path is prepared and cleared for further iniquity. Thus, by the repetition of sinful deeds, restraints are overborne, depraved habits are engendered, vice acquires a mastery over the man, and he becomes a

[1] Whedon, "Freedom of the Will," pp. 355–357.

slave. There is a deep humiliation in this sense of degradation and unworthiness. The sinner despises himself because of his weakness, and blushes in secret places at the remembrance of his own debasement.

The principal happiness or misery of man consists in the settled state of his own heart, and not in the outward conditions of his daily life. All human plaudits are as naught compared with the approval of one's own conscience; and no penal inflictions can compare with the anguish of remorse. The inward peace of the righteous soul, the disquietude and misery of the sinful soul, are the blossom and the fruitage of the seed which has been sown, and the stem and branches which have been nurtured by the voluntary choices and acts of man. "He that soweth to his flesh shall of the flesh reap corruption; but he that soweth to the spirit shall of the spirit reap life everlasting." The connection between sin and punishment is no arbitrary or accidental connection. It is just as much a relation between cause and effect as the relation between sowing and reaping in the physical world. "To cause the mind to punish itself, to work a retribution out of ourselves, to secure it by fixed nature, to inflict it by inflexible necessity, to convert the capacity of sin into the instrument of suffering, is the prerogative of Divine rule."[1]

IV. *The end of moral government.*—We have said that the end of government, in general, is the maintenance of order. The end of moral government is the maintenance of *moral order* in the realm of free self-determined powers. The moral order must consist in conformity to the idea of the *absolute good.* The personality of God (the essential momenta of which are reason and freedom, holiness and love) is *per se*, in its totality, the absolute good.

[1] Hamilton, "Revealed Doctrine of Rewards and Punishments," p. 88.

Infinite Personality is but another name for Absolute Perfection.

The highest good for a created dependent personality is "to resemble God" in all those attributes or perfections which constitute personality. It is to be fully established in harmony with God's moral character, unified with Him in will, glorified with Him in holiness, and perfected with Him in the blessedness of love. The highest perfection of personal being is moral order, and therefore human personality, conceived in its purity and perfection, is the end of the Divine government.[1]

This we have called "the ideal order of moral life," because it is not yet realized in the world. We must believe, however, that the final triumph of goodness is a part of the great world-plan. We must not only believe, but know, that the great design of creation, the reason for which the world exists at all, is that in it goodness may come to its final realization. And this conviction is grounded on the fact that the moral life of humanity has its source in the same Being who called the world into existence, and who is conducting this present dispensation to a glorious consummation, in which He shall "reconcile all things unto Himself, . . . whether they be things in earth or things in heaven," and "gather together in one all things in Christ," that "God may be all in all."

Christianity bases all the obligations and sanctions of morality on the great truths that God is near to man, that He sustains him every moment in life, that He is the Father of the human spirit, and that He governs man in order to perfect his nature and bring him into an everlasting fel-

[1] "The formation of noble human characters is the highest work that man, or, so far as we know, that God can be engaged in."—Murphy, "Scientific Basis of Faith," p. 39.

lowship with Himself. Christianity knows nothing of "a science of morals" which is not based upon the correlations between man and God, nor of a morality which forgets God and disregards the most sacred and fundamental of all duties, namely, the duties we owe to God. A morality based solely upon the relations in which we stand to our fellow-men is at best but secular and utilitarian. A morality which is grounded upon the relation of volition to the state of the sensibility, and regards "happiness as our being's end and aim," is egoistic and selfish. A morality which rests upon our relation to God, the absolute good, and which looks backward rather than forward for its motive, is unselfish and Christian.

INDEX.

THE END.

VALUABLE AND INTERESTING WORKS

FOR

PUBLIC & PRIVATE LIBRARIES,

PUBLISHED BY HARPER & BROTHERS, NEW YORK.

MACAULAY'S ENGLAND. The History of England from the Accession of James II. By THOMAS BABINGTON MACAULAY. New Edition, from new Electrotype Plates. 8vo, Cloth, with Paper Labels, Uncut Edges and Gilt Tops, 5 vols. in a Box, $10 00 per set. Sold only in Sets. Cheap Edition, 5 vols. in a Box, 12mo, Cloth, $2 50; Sheep, $3 75.

MACAULAY'S LIFE AND LETTERS. The Life and Letters of Lord Macaulay. By his Nephew, G. OTTO TREVELYAN, M.P. With Portrait on Steel. Complete in 2 vols., 8vo, Cloth, Uncut Edges and Gilt Tops, $5 00; Sheep, $6 00; Half Calf, $9 50. Popular Edition, two vols. in one, 12mo, Cloth, $1 75.

HUME'S ENGLAND. The History of England, from the Invasion of Julius Cæsar to the Abdication of James II., 1688. By DAVID HUME. New and Elegant Library Edition, from new Electrotype Plates. 6 vols. in a Box, 8vo, Cloth, with Paper Labels, Uncut Edges and Gilt Tops, $12 00. Sold only in Sets. Popular Edition, 6 vols. in a Box, 12mo, Cloth, $3 00; Sheep, $4 50.

GIBBON'S ROME. The History of the Decline and Fall of the Roman Empire. By EDWARD GIBBON. With Notes by Dean MILMAN, M. GUIZOT, and Dr. WILLIAM SMITH. New Edition, from new Electrotype Plates. 6 vols., 8vo, Cloth, with Paper Labels, Uncut Edges and Gilt Tops, $12 00. Sold only in Sets. Popular Edition, 6 vols. in a Box, 12mo, Cloth, $3 00; Sheep, $4 50.

HILDRETH'S UNITED STATES. History of the United States. FIRST SERIES: From the Discovery of the Continent to the Organization of the Government under the Federal Constitution. SECOND SERIES: From the Adoption of the Federal Constitution to the End of the Sixteenth Congress. By RICHARD HILDRETH. Popular Edition, 6 vols. in a Box, 8vo, Cloth, with Paper Labels, Uncut Edges and Gilt Tops, $12 00. Sold only in Sets.

MOTLEY'S DUTCH REPUBLIC. The Rise of the Dutch Republic. A History. By JOHN LOTHROP MOTLEY, LL.D., D.C.L. With a Portrait of William of Orange. Cheap Edition, 3 vols. in a Box, 8vo, Cloth, with Paper Labels, Uncut Edges and Gilt Tops, $6 00. Sold only in Sets. Original Library Edition, 3 vols., 8vo, Cloth, $10 50; Sheep, $12 00; Half Calf, $17 25.

MOTLEY'S UNITED NETHERLANDS. History of the United Netherlands: from the Death of William the Silent to the Twelve Years' Truce—1584-1609. With a full View of the English-Dutch Struggle against Spain and of the Origin and Destruction of the Spanish Armada. By JOHN LOTHROP MOTLEY, LL.D., D.C.L. Portraits. Cheap Edition, 4 vols. in a Box, 8vo, Cloth, with Paper Labels, Uncut Edges and Gilt Tops, $8 00. Sold only in Sets. Original Library Edition, 4 vols., 8vo, Cloth, $14 00; Sheep, $16 00; Half Calf, $23 00.

MOTLEY'S LIFE AND DEATH OF JOHN OF BARNEVELD. The Life and Death of John of Barneveld, Advocate of Holland: with a View of the Primary Causes and Movements of "The Thirty Years' War." By JOHN LOTHROP MOTLEY, LL.D., D.C.L. Illustrated. Cheap Edition, 2 vols. in a Box, 8vo, Cloth, with Paper Labels, Uncut Edges and Gilt Tops, $4 00. Sold only in Sets. Original Library Edition, 2 vols., 8vo, Cloth, $7 00; Sheep, $8 00; Half Calf, $11 50.

GEDDES'S HISTORY OF JOHN DE WITT. History of the Administration of John De Witt, Grand Pensionary of Holland. By JAMES GEDDES. Vol. I.—1623-1654. With a Portrait. 8vo, Cloth, $2 50.

SKETCHES AND STUDIES IN SOUTHERN EUROPE. By JOHN ADDINGTON SYMONDS. In Two Volumes. Post 8vo, Cloth, $4 00.

SYMONDS'S GREEK POETS. Studies of the Greek Poets. By JOHN ADDINGTON SYMONDS. 2 vols., Square 16mo, Cloth, $3 50.

BENJAMIN'S CONTEMPORARY ART. Contemporary Art in Europe. By S. G. W. BENJAMIN. Illustrated. 8vo, Cloth, $3 50.

BENJAMIN'S ART IN AMERICA. Art in America. By S. G. W. BENJAMIN. Illustrated. 8vo, Cloth, $4 00.

HUDSON'S HISTORY OF JOURNALISM. Journalism in the United States, from 1690 to 1872. By FREDERIC HUDSON. 8vo, Cloth, $5 00; Half Calf, $7 25.

KINGLAKE'S CRIMEAN WAR. The Invasion of the Crimea: its Origin, and an Account of its Progress down to the Death of Lord Raglan. By ALEXANDER WILLIAM KINGLAKE. With Maps and Plans. Three Volumes now ready. 12mo, Cloth, $2 00 per vol.

JEFFERSON'S LIFE. The Domestic Life of Thomas Jefferson: Compiled from Family Letters and Reminiscences, by his Great-granddaughter, SARAH N. RANDOLPH. Illustrated. Crown 8vo, Cloth, $2 50.

LAMB'S COMPLETE WORKS. The Works of Charles Lamb. Comprising his Letters, Poems, Essays of Elia, Essays upon Shakspeare, Hogarth, etc., and a Sketch of his Life, with the Final Memorials, by T. NOON TALFOURD. With Portrait. 2 vols., 12mo, Cloth, $3 00.

LAWRENCE'S HISTORICAL STUDIES. Historical Studies. By EUGENE LAWRENCE. Containing the following Essays: The Bishops of Rome.—Leo and Luther.—Loyola and the Jesuits.—Ecumenical Councils.—The Vaudois.—The Huguenots.—The Church of Jerusalem.—Dominic and the Inquisition.—The Conquest of Ireland.—The Greek Church. 8vo, Cloth, Uncut Edges and Gilt Tops, $3 00.

LOSSING'S FIELD-BOOK OF THE REVOLUTION. Pictorial Field-Book of the Revolution: or, Illustrations by Pen and Pencil of the History, Biography, Scenery, Relics, and Traditions of the War for Independence. By BENSON J. LOSSING. 2 vols., 8vo, Cloth, $14 00; Sheep or Roan, $15 00; Half Calf, $18 00.

LOSSING'S FIELD-BOOK OF THE WAR OF 1812. Pictorial Field-Book of the War of 1812; or, Illustrations by Pen and Pencil of the History, Biography, Scenery, Relics, and Traditions of the last War for American Independence. By BENSON J. LOSSING. With several hundred Engravings on Wood by Lossing and Barritt, chiefly from Original Sketches by the Author. 1088 pages, 8vo, Cloth, $7 00; Sheep, $8 50; Roan, $9 00; Half Calf, $10 00.

FORSTER'S LIFE OF DEAN SWIFT. The Early Life of Jonathan Swift (1667–1711). By JOHN FORSTER. With Portrait. 8vo, Cloth, Uncut Edges and Gilt Tops, $2 50.

GREEN'S ENGLISH PEOPLE. History of the English People. By JOHN RICHARD GREEN, M.A. 3 volumes ready. 8vo, Cloth, $2 50 per volume.

SHORT'S NORTH AMERICANS OF ANTIQUITY. The North Americans of Antiquity. Their Origin, Migrations, and Type of Civilization Considered. By JOHN T. SHORT. Illustrated. 8vo, Cloth, $3 00.

SQUIER'S PERU. Peru: Incidents of Travel and Exploration in the Land of the Incas. By E. GEORGE SQUIER, M.A., F.S.A., late U.S. Commissioner to Peru. With Illustrations. 8vo, Cloth, $5 00.

MYERS'S LOST EMPIRES. Remains of Lost Empires: Sketches of the Ruins of Palmyra, Nineveh, Babylon, and Persepolis. By P. V. N. MYERS. Illustrated. 8vo, Cloth, $3 50.

MAURY'S PHYSICAL GEOGRAPHY OF THE SEA. The Physical Geography of the Sea, and its Meteorology. By M. F. MAURY, LL.D. 8vo, Cloth, $4 00.

SCHWEINFURTH'S HEART OF AFRICA. The Heart of Africa. Three Years' Travels and Adventures in the Unexplored Regions of the Centre of Africa—from 1868 to 1871. By Dr. GEORG SCHWEINFURTH. Translated by ELLEN E. FREWER. With an Introduction by WINWOOD READE. Illustrated by about 130 Wood-cuts from Drawings made by the Author, and with two Maps. 2 vols., 8vo, Cloth, $8 00.

M'CLINTOCK & STRONG'S CYCLOPÆDIA. Cyclopædia of Biblical, Theological, and Ecclesiastical Literature. Prepared by the Rev. JOHN M'CLINTOCK, D.D., and JAMES STRONG, S.T.D. 9 *vols. now ready.* Royal 8vo. Price per vol., Cloth, $5 00; Sheep, $6 00; Half Morocco, $8 00. (*Sold by Subscription.*)

MOHAMMED AND MOHAMMEDANISM: Lectures Delivered at the Royal Institution of Great Britain in February and March, 1874. By R. BOSWORTH SMITH, M.A., Assistant Master in Harrow School; late Fellow of Trinity College, Oxford. With an Appendix containing Emanuel Deutsch's Article on "Islam." 12mo, Cloth, $1 50.

MOSHEIM'S CHURCH HISTORY. Ecclesiastical History, Ancient and Modern; in which the Rise, Progress, and Variation of Church Power are considered in their connection with the State of Learning and Philosophy, and the Political History of Europe during that Period. Translated, with Notes, etc., by A. MACLAINE, D.D. Continued to 1826 by C. COOTE, LL.D. 2 vols., 8vo, Cloth, $4 00; Sheep, $5 00.

HARPER'S NEW CLASSICAL LIBRARY. Literal Translations.
The following volumes are now ready. 12mo, Cloth, $1 50 each.

CÆSAR.—VIRGIL.—SALLUST.—HORACE.—CICERO'S ORATIONS.—CICERO'S OFFICES, etc.—CICERO ON ORATORY AND ORATORS.—TACITUS (2 vols.).—TERENCE.—SOPHOCLES.—JUVENAL.—XENOPHON.—HOMER'S ILIAD.—HOMER'S ODYSSEY.—HERODOTUS.—DEMOSTHENES (2 vols.).—THUCYDIDES.—ÆSCHYLUS.—EURIPIDES (2 vols.).—LIVY (2 vols.).—PLATO [Select Dialogues].

VINCENT'S LAND OF THE WHITE ELEPHANT. The Land of the White Elephant: Sights and Scenes in Southeastern Asia. A Personal Narrative of Travel and Adventure in Farther India, embracing the Countries of Burma, Siam, Cambodia, and Cochin-China (1871–2). By FRANK VINCENT, Jr. Illustrated with Maps, Plans, and Wood-cuts. Crown 8vo, Cloth, $3 50.

LIVINGSTONE'S SOUTH AFRICA. Missionary Travels and Researches in South Africa: including a Sketch of Sixteen Years' Residence in the Interior of Africa, and a Journey from the Cape of Good Hope to Loanda on the West Coast; thence across the Continent, down the River Zambesi, to the Eastern Ocean. By DAVID LIVINGSTONE, LL.D., D.C.L. With Portrait, Maps, and Illustrations. 8vo, Cloth, $4 50; Sheep, $5 00; Half Calf, $6 75.

LIVINGSTONE'S ZAMBESI. Narrative of an Expedition to the Zambesi and its Tributaries, and of the Discovery of the Lakes Shirwa and Nyassa, 1858–1864. By DAVID and CHARLES LIVINGSTONE. Map and Illustrations. 8vo, Cloth, $5 00; Sheep, $5 50; Half Calf, $7 25.

LIVINGSTONE'S LAST JOURNALS. The Last Journals of David Livingstone in Central Africa, from 1865 to his Death. Continued by a Narrative of his Last Moments and Sufferings, obtained from his Faithful Servants Chuma and Susi. By HORACE WALLER, F.R.G.S., Rector of Twywell, Northampton. With Portrait, Maps, and Illustrations. 8vo, Cloth, $5 00; Sheep, $5 50; Half Calf, $7 25. Cheap Popular Edition, 8vo, Cloth, with Map and Illustrations, $2 50.

GROTE'S HISTORY OF GREECE. 12 vols., 12mo, Cloth, $18 00; Sheep, $22 80; Half Calf, $39 00.

RECLUS'S EARTH. The Earth: a Descriptive History of the Phenomena of the Life of the Globe. By ÉLISÉE RECLUS. With 234 Maps and Illustrations, and 23 Page Maps printed in Colors. 8vo, Cloth, $5 00.

RECLUS'S OCEAN. The Ocean, Atmosphere, and Life. Being the Second Series of a Descriptive History of the Life of the Globe. By ÉLISÉE RECLUS. Profusely Illustrated with 250 Maps or Figures, and 27 Maps printed in Colors. 8vo, Cloth, $6 00.

NORDHOFF'S COMMUNISTIC SOCIETIES OF THE UNITED STATES. The Communistic Societies of the United States, from Personal Visit and Observation; including Detailed Accounts of the Economists, Zoarites, Shakers, the Amana, Oneida, Bethel, Aurora, Icarian, and other existing Societies. With Particulars of their Religious Creeds and Practices, their Social Theories and Life, Numbers, Industries, and Present Condition. By CHARLES NORDHOFF. Illustrations. 8vo, Cloth, $4 00.

NORDHOFF'S CALIFORNIA. California: for Health, Pleasure, and Residence. A Book for Travellers and Settlers. Illustrated. 8vo, Cloth, $2 50.

NORDHOFF'S NORTHERN CALIFORNIA AND THE SANDWICH ISLANDS. Northern California, Oregon, and the Sandwich Islands. By CHARLES NORDHOFF. Illustrated. 8vo, Cloth, $2 50.

SHAKSPEARE. The Dramatic Works of William Shakspeare. With Corrections and Notes. Engravings. 6 vols., 12mo, Cloth, $9 00. 2 vols., 8vo, Cloth, $4 00; Sheep, $5 00. In one vol., 8vo, Sheep, $4 00.

BAKER'S ISMAILÏA. Ismailïa: a Narrative of the Expedition to Central Africa for the Suppression of the Slave-trade, organized by Ismail, Khedive of Egypt. By Sir SAMUEL WHITE BAKER, PASHA, F.R.S., F.R.G.S. With Maps, Portraits, and Illustrations. 8vo, Cloth, $5 00; Half Calf, $7 25.

GRIFFIS'S JAPAN. The Mikado's Empire: Book I. History of Japan, from 660 B.C. to 1872 A.D. Book II. Personal Experiences, Observations, and Studies in Japan, 1870–1874. By WILLIAM ELLIOT GRIFFIS, A.M., late of the Imperial University of Tōkiō, Japan. Copiously Illustrated. 8vo, Cloth, $4 00; Half Calf, $6 25.

SMILES'S HISTORY OF THE HUGUENOTS. The Huguenots: their Settlements, Churches, and Industries in England and Ireland. By SAMUEL SMILES. With an Appendix relating to the Huguenots in America. Crown 8vo, Cloth, $2 00.

SMILES'S HUGUENOTS AFTER THE REVOCATION. The Huguenots in France after the Revocation of the Edict of Nantes; with a Visit to the Country of the Vaudois. By SAMUEL SMILES. Crown 8vo, Cloth, $2 00.

SMILES'S LIFE OF THE STEPHENSONS. The Life of George Stephenson, and of his Son, Robert Stephenson; Comprising, also, a History of the Invention and Introduction of the Railway Locomotive. By SAMUEL SMILES. With Steel Portraits and numerous Illustrations. 8vo, Cloth, $3 00.

RAWLINSON'S MANUAL OF ANCIENT HISTORY. A Manual of Ancient History, from the Earliest Times to the Fall of the Western Empire. Comprising the History of Chaldæa, Assyria, Media, Babylonia, Lydia, Phœnicia, Syria, Judæa, Egypt, Carthage, Persia, Greece, Macedonia, Parthia, and Rome. By GEORGE RAWLINSON, M.A., Camden Professor of Ancient History in the University of Oxford. 12mo, Cloth, $1 25.

ALISON'S HISTORY OF EUROPE. FIRST SERIES: From the Commencement of the French Revolution, in 1789, to the Restoration of the Bourbons in 1815. [In addition to the Notes on Chapter LXXVI., which correct the errors of the original work concerning the United States, a copious Analytical Index has been appended to this American Edition.] SECOND SERIES: From the Fall of Napoleon, in 1815, to the Accession of Louis Napoleon, in 1852. 8 vols., 8vo, Cloth, $16 00; Sheep, $20 00; Half Calf, $34 00.

www.ingramcontent.com/pod-product-compliance
Lightning Source LLC
LaVergne TN
LVHW021147110826
845150LV00005B/1145

* 9 7 8 1 4 2 5 5 4 7 6 8 4 *